CAMARO & FIREBIRD
1982-1986
SHOP MANUAL

By
KALTON C. LAHUE

ALAN AHLSTRAND
Editor

JEFF ROBINSON
Publisher

CLYMER PUBLICATIONS

*World's largest publisher of books
devoted exclusively to automobiles and motorcycles*

12860 MUSCATINE STREET • P.O. BOX 4520 • ARLETA, CALIFORNIA 91333-4520

FIRST EDITION
First Printing September, 1983

SECOND EDITION
*Revised by Kalton C. Lahue to include 1983-1984
models*
First Printing July, 1984

THIRD EDITION
Revised by Kalton C. Lahue to include 1985 models
First Printing April, 1985
Second Printing October, 1985

FOURTH EDITION
Updated by Kalton C. Lahue to include 1986 models
First Printing July, 1986

Printed in U.S.A.

ISBN: 0-89287-377-9

*Production Coordinators, Steven Shepard & Victor
Williams*

*Technical assistance from General Motors Product Service Training, Detroit, Michigan and Burbank, California.
Technical illustration courtesy of General Motors Corporation.*

*COVER: Photographed by Michael Brown Photographic Productions, Los Angeles, California. Assisted by Bill
Masho. Cars courtesy of Chevrolet Motor Division and Pontiac Motor Division, General Motors Corporation.*

CONTENTS

CAMARO & FIREBIRD
1982-1986
SHOP MANUAL

QUICK REFERENCE DATA

RECOMMENDED LUBRICANTS

Engine crankcase	API Service SF, SF/CC or SF/CD oil
Engine coolant	Prestone II or equivalent
Brake fluid	Delco Supreme 11 or other DOT 3 or DOT 4 fluid
Power steering pump	GM power steering fluid or equivalent
Manual steering gear	GM lubricant part No. 1051052 or equivalent
Manual transmission	SAE 80W or SAE 80W/90 GL-5 gear lubricant
Rear axle (standard)	SAE 80W or SAE 80W/90 GL-5 gear lubricant
Rear axle (limited slip)	GM part No. 1052271 or equivalent plus 4 oz. GM part No. 1052358 additive or equivalent
Automatic transmission	DEXRON II automatic transmission fluid
Shift linkage	Engine oil
Front wheel bearings	GM lubricant part No. 1051344 or equivalent
Chassis lubrication	GM chassis grease meeting 6031-M specification
Hood latch, all hinges	Engine oil
Windshield washer	GM Optikleen washer solvent or equivalent
Key lock cylinders	WD-40 or equivalent

APPROXIMATE REFILL CAPACITIES

	qt.	pt.
Engine crankcase		
4-cylinder	3.0*	
V6 engine	4.0*	
V8 engine	4.0**	
Automatic transmission		
THM 200C		
After rebuild		10.0
After fluid change		7.0
THM 700 R4		
After rebuild		23.0
After fluid change		10.0
Manual transmission		
4-speed	3.5	
5-speed	3.5	
Differential		3.5
Cooling system		
4-cylinder		
With air conditioning	9.1	
Without air conditioning	8.8	
V6	12.5	
V8	15.0	

* With or without filter change.
** Add 1 qt. with filter change.

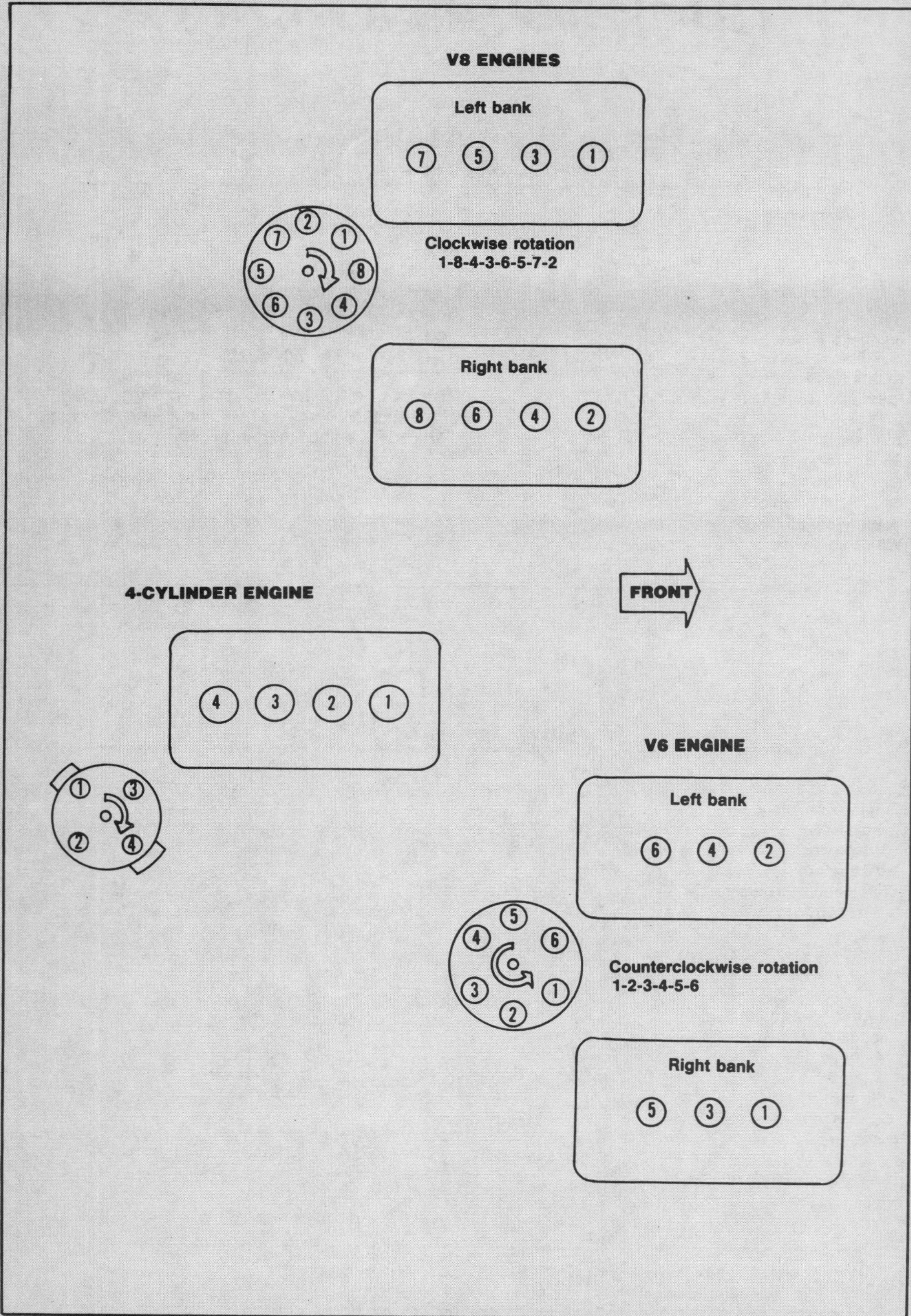

V8 ENGINES

Left bank

⑦ ⑤ ③ ①

**Clockwise rotation
1-8-4-3-6-5-7-2**

⑦ ② ①
⑤ ⑧
⑥ ③ ④

Right bank

⑧ ⑥ ④ ②

4-CYLINDER ENGINE

④ ③ ② ①

① ③
② ④

FRONT →

V6 ENGINE

Left bank

⑥ ④ ②

⑤
④ ⑥
③ ①
②

**Counterclockwise rotation
1-2-3-4-5-6**

Right bank

⑤ ③ ①

MAINTENANCE SCHEDULE

Every 7,500 miles **(12 months)**	• Engine oil[1] • Chassis lubrication • Inspect suspension and steering • Check brake lines • Check exhaust system
First 7,500 miles, then **every 15,000 miles**	• Engine oil filter[1] • Check and rotate tires • Check disc brakes • Check and adjust drive belts
First 7,500 miles, then **every 30,000 miles**	• Check carburetor choke and hoses • Check carburetor/throttle body mounting torque • Have idle speed checked and adjusted
Every 15,000 miles	• Check cooling system[2] • Check rear brakes and parking brake • Check throttle linkage • Inspect fuel tank, cap and lines • Change fuel filter
Every 30,000 miles	• Replace spark plugs[1] • Check and adjust ignition timing • Check ignition wiring • Drain/refill cooling system • Inspect manual steering gear seals • Check air cleaner system • Replace air cleaner filter • Replace crankcase vent filter • Replace PCV valve • Replace oxygen sensor[3] • Check EGR system operation • Repack and adjust wheel bearings[1]
Every 100,000 miles	• Change automatic transmission fluid

1. Severe service operation: If the vehicle is operated under any of the following conditions, change engine oil @ 3,000 mile or 3 month intervals and oil filter @ alternate oil changes. Clean and regap spark plugs every 6,000 miles. Repack wheel bearings and change automatic transmission fluid/strainer/filter every 15,000 miles.

  a. Extended idle or low-speed operation (short trips, stop-and-go driving).

  b. Trailer towing.

  c. Operation @ temperatures below 10° F for 60 days or more with most trips under 10 miles.

  d. Very dusty or muddy conditions.

2. Check coolant protection once a year.

3. Some 1982 engines only; see your dealer.

SAE VISCOSITY GRADES

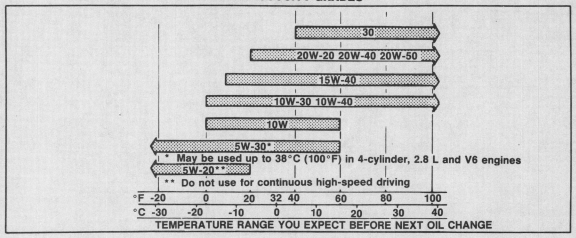

* May be used up to 38°C (100°F) in 4-cylinder, 2.8 L and V6 engines

** Do not use for continuous high-speed driving

TEMPERATURE RANGE YOU EXPECT BEFORE NEXT OIL CHANGE

DRIVE BELT TENSION

Belt size	Tension in lb.	
	New	Used*
1982		
5/16 in.	80	50
3/8 in.	140	70
7/16 in.	165	90
15/32 in.	165	90
1983-ON		
4-cylinder		
Air conditioning	135-165	65
All others	120-150	55
V6		
Air pump	100	45
Power steering pump	135	65-80
All others	145	65-80
V8		
Air conditioning	145	65-95
All others	130	65-80

* A belt is considered used after the engine has made more than one revolution and the belt has stretched or seated into the pulley groove.

TUNE-UP SPECIFICATIONS (1982)*

Engine	Ignition timing (Degrees BTDC @ rpm)	Spark plug	
		Type	Gap
4-cylinder	8 @ 1,050	R44TSX	0.060 in.
V6			
Automatic	10 @ 600	R43TS	0.045 in.
Manual	10 @ 850		
V8	6 @ 500	R45TS	0.045 in.

* See Vehicle Emissions Control Information (VECI) label in engine compartment for 1983 and later specifications.

—NOTES—

INTRODUCTION

This detailed, comprehensive manual covers the 1982-1986 Chevrolet Camaro and Pontiac Firebird. The expert text gives complete information on maintenance, repair and overhaul. Hundreds of photos and drawings guide you through every step. The book includes all you need to know to keep your Camaro or Firebird running right.

Chapters One through Thirteen contain general information on all models and specific information on 1982 models. The Supplement at the end of the book contains specific information on 1983 and later models which differs from that in the main book.

Where repairs are practical for the owner/mechanic, complete procedures are given. Equally important, difficult jobs are pointed out. Such operations are usually more economically performed by a dealer or independent garage.

Where special tools are required or recommended, the tool numbers are provided. These tools can sometimes be rented from rental dealers, but they can always be purchased from Kent-Moore Tool Division, 28635 Mound Road, Warren, Michigan 48092.

A shop manual is a reference. You want to be able to find information fast. As in all Clymer books, this one is designed with such use in mind. All chapters are thumb tabbed. Important items are indexed at the rear of the book. All the most frequently used specifications and capacities are summarized on the *Quick Reference* pages at the front of the book.

Keep the book handy. Carry it in your glove box. It will help you to better understand your car, lower repair and maintenance costs and generally improve your satisfaction with your vehicle.

CHAPTER ONE

GENERAL INFORMATION

The troubleshooting, tune-up, maintenance, and step-by-step repair procedures in this book are written for the owner and home mechanic. The text is accompanied by useful photos and diagrams to make the job as clear and correct as possible.

Troubleshooting, tune-up, maintenance, and repair are not difficult if you know what tools and equipment to use and what to do. Anyone not afraid to get their hands dirty, of average intelligence, and with some mechanical ability can perform most of the procedures in this book.

In some cases, a repair job may require tools or skills not reasonably expected of the home mechanic. These procedures are noted in each chapter and it is recommended that you take the job to your dealer, a competent mechanic, or machine shop.

MANUAL ORGANIZATION

This chapter provides general information and safety and service hints. Also included are lists of recommended shop and emergency tools as well as a brief description of troubleshooting and tune-up equipment.

Chapter Two provides methods and suggestions for quick and accurate diagnosis and repair of problems. Troubleshooting procedures discuss typical symptoms and logical methods to pinpoint the trouble.

Chapter Three explains all periodic lubrication and routine maintenance necessary to keep your vehicle running well. Chapter Three also includes recommended tune-up procedures, eliminating the need to constantly consult chapters on the various subassemblies.

Subsequent chapters cover specific systems such as the engine, transmission, and electrical systems. Each of these chapters provides disassembly, repair, and assembly procedures in a simple step-by-step format. If a repair requires special skills or tools, or is otherwise impractical for the home mechanic, it is so indicated. In these cases it is usually faster and less expensive to have the repairs made by a dealer or competent repair shop. Necessary specifications concerning a particular system are included at the end of the appropriate chapter.

When special tools are required to perform a procedure included in this manual, the tool is illustrated either in actual use or alone. It may be possible to rent or borrow these tools. The inventive mechanic may also be able to find a suitable substitute in his tool box, or to fabricate one.

The terms NOTE, CAUTION, and WARNING have specific meanings in this manual. A NOTE provides additional or explanatory information. A CAUTION is used to emphasize areas where equipment damage could result if proper precautions are not taken. A WARNING is used to stress those areas where personal injury or death could result from negligence, in addition to possible mechanical damage.

SERVICE HINTS

Observing the following practices will save time, effort, and frustration, as well as prevent possible injury.

Throughout this manual keep in mind two conventions. "Front" refers to the front of the vehicle. The front of any component, such as the transmission, is that end which faces toward the front of the vehicle. The "left" and "right" sides of the vehicle refer to the orientation of a person sitting in the vehicle facing forward. For example, the steering wheel is on the left side. These rules are simple, but even experienced mechanics occasionally become disoriented.

Most of the service procedures covered are straightforward and can be performed by anyone reasonably handy with tools. It is suggested, however, that you consider your own capabilities carefully before attempting any operation involving major disassembly of the engine.

Some operations, for example, require the use of a press. It would be wiser to have these performed by a shop equipped for such work, rather than to try to do the job yourself with makeshift equipment. Other procedures require precision measurements. Unless you have the skills and equipment required, it would be better to have a qualified repair shop make the measurements for you.

Repairs go much faster and easier if the parts that will be worked on are clean before you begin. There are special cleaners for washing the engine and related parts. Brush or spray on the cleaning solution, let it stand, then rinse it away with a garden hose. Clean all oily or greasy parts with cleaning solvent as you remove them.

WARNING
Never use gasoline as a cleaning agent. It presents an extreme fire hazard. Be sure to work in a well-ventilated area when using cleaning solvent. Keep a fire extinguisher, rated for gasoline fires, handy in any case.

Much of the labor charge for repairs made by dealers is for the removal and disassembly of other parts to reach the defective unit. It is frequently possible to perform the preliminary operations yourself and then take the defective unit in to the dealer for repair, at considerable savings.

Once you have decided to tackle the job yourself, make sure you locate the appropriate section in this manual, and read it entirely. Study the illustrations and text until you have a good idea of what is involved in completing the job satisfactorily. If special tools are required, make arrangements to get them before you start. Also, purchase any known defective parts prior to starting on the procedure. It is frustrating and time-consuming to get partially into a job and then be unable to complete it.

Simple wiring checks can be easily made at home, but knowledge of electronics is almost a necessity for performing tests with complicated electronic testing gear.

During disassembly of parts keep a few general cautions in mind. Force is rarely needed to get things apart. If parts are a tight fit, like a bearing in a case, there is usually a tool designed to separate them. Never use a screwdriver to pry apart parts with machined surfaces such as cylinder head and valve cover. You will mar the surfaces and end up with leaks.

Make diagrams wherever similar-appearing parts are found. You may think you can remember where everything came from — but mistakes are costly. There is also the possibility you may get sidetracked and not return to work for days or even weeks — in which interval, carefully laid out parts may have become disturbed.

Tag all similar internal parts for location, and mark all mating parts for position. Record number and thickness of any shims as they are removed. Small parts such as bolts can be identified by placing them in plastic sandwich bags that are sealed and labeled with masking tape.

Wiring should be tagged with masking tape and marked as each wire is removed. Again, do not rely on memory alone.

When working under the vehicle, do not trust a hydraulic or mechanical jack to hold the vehicle up by itself. Always use jackstands. See **Figure 1**.

Disconnect battery ground cable before working near electrical connections and before disconnecting wires. Never run the engine with the battery disconnected; the alternator could be seriously damaged.

Protect finished surfaces from physical damage or corrosion. Keep gasoline and brake fluid off painted surfaces.

Frozen or very tight bolts and screws can often be loosened by soaking with penetrating oil like Liquid Wrench or WD-40, then sharply striking the bolt head a few times with a hammer and punch (or screwdriver for screws). Avoid heat unless absolutely necessary, since it may melt, warp, or remove the temper from many parts.

Avoid flames or sparks when working near a charging battery or flammable liquids, such as brake fluid or gasoline.

No parts, except those assembled with a press fit, require unusual force during assembly. If a part is hard to remove or install, find out why before proceeding.

Cover all openings after removing parts to keep dirt, small tools, etc., from falling in.

When assembling two parts, start all fasteners, then tighten evenly.

The clutch plate, wiring connections, brake shoes, drums, pads, and discs should be kept clean and free of grease and oil.

When assembling parts, be sure all shims and washers are replaced exactly as they came out.

Whenever a rotating part butts against a stationary part, look for a shim or washer. Use new gaskets if there is any doubt about the condition of old ones. Generally, you should apply gasket cement to one mating surface only, so the parts may be easily disassembled in the future. A thin coat of oil on gaskets helps them seal effectively.

Heavy grease can be used to hold small parts in place if they tend to fall out during assembly. However, keep grease and oil away from electrical, clutch, and brake components.

High spots may be sanded off a piston with sandpaper, but emery cloth and oil do a much more professional job.

Carburetors are best cleaned by disassembling them and soaking the parts in a commercial carburetor cleaner. Never soak gaskets and rubber parts in these cleaners. Never use wire to clean out jets and air passages; they are easily damaged. Use compressed air to blow out the carburetor, but only if the float has been removed first.

Take your time and do the job right. Do not forget that a newly rebuilt engine must be broken in the same as a new one. Refer to your owner's manual for the proper break-in procedures.

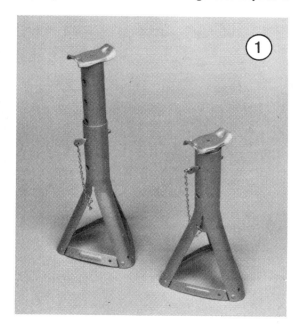

SAFETY FIRST

Professional mechanics can work for years and never sustain a serious injury. If you observe a few rules of common sense and safety, you can enjoy many safe hours servicing your vehicle. You could hurt yourself or damage the vehicle if you ignore these rules.

1. Never use gasoline as a cleaning solvent.

2. Never smoke or use a torch in the vicinity of flammable liquids such as cleaning solvent in open containers.

3. Never smoke or use a torch in an area where batteries are being charged. Highly explosive hydrogen gas is formed during the charging process.

4. Use the proper sized wrenches to avoid damage to nuts and injury to yourself.

5. When loosening a tight or stuck nut, be guided by what would happen if the wrench should slip. Protect yourself accordingly.

6. Keep your work area clean and uncluttered.

7. Wear safety goggles during all operations involving drilling, grinding, or use of a cold chisel.

8. Never use worn tools.

9. Keep a fire extinguisher handy and be sure it is rated for gasoline (Class B) and electrical (Class C) fires.

EXPENDABLE SUPPLIES

Certain expendable supplies are necessary. These include grease, oil, gasket cement, wiping rags, cleaning solvent, and distilled water.

Also, special locking compounds, silicone lubricants, and engine cleaners may be useful. Cleaning solvent is available at most service stations and distilled water for the battery is available at most supermarkets.

SHOP TOOLS

For proper servicing, you will need an assortment of ordinary hand tools (**Figure 2**).

As a minimum, these include:

  a. Combination wrenches

  b. Sockets

  c. Plastic mallet

  d. Small hammer

  e. Snap ring pliers

  f. Gas pliers

  g. Phillips screwdrivers

  h. Slot (common) screwdrivers

  i. Feeler gauges

  j. Spark plug gauge

  k. Spark plug wrench

Special tools necessary are shown in the chapters covering the particular repair in which they are used.

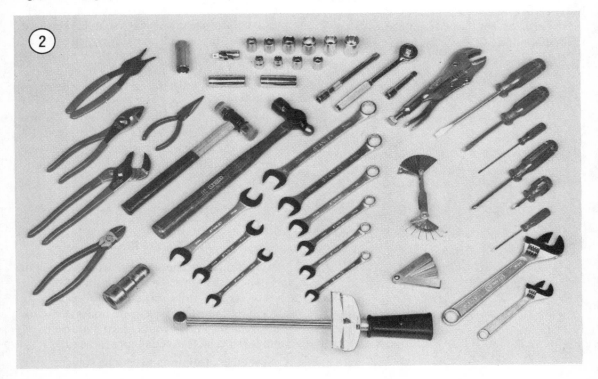

Engine tune-up and troubleshooting procedures require other special tools and equipment. These are described in detail in the following sections.

EMERGENCY TOOL KIT

A small emergency tool kit kept in the trunk is handy for road emergencies which otherwise could leave you stranded. The tools listed below and shown in **Figure 3** will let you handle most roadside repairs.

  a. Combination wrenches

  b. Crescent (adjustable) wrench

  c. Screwdrivers — common and Phillips

  d. Pliers — conventional (gas) and needle nose

  e. Vise Grips

  f. Hammer — plastic and metal

  g. Small container of waterless hand cleaner

  h. Rags for clean up

  i. Silver waterproof sealing tape (duct tape)

  j. Flashlight

  k. Emergency road flares — at least four

  l. Spare drive belts (water pump, alternator, etc.)

TROUBLESHOOTING AND TUNE-UP EQUIPMENT

Voltmeter, Ohmmeter, and Ammeter

For testing the ignition or electrical system, a good voltmeter is required. For automotive use, an instrument covering 0-20 volts is satisfac-

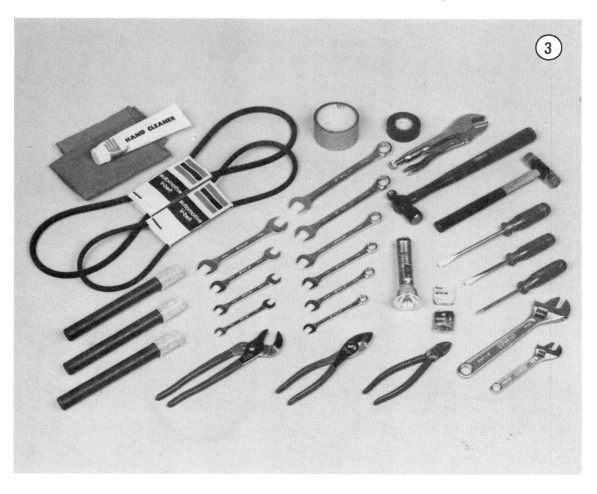

tory. One which also has a 0-2 volt scale is necessary for testing relays, points, or individual contacts where voltage drops are much smaller. Accuracy should be ± ½ volt.

An ohmmeter measures electrical resistance. This instrument is useful for checking continuity (open and short circuits), and testing fuses and lights.

The ammeter measures electrical current. Ammeters for automotive use should cover 0-50 amperes and 0-250 amperes. These are useful for checking battery charging and starting current.

Several inexpensive VOM's (volt-ohm-milli-ammeter) combine all three instruments into one which fits easily in any tool box. See **Figure 4**. However, the ammeter ranges are usually too small for automotive work.

Hydrometer

The hydrometer gives a useful indication of battery condition and charge by measuring the specific gravity of the electrolyte in each cell. See **Figure 5**. Complete details on use and interpretation of readings are provided in the electrical chapter.

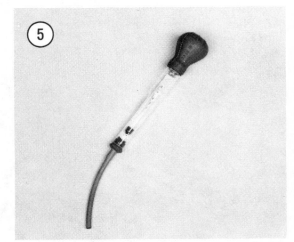

Compression Tester

The compression tester measures the compression pressure built up in each cylinder. The results, when properly interpreted, can indicate general cylinder and valve condition. See **Figure 6**.

Vacuum Gauge

The vacuum gauge (**Figure 7**) is one of the easiest instruments to use, but one of the most difficult for the inexperienced mechanic to interpret. The results, when interpreted with other findings, can provide valuable clues to possible trouble.

To use the vacuum gauge, connect it to a vacuum hose that goes to the intake manifold. Attach it either directly to the hose or to a T-fitting installed into the hose.

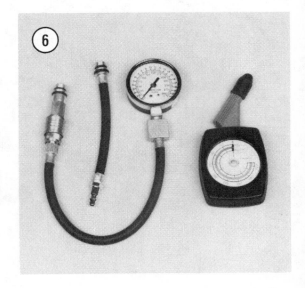

NOTE: *Subtract one inch from the reading for every 1,000 ft. elevation.*

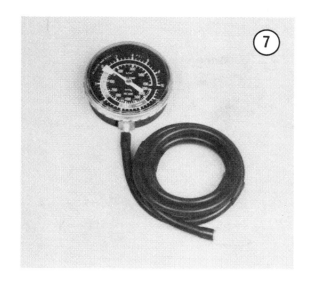

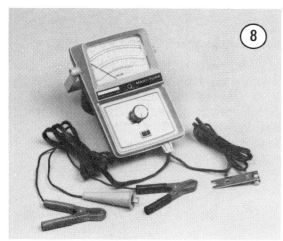

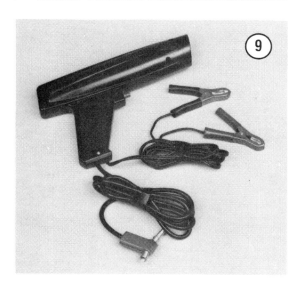

Fuel Pressure Gauge

This instrument is invaluable for evaluating fuel pump performance. Fuel system troubleshooting procedures in this manual use a fuel pressure gauge. Usually a vacuum gauge and fuel pressure gauge are combined.

Dwell Meter (Contact Breaker Point Ignition Only)

A dwell meter measures the distance in degrees of cam rotation that the breaker points remain closed while the engine is running. Since this angle is determined by breaker point gap, dwell angle is an accurate indication of breaker point gap.

Many tachometers intended for tuning and testing incorporate a dwell meter as well. See **Figure 8**. Follow the manufacturer's instructions to measure dwell.

Tachometer

A tachometer is necessary for tuning. See **Figure 8**. Ignition timing and carburetor adjustments must be performed at the specified idle speed. The best instrument for this purpose is one with a low range of 0-1,000 or 0-2,000 rpm for setting idle, and a high range of 0-4,000 or more for setting ignition timing at 3,000 rpm. Extended range (0-6,000 or 0-8,000 rpm) instruments lack accuracy at lower speeds. The instrument should be capable of detecting changes of 25 rpm on the low range.

Strobe Timing Light

This instrument is necessary for tuning, as it permits very accurate ignition timing. The light flashes at precisely the same instant that No. 1 cylinder fires, at which time the timing marks on the engine should align. Refer to Chapter Three for exact location of the timing marks for your engine.

Suitable lights range from inexpensive neon bulb types ($2-3) to powerful xenon strobe lights ($20-40). See **Figure 9**. Neon timing lights are difficult to see and must be used in dimly lit areas. Xenon strobe timing lights can be used outside in bright sunlight. Both types work on this vehicle; use according to the manufacturer's instructions.

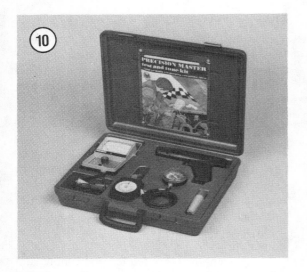

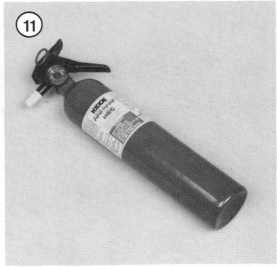

Tune-up Kits

Many manufacturer's offer kits that combine several useful instruments. Some come in a convenient carry case and are usally less expensive than purchasing one instrument at a time. **Figure 10** shows one of the kits that is available. The prices vary with the number of instruments included in the kit.

Fire Extinguisher

A fire extinguisher is a necessity when working on a vehicle. It should be rated for both *Class B* (flammable liquids—gasoline, oil, paint, etc.) and *Class C* (electrical—wiring, etc.) type fires. It should always be kept within reach. See **Figure 11**.

CHAPTER TWO

TROUBLESHOOTING

Troubleshooting can be a relatively simple matter if it is done logically. The first step in any troubleshooting procedure must be defining the symptoms as closely as possible. Subsequent steps involve testing and analyzing areas which could cause the symptoms. A haphazard approach may eventually find the trouble, but in terms of wasted time and unnecessary parts replacement, it can be very costly.

The troubleshooting procedures in this chapter analyze typical symptoms and show logical methods of isolation. These are not the only methods. There may be several approaches to a problem, but all methods must have one thing in common — a logical, systematic approach.

STARTING SYSTEM

The starting system consists of the starter motor and the starter solenoid. The ignition key controls the starter solenoid, which mechanically engages the starter with the engine flywheel, and supplies electrical current to turn the starter motor.

Starting system troubles are relatively easy to find. In most cases, the trouble is a loose or dirty electrical connection. **Figures 1 and 2** provide routines for finding the trouble.

CHARGING SYSTEM

The charging system consists of the alternator (or generator on older vehicles), voltage regulator, and battery. A drive belt driven by the engine crankshaft turns the alternator which produces electrical energy to charge the battery. As engine speed varies, the voltage from the alternator varies. A voltage regulator controls the charging current to the battery and maintains the voltage to the vehicle's electrical system at safe levels. A warning light or gauge on the instrument panel signals the driver when charging is not taking place. Refer to **Figure 3** for a typical charging system.

Complete troubleshooting of the charging system requires test equipment and skills which the average home mechanic does not possess. However, there are a few tests which can be done to pinpoint most troubles.

Charging system trouble may stem from a defective alternator (or generator), voltage regulator, battery, or drive belt. It may also be caused by something as simple as incorrect drive belt tension. The following are symptoms of typical problems you may encounter.

1. *Battery dies frequently, even though the warning lamp indicates no discharge* — This can be caused by a drive belt that is slightly too

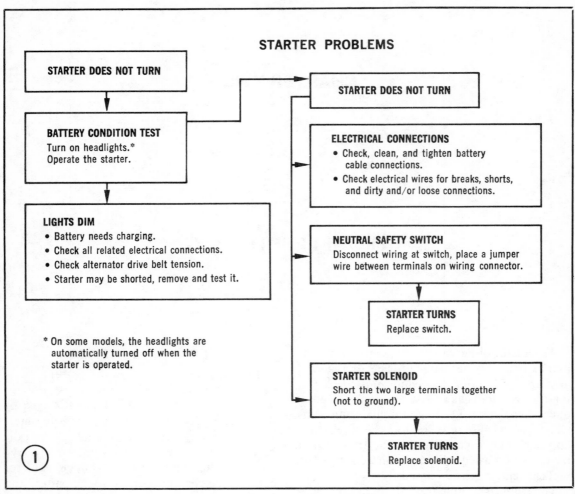

STARTER PROBLEMS

STARTER DOES NOT TURN

BATTERY CONDITION TEST
Turn on headlights.*
Operate the starter.

LIGHTS DIM
• Battery needs charging.
• Check all related electrical connections.
• Check alternator drive belt tension.
• Starter may be shorted, remove and test it.

* On some models, the headlights are
automatically turned off when the
starter is operated.

STARTER DOES NOT TURN

ELECTRICAL CONNECTIONS
• Check, clean, and tighten battery
  cable connections.
• Check electrical wires for breaks, shorts,
  and dirty and/or loose connections.

NEUTRAL SAFETY SWITCH
Disconnect wiring at switch, place a jumper
wire between terminals on wiring connector.

STARTER TURNS
Replace switch.

STARTER SOLENOID
Short the two large terminals together
(not to ground).

STARTER TURNS
Replace solenoid.

①

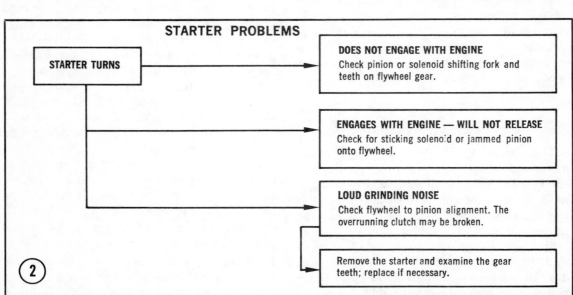

STARTER PROBLEMS

STARTER TURNS

DOES NOT ENGAGE WITH ENGINE
Check pinion or solenoid shifting fork and
teeth on flywheel gear.

ENGAGES WITH ENGINE — WILL NOT RELEASE
Check for sticking solenoid or jammed pinion
onto flywheel.

LOUD GRINDING NOISE
Check flywheel to pinion alignment. The
overrunning clutch may be broken.

Remove the starter and examine the gear
teeth; replace if necessary.

②

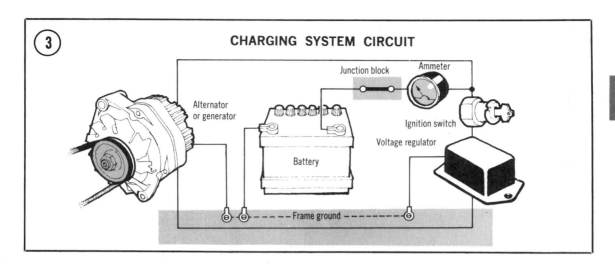

③ **CHARGING SYSTEM CIRCUIT**

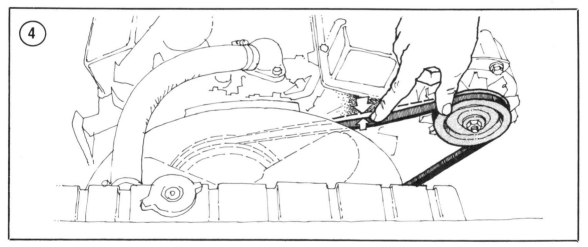

④

loose. Grasp the alternator (or generator) pulley and try to turn it. If the pulley can be turned without moving the belt, the drive belt is too loose. As a rule, keep the belt tight enough that it can be deflected about ½ in. under moderate thumb pressure between the pulleys (**Figure 4**). The battery may also be at fault; test the battery condition.

2. *Charging system warning lamp does not come on when ignition switch is turned on —* This may indicate a defective ignition switch, battery, voltage regulator, or lamp. First try to start the vehicle. If it doesn't start, check the ignition switch and battery. If the car starts, remove the warning lamp; test it for continuity with an ohmmeter or substitute a new lamp. If the lamp is good, locate the voltage regulator

and make sure it is properly grounded (try tightening the mounting screws). Also the alternator (or generator) brushes may not be making contact. Test the alternator (or generator) and voltage regulator.

3. *Alternator (or generator) warning lamp comes on and stays on —* This usually indicates that no charging is taking place. First check drive belt tension (**Figure 4**). Then check battery condition, and check all wiring connections in the charging system. If this does not locate the trouble, check the alternator (or generator) and voltage regulator.

4. *Charging system warning lamp flashes on and off intermittently —* This usually indicates the charging system is working intermittently.

Check the drive belt tension (**Figure 4**), and check all electrical connections in the charging system. Check the alternator (or generator). *On generators only*, check the condition of the commutator.

5. *Battery requires frequent additions of water, or lamps require frequent replacement* — The alternator (or generator) is probably overcharging the battery. The voltage regulator is probably at fault.

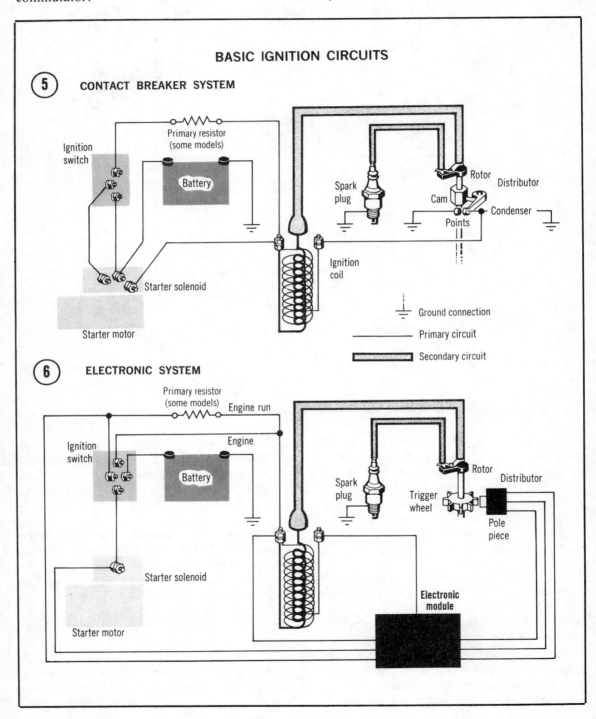

BASIC IGNITION CIRCUITS

⑤ **CONTACT BREAKER SYSTEM**

Primary resistor (some models)
Ignition switch
Battery
Spark plug
Rotor
Distributor
Cam
Condenser
Points
Ignition coil
Starter solenoid
Starter motor

⊥ Ground connection
── Primary circuit
▭ Secondary circuit

⑥ **ELECTRONIC SYSTEM**

Primary resistor (some models)
Engine run
Engine
Ignition switch
Battery
Spark plug
Trigger wheel
Rotor
Distributor
Pole piece
Starter solenoid
Electronic module
Starter motor

6. *Excessive noise from the alternator (or generator)* — Check for loose mounting brackets and bolts. The problem may also be worn bearings or the need of lubrication in some cases. If an alternator whines, a shorted diode may be indicated.

IGNITION SYSTEM

The ignition system may be either a conventional contact breaker type or an electronic ignition. See electrical chapter to determine which type you have. **Figures 5 and 6** show simplified diagrams of each type.

Most problems involving failure to start, poor performance, or rough running stem from trouble in the ignition system, particularly in contact breaker systems. Many novice trouble-shooters get into trouble when they assume that these symptoms point to the fuel system instead of the ignition system.

Ignition system troubles may be roughly divided between those affecting only one cylinder and those affecting all cylinders. If the trouble affects only one cylinder, it can only be in the spark plug, spark plug wire, or portion of the distributor associated with that cylinder. If the trouble affects all cylinders (weak spark or no spark), then the trouble is in the ignition coil, rotor, distributor, or associated wiring.

The troubleshooting procedures outlined in **Figure 7** (breaker point ignition) or **Figure 8**

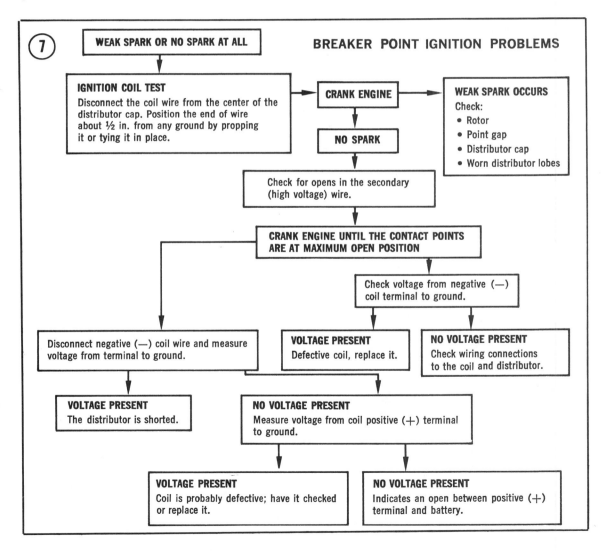

(electronic ignition) will help you isolate ignition problems fast. Of course, they assume that the battery is in good enough condition to crank the engine over at its normal rate.

ENGINE PERFORMANCE

A number of factors can make the engine difficult or impossible to start, or cause rough running, poor performance and so on. The majority of novice troubleshooters immediately suspect the carburetor or fuel injection system. In the majority of cases, though, the trouble exists in the ignition system.

The troubleshooting procedures outlined in **Figures 9 through 14** will help you solve the majority of engine starting troubles in a systematic manner.

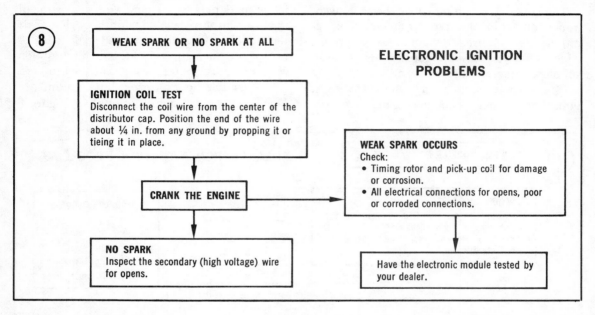

⑧

WEAK SPARK OR NO SPARK AT ALL

ELECTRONIC IGNITION PROBLEMS

IGNITION COIL TEST
Disconnect the coil wire from the center of the distributor cap. Position the end of the wire about ¼ in. from any ground by propping it or tieing it in place.

WEAK SPARK OCCURS
Check:
• Timing rotor and pick-up coil for damage or corrosion.
• All electrical connections for opens, poor or corroded connections.

CRANK THE ENGINE

NO SPARK
Inspect the secondary (high voltage) wire for opens.

Have the electronic module tested by your dealer.

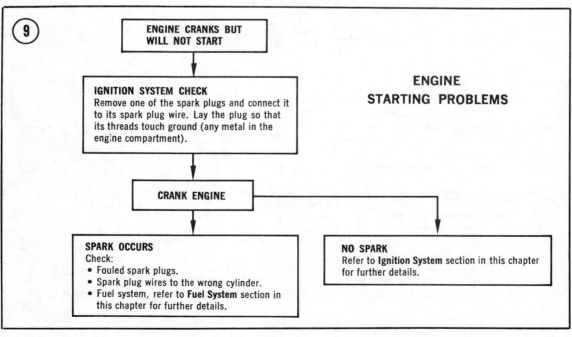

⑨

ENGINE CRANKS BUT WILL NOT START

ENGINE STARTING PROBLEMS

IGNITION SYSTEM CHECK
Remove one of the spark plugs and connect it to its spark plug wire. Lay the plug so that its threads touch ground (any metal in the engine compartment).

CRANK ENGINE

SPARK OCCURS
Check:
• Fouled spark plugs.
• Spark plug wires to the wrong cylinder.
• Fuel system, refer to **Fuel System** section in this chapter for further details.

NO SPARK
Refer to **Ignition System** section in this chapter for further details.

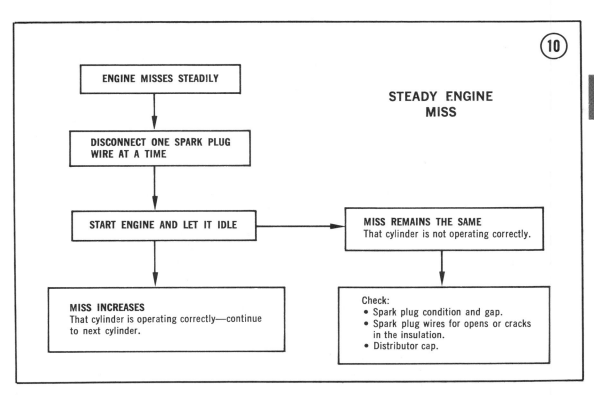

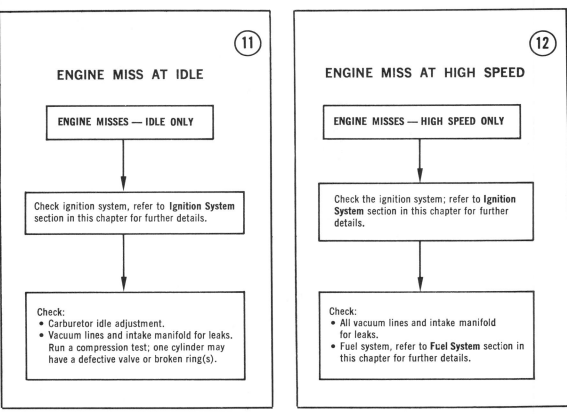

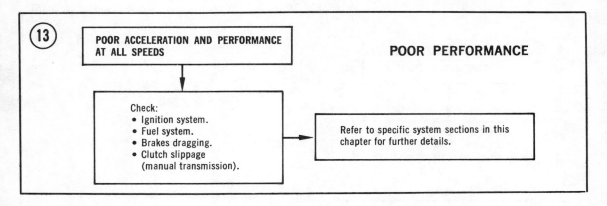

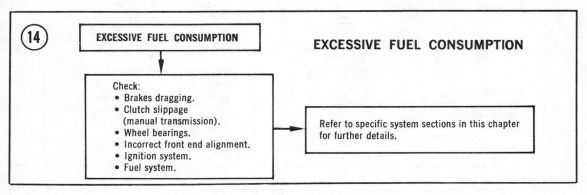

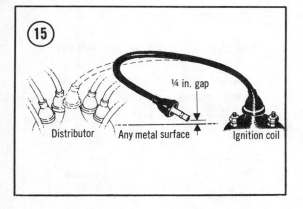

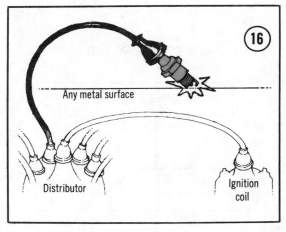

Some tests of the ignition system require running the engine with a spark plug or ignition coil wire disconnected. The safest way to do this is to disconnect the wire with the engine stopped, then prop the end of the wire next to a metal surface as shown in **Figures 15 and 16**.

WARNING
Never disconnect a spark plug or ignition coil wire while the engine is running. The high voltage in an ignition system, particularly the newer high-energy electronic ignition systems could cause serious injury or even death.

Spark plug condition is an important indication of engine performance. Spark plugs in a properly operating engine will have slightly pitted electrodes, and a light tan insulator tip. **Figure 17** shows a normal plug, and a number of others which indicate trouble in their respective cylinders.

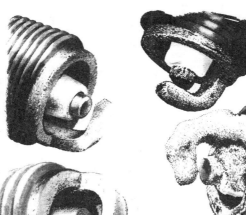

2

- Appearance—Firing tip has deposits of light gray to light tan.
- Can be cleaned, regapped and reused.

- Appearance—Dull, dry black with fluffy carbon deposits on the insulator tip, electrode and exposed shell.
- Caused by—Fuel/air mixture too rich, plug heat range too cold, weak ignition system, dirty air cleaner, faulty automatic choke or excessive idling.
- Can be cleaned, regapped and reused.

- Appearance—Wet black deposits on insulator and exposed shell.
- Caused by—Excessive oil entering the combustion chamber through worn rings, pistons, valve guides or bearings.
- Replace with new plugs (use a hotter plug if engine is not repaired).

- Appearance — Yellow insulator deposits (may sometimes be dark gray, black or tan in color) on the insulator tip.
- Caused by—Highly leaded gasoline.
- Replace with new plugs.

- Appearance—Yellow glazed deposits indicating melted lead deposits due to hard acceleration.
- Caused by—Highly leaded gasoline.
- Replace with new plugs.

- Appearance—Glazed yellow deposits with a slight brownish tint on the insulator tip and ground electrode.
- Replace with new plugs.

- Appearance — Brown colored hardened ash deposits on the insulator tip and ground electrode.
- Caused by—Fuel and/or oil additives.
- Replace with new plugs.

- Appearance — Severely worn or eroded electrodes.
- Caused by—Normal wear or unusual oil and/or fuel additives.
- Replace with new plugs.

- Appearance — Melted ground electrode.
- Caused by—Overadvanced ignition timing, inoperative ignition advance mechanism, too low of a fuel octane rating, lean fuel/air mixture or carbon deposits in combustion chamber.

- Appearance—Melted center electrode.
- Caused by—Abnormal combustion due to overadvanced ignition timing or incorrect advance, too low of a fuel octane rating, lean fuel/air mixture, or carbon deposits in combustion chamber.
- Correct engine problem and replace with new plugs.

- Appearance—Melted center electrode and white blistered insulator tip.
- Caused by—Incorrect plug heat range selection.
- Replace with new plugs.

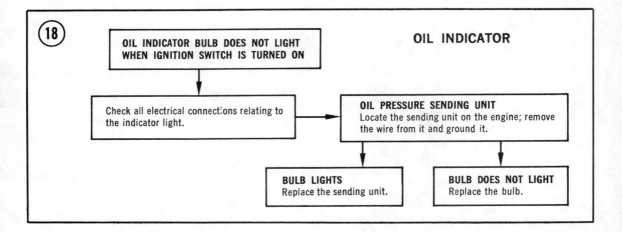

ENGINE OIL PRESSURE LIGHT

Proper oil pressure to the engine is vital. If oil pressure is insufficient, the engine can destroy itself in a comparatively short time.

The oil pressure warning circuit monitors oil pressure constantly. If pressure drops below a predetermined level, the light comes on.

Obviously, it is vital for the warning circuit to be working to signal low oil pressure. Each time you turn on the ignition, but before you start the car, the warning light should come on. If it doesn't, there is trouble in the warning circuit, not the oil pressure system. See **Figure 18** to troubleshoot the warning circuit.

Once the engine is running, the warning light should stay off. If the warning light comes on or acts erratically while the engine is running there is trouble with the engine oil pressure system. *Stop the engine immediately*. Refer to **Figure 19** for possible causes of the problem.

FUEL SYSTEM (CARBURETTED)

Fuel system problems must be isolated to the fuel pump (mechanical or electric), fuel lines, fuel filter, or carburetor. These procedures assume the ignition system is working properly and is correctly adjusted.

1. *Engine will not start* — First make sure that fuel is being delivered to the carburetor. Remove the air cleaner, look into the carburetor throat, and operate the accelerator

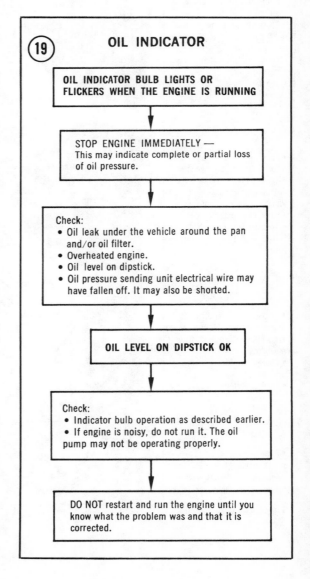

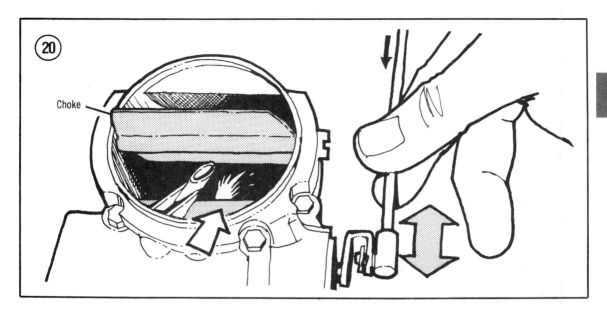

linkage several times. There should be a stream of fuel from the accelerator pump discharge tube each time the accelerator linkage is depressed **(Figure 20)**. If not, check fuel pump delivery (described later), float valve, and float adjustment. If the engine will not start, check the automatic choke parts for sticking or damage. If necessary, rebuild or replace the carburetor.

2. *Engine runs at fast idle* — Check the choke setting. Check the idle speed, idle mixture, and decel valve (if equipped) adjustment.

3. *Rough idle or engine miss with frequent stalling* — Check idle mixture and idle speed adjustments.

4. *Engine "diesels" (continues to run) when ignition is switched off* — Check idle mixture (probably too rich), ignition timing, and idle speed (probably too fast). Check the throttle solenoid (if equipped) for proper operation. Check for overheated engine.

5. *Stumbling when accelerating from idle* — Check the idle speed and mixture adjustments. Check the accelerator pump.

6. *Engine misses at high speed or lacks power* — This indicates possible fuel starvation. Check fuel pump pressure and capacity as described in this chapter. Check float needle valves. Check for a clogged fuel filter or air cleaner.

7. *Black exhaust smoke* — This indicates a badly overrich mixture. Check idle mixture and idle speed adjustment. Check choke setting. Check for excessive fuel pump pressure, leaky floats, or worn needle valves.

8. *Excessive fuel consumption* — Check for overrich mixture. Make sure choke mechanism works properly. Check idle mixture and idle speed. Check for excessive fuel pump pressure, leaky floats, or worn float needle valves.

FUEL SYSTEM (FUEL INJECTED)

Troubleshooting a fuel injection system requires more thought, experience, and know-how than any other part of the vehicle. A logical approach and proper test equipment are essential in order to successfully find and fix these troubles.

It is best to leave fuel injection troubles to your dealer. In order to isolate a problem to the injection system make sure that the fuel pump is operating properly. Check its performance as described later in this section. Also make sure that fuel filter and air cleaner are not clogged.

FUEL PUMP TEST (MECHANICAL AND ELECTRIC)

1. Disconnect the fuel inlet line where it enters the carburetor or fuel injection system.

2. Fit a rubber hose over the fuel line so fuel can be directed into a graduated container with about one quart capacity. See **Figure 21**.

3. To avoid accidental starting of the engine, disconnect the secondary coil wire from the coil or disconnect and insulate the coil primary wire.

4. Crank the engine for about 30 seconds.

5. If the fuel pump supplies the specified amount (refer to the fuel chapter later in this book), the trouble may be in the carburetor or fuel injection system. The fuel injection system should be tested by your dealer.

6. If there is no fuel present or the pump cannot supply the specified amount, either the fuel pump is defective or there is an obstruction in the fuel line. Replace the fuel pump and/or inspect the fuel lines for air leaks or obstructions.

7. Also pressure test the fuel pump by installing a T-fitting in the fuel line between the fuel pump and the carburetor. Connect a fuel pressure gauge to the fitting with a short tube **(Figure 22)**.

8. Reconnect the coil wire, start the engine, and record the pressure. Refer to the fuel chapter later in this book for the correct pressure. If the pressure varies from that specified, the pump should be replaced.

9. Stop the engine. The pressure should drop off very slowly. If it drops off rapidly, the outlet valve in the pump is leaking and the pump should be replaced.

EMISSION CONTROL SYSTEMS

Major emission control systems used on nearly all U.S. models include the following:

a. Positive crankcase ventilation (PCV)

b. Thermostatic air cleaner

c. Air injection reaction (AIR)

d. Fuel evaporation control

e. Exhaust gas recirculation (EGR)

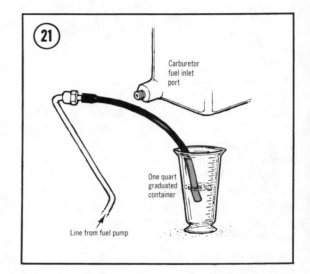
Carburetor fuel inlet port

One quart graduated container

Line from fuel pump

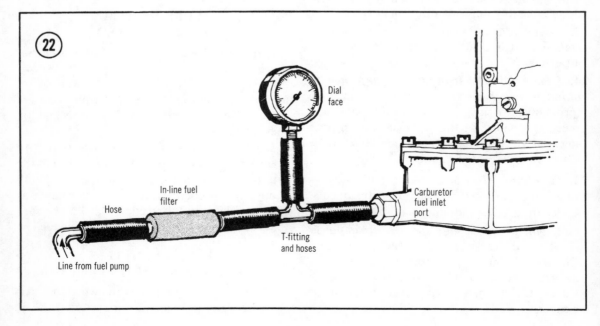
Dial face

In-line fuel filter

Hose

Carburetor fuel inlet port

T-fitting and hoses

Line from fuel pump

Emission control systems vary considerably from model to model. Individual models contain variations of the four systems described here. In addition, they may include other special systems. Use the index to find specific emission control components in other chapters.

Many of the systems and components are factory set and sealed. Without special expensive test equipment, it is impossible to adjust the systems to meet state and federal requirements.

Troubleshooting can also be difficult without special equipment. The procedures described below will help you find emission control parts which have failed, but repairs may have to be entrusted to a dealer or other properly equipped repair shop.

With the proper equipment, you can test the carbon monoxide and hydrocarbon levels.

Figure 23 provides some sources of trouble if the readings are not correct.

Positive Crankcase Ventilation

Fresh air drawn from the air cleaner housing scavenges emissions (e.g., piston blow-by) from the crankcase, then the intake manifold vacuum draws emissions into the intake manifold. They can then be reburned in the normal combustion process. **Figure 24** shows a typical system. **Figure 25** provides a testing procedure.

Thermostatic Air Cleaner

The thermostatically controlled air cleaner maintains incoming air to the engine at a predetermined level, usually about 100°F or higher. It mixes cold air with heated air from the exhaust manifold region. The air cleaner in-

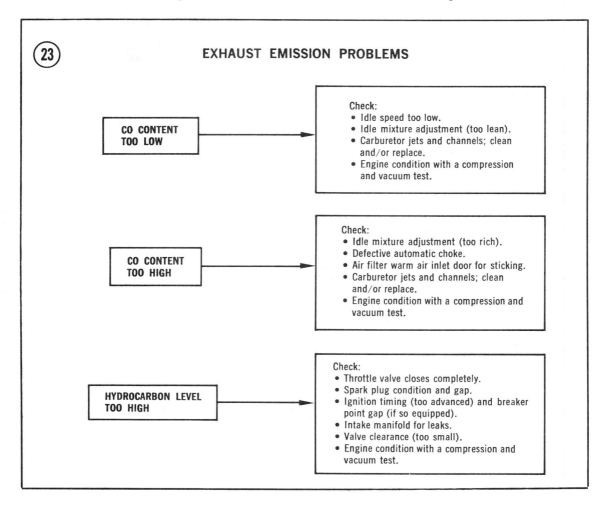

(23) **EXHAUST EMISSION PROBLEMS**

CO CONTENT TOO LOW

Check:
- Idle speed too low.
- Idle mixture adjustment (too lean).
- Carburetor jets and channels; clean and/or replace.
- Engine condition with a compression and vacuum test.

CO CONTENT TOO HIGH

Check:
- Idle mixture adjustment (too rich).
- Defective automatic choke.
- Air filter warm air inlet door for sticking.
- Carburetor jets and channels; clean and/or replace.
- Engine condition with a compression and vacuum test.

HYDROCARBON LEVEL TOO HIGH

Check:
- Throttle valve closes completely.
- Spark plug condition and gap.
- Ignition timing (too advanced) and breaker point gap (if so equipped).
- Intake manifold for leaks.
- Valve clearance (too small).
- Engine condition with a compression and vacuum test.

cludes a temperature sensor, vacuum motor, and a hinged door. See **Figure 26**.

The system is comparatively easy to test. See **Figure 27** for the procedure.

Air Injection Reaction System

The air injection reaction system reduces air pollution by oxidizing hydrocarbons and carbon monoxide as they leave the combustion chamber. See **Figure 28**.

The air injection pump, driven by the engine, compresses filtered air and injects it at the exhaust port of each cylinder. The fresh air mixes with the unburned gases in the exhaust and promotes further burning. A check valve prevents exhaust gases from entering and damaging the air pump if the pump becomes inoperative, e.g., from a fan belt failure.

Figure 29 explains the testing procedure for this system.

Fuel Evaporation Control

Fuel vapor from the fuel tank passes through the liquid/vapor separator to the carbon canister. See **Figure 30**. The carbon absorbs and

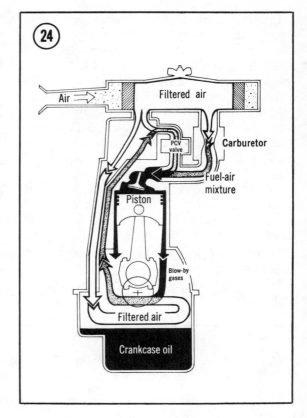

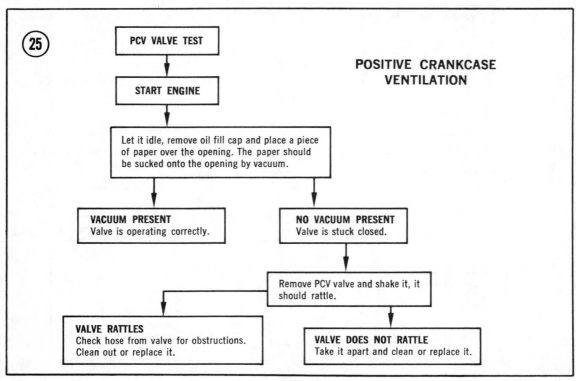

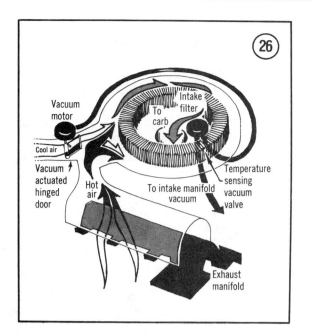

26

- Vacuum motor
- Intake filter
- To carb
- Cool air
- Vacuum actuated hinged door
- Hot air
- To intake manifold vacuum
- Temperature sensing vacuum valve
- Exhaust manifold

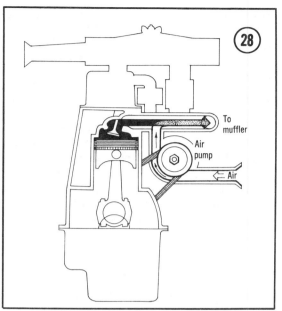

28

- To muffler
- Air pump
- Air

2

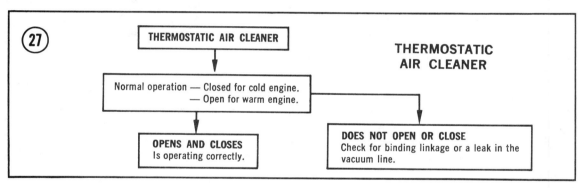

27

THERMOSTATIC AIR CLEANER

↓

Normal operation — Closed for cold engine.
— Open for warm engine.

**THERMOSTATIC
AIR CLEANER**

↓   ↓

OPENS AND CLOSES
Is operating correctly.

DOES NOT OPEN OR CLOSE
Check for binding linkage or a leak in the
vacuum line.

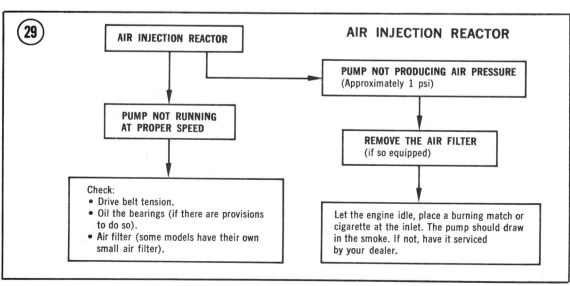

29

AIR INJECTION REACTOR

AIR INJECTION REACTOR

↓

PUMP NOT PRODUCING AIR PRESSURE
(Approximately 1 psi)

**PUMP NOT RUNNING
AT PROPER SPEED**

↓

REMOVE THE AIR FILTER
(if so equipped)

↓

Check:
- Drive belt tension.
- Oil the bearings (if there are provisions to do so).
- Air filter (some models have their own small air filter).

↓

Let the engine idle, place a burning match or
cigarette at the inlet. The pump should draw
in the smoke. If not, have it serviced
by your dealer.

stores the vapor when the engine is stopped. When the engine runs, manifold vacuum draws the vapor from the canister. Instead of being released into the atmosphere, the fuel vapor takes part in the normal combustion process.

Exhaust Gas Recirculation

The exhaust gas recirculation (EGR) system is used to reduce the emission of nitrogen oxides (NOx). Relatively inert exhaust gases are introduced into the combustion process to slightly reduce peak temperatures. This reduction in temperature reduces the formation of NOx.

Figure 31 provides a simple test of this system.

ENGINE NOISES

Often the first evidence of an internal engine trouble is a strange noise. That knocking, clicking, or tapping which you never heard before may be warning you of impending trouble.

While engine noises can indicate problems, they are sometimes difficult to interpret correctly; inexperienced mechanics can be seriously misled by them.

Professional mechanics often use a special stethoscope which looks similar to a doctor's stethoscope for isolating engine noises. You can do nearly as well with a "sounding stick" which can be an ordinary piece of doweling or a section of small hose. By placing one end in contact with the area to which you want to listen and the other end near your ear, you can hear

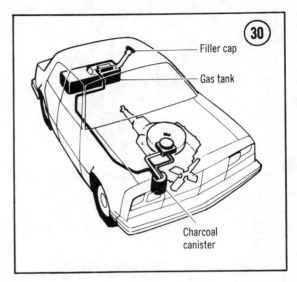

30

Filler cap

Gas tank

Charcoal canister

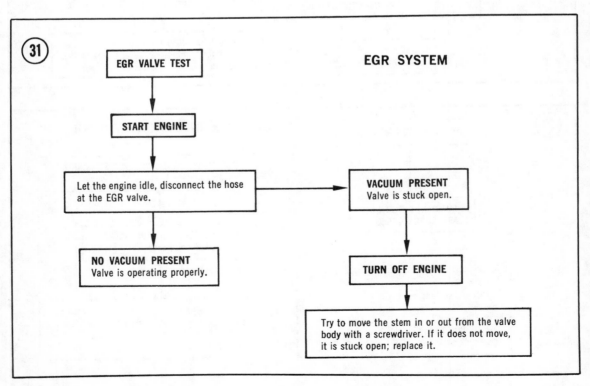

31

EGR SYSTEM

EGR VALVE TEST

START ENGINE

Let the engine idle, disconnect the hose at the EGR valve.

NO VACUUM PRESENT
Valve is operating properly.

VACUUM PRESENT
Valve is stuck open.

TURN OFF ENGINE

Try to move the stem in or out from the valve body with a screwdriver. If it does not move, it is stuck open; replace it.

sounds emanating from that area. The first time you do this, you may be horrified at the strange noises coming from even a normal engine. If you can, have an experienced friend or mechanic help you sort the noises out.

Clicking or Tapping Noises

Clicking or tapping noises usually come from the valve train, and indicate excessive valve clearance.

If your vehicle has adjustable valves, the procedure for adjusting the valve clearance is explained in Chapter Three. If your vehicle has hydraulic lifters, the clearance may not be adjustable. The noise may be coming from a collapsed lifter. These may be cleaned or replaced as described in the engine chapter.

A sticking valve may also sound like a valve with excessive clearance. In addition, excessive wear in valve train components can cause similar engine noises.

Knocking Noises

A heavy, dull knocking is usually caused by a worn main bearing. The noise is loudest when the engine is working hard, i.e., accelerating hard at low speed. You may be able to isolate the trouble to a single bearing by disconnecting

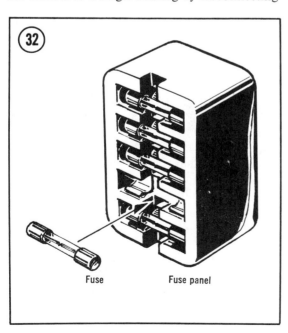

Fuse   Fuse panel

the spark plugs one at a time. When you reach the spark plug nearest the bearing, the knock will be reduced or disappear.

Worn connecting rod bearings may also produce a knock, but the sound is usually more "metallic." As with a main bearing, the noise is worse when accelerating. It may even increase further just as you go from accelerating to coasting. Disconnecting spark plugs will help isolate this knock as well.

A double knock or clicking usually indicates a worn piston pin. Disconnecting spark plugs will isolate this to a particular piston, however, the noise will *increase* when you reach the affected piston.

A loose flywheel and excessive crankshaft end play also produce knocking noises. While similar to main bearing noises, these are usually intermittent, not constant, and they do not change when spark plugs are disconnected.

Some mechanics confuse piston pin noise with piston slap. The double knock will distinguish the piston pin noise. Piston slap is identified by the fact that it is always louder when the engine is cold.

ELECTRICAL ACCESSORIES

Lights and Switches (Interior and Exterior)

1. *Bulb does not light* — Remove the bulb and check for a broken element. Also check the inside of the socket; make sure the contacts are clean and free of corrosion. If the bulb and socket are OK, check to see if a fuse has blown or a circuit breaker has tripped. The fuse panel (**Figure 32**) is usually located under the instrument panel. Replace the blown fuse or reset the circuit breaker. If the fuse blows or the breaker trips again, there is a short in that circuit. Check that circuit all the way to the battery. Look for worn wire insulation or burned wires.

If all the above are all right, check the switch controlling the bulb for continuity with an ohmmeter at the switch terminals. Check the switch contact terminals for loose or dirty electrical connections.

2. *Headlights work but will not switch from either high or low beam* — Check the beam selector switch for continuity with an ohmmeter

at the switch terminals. Check the switch contact terminals for loose or dirty electrical connections.

3. *Brake light switch inoperative* — On mechanically operated switches, usually mounted near the brake pedal arm, adjust the switch to achieve correct mechanical operation. Check the switch for continuity with an ohmmeter at the switch terminals. Check the switch contact terminals for loose or dirty electrical connections.

4. *Back-up lights do not operate* — Check light bulb as described earlier. Locate the switch, normally located near the shift lever. Adjust switch to achieve correct mechanical operation. Check the switch for continuity with an ohmmeter at the switch terminals. Bypass the switch with a jumper wire; if the lights work, replace the switch.

Directional Signals

1. *Directional signals do not operate* — If the indicator light on the instrument panel burns steadily instead of flashing, this usually indicates that one of the exterior lights is burned out. Check all lamps that normally flash. If all are all right, the flasher unit may be defective. Replace it with a good one.

2. *Directional signal indicator light on instrument panel does not light up* — Check the light bulbs as described earlier. Check all electrical connections and check the flasher unit.

3. *Directional signals will not self-cancel* — Check the self-cancelling mechanism located inside the steering column.

4. *Directional signals flash slowly* — Check the condition of the battery and the alternator (or generator) drive belt tension (**Figure 4**). Check the flasher unit and all related electrical connections.

Windshield Wipers

1. *Wipers do not operate* — Check for a blown fuse or circuit breaker that has tripped; replace or reset. Check all related terminals for loose or dirty electrical connections. Check continuity of the control switch with an ohmmeter at the switch terminals. Check the linkage and arms for loose, broken, or binding parts. Straighten out or replace where necessary.

2. *Wiper motor hums but will not operate* — The motor may be shorted out internally; check and/or replace the motor. Also check for broken or binding linkage and arms.

3. *Wiper arms will not return to the stowed position when turned off* — The motor has a special internal switch for this purpose. Have it inspected by your dealer. Do not attempt this yourself.

Interior Heater

1. *Heater fan does not operate* — Check for a blown fuse or circuit breaker that has tripped. Check the switch for continuity with an ohmmeter at the switch terminals. Check the switch contact terminals for loose or dirty electrical connections.

2. *Heat output is insufficient* — Check the heater hose/engine coolant control valve usually located in the engine compartment; make sure it is in the open position. Ensure that the heater door(s) and cable(s) are operating correctly and are in the open position. Inspect the heat ducts; make sure that they are not crimped or blocked.

COOLING SYSTEM

The temperature gauge or warning light usually signals cooling system troubles before there is any damage. As long as you stop the vehicle at the first indication of trouble, serious damage is unlikely.

In most cases, the trouble will be obvious as soon as you open the hood. If there is coolant or steam leaking, look for a defective radiator, radiator hose, or heater hose. If there is no evidence of leakage, make sure that the fan belt is in good condition. If the trouble is not obvious, refer to **Figures 33 and 34** to help isolate the trouble.

Automotive cooling systems operate under pressure to permit higher operating temperatures without boil-over. The system should be checked periodically to make sure it can withstand normal pressure. **Figure 35** shows the equipment which nearly any service station has for testing the system pressure.

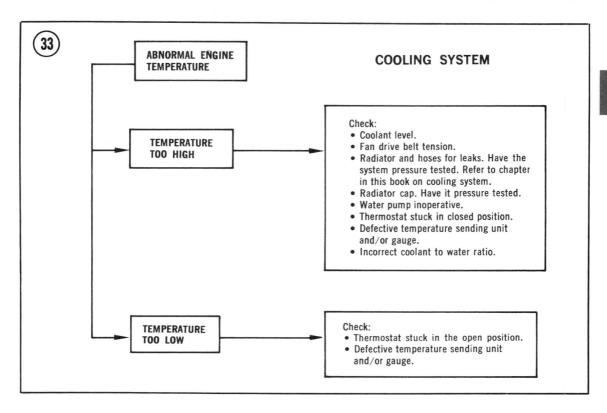

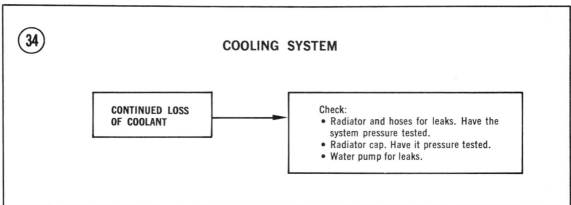

CLUTCH

All clutch troubles except adjustments require transmission removal to identify and cure the problem.

1. *Slippage* — This is most noticeable when accelerating in a high gear at relatively low speed. To check slippage, park the vehicle on a level surface with the handbrake set. Shift to 2nd gear and release the clutch as if driving off. If the clutch is good, the engine will slow and stall. If the clutch slips, continued engine speed will give it away.

Slippage results from insufficient clutch pedal free play, oil or grease on the clutch disc, worn pressure plate, or weak springs.

2. *Drag or failure to release* — This trouble usually causes difficult shifting and gear clash, especially when downshifting. The cause may be excessive clutch pedal free play, warped or bent pressure plate or clutch disc, broken or

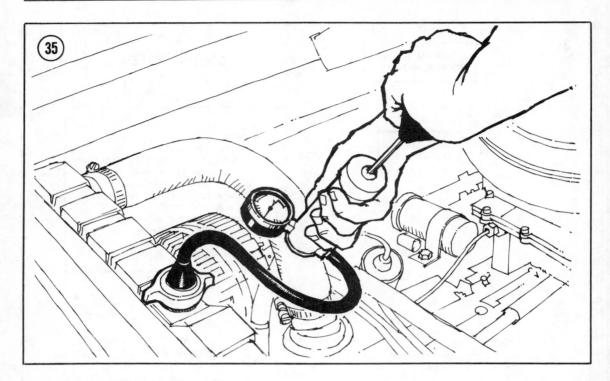

loose linings, or lack of lubrication in pilot bearing. Also check condition of transmission main shaft splines.

3. *Chatter or grabbing* — A number of things can cause this trouble. Check tightness of engine mounts and engine-to-transmission mounting bolts. Check for worn or misaligned pressure plate and misaligned release plate.

4. *Other noises* — Noise usually indicates a dry or defective release or pilot bearing. Check the bearings and replace if necessary. Also check all parts for misalignment and uneven wear.

MANUAL
TRANSMISSION/TRANSAXLE

Transmission and transaxle troubles are evident when one or more of the following symptoms appear:

   a. Difficulty changing gears
   b. Gears clash when downshifting
   c. Slipping out of gear
   d. Excessive noise in NEUTRAL
   e. Excessive noise in gear
   f. Oil leaks

Transmission and transaxle repairs are not recommended unless the many special tools required are available.

Transmission and transaxle troubles are sometimes difficult to distinguish from clutch troubles. Eliminate the clutch as a source of trouble before installing a new or rebuilt transmission or transaxle.

AUTOMATIC TRANSMISSION

Most automatic transmission repairs require considerable specialized knowledge and tools. It is impractical for the home mechanic to invest in the tools, since they cost more than a properly rebuilt transmission.

Check fluid level and condition frequently to help prevent future problems. If the fluid is orange or black in color or smells like varnish, it is an indication of some type of damage or failure within the transmission. Have the transmission serviced by your dealer or competent automatic transmission service facility.

BRAKES

Good brakes are vital to the safe operation of the vehicle. Performing the maintenance speci-

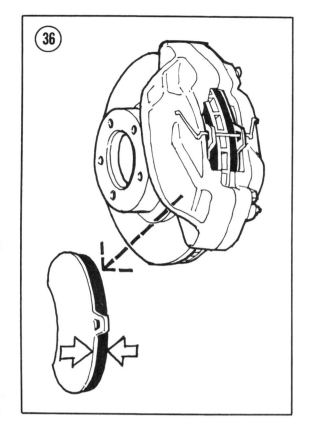

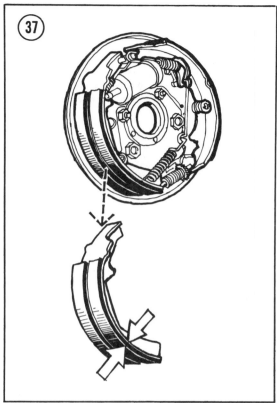

fied in Chapter Three will minimize problems with the brakes. Most importantly, check and maintain the level of fluid in the master cylinder, and check the thickness of the linings on the disc brake pads (**Figure 36**) or drum brake shoes (**Figure 37**).

If trouble develops, **Figures 38 through 40** will help you locate the problem. Refer to the brake chapter for actual repair procedures.

STEERING AND SUSPENSION

Trouble in the suspension or steering is evident when the following occur:

  a. Steering is hard
  b. Car pulls to one side
  c. Car wanders or front wheels wobble
  d. Steering has excessive play
  e. Tire wear is abnormal

Unusual steering, pulling, or wandering is usually caused by bent or otherwise misaligned suspension parts. This is difficult to check

without proper alignment equipment. Refer to the suspension chapter in this book for repairs that you can perform and those that must be left to a dealer or suspension specialist.

If your trouble seems to be excessive play, check wheel bearing adjustment first. This is the most frequent cause. Then check ball-joints (refer to Suspension chapter). Finally, check tie rod end ball-joints by shaking each tie rod. Also check steering gear, or rack-and-pinion assembly to see that it is securely bolted down.

TIRE WEAR ANALYSIS

Abnormal tire wear should be analyzed to determine its causes. The most common causes are the following:

  a. Incorrect tire pressure
  b. Improper driving
  c. Overloading
  d. Bad road surfaces
  e. Incorrect wheel alignment

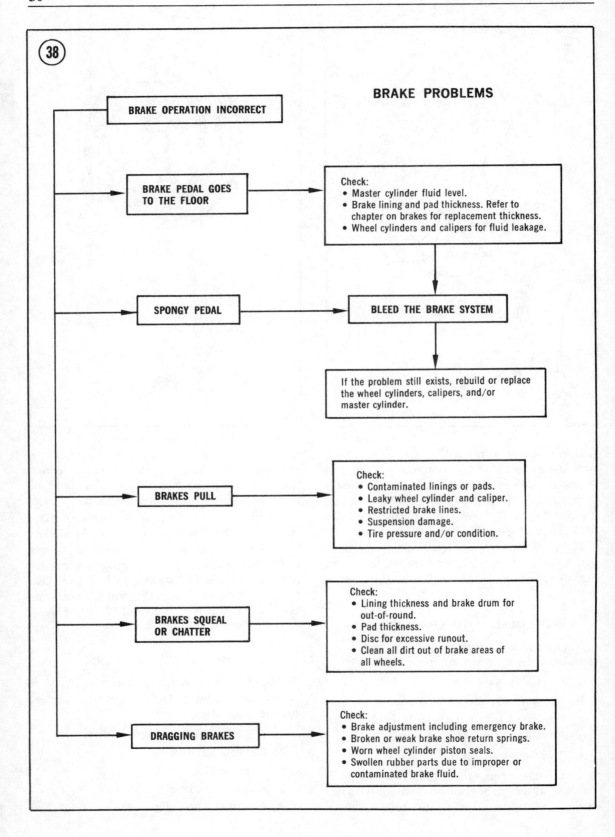

(38)

BRAKE PROBLEMS

BRAKE OPERATION INCORRECT

BRAKE PEDAL GOES
TO THE FLOOR

Check:
- Master cylinder fluid level.
- Brake lining and pad thickness. Refer to chapter on brakes for replacement thickness.
- Wheel cylinders and calipers for fluid leakage.

SPONGY PEDAL

BLEED THE BRAKE SYSTEM

If the problem still exists, rebuild or replace the wheel cylinders, calipers, and/or master cylinder.

BRAKES PULL

Check:
- Contaminated linings or pads.
- Leaky wheel cylinder and caliper.
- Restricted brake lines.
- Suspension damage.
- Tire pressure and/or condition.

BRAKES SQUEAL
OR CHATTER

Check:
- Lining thickness and brake drum for out-of-round.
- Pad thickness.
- Disc for excessive runout.
- Clean all dirt out of brake areas of all wheels.

DRAGGING BRAKES

Check:
- Brake adjustment including emergency brake.
- Broken or weak brake shoe return springs.
- Worn wheel cylinder piston seals.
- Swollen rubber parts due to improper or contaminated brake fluid.

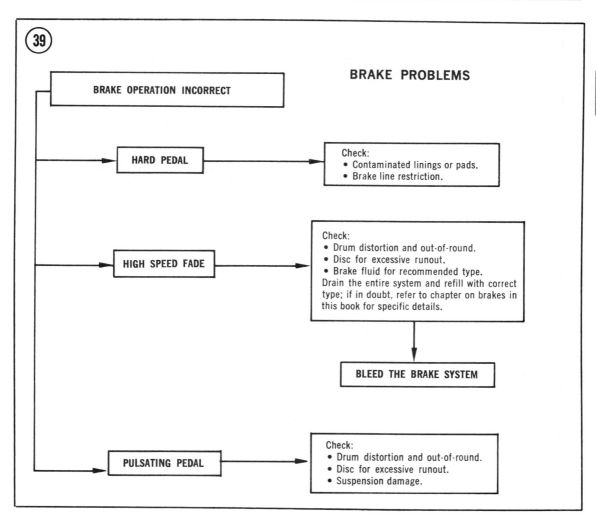

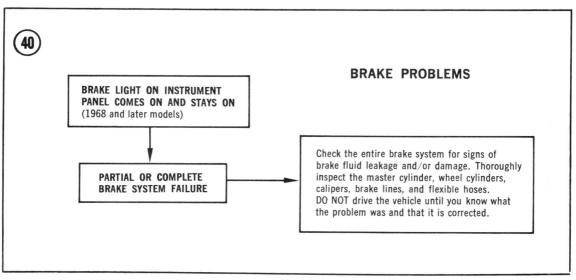

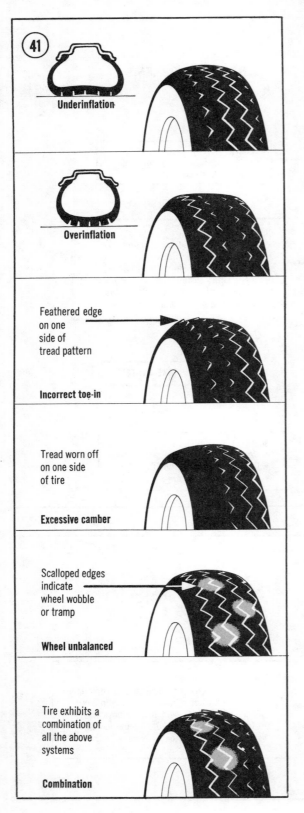

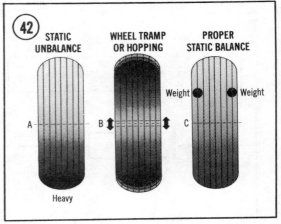

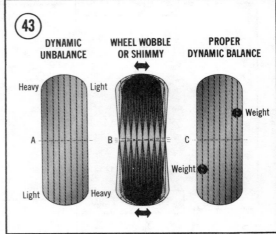

Figure 41 identifies wear patterns and indicates the most probable causes.

WHEEL BALANCING

All four wheels and tires must be in balance along two axes. To be in static balance (**Figure 42**), weight must be evenly distributed around the axis of rotation. (A) shows a statically unbalanced wheel; (B) shows the result — wheel tramp or hopping; (C) shows proper static balance.

To be in dynamic balance (**Figure 43**), the centerline of the weight must coincide with the centerline of the wheel. (A) shows a dynamically unbalanced wheel; (B) shows the result — wheel wobble or shimmy; (C) shows proper dynamic balance.

NOTE: If you own a 1983 or later model, first check the Supplement at the back of the book for any new service information.

CHAPTER THREE

3

LUBRICATION, MAINTENANCE AND TUNE-UP

This chapter deals with the normal maintenance necessary to keep your Camaro or Firebird running properly. **Table 1** lists the maintenance intervals for cars given normal use. Some procedures are done at fuel stops; others are done at specified mileage or time intervals.

Cars driven under severe conditions require more frequent maintenance. This is specified in **Table 1**. Such conditions include:

    a. Frequent short trips.
    b. Stop-and-go driving.
    c. Extremely cold weather.
    d. Trailer towing.
    e. Dusty conditions.

Some maintenance procedures are included in the *Tune-up* section at the end of the chapter and detailed instructions will be found there. Other steps are described in the following chapters. Chapter references are included with these steps.

Tables 1-6 are at the end of the chapter.

HOISTING, JACKING AND LIFTING POINTS

Camaro/Firebird design requires that special precautions be taken when raising the car with a jack or a hoist and when positioning jackstands. Incorrect jack or jackstand placement can cause suspension or drive train damage. The service jack provided with the car is intended only for emergency use in changing a flat tire. Refer to the Owner's Manual when using this jack. Do not use it to lift the car up while performing other service.

A floor jack or other type of hydraulic jack is recommended for raising the front or rear of the car when required for service. Always place jackstands at the appropriate points to hold the car stable. Relying upon a single jack to hold the car without the use of jackstands can lead to serious physical injury.

When lifting the front of the car, place your jack (and jackstand) under the lift pad located to the rear of the front tire. A similar lift point for the rear of the car is located just forward of the rear tire. The use of a suspension contact hoist is recommended; it should be positioned as shown in **Figure 1** and **Figure 2**.

FUEL STOP CHECKS

1. With the engine cold and off, pull out the dipstick. See **Figure 3** for the 4-cylinder

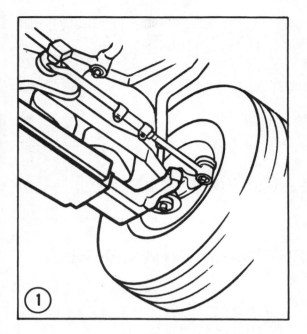

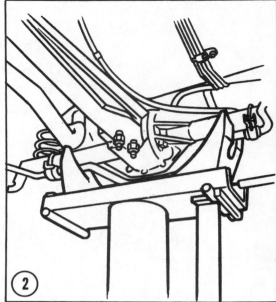

engine, **Figure 4** for the V6 engine and **Figure 5** for the V8 engine. Wipe dipstick with a clean rag, insert it and pull it out again. Check the oil level on the dipstick.

NOTE
Some dipsticks have "ADD" and "FULL" lines. Others read "ADD 1 QT." and "OPERATING RANGE." In either case, keep the oil level above the "ADD" line.

2. Top up to the "FULL" or "OPERATING RANGE" mark on the dipstick if necessary, using *only* an SF grade oil. See **Table 2** for proper oil viscosity. Add oil through the hole in the valve cover. See **Figure 6** (4-cylinder engine), **Figure 7** (V6 engine) or **Figure 8** (V8 engine).

3. Check coolant level in the recovery tank (**Figure 9**). It should be at the "FULL COLD" mark when the engine is cold and at the "FULL HOT" mark when the engine is hot. Top up as needed. If the tank is empty, check the radiator level as well.

WARNING
The radiator cap should not be removed when the engine is warm or hot. If this is unavoidable, cover the cap with a thick rag or wear heavy leather gloves. Turn the cap slowly counterclockwise

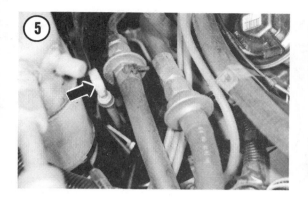

3

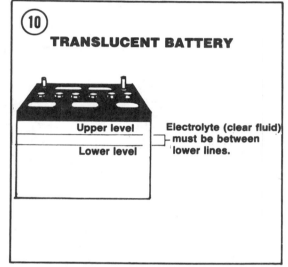

TRANSLUCENT BATTERY

Upper level

Lower level

Electrolyte (clear fluid) must be between lower lines.

against the first stop (about 1/4 turn). Let all pressure (hot coolant and steam) escape. Then press the cap down and turn counterclockwise to remove. If the cap is removed too soon, scalding coolant may escape and cause a serious burn.

4. Check battery electrolyte level (not required on maintenance-free batteries). On translucent batteries, it should be between the marks on the battery case (**Figure 10**). On black batteries, it should be even with the bottom of the filler wells. See **Figure 11**.

5. Check fluid in the windshield washer jar. See **Figure 12**. It should be kept full, except during winter months when filling it only 3/4 full will allow for expansion if the fluid freezes. Use windshield washer solvent, following the manufacturer's instructions.

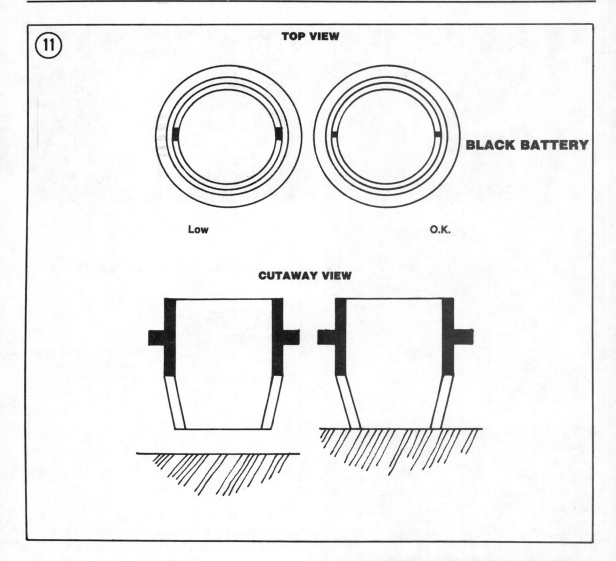

⑪ TOP VIEW

BLACK BATTERY

Low   O.K.

CUTAWAY VIEW

6. Check fluid level in the brake master
cylinder (**Figure 13**). Clean the area around
the master cylinder reservoir cover. Lift up on
the cover tabs on one side and remove the
cover (**Figure 14**). Make sure the brake fluid
in both sections is within 1/4 in. of the lowest
edge of each filler opening. Top up if
necessary with DOT 3 or DOT 4 brake fluid.

⑫

Brake fluid absorbs moisture; moisture in the brake lines can reduce braking efficiency.

7. Check fluid level in the power steering pump reservoir (**Figure 15**), if so equipped. With the engine at normal operating temperature (upper radiator hose hot), turn the steering wheel lock-to-lock several times, then shut the engine off and remove the

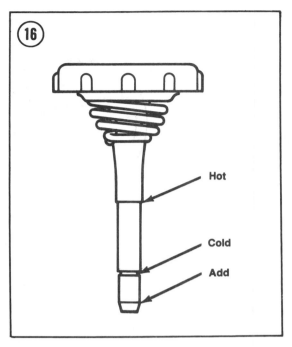

power steering pump dipstick. The fluid should be between the "HOT" and "COLD" marks on the dipstick (**Figure 16**). Top up, if necessary, with power steering fluid.

8. Check tire pressures. This should be done when the tires are cold in the morning or after the car has been parked for at least 3 hours after being driven less than one mile. When the tires heat up from driving, the air inside them expands and gives false high-pressure readings. See the tire placard affixed to the left front door edge for recommended tire pressures.

NOTE
Maintain the compact spare tire at 60 psi.

**EVERY 7,500 MILES
(12 MONTHS)**

Engine Oil and Filter

If the car is given normal use, change the oil every 7,500 miles or 12 months, whichever comes first. If it is used in dusty areas or for frequent short trips, stop-and-go driving or in extremely cold weather, change the oil every 3,000 miles or 3 months. Change the oil filter at every second oil change.

Use an SF grade oil only. Multi-viscosity oils are recommended. To select the exact viscosity range, refer to **Table 2**. The rating and viscosity range are usually printed on top of the can.

To drain the oil and change the filter, you will need:

a. Drain pan (6 quarts or more capacity).
b. Oil can spout or can opener and funnel.
c. Filter wrench.
d. 3-4 quarts of SF grade oil (see **Table 4**).
e. Adjustable wrench.
f. New oil filter.

There are several ways to discard the old oil safely. Some service stations accept oil for recycling. Check local regulations before disposing of oil in the trash.

The drain pan can be cleaned with solvent or paint thinner, if available. If not, hot water and dishwashing liquid will work.

1. Warm the engine to operating temperature, then shut it off.
2. Place the drain pan under the crankcase drain plug. See **Figure 17** for the 4-cylinder engine drain plug; the V6 and V8 are similar. Remove the plug with the wrench and let the oil drain for at least 10 minutes. Check condition of the drain plug gasket and replace if damaged. Reinstall the plug and gasket and tighten the plug to 15-20 ft.-lb. (20-27 N•m).
3. Move the drain pan beneath the oil filter. See **Figure 18** for filter location on each engine. Unscrew the oil filter counterclockwise. Use a filter wrench if the filter is too tight or too hot to remove by hand.
4. Wipe the gasket surface on the engine block clean with a paper towel.
5. Coat the neoprene gasket on the new filter with clean engine oil.
6. Screw the filter onto the engine *by hand* until the gasket just touches the engine block. At this point, there will be a very slight resistance when turning the filter.
7. Tighten the filter another 3/4 turn *by hand*. If the filter wrench is used, the filter will probably be overtightened. This can cause an oil leak.
8. Remove the oil filler cap from the valve cover. See **Figure 19** (4-cylinder engine),

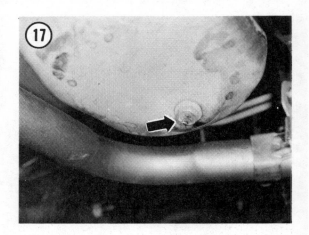

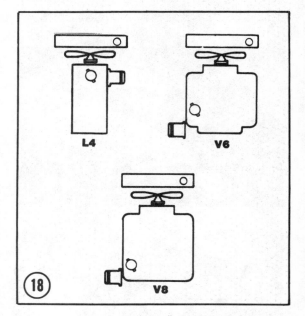

L4

V6

V8

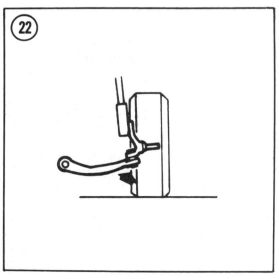

Figure 20 (V6 engine) or Figure 21 (V8 engine).

9. Pour the oil into the engine. Wipe up any spills on the valve cover or oil filler tube with a clean cloth. The crankcase capacities of the 4-cylinder and V6 engines are the same, whether or not the filter is changed. The V8 engine requires an additional quart when the filter is changed. See Table 4.

10. Start the engine and let it idle. The instrument panel oil pressure light will remain on for a few seconds, then go out. If equipped with an oil pressure gauge, the needle will gradually move into a normal operating position.

CAUTION
Do not race the engine to make the oil pressure light go out or the pressure indicator needle move. It takes time for the oil to reach all parts of the engine and racing it could damage dry parts.

11. While the engine is running, check the area under and around the drain plug and oil filter for leaks.

12. Turn the engine off. Let the oil settle for several minutes, then recheck the level on the dipstick. Add oil, if necessary, to bring the level up to the "FULL" or "OPERATING RANGE" mark, but *do not overfill*.

Chassis and Suspension Lubrication

Inspect and lubricate the following components or systems. If the car is driven under severe service conditions as described in Table 1, perform this service every 3,000 miles or 3 months.

   a. Upper and lower control arm ball-joints (Figure 22).
   b. Steering linkage (Figure 23).
   c. Transmission shift linkage contacting faces.
   d. Hood latch and hinges.
   e. Door hinges, jamb switch and lock cylinder.
   f. Tailgate hinges, latch and lock.
   g. Gas tank filler door hinge.
   h. Parking brake pulley, cable and linkage.
   i. Throttle linkage.

Brake Lines

Check brake lines and hoses for proper routing and connection. Look for binding, leaking, chafing, cracks or other defects. Replace any damaged hoses and correct other defects, if found.

Exhaust System

Inspect the complete exhaust system including the catalytic converter for open holes, seams, loose connections or other unsafe conditions. Check for broken, damaged, missing or out-of-position components. Whenever the muffler requires replacement, replace the exhaust pipe(s) and resonator to the rear of the muffler to maintain exhaust system integrity.

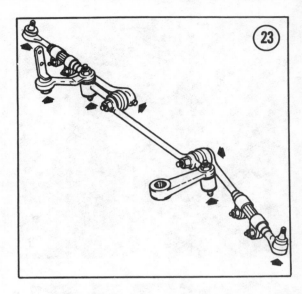

FIRST 7,500 MILES, EVERY 15,000 MILES

Tire Rotation

Inspect the tires for cracks, bumps, bulges or other defects. Look for signs of excessive wear. Built-in tread wear indicators will appear between the tread grooves when the tread depth is worn to 1/16 in. (1.6 mm) or less. Replace the tire when the indicators can be seen in 2 or more adjacent grooves at 3 points around the tire.

Rotate the tires according to **Figure 24**. Readjust tire pressure to the specifications listed on the tire placard affixed to the left front door edge.

Disc Brakes

Check the surface of the rotors when the tires are removed for rotation. Check the lining thickness through the inspection hole in the top of the caliper. If the lining is worn to the approximate thickness of the pad, remove the brake pads and measure the lining. Replace all pads if any lining is worn to within 1/32 in. of a rivet or any other point on the pad.

All front disc brakes use a wear indicator to make noise when the linings require replacement. The indicator is a spring clip (**Figure 25**) that is an integral part of the

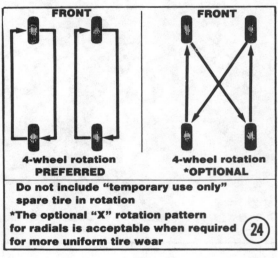

inboard pad. As the lining wears, the clip touches the rotor and makes a warning sound.

Drive Belts

Drive belt tension can be checked according to belt deflection, but GM recommends the use of a belt tension gauge. If the deflection method is used, press downward firmly on the belt at a point midway between the 2 pulleys. If the distance between the pulleys is less than 12 inches, the belt should deflect 1/3-1/4 in. Drive belts with a greater span should deflect 1/4-3/8 in.

Adjust drive belt tension with a tension gauge as follows:

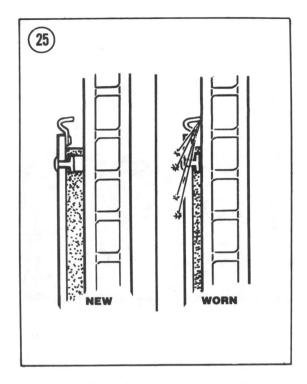

1. Install the belt tension gauge and take a reading. Compare to the specifications in **Table 5**.

2. Loosen the accessory pivot bolt and/or adjusting bolt.

3. Move the accessory unit toward or away from the engine as required.

4. Tighten the adjusting bolt, then tighten the pivot bolt.

5. Recheck belt tension. If necessary, repeat the procedure to obtain the correct tension.

FIRST 7,500 MILES, EVERY 30,000 MILES

Carburetor Choke and Hoses

Make sure that the choke and vacuum break assembly work freely and properly. Spray choke shaft with choke cleaner to remove any gum or varnish buildup. Inspect hoses for proper routing and connection. Check hose condition and replace any that are cracked, split or deteriorated.

Throttle Body Hoses

Check hoses for proper routing and connection. Check hose condition and replace any that are cracked, split or deteriorated.

Carburetor or Throttle Body Mounting Nuts/Bolts

Check carburetor mounting nut/bolt torque. If less than 5 ft.-lb. (7 N•m), retorque to 8 ft.-lb. (11 N•m). If greater than 5 ft.-lb. (7 N•m), do not retorque. If equipped with fuel injection, check throttle body nut/bolt torque. It should be 10-14 ft.-lb. (14-19 N•m).

Idle Speed

Check and adjust to the specifications shown on the Vehicle Emissions Control Information (VECI) label under the hood.

EVERY 15,000 MILES

Automatic Transmission Fluid

Under normal driving conditions, the transmission fluid is changed at 100,000 mile intervals. If the car has been driven under severe service conditions such as those stated in **Table 1**, drain and refill the fluid at this interval.

1. Raise the front of the car with a jack and place it on jackstands.

2. Place a drain pan under the transmission.

3. Loosen all pan attaching bolts (**Figure 26**) a few turns. Tap one corner of the pan with a rubber hammer to break it loose and let the fluid drain.

4. When the fluid has drained to the level of the pan flange, remove the pan bolts at the

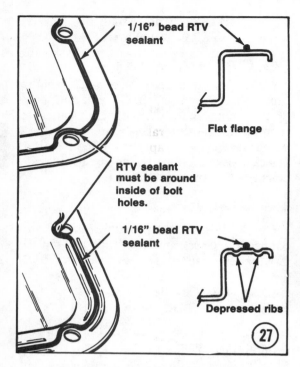

1/16" bead RTV sealant

Flat flange

RTV sealant must be around inside of bolt holes.

1/16" bead RTV sealant

Depressed ribs

(27)

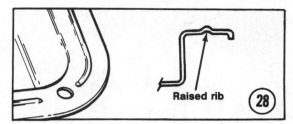

Raised rib (28)

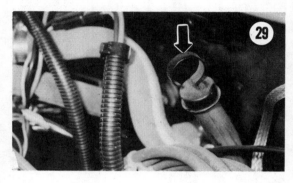

(29)

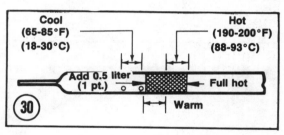

Cool (65-85°F) (18-30°C)   Hot (190-200°F) (88-93°C)

Add 0.5 liter (1 pt.)   Full hot

(30)   Warm

rear and along both sides of the pan. This will let the pan drop at one end and drain slowly.

5. When all fluid has drained, remove the pan and let the strainer drain.

6. Discard the gasket and clean the pan thoroughly with solvent and lint-free cloths or paper towels.

7. Remove the screen/filter-to-valve body bolts. Remove the screen/filter.

8. Clean screen assembly thoroughly in solvent and dry with compressed air. Replace paper or felt-type filters.

9. Install a new gasket or O-ring to the screen/filter assembly, as required. Install the screen/filter to the valve body and tighten attaching bolts securely.

10. Apply a 1/16 in. bead of RTV sealant to the pan mounting flange. See **Figure 27** and *Gasket Sealant*, Chapter Four.

NOTE
*If the pan flange has a raised rib as shown in **Figure 28**, do not use RTV sealant. This pan design requires the use of a gasket.*

11. Install the pan on the transmission and tighten the attaching bolts in a crisscross pattern to 10-13 ft.-lb. (14-18 N•m).

12. Fill the transmission through the dipstick tube with approximately 4 quarts of DEXRON II automatic transmission fluid. Start the engine and let it idle for 2 minutes.

13. Set the parking brake, block the wheels and place the transmission in PARK. Move the selector lever through each gear range, pausing long enough for the transmission to engage. Return to the PARK position.

14. Remove the dipstick (**Figure 29**) and wipe it clean. Reinsert the dipstick in the filler tube until it seats completely.

15. Remove the dipstick and check the fluid level. It should be in the crosshatch area between the "ADD" and "FULL HOT" marks (**Figure 30**). Install the dipstick.

NOTE
Do not overfill the transmission. This will cause foaming and a loss of fluid through the vent, which will result in a premature transmission failure.

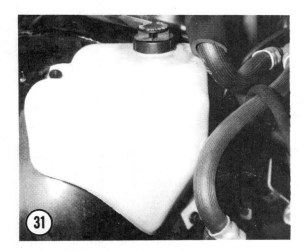

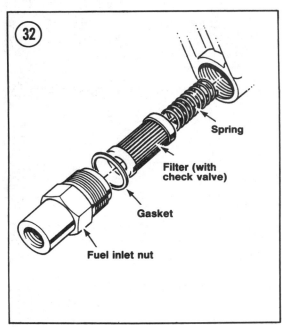

Spring

Filter (with
check valve)

Gasket

Fuel inlet nut

Cooling System

WARNING
*Personal injury is possible. Perform the
cooling system service when the engine
is cold.*

Visually inspect the level and condition of
the coolant in the recovery tank (**Figure 31**).
Top up, if necessary, with a 50/50 mixture of
ethylene glycol antifreeze and water. If the
coolant looks dirty or rusty, flush the radiator
and replace the coolant as described in
Chapter Seven. Inspect all radiator and heater

hoses. Replace any hoses that are cracked,
deteriorated or extremely soft or spongy.
Make sure all hoses are correctly installed and
all clamps are securely tightened.

Rear Brakes and Parking Brake

1. Check the rear brake linings and drums.
See *Rear Brakes*, Chapter Twelve.
2. Check the parking brake adjustment. See
Adjustment, Chapter Twelve.
3. Check the brake lines and hoses for leaks,
cracks or kinking. Make sure no brake lines or
hoses are rubbing against the car.
4. Check brake fluid level in the master
cylinder. See *Fuel Stop Checks* in this chapter.

Throttle Linkage

Check for damaged or missing parts. Work
the throttle lever back and forth to check for
interference or binding. Spray the linkage
with carburetor cleaner and lubricate with
WD-40.

Fuel Tank, Cap and Lines

Inspect the fuel tank, cap and lines for leaks
or damage. Remove the fuel cap and check
the gasket for an even filler neck imprint.

Fuel Filter (Carburetted Engine)

Carburetted engines use a pleated paper
filter and check valve assembly located in the
carburetor fuel inlet (**Figure 32**). To replace
the filter:
1. Hold the inlet nut with an open-end
wrench and loosen the fuel line attaching nut
with a second open-end wrench.
2. Disconnect the fuel line from the inlet nut.
Cap the line and move it out of the way.
3. Remove the fuel inlet nut. Remove the
filter and spring.
4. Install spring and filter element as shown
in **Figure 32**. The hole in the filter must face
toward the nut.
5. Install new gasket on inlet nut. Install nut
in carburetor and tighten to 25 ft.-lb. (34
N•m).

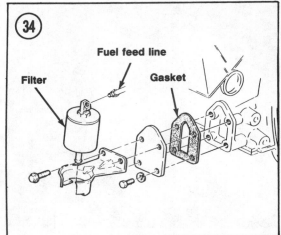

Fuel feed line

Filter

Gasket

6. Install fuel line to inlet nut. Hold inlet nut with an open-end wrench and tighten fuel line fitting to 18 ft.-lb. (24 N•m).

Fuel Filter (Fuel Injected Engine)

Fuel injected engines use a disposable inline filter canister (**Figure 33**). The V8 filter is bracket-mounted to the engine block (**Figure 34**). To replace the filter:

1. Relieve fuel system pressure as described in Chapter Six, *Relieving System Pressure*.
2. Loosen the fuel inlet and outlet fittings at the filter. Remove the inlet and outlet lines.
3. Loosen the bracket clamp screw. Pull the filter from the bracket.
4. Installation is the reverse of removal. Be sure the arrow on the filter canister faces in the direction of fuel flow.

EVERY 30,000 MILES

Spark Plugs, Engine Timing and Ignition Wiring

See *Tune-up* in this chapter.

Cooling System

Drain, flush and refill every 2 years or 30,000 miles. See *Cooling System Flushing* in Chapter Seven.

Manual Steering Gear Seals

No lubrication is necessary for the life of the steering gearbox. However, the seal should be checked for possible leakage. If

solid grease is found, replace the seal. An oily film can be ignored, as this is normal.

Air Cleaner System and Filter

Inspect the system as described under *Thermostatic Air Cleaner (Thermac)* in Chapter Six.

Remove the air cleaner cover and lift out the old filter. **Figure 35** shows the 4-cylinder engine; the V6 and V8 air cleaners are similar. Wipe the inside of the air cleaner housing with a damp paper towel to remove dust, dirt and debris. Install a new filter. Do not install the cover before changing the crankcase vent filter, if so equipped.

Crankcase Vent Filter

While the air cleaner cover is off to change the air cleaner filter, remove the retaining clip from the crankcase vent filter (**Figure 36**).

Replace the filter and install the retaining clip. Install the air cleaner cover.

Oxygen Sensor

The oxygen sensor is installed in the exhaust manifold. See **Figure 37** (4-cylinder engine) or **Figure 38** (V6 and V8 engine). It may be difficult to remove when engine temperature is less than 120° F (48° C). Do not use force to remove the sensor.

1. Disconnect the sensor pigtail electrical connector.
2. Remove the sensor from the exhaust manifold.

> *NOTE*
> *If the same sensor is to be reinstalled, coat the threads with GM antiseize compound part No. 5613695 or equivalent electrically conductive antiseize compound. New sensors already have the compound on the threads.*

3. Install the sensor and tighten to 30 ft.-lb. (41 N•m). Reconnect the electrical connector.

Exhaust Gas Recirculation (EGR) System

Inspect the system as described in Chapter Six.

PCV Valve

Replace the PCV valve. Disconnect the valve from the rocker cover and remove from hose. Install new valve bearing same part No. in end of hose and press valve into rocker cover grommet until fully seated. **Figure 39** shows the 4-cylinder engine. **Figure 40** shows the V6 and V8 engine installation.

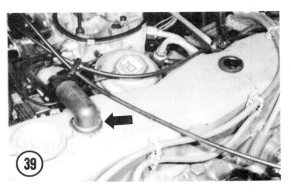

Wheel Bearings

Repack and adjust the wheel bearings. See Chapter Ten.

TUNE-UP

A tune-up consists of the following:
a. Compression check.
b. Ignition system work.
c. Carburetor inspection and adjustment.

Compression Test

Whenever the spark plugs are removed from the engine, it is a good idea to run a compression test. The compression test measures the compression pressure built up in each cylinder. Its results can be used to assess general cylinder and valve condition. In addition, it can warn of developing problems inside the engine.

1. Warm the engine to normal operating temperature (upper radiator hose hot). Shut off the engine. Make sure the choke and throttle valves are wide open.
2. Remove all spark plugs. See *Spark Plug Removal* in this chapter.
3. Disconnect the pink ignition switch feed wire at the distributor.

4. Connect a remote start switch to the starter solenoid according to manufacturer's instructions. Leave the ignition key in the OFF position.
5. Connect a compression tester to the No. 1 cylinder following the manufacturer's instructions.

NOTE
The No. 1 cylinder is the front cylinder on the 4-cylinder engine, the front cylinder in the right bank on the V6 and the front cylinder in the left bank on the V8. See **Figure 41**.

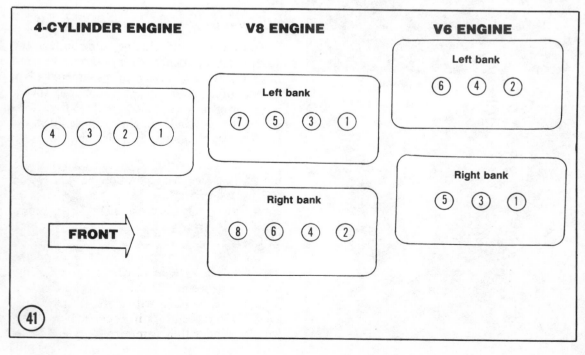

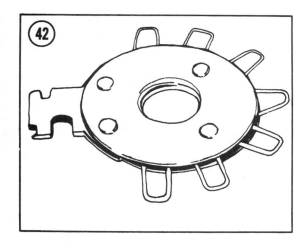

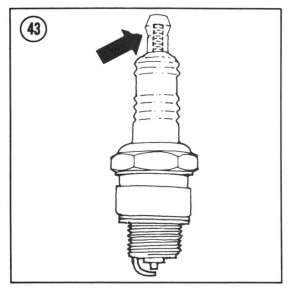

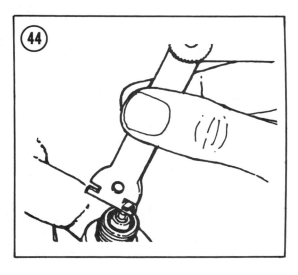

6. Crank the engine at least 5 turns with the remote start switch, or until there is no further increase in compression shown on the tester gauge.

7. Remove the compression tester and record the reading. Relieve the tester pressure valve.

8. Repeat Steps 5-7 for each cylinder.

When interpreting the results, actual readings are not as important as the differences in readings. The lowest must be within 75 percent of the highest. A greater difference indicates worn or broken rings, leaking or sticking valves or a combination of these problems.

If the compression test indicates a problem (low reading or excessive variation in readings), isolate the cause with a wet compression test. This is done in the same way as the dry compression test, except that about 1 tablespoon of oil is poured down the spark plug hole before performing Steps 5-7. If the wet compression readings are much greater than the dry compression readings, the trouble is probably due to worn or broken rings. If there is little difference between the wet and dry readings, the problem is probably due to leaky or sticking valves. If 2 adjacent cylinders read low, the head gasket may be damaged.

Spark Plug Removal

Spark plugs should be replaced every 30,000 miles.

CAUTION
Whenever the spark plugs are removed, dirt from around them can fall into the spark plug holes. This can cause expensive engine damage.

1. Blow out any foreign matter from around the spark plugs with compressed air. Use a compressor if you have one. Cans of compressed inert gas are available from photo stores.

2. Disconnect the spark plug wires by twisting the wire boot back and forth on the plug insulator while pulling upward. Pulling on the wire instead of the boot may break it.

3. Remove the plugs with a 5/8 in. spark plug socket. Keep the plugs in order so you know which cylinder they came from.

4. Examine each spark plug. Compare its condition with the illustrations in Chapter Two. Spark plug condition indicates engine condition and can warn of developing trouble.

5. Discard the plugs. Although they could be cleaned, regapped and reused if in good condition, they seldom last very long. New plugs are inexpensive and far more reliable.

Gapping and Installing the Plugs

New plugs should be carefully gapped to ensure a reliable, consistent spark. Use a special spark plug tool with a wire gauge. See **Figure 42** for one common type.

1. Remove the plugs from the box. Tapered plugs do not use gaskets. Some plug brands may have small end pieces that must be screwed on (**Figure 43**) before the plugs can be used.

> *NOTE*
> *The 4-cylinder engine uses a 0.060 in. spark plug gap; the V6 and V8 use a 0.045 in. gap. Refer to the Vehicle Emission Control Information (VECI) label located under the hood for the proper plug type and gap for your engine. If the label cannot be read, refer to **Table 6**.*

2. Determine the correct gap setting from the VECI label. Insert the appropriate size wire gauge between the electrodes. If the gap is correct, there will be a slight drag as the wire is pulled through. If there is no drag or if the wire will not pull through, bend the side electrode with the gapping tool (**Figure 44**) to change the gap and then remeasure with the wire gauge.

> *NOTE*
> *Never try to close the electrode gap by tapping the spark plug on a solid surface. This can damage the plug internally. Always use the special tool to open or close the gap.*

3. Screw each plug in by hand until it seats. Very little effort is required. If force is necessary, the plug is cross-threaded. Unscrew it and try again.

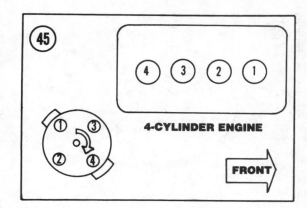

4-CYLINDER ENGINE

FRONT

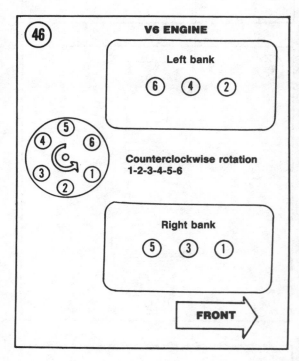

V6 ENGINE

Left bank

Counterclockwise rotation
1-2-3-4-5-6

Right bank

FRONT

4. Tighten the spark plugs. If you have a torque wrench, tighten to 15 ft.-lb. (20 N•m). If not, tighten the plugs with your fingers, then tighten an additional 1/16 turn with the plug wrench.

5. Install the wires to their correct cylinder location. Refer to **Figures 45-47**.

Distributor Cap, Wires and Rotor

The distributor cap, wires and rotor should be inspected every 30,000 miles.

1. Depress the 2 distributor cap latch screws and turn 90°. Lift the cap straight up and off to prevent rotor blade damage.

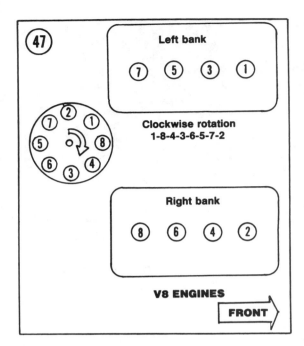

Left bank

⑦ ⑤ ③ ①

**Clockwise rotation
1-8-4-3-6-5-7-2**

Right bank

⑧ ⑥ ④ ②

V8 ENGINES

FRONT ▷

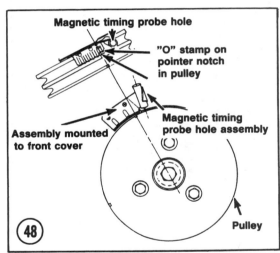

Magnetic timing probe hole

"O" stamp on pointer notch in pulley

Assembly mounted to front cover

Magnetic timing probe hole assembly

Pulley

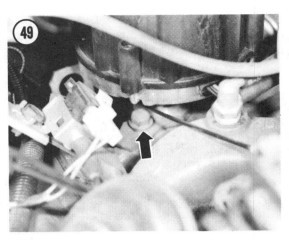

2. Check the carbon button and electrodes inside the distributor cap for dirt, corrosion or arcing. Check the cap for cracks. Replace the cap and rotor as a set, if necessary.

3. Replace the wires if the insulation is melted, brittle or cracked.

4. Loosen the 2 rotor screws. Lift the rotor straight up and off.

5. Wipe the rotor with a clean, damp cloth. Check for burns, arcing, cracks or other defects. Replace the cap and rotor as a set, if necessary.

6. Install the rotor.

7. Install the distributor cap. Depress and rotate the cap latch screws 90° to lock the cap in place.

Ignition Timing

Ignition timing should be checked at every tune-up or at 30,000 mile intervals.

*NOTE
Refer to the VECI label in the engine compartment. Follow all instructions on the label.*

1. Connect a timing light and tachometer to the engine according to the manufacturer's instructions. Refer to **Figures 45-47** as required for the No. 1 cylinder plug wire.

2. Check the idle speed and compare to the specification provided on the VECI label under the hood. If idle speed is not correct, see *Idle Speed Adjustment* in this chapter.

3. Locate the timing mark on the crankshaft balancer or pulley and mark it with white paint. See **Figure 48**. The paint makes the marks easier to see under the timing light.

4. Start the engine and let it idle. Point the timing light at the marks. They will appear to stand still or waver slightly under the light.

*WARNING
Keep your hands and hair clear of all drive belts and pulleys. Although they seem to be standing still, they are actually spinning at more than 10 times per second and can cause serious injury.*

5. If the timing is incorrect, loosen the distributor hold-down bolt enough to rotate the distributor body. **Figure 49** shows the V6 and V8 distributor. The 4-cylinder engine's hold-down bolt must be reached from underneath (**Figure 50**).

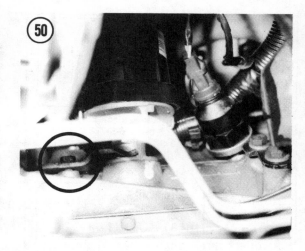

> *WARNING*
> *Never touch the distributor's thick wires when the engine is running. This can cause a painful shock, even if the insulation is in perfect condition.*

6. Grasp the distributor cap and rotate the body clockwise or counterclockwise as required to align the timing marks. Tighten

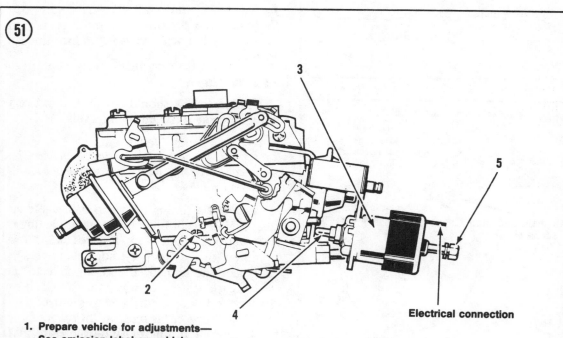

Electrical connection

1. Prepare vehicle for adjustments—
   See emission label on vehicle.
   Note: Ignition timing set per label.

2. Turn idle speed screw to set curb idle speed to specifications—A/C off (see emission label)

3. Solenoid energized—A/C compressor lead disconnected at A/C compressor, A/C on, A/T in DRIVE, M/T in NEUTRAL.

4. Open throttle slightly to allow solenoid plunger to fully extend.

5. Turn solenoid screw to adjust to specified rpm. (Reconnect A/C compressor lead after adjustment).

the distributor hold-down bolt snugly and recheck the timing.

7. Shut the engine off. Remove the test equipment. Perform any other steps specified on the VECI label.

Idle Speed Adjustment

Fuel injected engine

No attempt should be made to adjust the idle speed on 4-cylinder and V8 engines equipped with fuel injection. An idle air control (IAC) assembly mounted on the throttle body maintains the correct idle speed according to electrical impulses from the electronic control module (ECM). Attempting to adjust the system will only make matters worse. If idle speed requires adjustment, see your GM dealer.

Carburetted V6 engine

Refer to **Figure 51** for idle speed adjustment if equipped with air conditioning. Refer to **Figure 52** if not equipped with air conditioning.

Carburetted V8 engine

All adjustments are factory-set and adjustment points sealed to prevent unauthorized adjustment. If idle speed requires adjustment, see your GM dealer.

Idle Mixture Adjustment

The idle mixture screw is located under a plug seal on all carburetors in accordance with Federal regulations governing unauthorized adjustment. The carburetors are flow-tested and pre-set at the factory. Idle mixture on fuel injected engines is computer-controlled. If the idle mixture requires adjustment for any reason, see your GM dealer.

Fast Idle Speed Adjustment

Fuel injected engines

The fast idle speed is controlled by the ECM and ISC assembly and cannot be adjusted.

Carburetted V6 engine

Refer to **Figure 53**.

Carburetted V8 engine

Refer to **Figure 54**.

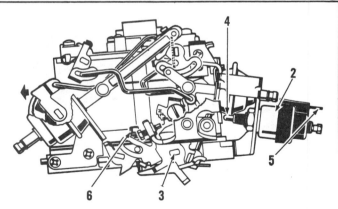

1. Prepare vehicle for adjustments—
See emission label on vehicle.
Note: Ignition timing set per label
2. Solenoid energized—
A/T in DRIVE, M/T in NEUTRAL.
3. Open throttle slightly to allow
solenoid plunger to fully extend
4. Turn solenoid screw to adjust curb idle speed to
specified rpm (solenoid energized).
5. Disconnect electrical lead to de-energize solenoid
6. Turn idle speed screw to set
basic idle speed to specifications.
Reconnect solenoid electrical
lead after adjustment.

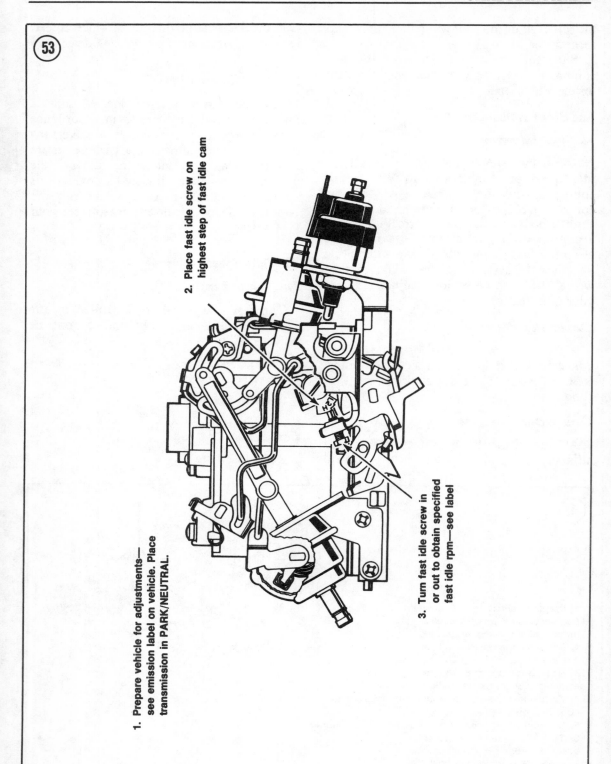

(53)

1. Prepare vehicle for adjustments—
   see emission label on vehicle. Place
   transmission in PARK/NEUTRAL.

2. Place fast idle screw on
   highest step of fast idle cam

3. Turn fast idle screw in
   or out to obtain specified
   fast idle rpm—see label

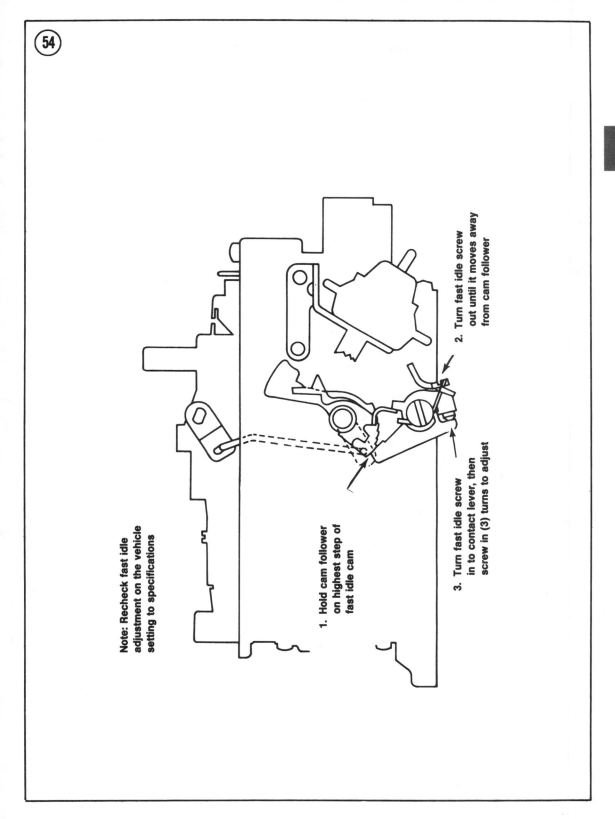

(54)

3

Note: Recheck fast idle
adjustment on the vehicle
setting to specifications

1. Hold cam follower
on highest step of
fast idle cam

2. Turn fast idle screw
out until it moves away
from cam follower

3. Turn fast idle screw
in to contact lever, then
screw in (3) turns to adjust

Table 1 MAINTENANCE SCHEDULE

Every 7,500 miles **(12 months)**	• Engine oil[1] • Chassis lubrication • Inspect suspension and steering • Check brake lines • Check exhaust system
First 7,500 miles, then **every 15,000 miles**	• Engine oil filter[1] • Check disc brakes • Check and rotate tires • Check and adjust drive belts
First 7,500 miles, then **every 30,000 miles**	• Check carburetor choke and hoses • Check carburetor/throttle body mounting torque • Have idle speed checked and adjusted
Every 15,000 miles	• Check cooling system[2] • Check rear brakes and parking brake • Check throttle linkage • Inspect fuel tank, cap and lines • Change fuel filter
Every 30,000 miles	• Replace spark plugs[1] • Check and adjust ignition timing • Check ignition wiring • Drain/refill cooling system • Inspect manual steering gear seals • Check air cleaner system • Replace air cleaner filter • Replace crankcase vent filter • Replace PCV valve • Replace oxygen sensor • Check EGR system operation • Repack and adjust wheel bearings[1]
Every 100,000 miles	• Change automatic transmission fluid

1. Severe service operation: If the vehicle is operated under any of the following conditions, change engine oil @ 3,000 mile or 3 month intervals and oil filter @ alternate oil changes. Clean and regap spark plugs every 6,000 miles. Repack wheel bearings and change automatic transmission fluid/strainer/filter every 15,000 miles.
  a. Extended idle or low-speed operation (short trips, stop-and-go driving).
  b. Trailer towing.
  c. Operation @ temperatures below 10° F for 60 days or more with most trips under 10 miles.
  d. Very dusty or muddy conditions.
2. Check coolant protection once a year.

Table 2 SAE VISCOSITY GRADES

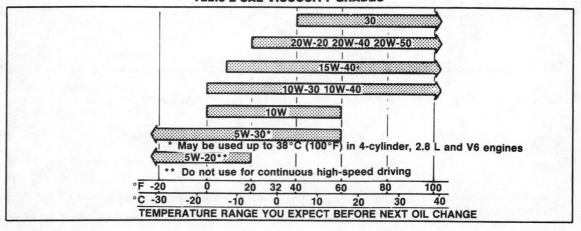

* May be used up to 38°C (100°F) in 4-cylinder, 2.8 L and V6 engines

** Do not use for continuous high-speed driving

TEMPERATURE RANGE YOU EXPECT BEFORE NEXT OIL CHANGE

3

Table 3 RECOMMENDED LUBRICANTS

Engine crankcase	API Service SF, SF/CC or SF/CD oil
Engine coolant	Prestone II or equivalent
Brake fluid	Delco Supreme 11 or other DOT 3 or DOT 4 fluid
Power steering pump	GM power steering fluid or equivalent
Manual steering gear	GM lubricant part No. 1051052 or equivalent
Manual transmission	SAE 80W or SAE 80W/90 GL-5 gear lubricant
Rear axle (standard)	SAE 80W or SAE 80W/90 GL-5 gear lubricant
Rear axle (limited slip)	GM part No. 1052271 or equivalent plus 4 oz. GM part No. 1052358 additive or equivalent
Automatic transmission	DEXRON II automatic transmission fluid
Shift linkage	Engine oil
Front wheel bearings	GM lubricant part No. 1051344 or equivalent
Chassis lubrication	GM chassis grease meeting 6031-M specification
Hood latch, all hinges	Engine oil
Windshield washer	GM Optikleen washer solvent or equivalent
Key lock cylinders	WD-40 or equivalent

TABLE 4 APPROXIMATE REFILL CAPACITIES

	qt.	pt.
Engine crankcase		
4-cylinder	3.0 *	
V6 engine	4.0 *	
V8 engine	4.0 **	
Automatic transmission		
After rebuild		10.0
After fluid change		7.0
Manual transmission	3.5	
Differential		3.5
Cooling system		
4-cylinder engine		
With air conditioning	9.1	
Without air conditioning	8.8	
V6 engine	12.5	
V8 engine	15.0	

* With or without filter change.
** Add 1 qt. with filter change.

Table 5 DRIVE BELT TENSION

	Tension in lb.	
Belt size	New	Used*
5/16 in.	80	50
3/8 in.	140	70
7/16 in.	165	90
15/32 in.	165	90

* A belt is considered used after the engine has made more than one rotation and the belt has stretched or seated into the pulley groove.

Table 6 TUNE-UP SPECIFICATIONS

Engine	Ignition timing (Degrees BTDC @ rpm)	Spark plug Type	Gap
4-cylinder	8 @ 1,050	R44TSX	0.060 in.
V6			
Automatic	10 @ 600	R43TS	0.045 in.
Manual	10 @ 850		
V8	6 @ 500	R45TS	0.045 in.

NOTE: If you own a 1983 or later model, first check the Supplement at the back of the book for any new service information.

CHAPTER FOUR

4

4-CYLINDER ENGINE

The base engine for Camaro/Firebird models (except the Z28 and Trans Am) is a 151 cid (2.5 liter) 4-cylinder engine manufactured by Pontiac.

The cast iron cylinder head contains intake and exhaust valves with integral valve guides. Rocker arms are retained on individual threaded shoulder bolts. A ball pivot valve train is used, with camshaft motion transferred through the hydraulic lifters to the rocker arms by pushrods. The gear-driven camshaft is supported by 3 bearings.

The crankshaft is supported by 5 main bearings. The No. 5 bearing provides the crankshaft thrust surfaces.

The cylinder block is cast iron with full-length water jackets around each cylinder.

Figure 1 shows the cylinder head assembly. **Figure 2** shows the cylinder block assembly.

Specifications (**Table 1**) and tightening torques (**Table 2**) are at the end of the chapter.

ENGINE IDENTIFICATION

An engine identification number (EIN) is located on the top corner of the 4-cylinder engine above the starter (**Figure 3**). This information identifies the engine.

The engine code is the 8th digit/letter of the Vehicle Identification Number (VIN). The VIN is the official identification for title and vehicle registration. The VIN is stamped on a metal Vehicle Identification Plate attached to the left top of the instrument panel (**Figure 4**). It can be seen through the windshield from outside the vehicle.

GASKET SEALANT

Gasket sealant is used instead of pre-formed gaskets between numerous mating surfaces on late-model engines. Two types of gasket sealant are available: room temperature vulcanizing (RTV) and anaerobic. Since these 2 materials have different sealing properties, they cannot be used interchangeably.

Room Temperature Vulcanizing (RTV) Sealant

This black silicone gel is supplied in tubes and is available from your GM dealer. Moisture in the air causes RTV to cure. Always place the cap on the tube as soon as possible when using RTV. RTV has a shelf life of one year and will not cure properly when the shelf life has expired. Check the expiration date on RTV tubes before using and keep partially used tubes tightly sealed.

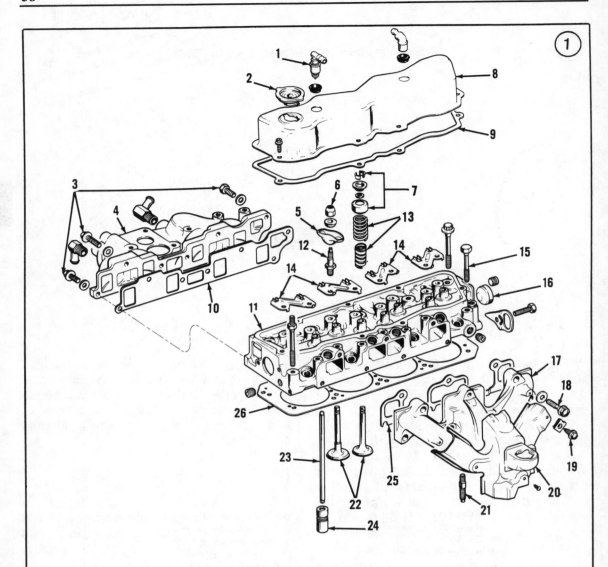

FOUR-CYLINDER ENGINE ASSEMBLY

1. PCV valve
2. Oil filler cap
3. Intake manifold
   attaching bolts
4. Intake manifold
5. Rocker arm
6. Rocker arm
   pivot ball and nut
7. Valve spring
   retainer assembly
8. Cylinder head cover
   (rocker cover)

9. Cylinder head
   cover gasket
10. Intake manifold gasket
11. Cylinder head
12. Rocker arm stud
13. Valve spring
14. Pushrod guide
15. Cylinder head bolts
16. Cylinder head core plug
17. Exhaust manifold
18. Exhaust manifold bolt

19. Oil level indicator
    tube attaching screw
20. Exhaust manifold heat
    shroud (heat shield)
21. Exhaust manifold to
    exhaust pipe stud
22. Valves
23. Pushrod
24. Lifter
25. Exhaust manifold gasket
26. Cylinder head gasket

FOUR-CYLINDER ENGINE ASSEMBLY

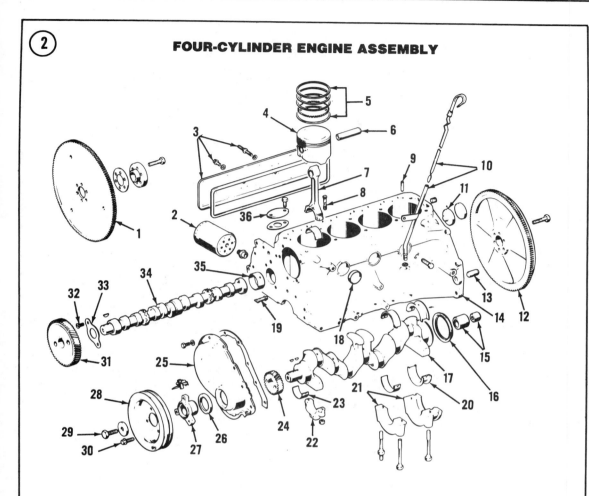

1. **Drive plate and ring (automatic transmission)**
2. **Oil filter**
3. **Pushrod cover and bolts**
4. **Piston**
5. **Piston ring**
6. **Piston pin**
7. **Connecting rod**
8. **Connecting rod bolt**
9. **Dowel**
10. **Oil level indicator and tube**
11. **Camshaft plug**
12. **Flywheel and ring gear (manual transmission)**
13. **Dowel**
14. **Cylinder block**
15. **Pilot and/or converter bushing**
16. **Rear oil seal**
17. **Crankshaft**
18. **Block core plug**
19. **Timing chain oiler**
20. **Main bearings**
21. **Main bearing caps**
22. **Connecting rod bearing cap**
23. **Connecting rod bearing**
24. **Crankshaft gear**
25. **Timing cover (front)**
26. **Timing cover oil seal**
27. **Crankshaft pulley hub**
28. **Crankshaft pulley**
29. **Crankshaft pulley hub bolt**
30. **Crankshaft pulley bolt**
31. **Camshaft timing gear**
32. **Camshaft thrust plate screw**
33. **Camshaft thrust plate**
34. **Camshaft**
35. **Camshaft bearing**
36. **Oil pump driveshaft retainer plate, gasket and bolt**

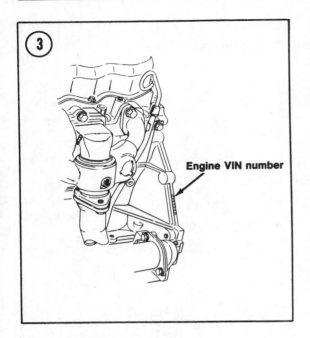

Engine VIN number

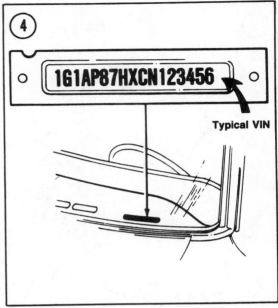

Typical VIN

Applying RTV Sealant

Clean all gasket residue from mating surfaces. They should be clean and free of oil and dirt. Remove all RTV gasket material from blind attaching holes, as it can cause a hydraulic effect and affect bolt torque.

Unless otherwise specified, apply RTV sealant in a continuous bead 3-5 mm (1/8-3/16 in.) thick. Apply the sealant on the inner side of all mounting holes. Torque mating parts within 10 minutes after application.

Anaerobic Sealant

This is a red gel supplied in tubes. It cures only in the absence of air, as when squeezed tightly between 2 machined mating surfaces. For this reason, it will not spoil if the cap is left off the tube. It should not be used if one mating surface is flexible.

Applying Anaerobic Sealant

Clean all gasket residue from mating surfaces. They must be clean and free of oil and dirt. Remove all gasket material from blind attaching holes, as it can cause a hydraulic effect and affect bolt torque.

Unless otherwise specified, apply anaerobic gasket material in a 1 mm or less (0.04 in.)

bead to one sealing surface. Apply the sealant on the inner side of all mounting holes. Torque mating parts within 15 minutes after application.

ENGINE REMOVAL

WARNING
*Before opening any fuel system lines on a fuel injected engine, relieve pressure in the system as described under **Relieving System Pressure** in Chapter Six.*

1. Disconnect the negative battery cable.
2. Remove the air cleaner assembly. See Chapter Six.
3. Remove the hood. See Chapter Thirteen.
4. Drain the cooling system. See *Cooling System Flushing*, Chapter Seven.
5. Remove the air conditioning compressor and brackets, if so equipped (**Figure 5**). Place compressor to one side without disconnecting any lines.
6. Remove the upper and lower radiator hoses at the engine.
7. Remove the fan assembly.
8. Remove the upper half of the radiator shroud on manual transmission models.

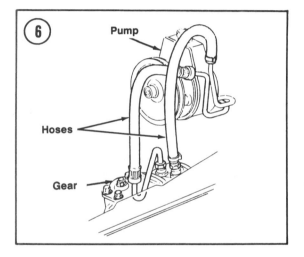

Pump

Hoses

Gear

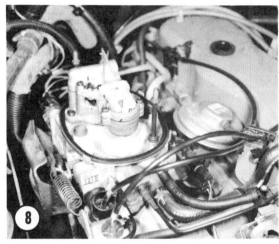

Remove the radiator and shroud assembly on automatic transmission models. See *Radiator Removal/Installation*, Chapter Seven.

9. Remove the power steering hoses at the power steering pump (**Figure 6**).

10. Disconnect the engine wiring harness at the bulkhead connection.

11. Disconnect the inlet and return fuel line at the flex hoses (**Figure 7**). Plug the lines to prevent leakage.

12. Remove the vacuum brake hose from the filter.

13. Remove the ground strap at the rear of the cylinder head.

14. Remove the right hush panel in the passenger compartment and disconnect the ECM harness. Remove splash shield from right fender and feed harness through from inside vehicle.

15. Remove heater hoses at the heater core.

16. Disconnect all electrical connectors and vacuum lines at the TBI assembly. Disconnect the throttle cable. Disconnect the cruise control cable, if so equipped. See **Figure 8**.

17. Raise the car with a jack and place it on jackstands.

18. Disconnect the speedometer cable and all electrical connections at the transmission.

19. Remove flywheel dust cover (**Figure 9**). Remove torque converter bolts on automatic transmission models.

20. Disconnect exhaust pipe at manifold. Remove exhaust pipe support at bellhousing.

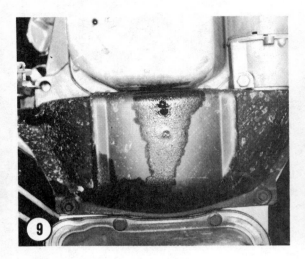

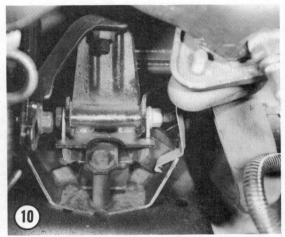

21. Disconnect catalytic converter at tailpipe joint. Remove converter and exhaust pipe assembly.
22. Remove bellhousing-to-engine bolts.
23. Remove starter. See Chapter Eight.
24. Remove motor mount through bolts. **Figure 10** shows the left mount; the right one is similar. Lower car to the ground.
25. Attach an engine hoist bracket or sling to the engine. Connect the bracket or sling to an engine hoist.
26. Position a floor jack with a block of wood under the transmission housing for support.
27. Remove the engine from the engine compartment with the hoist. If equipped with manual transmission, swing the engine slightly to the right to disengage the clutch arm from the ball.

ENGINE INSTALLATION

Engine installation is the reverse of removal, plus the following:
1. Lower the engine into the vehicle. Leave the hoist attached and holding the engine weight until the 2 upper bellhousing bolts are installed. Remove the transmission jack, lower the engine and remove the hoist.
2. Raise the car with a jack and place it on jackstands. Install the remaining bellhousing bolts. Install the front motor mount bolts.
3. Tighten all fasteners to specifications. See **Table 2**.
4. Fill the engine with an oil recommended in Chapter Three.

5. Fill the cooling system. See *Cooling System Flushing*, Chapter Seven.
6. Adjust the drive belts. See *Drive Belts*, Chapter Three.

DISASSEMBLY CHECKLIST

To use the checklists, remove and inspect each part in the order mentioned. To reassemble, go through the checklists backwards, installing the parts in order. Each major part is covered under its own heading in this chapter, unless otherwise noted.

Decarbonizing or Valve Service

1. Remove the rocker arm cover.
2. Remove the intake and exhaust manifolds.
3. Remove the rocker arms and camshaft.
4. Remove the cylinder head.
5. Remove and inspect the valves. Inspect valve guides and seats, repairing or replacing as required.
6. Assemble by reversing Steps 1-5.

Valve and Ring Service

1. Perform *Decarbonizing or Valve Service*.
2. Remove the oil pan.
3. Remove the pistons with the connecting rods.
4. Remove the piston rings. It is not necessary to separate the pistons from the connecting rods unless a piston, connecting rod or piston pin needs repair or replacement.
5. Assemble by reversing Steps 1-4.

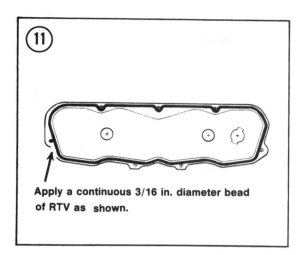

Apply a continuous 3/16 in. diameter bead of RTV as shown.

General Overhaul

1. Remove the engine. Remove the clutch (Chapter Nine) from manual transmission vehicles.
2. Remove the flywheel.
3. Remove the front mount brackets and oil pressure sending unit from the engine.
4. If available, mount the engine on an engine stand. These can be rented from equipment rental dealers. The stand is not absolutely necessary, but it will make the job much easier.
5. Check the engine for signs of coolant or oil leaks.
6. Clean the outside of the engine.
7. Remove the distributor. See Chapter Eight.
8. Remove all hoses and tubes connected to the engine.
9. Remove the intake and exhaust manifolds.
10. Remove the thermostat. See Chapter Seven.
11. Remove the rocker arms.
12. Remove the crankshaft pulley/vibration damper and timing gear cover.
13. Remove the camshaft.
14. Remove the water pump. See Chapter Seven.
15. Remove the cylinder head.
16. Remove the oil pan and oil pump.
17. Remove the pistons and connecting rods.
18. Remove the crankshaft.
19. Inspect the cylinder block.
20. Assemble by reversing Steps 1-18.

ROCKER ARM COVER

Removal/Installation

1. Remove the air cleaner assembly. See Chapter Six.
2. Disconnect the throttle cable at the TBI assembly.
3. Pull the PCV valve from the rocker arm cover.
4. Disconnect the spark plug wires from the plugs. Remove the wires and bracket clips from the cover.
5. Remove the rocker arm cover retaining bolts. Tap the end of the cover with a rubber mallet to break the RTV seal. Remove the cover.
6. Clean any RTV residue from the cylinder head and rocker arm cover with degreaser and a putty knife.

CAUTION
Keep sealant out of bolt holes in Step 7 to prevent a hydraulic effect which could damage the cylinder head.

7. Apply a continuous 3/16 in. bead of RTV sealant on the rocker arm cover as shown in **Figure 11**.
8. Install the cover on the cylinder head. Install the attaching bolts and tighten to 7 ft.-lb. (10 N•m).
9. Install the spark plug wires, PCV valve, throttle cable and air cleaner assembly.

INTAKE AND EXHAUST MANIFOLDS

Intake Manifold
Removal/Installation

1. Disconnect the negative battery cable.
2. Remove the air cleaner assembly. See Chapter Six.
3. Remove the PCV valve hose.
4. Drain the cooling system. See *Cooling System Flushing*, Chapter Seven.
5. Label and disconnect all vacuum lines and electrical connectors from the TBI assembly.
6. Disconnect the fuel line at the TBI assembly fuel inlet. Plug the line.
7. Disconnect the TBI throttle cable. Disconnect the cruise control cable, if so equipped.

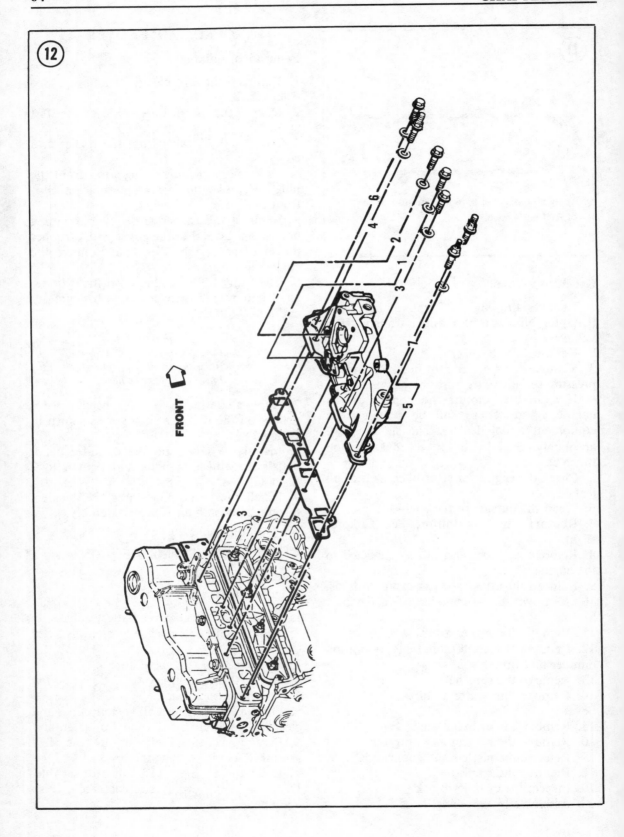

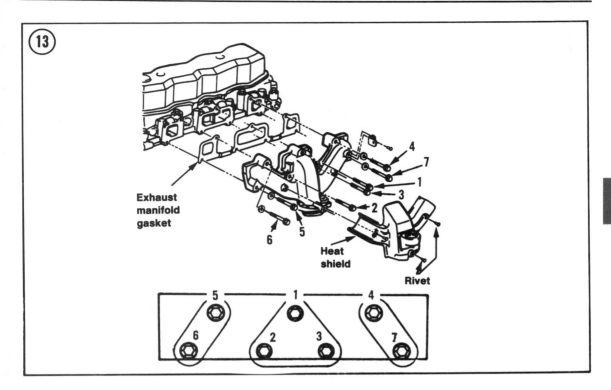

Exhaust manifold gasket

Heat shield

Rivet

8. Remove the TBI assembly. See *Throttle Body Assembly Removal*, Chapter Six.

9. Remove the ignition coil nuts and bolt.

10. Remove the coolant inlet and outlet hoses from the manifold.

11. Remove the air conditioning support brackets and compressor, if so equipped. Place to one side without disconnecting any lines.

12. Remove the manifold bolts. Remove the manifold.

13. Remove and discard the intake manifold gasket. Clean all gasket residue from the cylinder head sealing surfaces.

14. Installation is the reverse of removal.

   a. Use a new gasket and tighten all fasteners in the sequence shown in **Figure 12**.

   b. Tighten the No. 7 fastener to 37 ft.-lb. (50 N•m). Tighten all other fasteners to 25 ft.-lb. (34 N•m).

   c. Refill the cooling system.

Exhaust Manifold Removal/Installation

Refer to **Figure 13** for this procedure.

1. Remove the air cleaner assembly. See Chapter Six.

2. Remove the EFI preheat tube.

3. Remove the oxygen sensor from the exhaust manifold.

4. Remove the oil dipstick tube attaching bolt.

5. Raise the front of the vehicle with a jack and place it on jackstands.

6. Disconnect the exhaust pipe from the exhaust manifold. Lower the vehicle to the ground.

7. Remove the exhaust manifold bolts. Remove the manifold and gasket.

8. Clean any gasket residue from the cylinder head sealing surface.

9. Installation is the reverse of removal. Use a new gasket and tighten all fasteners to 44 ft.-lb. (60 N•m) in the sequence shown in **Figure 13**.

Manifold Inspection

1. Check the intake and exhaust manifolds for cracks or distortion. Replace if distorted or if cracks are found.

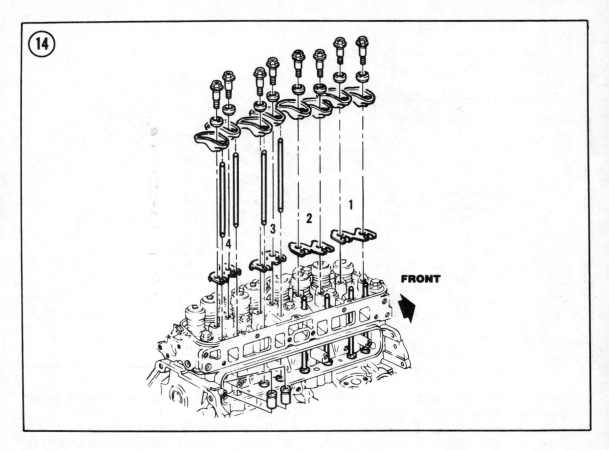

2. Check the gasket surfaces for nicks or burrs. Small burrs may be removed with an oilstone.

3. Place a straightedge across the manifold gasket surfaces. If there is any gap between the straightedge and the gasket surface, measure it with a feeler gauge. The gasket surface must be flat within 0.006 in. (0.15 mm) per foot of manifold length. If not, replace the manifold.

ROCKER ARMS AND PUSHROD COVER

Rocker Arm Removal/Installation

Each rocker arm moves on its own pivot ball. The rocker arm and pivot ball are retained by a capscrew. It is not necessary to remove the rocker arm for pushrod replacement; simply loosen the capscrew and move the arm away from the pushrod. Refer to **Figure 14** for the complete removal procedure.

1. Remove the rocker arm cover as described in this chapter.
2. Remove the rocker arm bolt and ball.
3. Remove the rocker arm. Remove the pushrod.
4. Installation is the reverse of removal. Tighten the bolt to 20 ft.-lb. (27 N•m).

Rocker Arm Inspection

Clean all parts with solvent and use compressed air to blow out the oil passages in the pushrod. Check each rocker arm, pivot ball and pushrod for scuffing, pitting or excessive wear. If the pushrod is worn from lack of oil, it will be necessary to replace the hydraulic valve tappet and rocker arm as well.

Pushrod Cover Removal/Installation

1. Remove the intake manifold as described in this chapter.

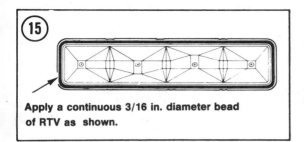

Apply a continuous 3/16 in. diameter bead of RTV as shown.

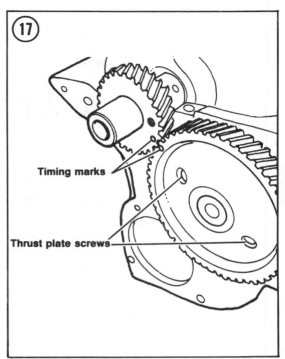

Timing marks

Thrust plate screws

2. Remove distributor. See Chapter Eight.

3. Remove 4 bolts holding pushrod cover. Remove pushrod cover.

4. Clean sealing surfaces on pushrod cover and cylinder block thoroughly.

5. Run a continuous 3/16 in. (5 mm) bead of RTV sealant along the pushrod cover as shown in **Figure 15**.

6. Install cover to block. Tighten attaching bolts to 75 in.-lb. (9 N•m).

7. Install distributor. Install intake manifold.

CAMSHAFT

Removal

1. Remove the engine from the vehicle as described in this chapter.

2. Remove the rocker arm cover as described in this chapter. Loosen the rocker arm bolts and move the rocker arms away from the pushrods.

3. Remove the pushrod cover, pushrods and valve tappets.

4. Remove the distributor. See Chapter Eight.

5. Remove the oil pump drive shaft and gear assembly.

6. Remove the front pulley hub and timing gear cover as described in this chapter.

7. Remove the 2 camshaft thrust plate screws through the holes in the camshaft gear (**Figure 16**).

8. Carefully withdraw the camshaft and gear assembly from the front of the engine block.

Installation

1. Lubricate the camshaft journals.

2. Carefully install the camshaft in the engine block.

3. Rotate the crankshaft and camshaft to align the valve timing marks on the gear teeth. See **Figure 17**. This places the No. 4 piston in its firing position.

4. Install the thrust plate screws and tighten to 75 in.-lb. (10 N•m).

5. Install the timing gear cover gasket and cover.

6. Align the hub keyway with the crankshaft key. Slide the hub onto the shaft. Install the center bolt and tighten to 160 ft.-lb. (212 N•m).

7. Install the valve tappets, pushrods and pushrod cover.

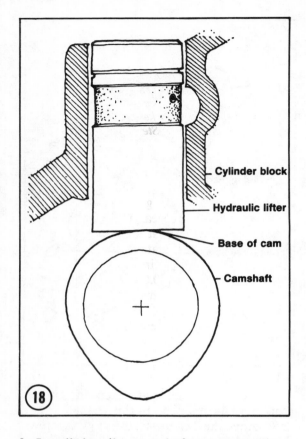

Cylinder block

Hydraulic lifter

Base of cam

Camshaft

8. Install the oil pump shaft/gear assembly.

9. Rotate the crankshaft 360° to bring the No. 1 piston into firing position. The timing notch on the vibration damper will align with the TDC mark on the timing scale.

10. Install the distributor with the rotor pointing toward the No. 1 cylinder electrode in the distributor cap.

11. Swing the rocker arms over the pushrods. With the lifters on the base circle or heel of the camshaft (**Figure 18**), tighten the rocker arm bolts to 20 ft.-lb. (27 N•m).

12. Install the rocker arm cover.

Inspection

1. Check the journals and lobes for signs of wear or scoring. Lobe pitting in the toe area is not sufficient reason for replacement, unless the lobe lift loss is excessive.

NOTE
If you do not have precision measuring equipment, have Step 2 done by a machine shop.

2. Measure the camshaft journals with a micrometer (**Figure 19**) and compare to specifications. Replace the camshaft if one or more journals do not meet specifications.

Bearing Replacement

A special bearing remover tool part No. J-21473-1 and extension tool part No. J-21054-1 are required for this procedure.

1. Remove the camshaft and flywheel/torque converter drive plate as described in this chapter.

2. Drive out the expansion plug from the rear cam bearing from inside the engine block.

3. Use tool part No. J-21473-1 to drive the front bearing toward the rear of the block and the rear bearing toward the front of the block.

4. Install extension part No. J-21054-1 to tool part No. J-21473-1 and drive the center bearing to the rear of the block (**Figure 20**).

5. Use the same tools to install new bearings. Install the center bearing first, then the rear and front bearings. Make sure the oil holes in

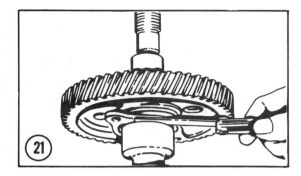

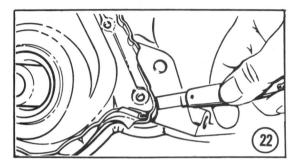

the bearings are correctly aligned with those in the block. Drive the front bearing in approximately 1/8 in. behind the front of the block to expose the oil hole for the timing gear oil nozzle.

Lobe Lift Measurement

1. Remove the rocker arm cover as described in this chapter.
2. Remove the rocker arm/pivot assemblies.
3. Remove the spark plugs.
4. Install a dial indicator on the end of a pushrod. A piece of rubber tubing will hold the dial indicator plunger in place on the center of the pushrod.
5. Rotate the crankshaft until the cam lobe heel is under the valve tappet (the pushrod will be down). Zero the dial indicator gauge.
6. Rotate the crankshaft until the pushrod reaches its maximum travel. Note the indicator reading. Correct cam lobe lift is 0.398 in. for both intake and exhaust.
7. Repeat Steps 4-6 for each pushrod. If all lobes are within the specifications in Step 6, reinstall the rocker arm assemblies.
8. If one or more lobes are worn beyond specifications, replace the camshaft as described in this chapter.

Timing Gear Replacement

1. Remove the camshaft as described in this chapter.

NOTE
Make sure the thrust plate is aligned with the Woodruff key in the camshaft before performing Step 2.

2. Install the camshaft in a press plate and use an arbor press to remove the camshaft from the gear.
3. Installation of the gear is the reverse of removal. Press the gear onto the camshaft until it bottoms against the gear spacer ring.
4. Check the thrust plate end clearance with a feeler gauge as shown in **Figure 21**. It should be 0.0015-0.0050 in. (0.038-0.127 mm). If less than 0.0015 in. (0.038 mm), replace the spacer ring. If greater than 0.0050 in. (0.127 mm), replace the thrust plate.

CRANKSHAFT HUB AND PULLEY

Removal/Installation

1. Remove the drive belt(s).
2. Remove the crankshaft bolt. Slide the pulley and hub from the crankshaft.
3. Installation is the reverse of removal. Tighten the crankshaft bolt to 160 ft.-lb. (212 N•m).

TIMING GEAR COVER

Removal/Installation

1. Disconnect the negative battery cable.
2. Remove the crankshaft pulley and hub as described in this chapter.
3. Remove the alternator mounting bracket and alternator. Place alternator to one side out of the way.
4. Remove the fan and shroud nuts. Loosen the drive belts. Remove the fan and shroud.
5. Remove the oil pan-to-front cover and front cover-to-block screws.
6. Pull the cover slightly forward and cut the oil pan front seal flush with the block at both sides of the cover (**Figure 22**) with a sharp knife.

4

7. Remove the timing gear cover with the cut portion of the oil pan front seal. Remove the cover gasket.

8. Carefully pry the seal from the timing gear cover. Work carefully to avoid bending or distorting the sheet metal cover.

9. Install a new seal with its helical lip facing the rear of the engine.

10. Clean the gasket surfaces on the block and timing gear cover.

11. Cut the tabs from a replacement oil pan front seal as shown in **Figure 23**.

12. Install the seal on the timing gear cover and press the tips into the cover holes.

13. Coat a new gasket with sealer and position it on the cover.

14. Run a 1/8 in. (3 mm) bead of RTV sealant along the joint formed at the oil pan and engine block. See **Figure 24**.

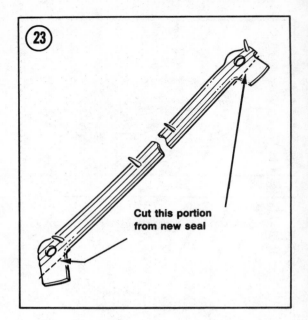

Cut this portion from new seal

> *NOTE*
> *The use of a centering tool in Step 15 is recommended to assure that the timing gear cover is properly aligned. If it is not, the crankshaft pulley hub may damage the seal when it is installed.*

15. Install centering tool part No. J-23042 in the timing gear cover seal and position the cover on the block (**Figure 25**).

16. Install and partially tighten 2 oil pan-to-timing gear cover screws. Install the cover-to-block screws.

17. Tighten cover attaching screws to specifications and remove the centering tool.

18. Install the alternator bracket.

19. Coat the seal contact area on the crankshaft pulley hub with engine oil. Install the pulley hub.

20. Install the fan assembly with the drive belts in position on their pulleys. Install the fan shroud. Tighten fasteners to 18 ft.-lb. (24 N•m).

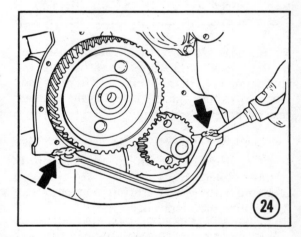

OIL PAN AND PUMP

Oil Pan Removal

Refer to **Figure 26** for this procedure.

1. Disconnect the negative battery cable.

2. Raise the front of the car with a jack and place it on jackstands.

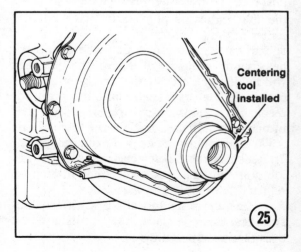

Centering tool installed

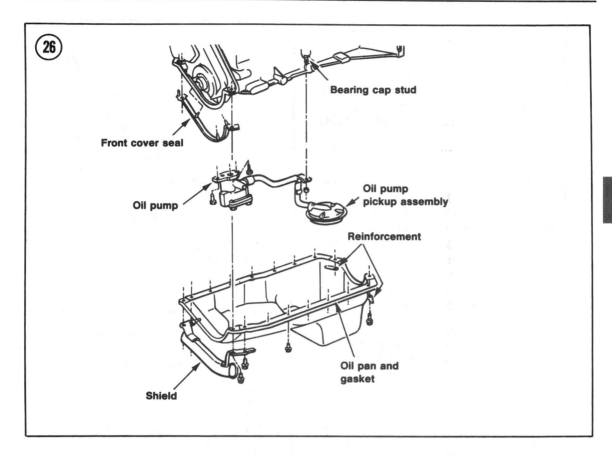

(26)

Bearing cap stud

Front cover seal

Oil pump

Oil pump pickup assembly

Reinforcement

Oil pan and gasket

Shield

3. Drain the engine oil. See *Engine Oil and Filter*, Chapter Three.

4. Disconnect the exhaust pipe at the manifold. Loosen the hanger bracket.

5. Remove the starter. See Chapter Eight.

6. Remove the flywheel dust cover.

7. Remove the front mount through bolts.

8. Attach a hoist to the engine and raise the engine to provide sufficient clearance for pan removal.

9. Remove the oil pan bolts. Remove the oil pan.

> *NOTE*
> *The oil pump pickup tube and screen are a press fit in the pump housing and should not be removed unless replacement is required.*

Oil Pan Inspection

1. Remove all gasket or RTV residue from the pan flange.

2. Clean the pan thoroughly in solvent.

3. Check the pan for dents or warped gasket surfaces. Straighten or replace the pan as necessary.

Oil Pan Installation

Refer to **Figure 26** for this procedure.

1. Install the rear pan gasket in the rear main bearing cap. Apply a small quantity of RTV sealant in the depressions where the pan gasket engages the block.

2. Install the front pan gasket on the timing gear cover. Press the gasket tips into the cover holes.

3. Smear a thin coat of grease along each pan flange and install the 2 pan side gaskets.

4. Run a 1/8 bead of RTV sealant 1/4 in. long at the split lines of the front and side gaskets.

> *NOTE*
> *Install the timing gear cover screws after the pan attaching screws. The*

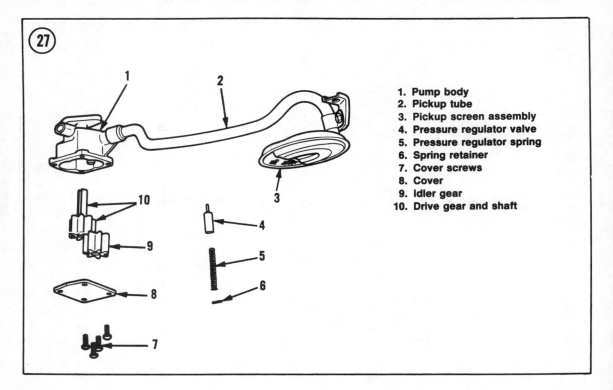

(27)

1. Pump body
2. Pickup tube
3. Pickup screen assembly
4. Pressure regulator valve
5. Pressure regulator spring
6. Spring retainer
7. Cover screws
8. Cover
9. Idler gear
10. Drive gear and shaft

cover screws are installed at an angle and the holes will not align until the rest of the pan bolts are tightened.

5. Install and tighten the pan attaching screws. Install and tighten the timing gear cover screws. Tighten all screws to 45 in.-lb. (5 N•m).
6. Reverse Steps 1-8 of *Oil Pan Removal* in this chapter to complete pan installation.

Oil Pump Removal/Installation

1. Remove the oil pan as described in this chapter.
2. Remove the 2 flange mounting bolts and nut from the main bearing cap bolt (**Figure 26**). Remove the oil pump and pickup assembly as a unit.
3. Align pump gear shaft tang with pump drive shaft slot.
4. Install pump-to-block positioning bracket over the oil pump drive shaft lower bushing.

NOTE
The oil pump should slide into place easily. If it does not, remove the shaft and realign the slot.

5. Install the pump attaching bolts. Tighten to 22 ft.-lb. (30 N•m).
6. Install the oil pan as described in this chapter.

Oil Pump Disassembly/Assembly

Refer to **Figure 27** for this procedure.
1. Remove the 4 cover attaching screws. Remove the cover.
2. Remove the idler gear, drive gear and shaft.
3. Remove the pressure regulator valve, spring and plunger.
4. Assembly is the reverse of disassembly. Tighten cover screws to 105 in.-lb. (9 N•m).

Oil Pump Inspection

The pump body and gears are serviced as an assembly. If one or the other is worn or damaged, replace the entire pump. No wear specifications are provided by General Motors.
1. Clean all parts thoroughly in solvent. Brush the inside of the body and the pressure regulator chamber to remove all dirt and metal particles. Dry with compressed air, if available.

2. Check the pump body and cover for cracks or signs of excessive wear.

3. Check the pump gears for damage or signs of excessive wear.

4. Check the drive gear shaft-to-body fit for excessive looseness.

5. Check the inside of the pump cover for wear that could allow oil to leak around the ends of the gears.

6. Check the pressure regulator valve for a proper fit.

CYLINDER HEAD

Removal

1. Disconnect and remove the negative battery cable.

2. Drain the cooling system. See *Cooling System Flushing*, Chapter Seven.

3. Remove the air conditioning compressor and bracket, if so equipped. Place to one side without disconnecting the lines.

4. Remove the alternator and brackets. Place to one side out of the way.

5. Remove the upper and lower radiator hoses at the engine.

6. Remove the engine ground and temperature sending unit wires.

7. Remove the rocker arm cover. Back off the rocker arm bolts and swivel the rocker arms to one side. Remove the pushrods.

8. Disconnect the fuel inlet and return lines.

9. Disconnect the exhaust pipe at the flex joint.

10. Remove the ignition coil.

11. Remove the cylinder head bolts.

12. Remove the cylinder head. Remove and discard the head gasket.

NOTE
Place the head on its side to prevent damage to the spark plugs or head gasket surface.

Decarbonizing

1. Without removing the valves, remove all deposits from the combustion chambers, intake ports and exhaust ports. Use a fine wire brush dipped in solvent or make a scraper from hardwood. Be careful not to scratch or gouge the combustion chambers.

2. After all carbon is removed from the combustion chambers and ports, clean the entire head in solvent.

3. Clean away all carbon on the piston tops. Do not remove the carbon ridge at the top of the cylinder bore.

4. Remove the valves as described in this chapter.

5. Clean the pushrod guides, valve guide bores and all bolt holes. Use a cleaning solvent to remove dirt and grease.

6. Clean the valves with a fine wire brush or buffing wheel.

Inspection

1. Check the cylinder head for signs of oil or water leaks before cleaning.

2. Clean the cylinder head thoroughly in solvent. While cleaning, look for cracks or other visible signs of damage. Look for corrosion or foreign material in the oil and water passages. Clean the passages with a stiff spiral brush, then blow them out with compressed air.

3. Check the cylinder head studs for damage and replace if necessary.

4. Check the threaded rocker arm bolt holes for damaged threads. Replace if necessary.

5. Check the flatness of the cylinder head-to-block surface with a straightedge and feeler gauge (**Figure 28**). If warped more than 0.004 in. (0.102 mm), replace the head.

Installation

1. Make sure the cylinder head and block gasket surfaces and bolt holes are clean. Dirt in the block bolt holes or on the head bolt threads will affect tightening torque.

2. Check all visible oil and water passages for cleanliness.

3. Install a new head gasket over the dowel pins on the cylinder block. Install the cylinder head.

4. Apply sealing compound to threads of bolt 9 and bolt 10 (**Figure 29**).

5. Install the head bolts and tighten to 85 ft.-lb. (115 N•m) in the sequence shown in **Figure 29**.

6. Reverse Steps 1-10 of *Cylinder Head Removal* in this chapter.

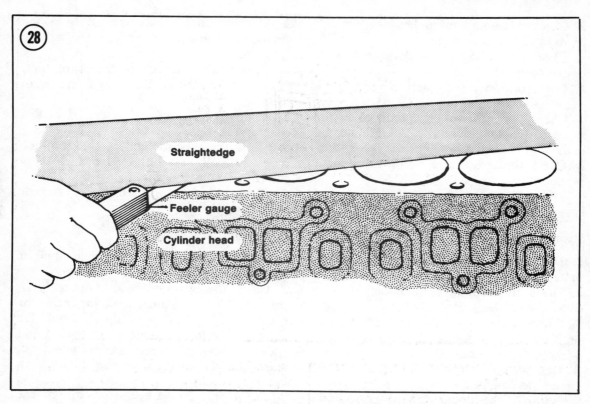

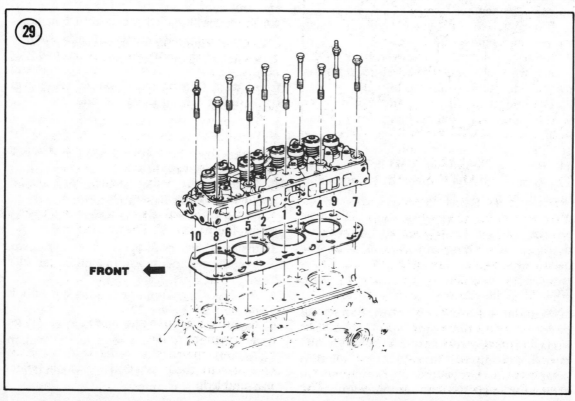

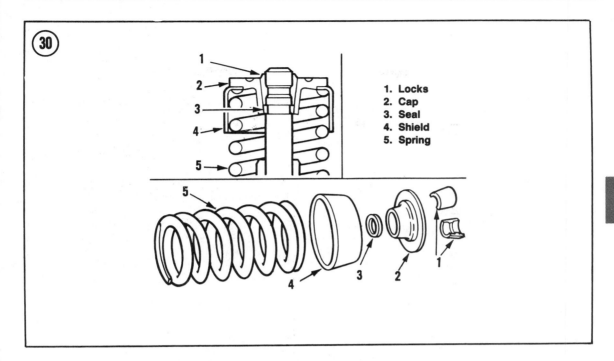

1. Locks
2. Cap
3. Seal
4. Shield
5. Spring

4

VALVES AND
VALVE SEATS

Some of the following procedures must be done by a dealer or machine shop, since they require special knowledge and expensive machine tools. Others, while possible for the home mechanic, are difficult or time-consuming. A general practice among those who do their own service is to remove the cylinder head, perform all disassembly except valve removal and take the head to a machine shop for inspection and service. Since the cost is low relative to the required effort and equipment, this is usually the best approach, even for experienced mechanics. The following procedures are given to acquaint the home mechanic with what the dealer or machine shop will do.

Valve Removal

Refer to **Figure 30** for this procedure.
1. Remove the cylinder head as described in this chapter.
2. Remove the rocker arm assemblies as described in this chapter.
3. Compress the valve spring with a compressor like the one shown in **Figure 31**. Remove the valve keys or cap locks and release the spring tension.
4. Remove the valve spring cap, shield, spring and damper assembly.
5. Remove the valve stem seal with a pair of pliers. See **Figure 32**. Discard the seal.

CAUTION
Remove any burrs from the valve stem lock grooves before removing the valves or the valve guides will be damaged.

6. Remove the valve and repeat Steps 3-5 on each remaining valve.
7. Arrange the parts in order so they can be returned to their original positions when reassembled.

Inspection

1. Clean the valves with a fine wire brush or buffing wheel. Discard any cracked, warped or burned valves.

2. Measure valve stems at the top, center and bottom for wear. A machine shop can do this when the valves are ground. Also measure the length of each valve and the diameter of each valve head.

3. Remove all carbon and varnish from the valve guides with a stiff spiral wire brush.

> *NOTE*
> *The next step assumes that all valve stems have been measured and are within specifications. Replace valves with worn stems before performing this step.*

4. Insert each valve into the guide from which it was removed. Holding the valve just slightly off its seat, rock it back and forth in a direction parallel with the rocker arms. This is the direction in which the greatest wear normally occurs. If the valve stem rocks more than slightly, the valve guide is probably worn.

5. If there is any doubt about valve guide condition after performing Step 4, have the valve guide measured with a valve stem clearance checking tool. Compare the results to specifications in **Table 1**. Worn guides must be reamed for the next oversize valve stem.

6. Test the valve springs under load on a spring tester (**Figure 33**). Replace any weak springs.

7. Inspect the valve seat inserts. If worn or burned, they must be reconditioned. This is a job for a dealer or machine shop, although the procedure is described in this chapter.

Valve Guide Reaming

Worn valve guides must be reamed to accept a valve with an oversize stem. These are available in 3 sizes for both intake and exhaust valves. Reaming must be done by hand (**Figure 34**) and is a job best left to an experienced machine shop. The valve seat must be refaced after the guide has been reamed.

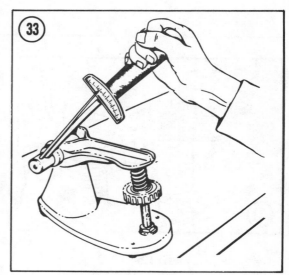

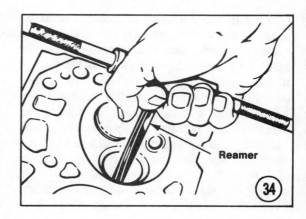
Reamer

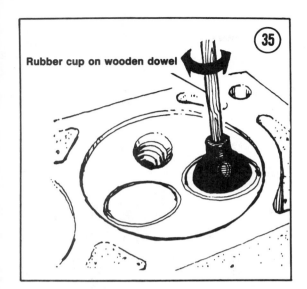

Rubber cup on wooden dowel   ㉟

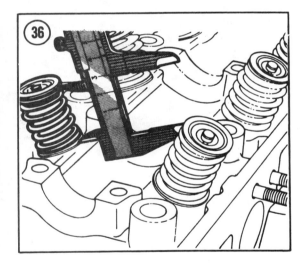

㊱

Valve Seat Reconditioning

1. Cut the valve seats to the specified angle (**Table 1**) with a dressing stone. Remove only enough metal to obtain a good finish.
2. Use tapered stones to obtain the specified seat width when necessary.

NOTE
Check the thickness of the valve edge or margin after the valves have been ground. Any valve with a margin of less than 1/32 in. (0.787 mm) should be discarded.

3. Coat the corresponding valve face with Prussian blue dye.

4. Insert the valve into the valve guide.
5. Apply light pressure to the valve and rotate it approximately 1/4 turn (**Figure 35**).
6. Lift the valve out. If it seats properly, the dye will transfer evenly to the valve face.
7. If the dye transfers to the top of the valve face, lower the seat. If it transfers to the bottom of the valve face, raise the seat.

Valve Installation

NOTE
Install all parts in the same position from which they were removed.

1. Coat the valves with oil and install them in the cylinder head.
2. Install new oil seals on each valve with a deep socket and hammer.
3. Drop the valve spring shim around the valve guide boss. Install the valve spring and cap.
4. Compress the springs and install the keys. Make sure both keys seat properly in the upper groove of the valve stem.
5. Measure the installed spring height between the top of the spring seat and the top of the valve spring, as shown in **Figure 36**. If greater than the specified height, install an extra spring seat shim about 1/16 in. thick and remeasure the height.

VALVE LIFTERS

Removal/Installation

1. Remove the rocker arm assemblies, pushrods and pushrod cover as described in this chapter.
2. Remove the valve lifters. This can be done without special tools, although tool part No. J-3049 will make the job easier and faster.
3. Installation is the reverse of removal.

Valve Lifter Inspection

Clean lifters in solvent and wipe dry with a clean, lint-free cloth.
Inspect all parts. If any lifter part shows signs of pitting, scoring, galling, non-rotation or excessive wear, replace the entire lifter. Check the side and face of the lifter for scuffing. Check the face for concave wear with

4

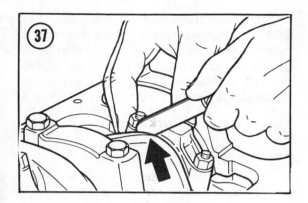

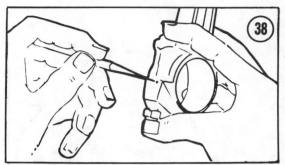

a straightedge. If the face is concave, the corresponding camshaft lobe is also worn. Replace both the lifter and the camshaft.

PISTON/CONNECTING ROD ASSEMBLY

Piston Removal

1. Remove the cylinder head and oil pan as described in this chapter.
2. Pack the cylinder bore with clean shop rags. Remove the carbon ridge at the top of the cylinder bores with a ridge reamer. These can be rented for use. Vacuum out the shavings, then remove the shop rags.
3. Rotate the crankshaft so the connecting rod is centered in the bore.
4. Measure the clearance between each connecting rod big end and the crankshaft journal flange with a feeler gauge (**Figure 37**). If the clearance exceeds specifications in **Table 1**, mark the parts for inspection after removal.

> *NOTE*
> *Mark the cylinder number on the top of each piston with quick-drying paint. Check for cylinder numbers or identification marks on the connecting rod and cap. If they are not visible, make your own (Figure 38).*

5. Remove the nuts holding the connecting rod cap. Lift off the cap, together with the lower bearing insert.

> *NOTE*
> *If the connecting rod caps are difficult to remove, tap the studs with a wooden hammer handle. See Figure 39.*

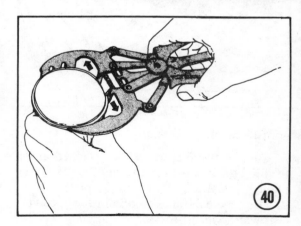

6. Use the wooden hammer handle to push the piston and connecting rod from the bore.
7. Remove the piston rings with a ring remover (**Figure 40**).

Piston Pin Removal/Installation

The piston pins are press-fitted to the connecting rods and hand-fitted to the

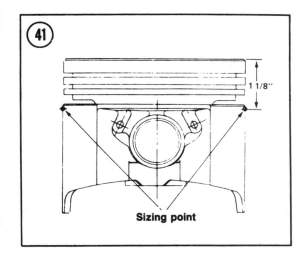

Sizing point

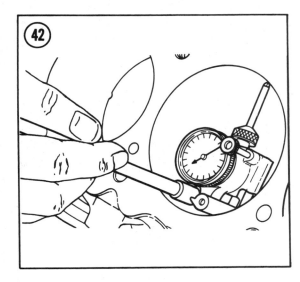

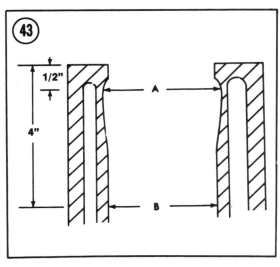

pistons. Removal requires the use of a press and support stand. This is a job for a dealer or machine shop equipped to fit the pistons to the pin, ream the pin bushings to the correct diameter and install the pistons and pins on the connecting rods.

Piston Clearance Check

If you do not have precision measuring equipment and know how to use it properly, have this procedure done by a machine shop.
1. Measure the piston diameter with a micrometer, at the sizing points shown in **Figure 41**.
2. Measure the cylinder bore diameter with a bore gauge (**Figure 42**). **Figure 43** shows the points of normal cylinder wear. If dimension A exceeds dimension B by more than 0.003 in., the cylinder must be rebored and a new piston/ring assembly installed.

Piston Ring Fit/Installation

1. Check the ring gap of each piston ring. To do this, position the ring at the top or bottom of the ring travel area and square it by tapping gently with an inverted piston. See **Figure 44**.

NOTE
If the cylinders have not been rebored, check the gap at the bottom of the ring travel, where the cylinder is least worn.

2. Measure the ring gap with a feeler gauge as shown in **Figure 45**. Compare with specifications in **Table 1**. If the measurement is not within specifications, the rings must be replaced as a set. Check gap of new rings and file ring ends if gap is too small.
3. Check the side clearance of the rings as shown in **Figure 46**. Place the feeler gauge alongside the ring all the way into the groove. If the measurement is not within specifications (**Table 1**), either the rings or the ring grooves are worn. Inspect and replace as necessary.
4. Using a ring expander tool (**Figure 47**), carefully install the oil control ring, then the compression rings.

NOTE
Oil rings consist of 3 segments. The wavy segment goes between the flat

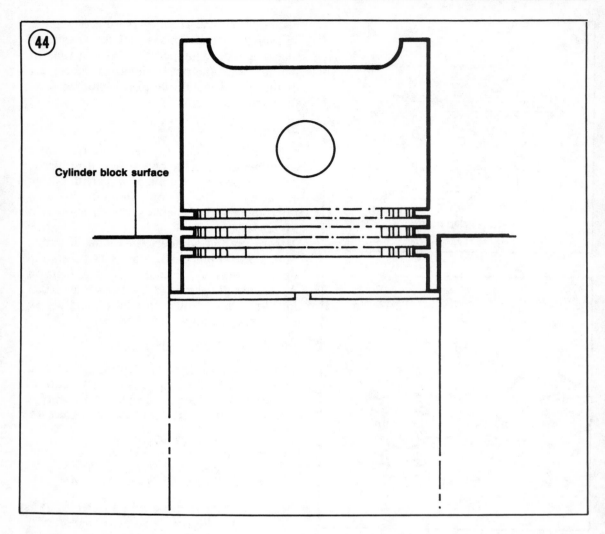

Cylinder block surface

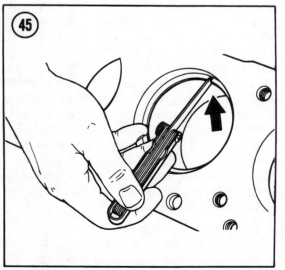

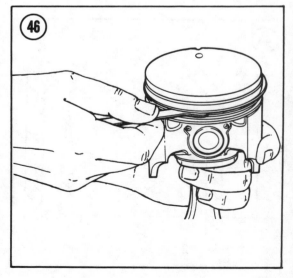

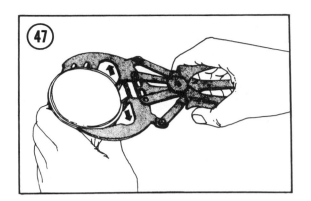

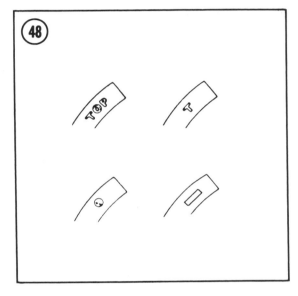

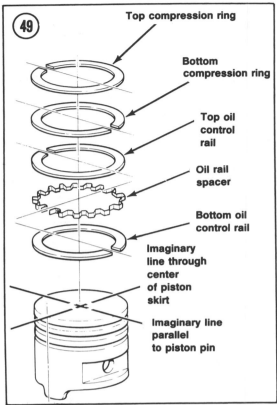

segments to act as a spacer. The upper and lower flat segments are interchangeable. The top sides of both compression rings are marked with one of the symbols shown in **Figure 48**. These markings must face upward.

5. Position the ring gaps 180° apart. See **Figure 49**.

Connecting Rod Inspection

Have the connecting rods checked for straightness by a dealer or a machine shop.

Connecting Rod Bearing Clearance Measurement

1. Place the connecting rods and upper bearing halves on the proper connecting rod journals.

2. Cut a piece of Plastigage the width of the bearing. Place the Plastigage on the journal (**Figure 50**), then install the lower bearing half and cap.

NOTE
Do not place Plastigage over the journal oil hole.

3. Tighten the connecting rod cap to 32 ft.-lb. (44 N•m). Do not rotate the crankshaft while the Plastigage is in place.

4. Remove the connecting rod caps. Bearing clearance is determined by comparing the width of the flattened Plastigage to the markings on the envelope. See **Figure 51**. If the clearance is excessive, the crankshaft must be reground and undersize bearings installed.

Installing Piston/Connecting Rod Assembly

1. Make sure the pistons are correctly installed on the connecting rod. See **Figure 52**.

2. Make sure the ring gaps are positioned as shown in **Figure 49**.

3. Slip short pieces of hose over the connecting rod studs to keep them from nicking the crankshaft. Tape will work if you do not have the right diameter hose, but it is more difficult to remove.

4. Immerse the entire piston in clean engine oil. Coat the cylinder wall with oil.

5. Install the piston/connecting rod assembly in its cylinder with a piston installer tool as shown in **Figure 53**. Make sure the number painted on the top of the piston before removal corresponds to the cylinder number, counting from the front of the engine.

6. Clean the connecting rod bearings carefully, including the back sides. Coat the journals and bearings with clean engine oil. Place the bearings in the connecting rod and cap.

7. Remove the protective hose or tape and install the connecting rod cap. Make sure the rod and cap marks align. Tighten the cap nuts to specifications.

8. Check the connecting rod big end play as described under *Piston Removal*.

CRANKSHAFT

Removal

1. Remove the engine from the vehicle.

2. Remove the spark plugs and the fan/pulley assembly.

3. Remove the crankshaft pulley/hub assembly as described in this chapter.

4. Remove the oil pan and pump assembly as described in this chapter.

5. Remove the timing gear cover and crankshaft timing gear as described in this chapter.

6. Remove the connecting rod bearing caps and bearings. Move the rod/piston assemblies away from the crankshaft.

7. Unbolt and remove the main bearing caps with bearing inserts.

NOTE
If the caps are difficult to remove, lift the bolts partway out, then pry them from side to side.

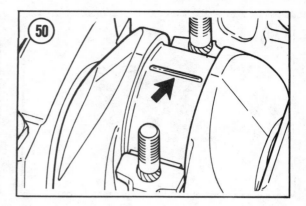

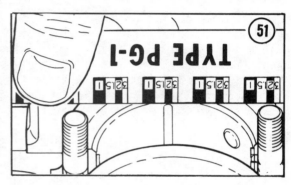

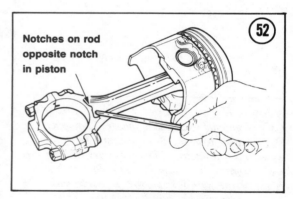

Notches on rod opposite notch in piston

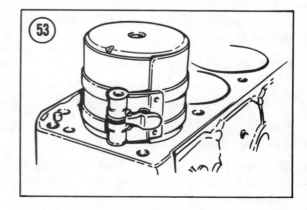

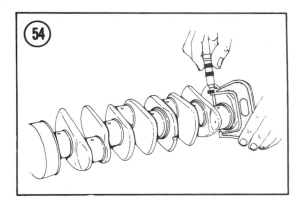

8. Check the caps for identification numbers or marks. If none are visible, clean the caps with a wire brush. If marks still cannot be seen, make your own with quick-drying paint.

9. Lift the crankshaft from the engine block. Lay the crankshaft, main bearings and bearing caps in order on a clean workbench.

Inspection

1. Clean the crankshaft thoroughly with solvent. Blow out the oil passages with compressed air.

NOTE
If you do not have precision measuring equipment, have a machine shop perform Step 2.

2. Check the crankpins and main bearing journals for wear, scoring and cracks. Check all journals against specifications for out-of-roundness and taper. See **Figure 54**. If necessary, have the crankshaft reground.

Main Bearing Clearance Measurement

Main bearing clearance is measured in the same manner as connecting rod bearing clearance, described in this chapter. Excessive clearance requires that the bearings be replaced, the crankshaft reground or both.

Installation

1. Install the main bearing inserts with their lubrication groove facing the cylinder block.
2. Lubricate the bolt threads with SAE 30W engine oil.
3. Install the cap bearing inserts.
4. Install the crankshaft in the block.

5. Install the bearing caps in their marked positions and tighten bolts finger-tight.
6. Check crankshaft end play as described in this chapter.
7. Tighten all main bearing caps to specifications.

End Play Measurement

1. Pry the crankshaft to the front of the engine with a large screwdriver.
2. Measure the crankshaft end play at the front of the No. 5 bearing with a feeler gauge. It should be 0.0015-0.0085 in. (0.0889-0.2159 mm).
3. If the end play is excessive, replace the No. 5 bearing. If less than specified, check the bearing faces for imperfections.

REAR MAIN BEARING SEAL REPLACEMENT

The one-piece rear main bearing oil seal can be replaced without removing the oil pan or crankshaft.

1. Disconnect the negative battery cable.
2. Raise the vehicle with a jack and place it on jackstands.
3. Remove the transmission. See Chapter Nine.
4. Remove the flywheel or torque converter drive plate as described in this chapter. If equipped with a manual transmission, remove the clutch pressure plate and disc assembly. See Chapter Nine.
5. Pry the rear main oil seal from the crankshaft with a small screwdriver. Work carefully to avoid damaging the crankshaft or seating groove.
6. Install a new seal with the seal lip facing toward the front of the engine. Tap the perimeter of the seal with a plastic hammer until it is fully seated in the groove.
7. Reverse Steps 1-4 to complete installation.

FLYWHEEL/DRIVE PLATE

Removal/Installation

Refer to **Figure 55** for this procedure.
1. Remove the clutch and transmission on manual transmission cars. Remove the torque converter and transmission on

automatic transmission cars. See Chapter Nine.

2. Unbolt the flywheel or drive plate from the engine. See **Figure 56**. Remove the bolts gradually in a diagonal pattern.

3. Installation is the reverse of removal. Tighten bolts to specifications in a diagonal pattern. Wipe all oil, grease and other contamination from the flywheel surface before installing the clutch on manual transmission cars.

Inspection

1. Visually check the flywheel surfaces for cracks, deep scoring, excessive wear, heat discoloration and checking.

2. Have the face runout checked with a dial indicator and compare to specifications.

3. Check surface flatness with a straightedge and feeler gauge.

4. Inspect the ring gear teeth for cracks, broken teeth or excessive wear. If severely worn, check the starter motor drive teeth for similar wear or damage. Replace as required.

NOTE
The ring gear can only be replaced on manual transmission vehicles. It is welded to and balanced as part of the torque converter drive plate assembly on autmatic transmission vehicles and must be replaced with the drive plate.

PILOT BUSHING REPLACEMENT

The pilot bushing is located inside the rear end of the crankshaft on manual transmission vehicles. It supports the transmission input shaft.

1. Remove the clutch and transmission. See Chapter Nine.

2. Soak a replacement bushing in engine oil while performing Steps 3-5.

3. Remove the bushing lubricating wick. Fill the crankshaft bushing bore with chassis grease.

4. Insert a dummy shaft or clutch aligning tool into the bushing and tap with a soft hammer. The hydraulic pressure caused by the grease should force the bushing out easily.

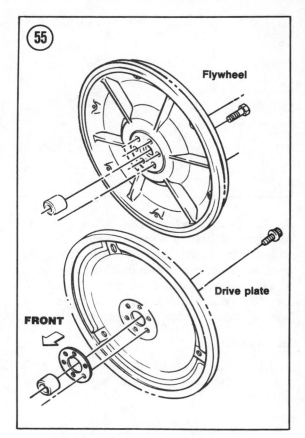

If it does not, remove the bushing with a bushing puller and slide hammer.

5. Clean the bore thoroughly of all grease.

6. Install the oil-soaked bushing on the end of the dummy shaft or clutch aligning tool.

7. Install the bushing using the dummy shaft or aligning tool as a driver.

8. Install the bushing lubricating wick. Install the clutch and transmission (Chapter Nine).

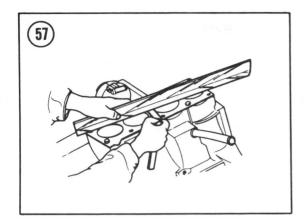

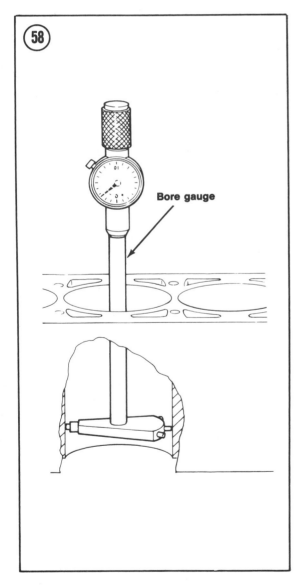

Bore gauge

CYLINDER BLOCK CLEANING AND INSPECTION

1. Clean the block thoroughly with solvent. Remove any RTV sealant residue from the machined surfaces. Check all freeze plugs for leaks and replace any that are suspect. See *Freeze Plug Replacement* in this chapter. Remove any plugs that seal oil passages. Check oil and coolant passages for sludge, dirt and corrosion while cleaning. If the passages are very dirty, have the block boiled out by a machine shop. Blow out all passages with compressed air. Check the threads in the head bolt holes to be sure they are clean. If dirty, use a tap to true up the threads and remove any deposits.

2. Examine the block for cracks. To confirm suspicions about possible leak areas, use a mixture of one part kerosene and 3 parts engine oil. Coat the suspected area with this solution, then wipe dry and immediately apply a solution of zinc oxide dissolved in wood alcohol. If any discoloration appears in the treated area, the block is cracked and should be replaced.

3. Check the cylinder block deck or top surface for flatness. Place an accurate straightedge on the block. If there is any gap between the block and straightedge, measure it with a feeler gauge as shown in **Figure 57**. Measure from end to end and from corner to corner. If gap exceeds 0.003 in., replace the block.

4. Measure the cylinder bores with a bore gauge (**Figure 58**) as described in *Piston Clearance Check* in this chapter. If the cylinders exceed maximum tolerances, they must be rebored. Reboring is also necessary if the cylinder walls are badly scuffed or scored.

NOTE
Before boring, install all main bearing caps and tighten the cap bolts to specifications.

FREEZE PLUG REPLACEMENT

The condition of all freeze plugs in the block should be checked whenever the engine is out of the vehicle for service. If any signs of leakage or corrosion are found around one freeze plug, replace them all.

NOTE
Do not drive freeze plugs into the engine casting. It will be impossible to retrieve them and they can restrict coolant circulation, resulting in serious engine damage.

1. Tap the bottom edge of the freeze plug with a hammer and drift. Use several sharp blows to push the bottom of the plug inward, tilting the top out (**Figure 59**).

2. Grip the top of the plug firmly with pliers. Pull the plug from its bore (**Figure 60**) and discard.

3. Clean the plug bore thoroughly to removal all traces of the old sealer.

4. Apply a light coat of Loctite Stud N' Bearing mount or equivalent to the plug bore.

5. Install the new core plug with an appropriate size driver or socket. The sharp edge of the plug should be at least 0.02 in. (0.5 mm) inside the lead-in chamfer.

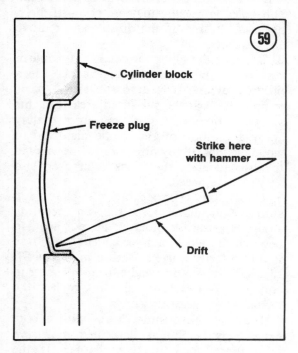

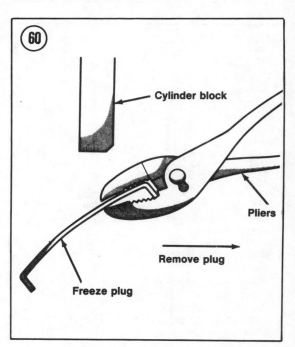

Table 1 ENGINE SPECIFICATIONS

Engine type	Inline 4-cylinder
Bore	4.00 in. (101.6 mm)
Stroke	3.00 in. (76.2 mm)
Displacement	151 cid (2.5 liter)
Firing order	1-3-4-2
Cylinder numbering	
(front to rear)	1-2-3-4
Cylinder bore	
Out-of-round (maximum)	0.0014 in. (0.0356 mm)
Taper (maximum)	0.0005 in. (0.0127 mm)
Valve system	
Clearance	
Intake	0.0010-0.0027 in. (0.0254-0.06858 mm)
Exhaust	
Top	0.0010-0.0027 in. (0.0254-0.06858 mm)
Bottom	0.0508-0.09398 in. (0.0020-0.0037 mm)
Head diameter	
Intake	1.72 in. (43.688 mm)
Exhaust	1.50 in. (38.1 mm)
Stem diameter	
Intake	0.3418-0.3425 in. (8.68172-8.6995 mm)
Exhaust	0.3418-0.3425 in. (8.68172-8.6995 mm)
Seat angle	46°
Face angle	45°
Installed height	1.69 in. (42.926 mm)
Valve spring load	
Closed	78-86 lb. @ 1.66 in.
Open	122-180 lb. @ 1.254 in.
Camshaft	
End play	0.0015-0.0050 in. (0.0381-0.127 mm)
Journal clearance	0.0007-0.0027 in. (0.1778-0.0685 mm)
Journal diameter	1.869 in. (47.4726 mm)
Crankshaft	
Main bearing journal	
Diameter	2.300 in. (59.182 mm)
Out-of-round (maximum)	0.0005 in.
Taper (maximum)	0.0005 in.
Clearance limit (new)	0.0005-0.0022 in. (0.05588 mm)
Crankshaft end play (new)	0.0035-0.0085 in. (0.889-0.2159 mm)
Rod bearing journal	
Diameter	2.000 in. (50.8 mm)
Out-of-round (maximum)	0.0005 in.
Taper (maximum)	0.0005 in.
Clearance limit (new)	0.0005-0.0026 in. (0.0127-0.06604 mm)
Rod side clearance	0.006-0.022 in. (0.1524-0.5588 mm)
Piston	
Clearance in bore	
Top	0.0025-0.0033 in. (0.635-0.838 mm)
Bottom	0.0017-0.0041 in. (0.043-0.1041 mm)
Piston-to-pin clearance	0.0003-0.0005 in. (loose)
Piston rings	
Clearance	
Top	0.0015-0.0030 in. (0.0762-0.0381 mm)
Second	0.0015-0.0030 in. (0.0762-0.0381 mm)
Ring gap	
Top	0.010-0.022 in. (0.381-0.635 mm)
Second	0.015-0.055 in. (0.381-1.397 mm)
Oil ring	0.010-0.027 in. (0.2286-0.4826 mm)

4

Table 2 TIGHTENING TORQUES

Fastener	ft.-lb.	in.-lb.	N•m
Main bearing cap to block bolt	70		95
Connecting rod nut	32		44
Cylinder head bolt	85		115
Crankshaft			
Harmonic balancer bolt	160		212
Flywheel bolt	44		60
Oil pan bolt		75	6
Oil pan drain plug	25		34
Oil pump			
To block	22		30
Cover	10		14
Intake manifold	29		40
Exhaust manifold	44		60
TBI assembly-to-manifold nut	15		20
TBI assembly-to-manifold bolt	15		20
Pushrod cover-to-block		90	10
Rocker arm cover	6		8
Rocker arm bolt	20		27
Fuel pump-to-block	18		25
Distributor retaining clamp	22		30
EGR valve-to-manifold	10		14
Water outlet/thermostat housing	20		27
Water pump-to-block	25		34
Timing cover bolt		90	10
Camshaft thrust plate	7		10

NOTE: If you own a 1983 or later model, first check the Supplement at the back of the book for any new service information.

CHAPTER FIVE

V6 AND V8 ENGINES

Camaro and Firebird models use the Chevrolet 173 cid (2.8L) V6 and 305 cid (5.0L) V8. The V6 firing order is 1-2-3-4-5-6. The V8 firing order is 1-8-4-3-6-5-7-2.

The V6 and V8 engines use a chain-driven camshaft. The V6 uses a 4-bearing camshaft; the V8 has a 5-bearing camshaft. A camshaft gear drives the distributor and oil pump. A camshaft eccentric operates the fuel pump on carburetted engines.

The cast iron cylinder heads have individual intake and exhaust ports. Integral valve guides are used, with rocker arms held on individual threaded studs. A ball pivot valve train is used, with camshaft motion transferred through hydraulic lifters to the rocker arms by pushrods.

The oil pump is driven by the camshaft and is mounted at the bottom of the engine block.

The V6 crankshaft is supported by 4 main bearings, with the No. 3 bearing providing the crankshaft thrust surfaces. The 5-bearing V8 crankshaft has the thrust surfaces on the No. 5 bearing.

The cylinder block is cast iron with full length water jackets around each cylinder.

Specifications (**Table 1** and **Table 2**) and tightening torques (**Table 3** and **Table 4**) are at the end of the chapter.

ENGINE IDENTIFICATION

The Vehicle Identification Number (VIN) is the official identification for title and vehicle registration. The V6 VIN is located on a pad at the front of the block below the cylinder head in one of 2 locations, as shown in **Figure 1**. The V8 VIN is located as shown in **Figure 2**. The engine code is the 8th digit/letter of the VIN.

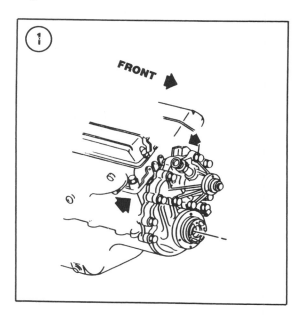

FRONT

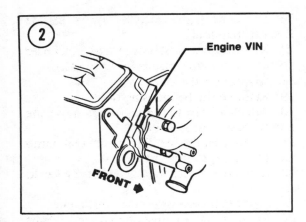

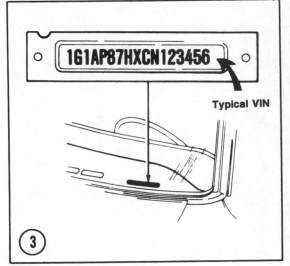

Typical VIN

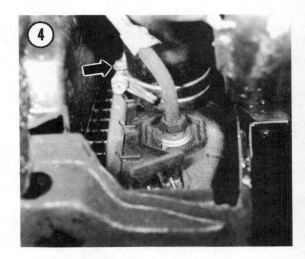

The VIN is also stamped on a gray-colored plate fastened to the upper left corner of the instrument panel close to the windshield on the driver's side (**Figure 3**). It can be read from outside the car.

GASKET SEALANT

Gasket sealant is used instead of pre-formed gaskets between numerous mating surfaces on the V6 and V8 engines. See *Gasket Sealant*, Chapter Four.

ENGINE REMOVAL

WARNING
*Before opening any fuel system line on a fuel injected engine, pressure in the system must be relieved as described under **Relieving System Pressure** in Chapter Six.*

If the car is equipped with air conditioning, have the system discharged by a dealer or air conditioning shop before starting this procedure.

1. Mark the location of the hinges and remove the hood. See Chapter Thirteen.
2. Disconnect the negative battery cable.
3. Remove the air cleaner. See Chapter Six.
4. Drain the cooling system. See *Cooling System Flushing*, Chapter Seven.
5. Disconnect the lower radiator hose (**Figure 4**).
6. Remove the upper radiator hose and coolant overflow line (**Figure 5**).
7. Remove upper fan shroud.
8. Disconnect and plug the oil cooler lines at the radiator.

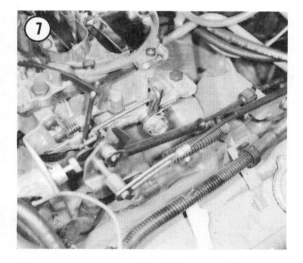

16. Disconnect the exhaust pipes at the exhaust manifold.

17. Remove the dust cover and converter bolts on automatic transmission models.

18. Disconnect the starter wires.

19. Remove the bellhousing bolts.

20. Attach a hoist to the engine. Remove the motor mount through bolts.

21. Disconnect the fuel lines at the fuel pump and plug lines to prevent leakage.

22. Remove the jackstands. Lower the car to the ground.

23. Support the transmission with a jack.

24. Remove the air injection/converter pipe bracket.

5

NOTE
At this point, there should be no wires, lines or hoses connecting the engine to the car. Recheck to make sure nothing will hamper engine removal.

25. Raise the engine slightly, then carefully disengage it from the transmission. Remove the engine from the engine compartment.

ENGINE INSTALLATION

Installation is the reverse of removal. Tighten all fasteners to specifications. Fill the engine with an oil recommended in Chapter Three. Fill the cooling system. See *Cooling System Flushing*, Chapter Seven. Adjust the drive belts. See *Drive Belts*, Chapter Three.

DISASSEMBLY CHECKLIST

To use the checklists, remove and inspect each part in the order mentioned. To reassemble, go through the checklists backwards, installing the parts in order. Each major part is covered under its own heading in this chapter, unless otherwise noted.

Decarbonizing or Valve Service

1. Remove the rocker arm covers.
2. Remove the intake and exhaust manifolds.
3. Remove the rocker arms and camshaft.
4. Remove the cylinder heads.
5. Remove and inspect the valves. Inspect valve guides and seats, repairing or replacing as required.
6. Assemble by reversing Steps 1-5.

9. Remove the fan assembly and radiator. See Chapter Seven.

10. Remove the heater hoses at the engine.

11. Disconnect all linkage at the carburetor or throttle body. **Figure 6** shows the V6 carburetor; **Figure 7** shows the V8 carburetor.

12. Remove the vacuum brake booster line.

13. Remove distributor cap and place to one side out of the way. It is not necessary to remove the wires from the cap.

14. Remove the power steering pump and air conditioning compressor, if so equipped, and place to one side out of the way. It is not necessary to disconnect the lines.

15. Raise the front of the car with a jack and place it on jackstands.

Valve and Ring Service

1. Perform Steps 1-5 of *Decarbonizing or Valve Service.*

2. Remove the oil pan.

3. Remove the pistons with the connecting rods.

4. Remove the piston rings. It is not necessary to separate the pistons from the connecting rods unless a piston, connecting rod or piston pin needs repair or replacement.

5. Assemble by reversing Steps 1-4.

General Overhaul

1. Remove the engine. Remove the clutch (Chapter Nine) from manual transmission cars.
2. Remove the flywheel.
3. Remove the mount brackets and oil pressure sending unit from the engine.
4. If available, mount the engine on an engine stand. These can be rented from equipment rental dealers. The stand is not absolutely necessary, but it will make the job much easier.
5. Check the engine for signs of coolant or oil leaks.
6. Clean the outside of the engine.
7. Remove the distributor. See Chapter Eight.
8. Remove all hoses and tubes connected to the engine.
9. Remove the fuel pump on carburetted engines. See Chapter Six.
10. Remove the intake and exhaust manifolds.
11. Remove the thermostat housing. See Chapter Seven.
12. Remove the rocker arms.
13. Remove the torsional damper, front cover, water pump, timing chain and sprockets.
14. Remove the camshaft.
15. Remove the cylinder heads.
16. Remove the oil pan and oil pump.
17. Remove the pistons and connecting rods.
18. Remove the crankshaft.
19. Inspect the cylinder block.
20. Assemble by reversing Steps 1-18.

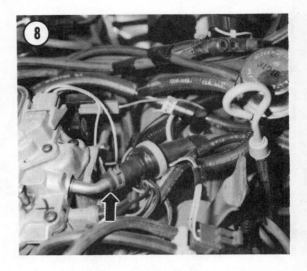

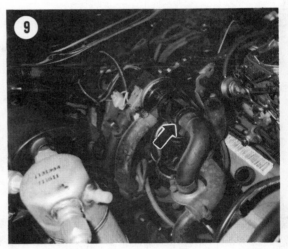

ROCKER ARM COVER

Removal/Installation (V6 Engine)

1. Disconnect the negative battery cable.
2. Remove the air cleaner. See Chapter Six.
3A. Right cover—Disconnect the air management hoses. See **Figure 8**.
3B. Left cover—Disconnect all hoses, wires and vacuum lines and move to one side. See **Figure 9**.
4. Remove the spark plug wires and clips from the retaining studs.
5A. Right cover—Disconnect carburetor controls and remove from bracket.
5B. Left cover—Disconnect and plug the fuel line at the carburetor.

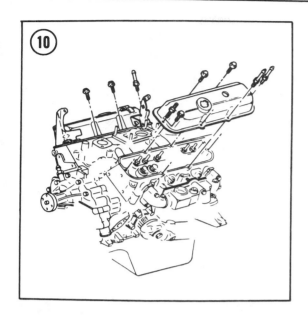

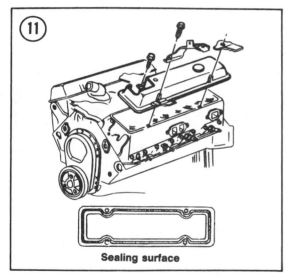

Sealing surface

6. Remove the rocker arm cover bolts (**Figure 10**).

> *NOTE*
> *If the cover refuses to come free in Step 9, bump the end with a rubber mallet. If this does not break the RTV seal, carefully pry the cover loose with a screwdriver. Use caution to prevent distorting the cover sealing flange.*

7. Remove the rocker arm cover. Clean any RTV residue from the cylinder head and rocker arm mating surfaces.

> *NOTE*
> *Keep sealant out of bolt holes in Step 10 to prevent a hydraulic condition which could damage the cylinder head.*

8. Run a 1/8 in. (3 mm) bead of RTV sealant around the rocker arm sealing surface. Flow the RTV on the inside of the bolt holes.

9. Install the rocker arm cover while the RTV is wet. Tighten the attaching bolts to 8 ft.-lb. (10 N•m).

10. Reverse Steps 1-5 to complete cover installation.

Removal/Installation
(V8 Engine)

1. Disconnect the negative battery cover.
2. Remove the air cleaner. See Chapter Six.
3A. Right cover—Disconnect all wires and hoses. Remove the EGR solenoid, air management valve bracket and tubes.
3B. Left cover—Remove power brake booster line, air injection hoses, PCV hose and wire harness. If equipped with fuel injection, relieve the fuel line pressure (Chapter Six) and remove the fuel return line.
4. Remove the rocker arm cover bolts. **Figure 11** shows the right cover; the left cover is similar.

> *NOTE*
> *If the cover refuses to come free in Step 6, bump the end with a rubber mallet. If this does not break the RTV seal, carefully pry the cover loose with a screwdriver. Use caution to prevent distorting the cover sealing flange.*

5. Remove the rocker arm cover. Clean any RTV residue from the cylinder head and rocker arm mating surfaces.

> *NOTE*
> *Keep sealant out of bolt holes in Step 7 to prevent a hydraulic condition which could damage the cylinder head.*

6. Run a 1/8 in. (3 mm) bead of RTV sealant around the rocker arm sealing surfaces. Flow the RTV on the inside of the bolt holes. See **Figure 11**.

7. Install the rocker arm cover while the RTV is wet. Tighten the attaching bolts to 40 in.-lb. (4.6 N•m).

5

8. Reverse Steps 1-3 to complete cover installation.

INTAKE MANIFOLD

Removal/Installation (V6 Engine)

1. Disconnect the negative battery cable.
2. Partially drain the cooling system. See *Cooling System Flushing*, Chapter Seven.
3. Remove the air cleaner. See Chapter Six.
4. Tag and disconnect all vacuum lines, electrical wiring and fuel lines to the carburetor.
5. Disconnect the throttle cable.
6. Disconnect the spark plug cables and coil wires.
7. Remove distributor cap. Mark distributor position. Remove hold-down bracket. Remove distributor.
8. Remove the air management hoses.
9. Disconnect the canister hoses. Remove tubing bracket from left valve cover.
10. Remove the left rocker cover bolts. Remove the rocker cover.
11. Remove the air management bracket.
12. Remove the right rocker cover.
13. Disconnect the upper radiator hose.
14. Disconnect the heater hose.
15. Remove the air conditioning compressor belt, if so equipped. Rotate the compressor out of the way without disconnecting any lines.
16. Disconnect all coolant switches.
17. Remove the manifold nuts and bolts.
18. Remove the manifold. Discard the gaskets. Remove all RTV sealant from the front and rear of the block.
19. Clean the gasket sealing surfaces on the intake manifold and cylinder head.

> *NOTE*
> *Gaskets are marked "RIGHT SIDE" or "LEFT SIDE." Install as marked. Cut gaskets where indicated to install behind pushrods.*

20. Run a 5 mm (3/16 in.) bead of RTV sealant at the front and rear block mating surfaces. Install gaskets and hold in place by

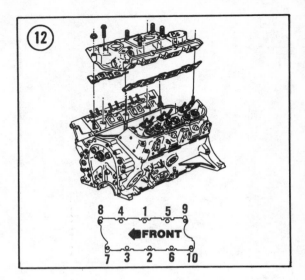

extending the RTV bead 6 mm (7/32 in.) onto the gasket ends.
21. Install the intake manifold. Tighten the bolts to 23 ft.-lb. (31 N•m) in the sequence shown in **Figure 12**.
23. Reverse Steps 1-16 to complete the installation.

Removal/Installation (Carburetted V8 Engine)

1. Disconnect the negative battery cable.
2. Remove the air cleaner. See Chapter Six.
3. Drain the cooling system. See *Cooling System Flushing*, Chapter Seven.
4. Disconnect the upper radiator hose and heater hose at the manifold.
5. Disconnect the carburetor linkage. Disconnect and plug fuel line at the carburetor (**Figure 13**).

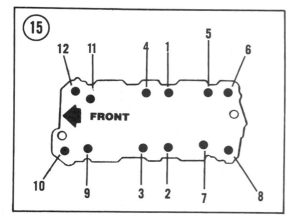

14. Clean gasket and seal surfaces on manifold, block and cylinder heads to remove all RTV sealant and gasket residue.

15. Install new gaskets on cylinder heads. Run a 3/16 in. (5 mm) bead of RTV sealant on the front and rear cylinder case ridges. Extend the bead 1/2 in. (13 mm) up each cylinder head to seal and retain manifold side gaskets. Use sealer at water passages.

16. Install manifold and tighten bolts to specifications in the sequence shown in **Figure 15**. Reverse Steps 1-11 to complete the installation.

Removal/Installation (Fuel Injected V8 Engine)

1. Disconnect the negative battery cable.
2. Remove the air cleaner. See Chapter Six.
3. Drain the cooling system. See *Cooling System Flushing*, Chapter Seven.

> *WARNING*
> *Relieve fuel system pressure before performing Step 4. See Chapter Six.*

4. Disconnect and plug the fuel line at the TBI assembly.
5. Remove the EGR solenoid.
6. Remove the alternator adjustment bracket.
7. Remove the power brake booster and fuel return lines.
8. Disconnect the throttle cable. Disconnect the cruise control cable, if so equipped.
9. Disconnect the PCV line and all vacuum hoses.
10. Remove the fuel balance tube.
11. Remove the throttle body assembly-to-manifold bolts. Remove the throttle body assembly plate.
12. Remove the distributor cap. Mark the distributor rotor position. Remove the distributor.
13. Remove the radiator hose at the thermostat housing. Disconnect the heater hose.
14. Remove the manifold. Discard the gaskets.
15. Remove all RTV sealant and gasket residue from the cylinder heads, manifold and block.

6. Disconnect all wires and hoses including the right bank of spark plug wires.
7. Remove the distributor cap. Mark the rotor position, then remove the distributor.
8. If equipped with air conditioning and/or cruise control, remove the compressor and/or servo and bracket assembly. Place to one side out of the way without disconnecting the lines.
9. Remove alternator upper mounting bracket (**Figure 14**).
10. Remove EGR solenoids and bracket.
11. Remove vacuum brake line at the manifold.
12. Remove the manifold bolts. Remove the manifold and discard the gaskets.
13. If replacing the manifold, transfer the carburetor, thermostat housing, EGR valve and all necessary switches and fittings.

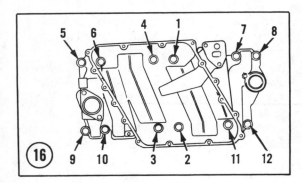

16. Run a 3/16 in. (5 mm) bead of RTV sealant at the front and rear block mating surfaces. Install gaskets and hold in place by extending the RTV bead 1/2 in. (13 mm) up each cylinder head. Use sealer at water passages.

17. Install intake manifold. Wipe bolt threads with Loctite and tighten to specifications in sequence shown in **Figure 16**. Reverse Steps 1-13 to complete installation.

EXHAUST MANIFOLDS

Removal/Installation
(V6 Engine)

Refer to **Figure 17** for this procedure.
1. Disconnect the negative battery cable.
2. Raise the front of the car with a jack and place it on jackstands.
3. Disconnect the exhaust pipe at the manifold.
4. Left manifold—Remove 4 rear bolts and one nut.
5. Remove the jackstands. Lower the car to the ground.
6. Right manifold—Remove the attaching bolts.
7. Disconnect the air management hose and any wires.
8. Left manifold—Remove the power steering bracket.
9. Remove the manifolds.
10. Installation is the reverse of removal. Tighten manifold bolts to 25 ft.-lb. (34 N•m).

Removal/Installation
(V8 Engine)

Refer to **Figure 18** for this procedure.
1. Disconnect the negative battery cable.

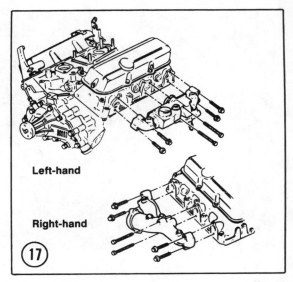

Left-hand

Right-hand

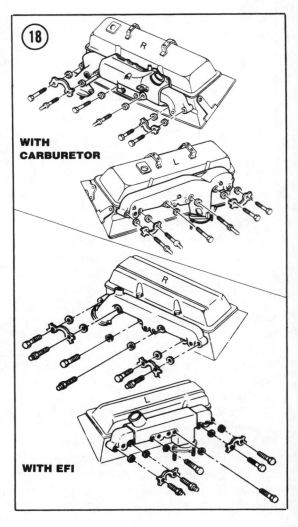

WITH CARBURETOR

WITH EFI

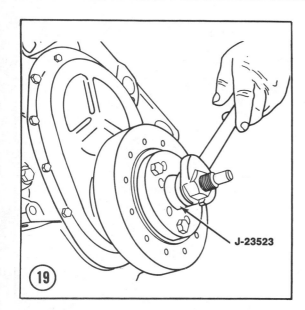

TORSIONAL DAMPER

NOTE
The inertial weight section of the damper is assembled to the hub by a rubber sleeve. Follow the procedure below using the specified tools or you may destroy the damper tuning.

Removal/Installation

This procedure requires the use of a GM puller part No. J-23523 for V6 and V8 engines. If working on the V6, GM installer part No. J-29113 is also required. Refer to **Figure 19** (V8 engine shown).
1. Disconnect the negative battery cable.
2. Loosen the accessory units and remove all drive belts.
3. Raise the front of the car with a jack and place it on jackstands.
4. Remove the accessory drive pulley. Remove the damper retaining bolt.
5. Remove the damper with tool part No. J-23523.
6. Lubricate the front cover seal contact area with SAE 30W engine oil.
7. Position the damper over the crankshaft key.
8A. V6 engine—Install tool part No. J-29113 in the crankshaft so that at least 6 mm of the tool threads are engaged.
8B. V8 engine—Install threaded end of tool part No. J-23523 in the crankshaft so that at least 13 mm of the tool threads are engaged. Install plate, thrust bearing and nut to complete tool installation.
9. Pull the damper into position as shown in **Figure 19**.
10. Reverse Steps 1-4 to complete installation. Adjust all drive belts. See *Drive Belts*, Chapter Three.

2. Disconnect spark plug wires and lay them back out of the way.
3. Disconnect the air injection hoses.
4. Right manifold—Remove air conditioning compressor and/or power steering pump, if so equipped. Move to one side out of the way without disconnecting the lines. Remove the air conditioning and power steering brackets.
5. Raise the car with a jack and place it on jackstands.
6. Disconnect the exhaust pipe at the exhaust manifold.
7. Remove the jackstands and lower the car to the ground.
8. Remove the manifold bolts. Remove the manifolds.

MANIFOLD INSPECTION

1. Check the intake and exhaust manifolds for cracks or distortion. Replace if distorted or if cracks are found.
2. Check the gasket surfaces for nicks or burrs. Small burrs may be removed with an oilstone.
3. Place a straightedge across the manifold gasket surfaces. If there is any gap between the straightedge and the gasket surface, measure it with a feeler gauge. The gasket surface must be flat within 0.006 in. (0.15 mm) per foot of manifold length. If not, replace the manifold.

CRANKCASE FRONT COVER

Removal/Installation
(V6 Engine)

Refer to **Figure 20** for this procedure.
1. Remove the water pump. See Chapter Seven.
2. If equipped with air conditioning, remove the compressor from the mounting bracket

5

without disconnecting any lines. Place the compressor out of the way. Remove the mounting bracket.

3. Remove the torsional damper as described in this chapter.

4. Disconnect the lower radiator hose at the front cover. Disconnect the heater hose at the water pump.

5. Remove front cover bolts and cover.

6. Clean block, oil pan and front cover sealing surfaces of all oil and grease. Apply a 3/32 in. (2 mm) bead of anaerobic sealant on cover-to-block sealing surface. Apply a 1/8 in. (3 mm) bead of RTV sealant on cover-to-oil pan sealing surface. See **Figure 21**. Install cover while sealant is wet.

7. Install stud bolt and bolts. Install water pump. Install retaining bolts and nut. Tighten fasteners to specifications within 5 minutes after installing the cover.

8. Install the torsional damper as described in this chapter.

9. Install the heater and lower radiator hoses.

10. Install the air conditioning compressor bracket and compressor, if removed.

11. Install and adjust accessory drive belts.

Removal/Installation
(V8 Engine)

Refer to **Figure 22** for this procedure.

1. Remove the torsional damper as described in this chapter.

2. Remove the water pump. See Chapter Seven.

3. Remove the front cover attaching screws. Remove the front cover and gasket. Discard the gasket.

4. Cut away any excess oil pan gasket material protruding at the oil pan-to-block joint.

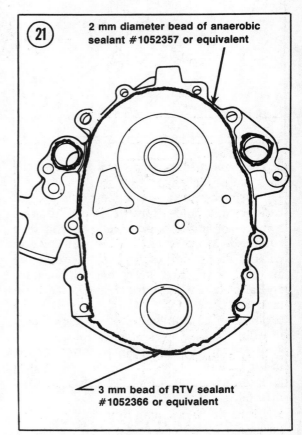

2 mm diameter bead of anaerobic sealant #1052357 or equivalent

3 mm bead of RTV sealant #1052366 or equivalent

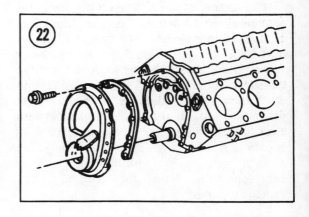

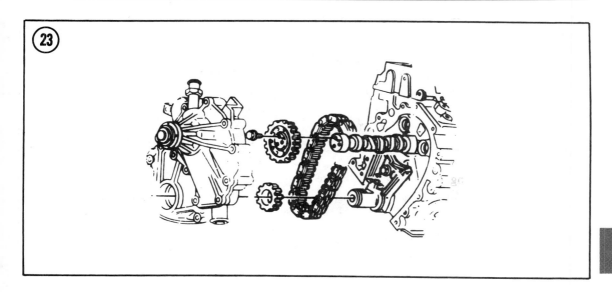

(23)

5

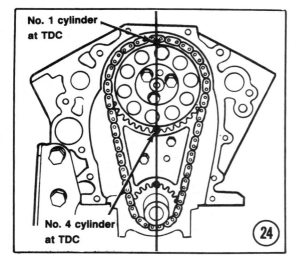

No. 1 cylinder at TDC

No. 4 cylinder at TDC

(24)

5. Clean the block and front cover sealing surfaces of all oil and grease. Apply a 1/8 in. (3 mm) bead of RTV sealant to the joint formed at the oil pan and cylinder block.

6. Install the gasket to the cover with gasket sealant.

7. Install the cover-to-oil pan seal. Coat the bottom of the seal with engine oil. Position cover over crankshaft end.

8. Install cover-to-block upper screws loosely.

NOTE
Do not force cover on dowels in Step 9 so the cover flange or holes are distorted.

9. Press downward on cover to align dowels in block with corresponding cover holes and tighten screws in a crisscross pattern.

10. Install remaining cover screws and tighten to specifications.

11. Install water pump. See Chapter Seven.

12. Install torsional damper as described in this chapter.

TIMING CHAIN AND SPROCKET

Removal

Refer to **Figure 23** (V6 engine shown) for this procedure.

1. Remove the spark plugs. See *Tune-up* in Chapter Three.

2. Remove the torsional damper as described in this chapter.

3. Remove the front cover as described in this chapter.

4. Rotate the crankshaft to position the No. 1 piston at TDC with the camshaft and crankshaft marks aligned as shown in **Figure 24** (V6 engine) or **Figure 25** (V8 engine).

NOTE
The camshaft sprocket is a light fit on the camshaft. A light blow with a plastic mallet on the lower sprocket edge should dislodge it.

5. Remove the camshaft sprocket bolts. Remove the sprocket and chain.

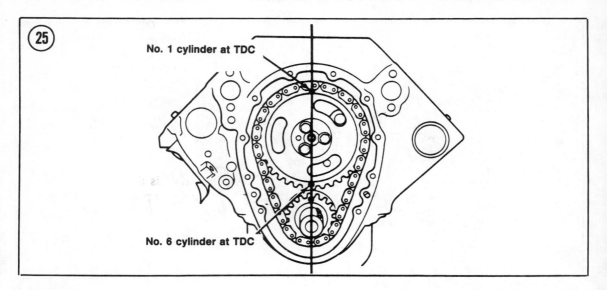

No. 1 cylinder at TDC

No. 6 cylinder at TDC

Installation

Refer to **Figure 23** (V6 engine shown) for this procedure.

1. Install the timing chain on the camshaft sprocket.

2. Hold the sprocket vertically with the chain hanging down. Align the camshaft and crankshaft sprocket marks as shown in **Figure 24** (V6 engine) or **Figure 25** (V8 engine).

3. Align the camshaft dowel with the sprocket hole. Install the sprocket on the camshaft.

4. Install the camshaft sprocket mounting bolts. Tighten bolts to draw the sprocket onto the camshaft. Tighten bolts to specifications.

5. Lubricate the timing chain with SAE 30W engine oil.

6. Install the front cover as described in this chapter.

7. Install the torsional damper as described in this chapter.

ROCKER ARMS

Removal/Installation

Refer to **Figure 26** (V8 engine shown) for this procedure.

1. Remove the rocker arm cover as described in this chapter.

2. Remove the rocker arm nuts, rocker arm balls, rocker arms and pushrods.

3. Place each rocker arm assembly in a separate container or use a rack to keep them

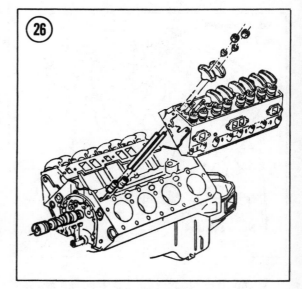

separated for reinstallation in the same position as before they were removed.

4. Remove the valve lifters with a pencil-type magnet. Do not pry lifters out with a screwdriver.

NOTE
When installing new valve lifters, rocker arms or rocker arm balls, coat the contact surfaces with Molykote or equivalent.

5. Install the valver lifters and pushrods. Seat each pushrod in its lifter and align in its retainer.

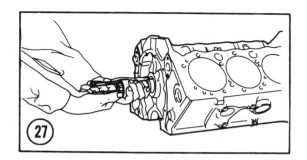

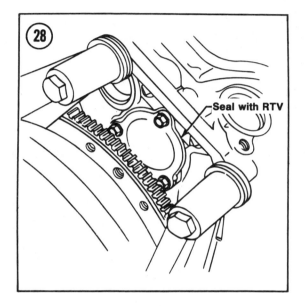

Seal with RTV

6. Install the rocker arms, rocker arm balls and rocker arm nuts. Tighten the nuts until all lash is removed.

7. Adjust the valves as described in this chapter.

8. Install the rocker arm cover as described in this chapter.

CAMSHAFT

Removal

1. Remove the engine from the car as described in this chapter.

2. Remove the rocker arm cover as described in this chapter.

3. Remove the rocker arms and valve lifters as described in this chapter.

4. Remove the torsional damper and front cover as described in this chapter.

5. Remove the fuel pump and pushrod on carburetted engines. See Chapter Six.

NOTE
All camshaft journals are the same diameter and care must be taken to prevent bearing damage while performing Step 6.

6. Withdraw camshaft from the block with a slow, careful rotating motion. See **Figure 27**.

Inspection

1. Check the journals and lobes for signs of wear or scoring. Lobe pitting in the toe area is not sufficient reason for replacement, unless the lobe lift loss exceeds specifications.

NOTE
If you do not have precision measuring equipment, have Step 2 done by a machine shop.

2. Measure the camshaft journal diameters with a micrometer. Replace the camshaft if the journals are more than 0.001 in. (0.025 mm) out-of-round.

Installation

NOTE
When installing a new camshaft, coat the lobes with GM EOS lubricant or equivalent.

1. Lubricate the camshaft journals with SAE 30W engine oil.

2. Install the camshaft with a rotating motion.

3. Reverse Steps 1-5 of *Camshaft Removal* in this chapter to complete installation.

Bearing Replacement

Camshaft bearings can be replaced without complete engine disassembly. Camshaft bearing remover/installer tool part No. J-6098 is required for bearing replacement.

1. Remove the camshaft and crankshaft as described in this chapter.

2A. V6 engine—Remove the camshaft rear cover (**Figure 28**) from the block.

2B. V8 engine—Drive camshaft rear plug from the block.

3. Install the nut and thrust washer to tool part No. J-6098. Index the tool pilot in the

front cam bearing. Install the puller screw through the pilot.

4. Install tool part No. J-6098 with its shoulder facing the front intermediate bearing and the threads engaging the bearing.

5. Hold the puller screw with one wrench. Turn the nut with a second wrench until the bearing has been pulled from its bore.

6. Repeat Steps 3-5 to remove remaining bearings (except front and rear).

7. Remove the tool and index it to the rear bearing to remove the rear intermediate bearing from the block.

8. Remove the front and rear bearings by driving them toward the center of the block.

9. Installation is the reverse of removal. Use the same tool to pull new bearings into their bores.

   a. On V6 engines, index the rear intermediate bearing oil holes at the 2:30 position. Index the front bearing oil holes at the 1:00 and 2:30 positions.

   b. On V8 engines, index the front bearing oil holes so they are equidistant from the 6:00 position. Index the rear bearing oil hole at the 12:00 position.

   c. Index all other bearing oil holes at the 5:00 position.

10A. V6 engine—Install the camshaft rear cover with a 1/8 in. bead of RTV sealant and tighten bolts immediately.

10B. V8 engine—Coat outer diameter of new camshaft rear plug with sealant and install flush to 1/32 in. deep.

Lobe Lift Measurement

Camshaft lobe lift is measured with the camshaft in the block and the cylinder head in place. Refer to **Figure 29**.

1. Remove the rocker arm cover and rocker arm assembly as described in this chapter.

2. Install a dial indicator with a ball socket adapter to fit over the pushrod. See **Figure 29**.

3. Turn the crankshaft in the direction of rotation until the valve lifter seats on the heel of the cam lobe. This positions the pushrod at its lowest point.

4. Zero the dial indicator, then slowly rotate the crankshaft until the pushrod is in its fully raised position. Record the total lift.

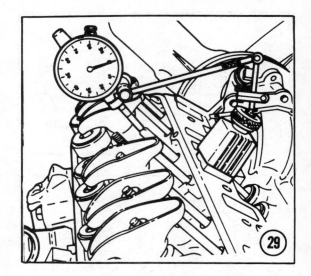

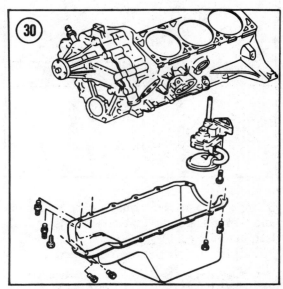

5. Repeat Steps 2-4 for each pushrod. If all lobes are within specifications (**Table 1** and **Table 2**), reinstall the rocker arm assemblies and adjust the valves as described in this chapter.

6. If one or more lobes are worn beyond specifications, replace the camshaft as described in this chapter.

OIL PAN AND PUMP

Oil Pan Removal

Figure 30 shows the V6 assembly; **Figure 31** shows the V8 pan and pump.

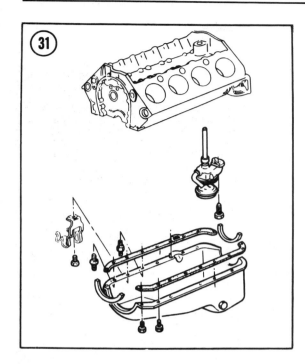

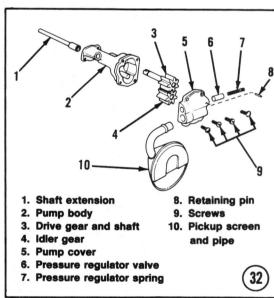

1. Shaft extension
2. Pump body
3. Drive gear and shaft
4. Idler gear
5. Pump cover
6. Pressure regulator valve
7. Pressure regulator spring
8. Retaining pin
9. Screws
10. Pickup screen and pipe

1. Disconnect the negative battery cable.
2. Remove the fan shroud.
3. Raise the car with a jack and place it on jackstands.
4. Drain the crankcase. See *Engine Oil and Filter*, Chapter Three.
5. Remove air injection pipe at converter.
6. Remove the converter hanger bolts.

7. Remove the starter bolts. Loosen brace and place starter to one side.
8. Attach a hoist to the engine. Remove the motor mount through bolts.
9. Raise the engine slightly with the hoist. Remove the oil pan bolts.
10. Make sure that the forward crankshaft throw and/or counterbalance weight do not extend downward and block pan removal. If necessary, turn crankshaft to place throw on a horizontal plane.
11. Remove the oil pan.

NOTE
The oil pump pickup tube and screen are a press fit in the pump housing and should not be removed unless replacement is required.

Oil Pan Inspection

1. Clean the pan thoroughly in solvent.
2. Check the pan for dents or warped gasket surfaces. Straighten or replace the pan as needed.
3. Check the pan for cracks. Repair or replace the pan as needed.

Oil Pan Installation

1. Clean any RTV sealant or gasket residue from the oil pan rail on the engine block.
2A. V6 engine—Run a 1/8 in. (3 mm) bead of RTV sealant along the oil pan block sealing flanges. Install oil pan.
2B. V8 engine—Install oil pan with new seals and gaskets.
3. Tighten pan bolts to specifications.
4. Reverse Steps 1-8 of *Oil Pan Removal* in this chapter to complete installation.

Oil Pump Removal/Installation

1. Remove the oil pan as described in this chapter.
2. Remove the pump-to-rear main bearing cap bolt. Remove the oil pump and drive shaft.
3. Installation is the reverse of removal.

Oil Pump Disassembly/Assembly

Refer to **Figure 32** for this procedure.
1. Remove the cover bolts and cover.

2. Scribe a mark on the gear teeth for reinstallation indexing.

3. Remove the idler gear, drive gear and shaft from the pump body.

4. Remove the pressure regulator valve pin, spring and valve.

5. Remove the pickup tube/screen *only* if it needs replacement. Secure the pump body in a soft-jawed vise and separate the tube from the cover.

> NOTE
> *Do not twist, shear or collapse the tube when installing it in Step 6.*

6. If the pickup tube/screen was removed, install a new one. Secure the pump body in a soft-jawed vise. Apply sealer to the new tube and tap in place with a plastic mallet.

7. Assembly is the reverse of disassembly. Use a new cover gasket and tighten cover bolts to 6-9 ft.-lb. (8-12 N•m).

Oil Pump Inspection

> NOTE
> *The pump body and gears are serviced as an assembly. If one or the other is worn or damaged, replace the entire pump. No wear specifications are provided by General Motors.*

1. Clean all parts thoroughly in solvent. Brush the inside of the body and the pressure regulator chamber to remove all dirt and metal particles. Dry with compressed air, if available.

2. Check the pump body and cover for cracks or excessive wear.

3. Check the pump gears for damage or excessive wear.

4. Check the drive gear shaft-to-body fit for excessive looseness.

5. Check the inside of the pump cover for wear that could allow oil to leak around the ends of the gears.

6. Check the pressure regulator valve for a proper fit.

CYLINDER HEAD

Removal

1. Remove the intake manifold as described in this chapter.

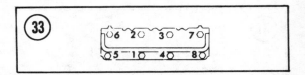

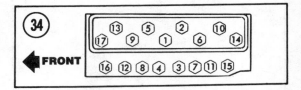

2. Disconnect the negative battery cable.

3. Drain the cooling system. See *Cooling System Flushing*, Chapter Seven.

4. Raise the front of the car with a jack and place it on jackstands.

5. Disconnect the exhaust pipe at the manifold.

6. Left head—Remove the dipstick tube attachment.

7. Remove the jacks and lower the car to the ground.

8. Loosen the rocker arms. Swivel rocker arms off pushrods and remove pushrods.

9. Right head—Remove the alternator mounting bracket.

10. Remove the head bolts. Remove the cylinder head. Remove and discard the gasket.

> NOTE
> *Place the head on its side to prevent damage to the spark plugs or head gasket surface.*

Decarbonizing

1. Without removing the valves, remove all deposits from the combustion chambers, intake ports and exhaust ports. Use a fine wire brush dipped in solvent or make a scraper from hardwood. Be careful not to scratch or gouge the combustion chambers.

2. After all carbon is removed from the combustion chambers and ports, clean the entire head in solvent.

3. Clean away all carbon on the piston tops. Do not remove the carbon ridge at the top of the cylinder bore.

4. Remove the valves as described in this chapter.

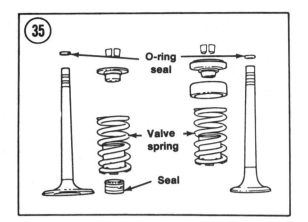

5. Clean the pushrod guides, valve guide bores and all bolt holes. Use a cleaning solvent to remove dirt and grease.
6. Clean the valves with a fine wire brush or buffing wheel.

Inspection

1. Check the cylinder head for signs of oil or water leaks before cleaning.
2. Clean the cylinder head thoroughly in solvent. While cleaning, check for cracks or other visible damage. Look for corrosion or foreign material in the oil and water passages. Clean the passages with a stiff spiral brush, then blow them out with compressed air.
3. Check the cylinder head studs for damage and replace if necessary.
4. Check the threaded rocker arm bolts for damaged threads and replace if necessary.

Installation

1. Be sure the cylinder head and block gasket surfaces and bolt holes are clean. Dirt in the block bolt holes or on the head bolt threads will affect bolt torque.
2. Check all visible oil and water passages for cleanliness.

NOTE
Use gasket sealer on V8 steel gaskets. Do not use sealer on V8 composition steel/asbestos gaskets.

3. Install a new head gasket on the cylinder head dowel pins in the block with the words "THIS SIDE UP" facing up. If not marked in this manner, be sure the bead faces up.

4. Carefully lower the cylinder head in place on the dowel pins and gasket.
5. Coat the head bolt threads with sealing compound and install the bolts finger-tight.
6. Tighten the head bolts to specifications. Follow the sequence shown in **Figure 33** for V6 engines and **Figure 34** for V8 engines.
7. Reverse Steps 1-9 of *Cylinder Head Removal* in this chapter to complete installation.

VALVES AND VALVE SEATS

Some of the following procedures must be done by a dealer or a machine shop, since they require special knowledge and expensive machine tools. Others, while possible for the home mechanic, are difficult or time-consuming. A general practice among those who do their own service is to remove the cylinder head, perform all disassembly except valve removal and take the head to a machine shop for inspection and service. Since the cost is low relative to the required effort and equipment, this is usually the best approach, even for experienced mechanics. The following procedures are given to acquaint the home mechanic with what the dealer or machine shop will do.

Valve Removal

Refer to **Figure 35** for this procedure.
1. Remove the cylinder head as described in this chapter.
2. Remove the rocker arm assemblies as described in this chapter.
3. Compress the valve spring with a compressor like the one shown in **Figure 36**. Remove the valve locks and release the spring tension.
4. Remove the valve spring cap, spring shield, valve spring and damper assembly.
5. Pry the stem seal off with a screwdriver blade and discard it.

CAUTION
Remove any burrs from the valve stem lock grooves before removing the valves or the valve guides will be damaged.

6. Remove the valve and repeat Steps 3-5 on each remaining valve.

7. Arrange the parts in order so they can be returned to their original positions when reassembled.

Inspection

1. Clean the valves with a fine wire brush or buffing wheel. Discard any cracked, warped or burned valves.

2. Measure valve stems at the top, center and bottom for wear. A machine shop can do this when the valves are ground. Also measure the length of each valve and the diameter of each valve head.

3. Remove all carbon and varnish from the valve guides with a stiff spiral wire brush.

> *NOTE*
> *The next step assumes that all valve stems have been measured and are within specifications. Replace valves with worn stems before performing this step.*

4. Insert each valve into the guide from which it was removed. Holding the valve just slightly off its seat, rock it back and forth in a direction parallel with the rocker arms. This is the direction in which the greatest wear normally occurs. If the valve stem rocks more than slightly, the valve guide is probably worn.

5. If there is any doubt about valve guide condition after performing Step 4, have the valve guide measured with a valve stem clearance checking tool. Compare the results to specifications (**Table 1** and **Table 2**). Worn guides must be reamed for the next oversize valve stem.

6. Test the valve springs under load on a spring tester (**Figure 37**). Replace any weak springs.

7. Inspect the valve seat inserts. If worn or burned, they must be reconditioned. This is a job for a dealer or machine shop, although the procedure is described in this chapter.

Valve Guide Reaming

Worn valve guides must be reamed to accept a valve with an oversize stem. These

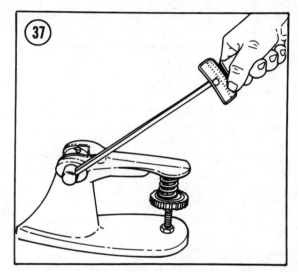

are available in 3 sizes for both intake and exhaust valves. Reaming must be done by hand and is a job best left to an experienced machine shop. The valve seat must be refaced after the guide has been reamed.

> *NOTE*
> *Valves with oversize stem diameters of 0.89, 0.394 and 0.775 mm are available. Do not attempt to ream the guide from stock directly to 0.775 mm oversize. Ream in 0.89, 0.394 and 0.775 mm increments to maintain proper guide-to-seat relationships.*

Valve Seat Reconditioning

1. Cut the valve seats to a 46° angle using a cutter or special stone.

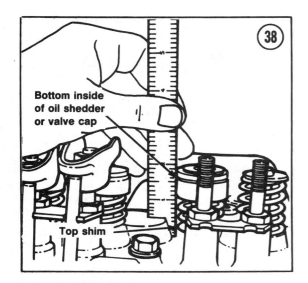

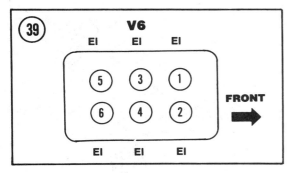

NOTE
Check the thickness of the valve edge or margin after the valves have been ground. Any valve with a margin of less than 1/32 in. (0.8 mm) should be discarded.

2. Coat the corresponding valve face with Prussian blue dye.
3. Insert the valve into the valve guide.
4. Apply light pressure to the valve and rotate it approximately 1/4 turn.
5. Lift the valve out. If it seats properly, the dye will transfer evenly to the valve face.
6. If the dye transfers to the top of the valve face, lower the seat. If it transfers to the bottom of the valve face, raise the seat.

Valve Installation

NOTE
Install all parts in the same position from which they were removed.

Refer to **Figure 35** for this procedure.
1. Coat the valves with oil and install them in the cylinder head.
2. Install new oil seals on each intake valve.
3. Install the valve springs, spring shields and valve rotators on exhaust valves. Install valve springs and caps on intake valves.
4. Compress the springs and install the square cut O-ring around the lower groove of the valve stem. Make sure it is not twisted.
5. Install the valve locks. Make sure both locks seat properly in the upper groove of the valve stem.
6. Measure the installed spring height. Measure between the top of the spring damper feet to the bottom inside of the oil shedder on exhaust valves and from the top of the spring damper feet to the bottom of the valve cap on intake valves. See **Figure 38**. If greater than the specified height, install an extra spring seat shim about 0.7 mm thick and remeasure the height.

VALVE LIFTERS

Removal/Installation

See *Rocker Arm Removal/Installation* in this chapter.

Inspection

Keep the lifters in proper sequence for replacement in their original position in the head. Clean lifters in solvent and wipe dry with a clean, lint-free cloth.

Inspect all parts. If any lifter shows signs of pitting, scoring, galling, non-rotation or excessive wear, replace the entire lifter. Check the lifter foot. It must be slightly convex. If the bottom of the body is scuffed or worn, check the camshaft lobe. If the pushrod seat is scuffed or worn, check the pushrod.

VALVE ADJUSTMENT

Valve lash adjustment is only required when the cylinder head valve train has been disassembled. Adjust the valves with the lifter on the base circle of the camshaft lobe. Cylinder position and valve arrangement are shown in **Figure 39** (V6) and **Figure 40** (V8).

1. Rotate the crankshaft until the pulley notch aligns with the zero mark on the timing tab. This positions the No. 1 piston at TDC. This position can be verified by placing a finger on the No. 1 rocker arms as the pulley notch nears the zero mark. If the valves are moving, the engine is in the No. 4 (V6) or No. 6 (V8) firing position. Rotate the crankshaft pulley one full turn to reach the No. 1 firing position.

2A. V6 engine—Adjust the No. 1, 2 and 3 exhaust valves and the No. 1, 5 and 6 intake valves. See **Figure 39**.

2B. V8 engine—Adjust the No. 1, 3, 4 and 8 exhaust valves, and the No. 1, 2, 5 and 7 intake valves. See **Figure 40**.

3. To adjust the valves, back off the adjusting nut until lash is felt at the pushrod, then turn the nut in to remove all lash. When lash has been removed, the pushrod cannot be rotated (**Figure 41**). Turn the nut in another full turn (V8) or 1 1/2 turns (V6) to center the lifter plunger.

4. Rotate the crankshaft pulley one full turn to realign the pulley notch and the timing tab zero mark. This is the No. 4 firing position for V6 engines and the No. 6 firing position for V8 engines.

5A. V6 engine—Adjust the No. 4, 5 and 6 exhaust valves and the No. 2, 3 and 4 intake valves. See **Figure 39**.

5B. V8 engine—Adjust the No. 2, 5, 6 and 7 exhaust valves and the No. 3, 4, 6 and 8 intake valves. See **Figure 40**.

6. Install the rocker arm covers as described in this chapter.

PISTON/CONNECTING ROD ASSEMBLY

Piston Removal

1. Remove the cylinder head and oil pan as described in this chapter.

2. Pack the cylinder bore with clean shop rags. Remove the carbon ridge at the top of the cylinder bores with a ridge reamer. These can be rented for use. Vacuum out the shavings, then remove the shop rags.

3. Rotate the crankshaft so the connecting rod is centered in the bore.

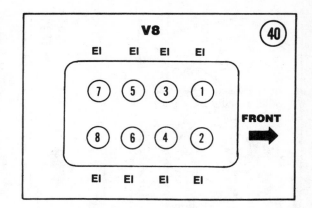

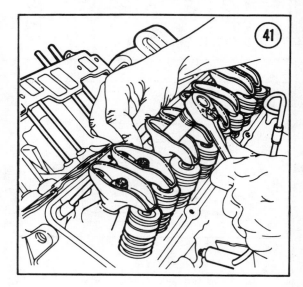

Measure between rod cap and crank throw

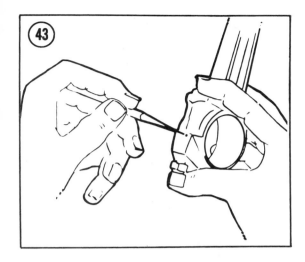

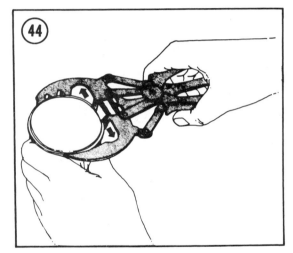

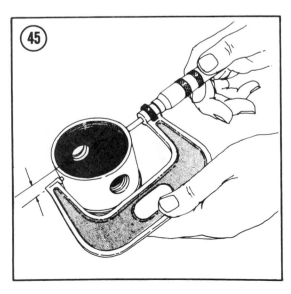

4. Measure the clearance between each connecting rod big end and the crankshaft rod cap with a feeler gauge (**Figure 42**). If the clearance exceeds specifications, replace the connecting rod during reassembly.

NOTE
*Mark the cylinder number on the top of each piston with quick-drying paint. Check for cylinder numbers stamped on the connecting rod and cap. If they are not visible, make your own (**Figure 43**).*

5. Remove the nuts holding the connecting rod cap. Lift off the cap, together with the lower bearing half.

NOTE
If the connecting rod caps are difficult to remove, tap the studs with a wooden hammer handle.

6. Use the wooden hammer handle to push the piston and connecting rod out of the bore.
7. Remove the piston rings with a ring remover (**Figure 44**).

Piston Pin Removal/Installation

The piston pins are press-fitted to the connecting rods and hand-fitted to the pistons. Removal requires the use of a press and support stand. This is a job for a dealer or machine shop equipped to fit the pistons to the pin, ream the pin bushings to the correct diameter and install the pistons and pins on the connecting rods.

Piston Clearance Check

If you do not have precision measuring equipment and know how to use it properly, have this procedure done by a machine shop.
1. Measure the piston diameter with a micrometer (**Figure 45**). Measure just below the rings at right angles to the piston pin bore.
2. Measure the cylinder bore diameter with a bore gauge (**Figure 46**). Measure at the top, center and bottom of the bore, in front-to-rear and side-to-side directions.
3. Subtract the piston diameter from the largest cylinder bore reading. If it exceeds the specifications in **Table 1** or **Table 2**, the cylinder must be rebored and oversized pistons installed.

Piston Ring Fit/Installation

1. Check the ring gap of each piston ring. To do this, position the ring at the top or bottom of the ring travel area and square it by tapping gently with an inverted piston. See **Figure 47**.

NOTE
If the cylinders have not been rebored, check the gap at the bottom of the ring travel, where the cylinder is least worn.

2. Measure ring gap with a feeler gauge as shown in **Figure 48** and compare with specifications. If the measurement is not within specifications, the rings must be replaced as a set. Check the gap of new rings and file the ends if the gap is too small.

3. Check the side clearance of the rings as shown in **Figure 49**. Place the feeler gauge alongside the ring all the way into the groove. If the measurement is not within specifications (**Table 1** or **Table 2**), either the rings or the ring grooves are worn. Inspect and replace as necessary.

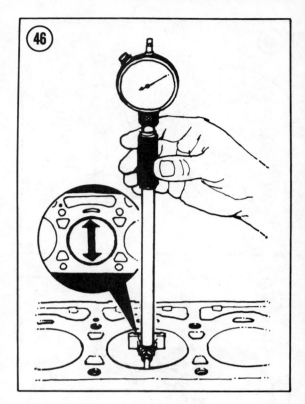

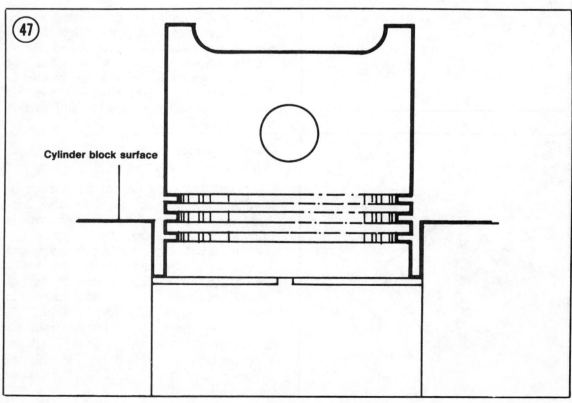

Cylinder block surface

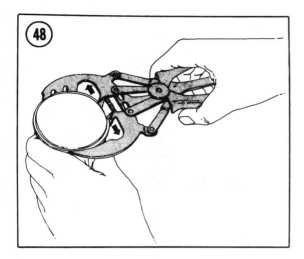

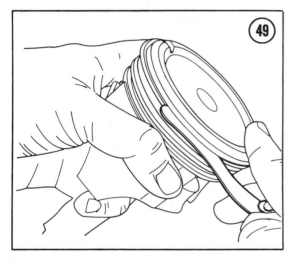

4. Using a ring expander tool (**Figure 48**), carefully install the oil control ring, then the compression rings. Oil rings consist of 3 segments. The wavy segment goes between the flat segment to act as a spacer. Upper and lower flat segments are interchangeable. The second compression ring is tapered. The top sides of both compression rings are marked and must face up.

5. Position the ring gaps as shown in **Figure 51**.

Connecting Rod Inspection

Have connecting rod straightness checked by a dealer or a machine shop.

Connecting Rod Bearing Clearance Measurement

1. Place the connecting rods and upper bearing halves on the proper connecting rod crankpin.

2. Cut a piece of Plastigage the width of the bearing. Place the Plastigage on the crankpin (**Figure 52**), then install the lower bearing half and cap.

> *NOTE*
> *Do not place Plastigage over crankpin oil hole or rotate crankshaft while Plastigage is in place.*

3. Tighten the connecting rod cap to specifications in **Table 2** or **Table 4**. Do not

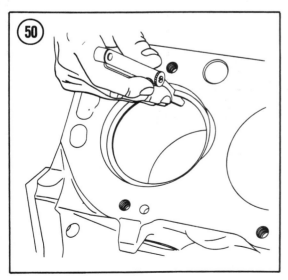

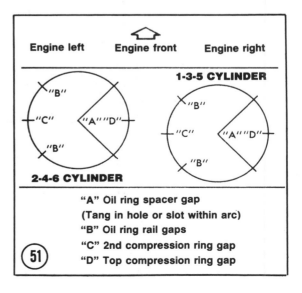

rotate the crankshaft while the Plastigage is in place.

4. Remove the connecting rod caps. Bearing clearance is determined by comparing the width of the flattened Plastigage to the markings on the envelope (**Figure 53**). If the clearance is excessive, select a new bearing of the correct size and remeasure the clearance. If clearance cannot be brought within specifications, the crankpin will have to be ground undersize and appropriate bearings installed.

Installing Piston/Connecting Rod Assembly

1. Make sure the pistons are correctly installed on the connecting rod. The machined hole or cast notch on the top of the piston (**Figure 54**) and the oil hole on the side of the connecting rod must both face the same way.

2. Be sure the ring gaps are positioned as shown in **Figure 51**.

3. Slip short pieces of hose over the connecting rod studs to keep them from nicking the crankshaft. Tape will work if you do not have the right diameter hose, but tape is more difficult to remove.

4. Immerse the entire piston in clean engine oil. Coat the cylinder wall with oil.

5. Install the piston/connecting rod assembly in its cylinder with a piston installer tool as shown in **Figure 55**. Tap lightly with a wooden hammer to insert the piston. Be sure the notch or hole at the top of the piston (**Figure 54**) faces toward the front of the engine and that the piston number painted on the top before removal corresponds to the cylinder number.

> *CAUTION*
> *Use extreme care not to let the connecting rod nick the crankshaft journal.*

6. Clean the connecting rod bearings carefully, including the back sides. Coat the journals and bearings with clean engine oil. Place the bearings in the connecting rod and cap.

7. Remove the protective hose or tape and install the connecting rod cap. Make sure the

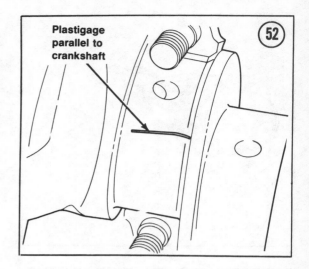
Plastigage parallel to crankshaft

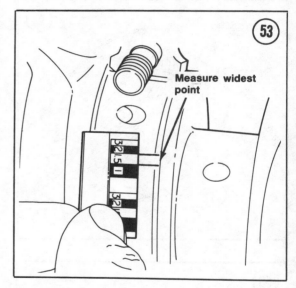
Measure widest point

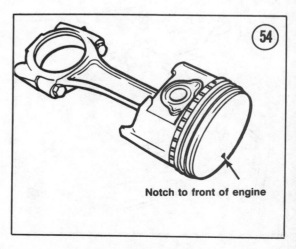
Notch to front of engine

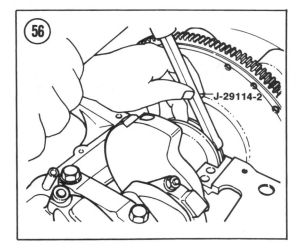

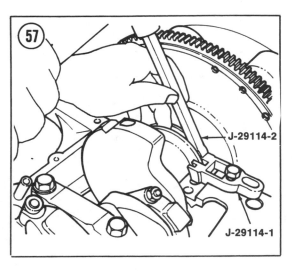

rod and cap marks align. Tighten the cap nuts to specifications.

8. Check the connecting rod big end play as described under *Piston Removal.*

REAR MAIN OIL SEAL

Replacement
(V6 Engine)

NOTE
See the Chapter Five section of the supplement (end of book) for replacement procedure for rubber split rear main oil seal.

The rear main oil seal is located under the rear main bearing cap. The seal is a 2-piece rope type and requires the use of tools part Nos. J-29114-1, J-29114-2 and J-29590 for replacement. The seal can be replaced without removing the engine from the car, if necessary.

1. Remove the oil pan and oil pump as described in this chapter.

2. Unbolt and remove the rear main bearing cap.

3. Carefully drive the upper seal into the groove on both sides about 1/4 in. with tool part No. J-29114-2 (**Figure 56**).

4. Measure how far the seal was driven up on one side and add 1/16 in. to the distance. Remove the old seal from the main bearing cap and cut that amount off it. Repeat this step for the other side of the seal.

5. Install tool part No. J-29114-1 to the cylinder block (**Figure 57**). Use tool part No. J-29114-2 to work the short pieces cut in Step 4 into tool part No. J-29114-1. Oil the short pieces and pack in the block groove.

6. Install a new rope seal in the main bearing cap. Position the seal with tool part No. J-29590, rotate the tool slightly and cut off each seal end flush with the block. See **Figure 58.**

7. Check rear main bearing clearance with Plastigage. See *Main Bearing Clearance Measurement* in this chapter.

8. If bearing clearance is out of specification, recheck seal ends for fraying and correct as required. Clean Plastigage from the journal and bearing.

9. Apply a thin coat of anaerobic sealant to the rear bearing cap as shown in **Figure 59**. The sealant should not touch the seal or bearing.

10. Apply a light coat of SAE 30W engine oil to the crankshaft surface that touches the seal.

11. Install the rear main bearing cap and tighten to 70 ft.-lb. (95 N•m).

12. Install the oil pump and oil pan as described in this chapter.

Replacement (V8 Engine)

1. Fabricate a seal installation tool as shown in **Figure 60** to protect the seal bead when positioning the new seal.

2. Remove the oil pan and oil pump as described in this chapter.

3. Remove the rear main bearing cap. Pry the oil seal from the bottom of the cap with a small screwdriver as shown in **Figure 61**.

4. Remove the upper half of the seal with a brass pin punch. Tap punch on one end of seal until other end protrudes far enough to be removed with pliers. See **Figure 62**.

5. Clean all sealant from bearing cap and crankshaft with a non-abrasive cleaner.

6. Coat new seal lips and bead with light engine oil. Do not let oil touch seal mating ends.

7. Position tip of seal installer tool (fabricated in Step 1) between crankshaft and seal seat. Position seal between crankshaft and tip of tool so seal bead touches tool tip. Make sure oil seal lip faces toward front of engine.

8. Use seal installer tool as a shoehorn and roll seal around crankshaft, protecting seal bead from sharp corners of seal seat surface. Keep tool in position until seal is properly seated, with both ends flush with the block.

9. Remove tool carefully to prevent pulling seal out with it.

10. Use seal installer tool as a shoehorn again and install seal half in bearing cap. Feed seal into cap with light thumb and finger pressure.

11. Apply sealant to the areas shown in **Figure 63**. Keep sealant off the seal split line.

12. Install bearing cap and tighten to 10-12 ft.-lb. (14-16 N•m). Tap end of crankshaft to

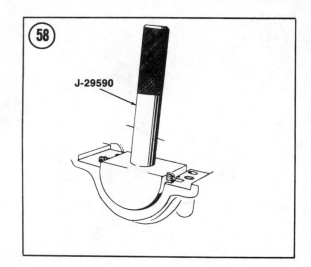

58

J-29590

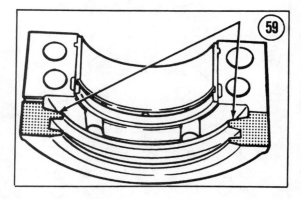

59

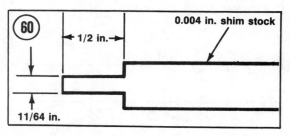

60

0.004 in. shim stock

1/2 in.

11/64 in.

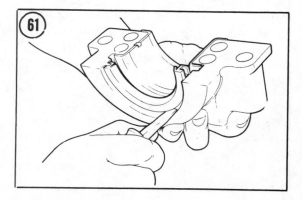

61

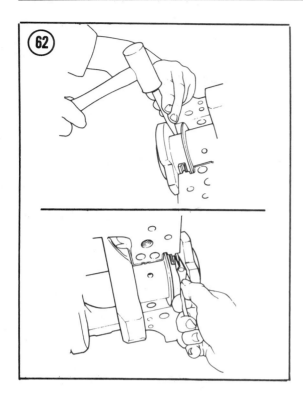

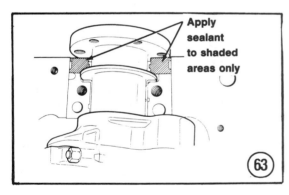

the rear, then to the front to line up thrust surfaces.
13. Retighten bearing cap to specifications.

CRANKSHAFT

Removal

1. If it is necessary to remove the crankshaft sprocket, use puller part No. J-5825.
2. Remove the flywheel or torque converter drive plate.
3. Unbolt and remove the main bearing caps and bearing inserts.

NOTE
If the caps are difficult to remove, lift the bolts partway out, then pry them from side to side.

4. Check the caps for identification numbers or marks. If none are visible, clean the caps with a wire brush. If marks still cannot be seen, make your own with quick-drying paint.
5. Lift the crankshaft from the engine block. Lay the crankshaft, main bearings and bearing caps in order on a clean workbench.

Inspection

1. Clean the crankshaft thoroughly with solvent. Blow out the oil passages with compressed air.

NOTE
If you do not have precision measuring equipment, have a machine shop perform Step 2.

2. Check the crankpins and main bearing journals for wear, scoring and cracks. Check all journals against specifications (**Table 1** or **Table 2**) for out-of-roundness and taper. If necessary, have the crankshaft reground.

Main Bearing Clearance Measurement

Main bearing clearance is measured in the same manner as connecting rod bearing clearance, described in this chapter. Excessive clearance requires that the bearings be replaced, the crankshaft reground or both.

Installation

1. If the crankshaft sprocket was removed, install it with tool part No. J-5590.
2. Install the main bearing shells with their lubrication groove facing the cylinder block. Bearing oil holes must align with block oil holes and bearing tabs must seat in the block tab slots.
3. Lubricate the bolt threads with SAE 30W engine oil.
4. Install the cap bearing shells.
5. Install the crankshaft in the block.
6. Install the bearing caps in their marked positions with the arrows pointing toward the front of the engine. Tighten finger-tight.

5

7A. V6 engine—Tighten all main bearing caps *except* the No. 3 main cap to 70 ft.-lb. (95 N•m). Tighten the No. 3 main cap to 11 ft.-lb. (15 N•m).

7B. V8 engine—Tighten all main bearing caps *except* the rear main cap to 70 ft.-lb. (95 N•m). Tighten the rear main cap to 10-12 ft.-lb. (14-16 N•m).

8. Tap end of crankshaft rearward, then forward to line up bearing thrust surfaces. Retighten all main bearing caps to 70 ft.-lb. (95 N•m).

9. Install the flywheel or drive plate. Place a block of wood between the crankshaft and cylinder block to prevent the crankshaft from rotating, then tighten the bolts to specifications.

End Play Measurement

1. Pry the crankshaft to the front of the engine with a large screwdriver.

2A. V6 engine—Measure the crankshaft end play at the front of the No. 3 main bearing with a feeler gauge (**Figure 64**). Compare to specifications.

2B. V8 engine—Measure the crankshaft end play at the front of the rear main bearing with a feeler gauge (**Figure 65**). Compare to specifications.

3. If the end play is excessive, replace the No. 3 bearing on V6 engines or the rear main bearing on V8 engines. If less than specified, check the bearing faces for imperfections.

Pilot Bearing

The pilot bearing is located inside the rear end of the crankshaft. It supports the transmission input shaft on manual transmission cars.

1. Check the bearing for visible wear or damage. Turn the bearing with a finger and make sure it turns easily. If wear, damage or stiff movement are found, remove the bearing with a puller. These are available from rental dealers.

2. Tap a new bearing in place with a drift until fully seated.

CAUTION
Do not tap too hard or you will damage the bearing.

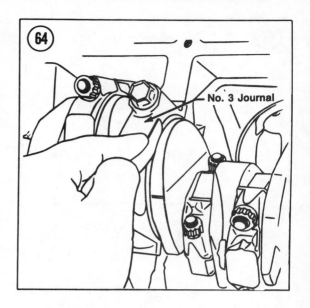

No. 3 Journal

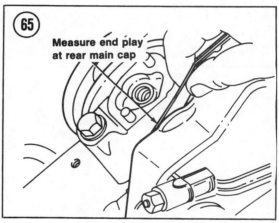

Measure end play at rear main cap

CYLINDER BLOCK CLEANING AND INSPECTION

1. Clean the block thoroughly with solvent. Remove any RTV sealant residue from the machined surfaces. Check all freeze plugs for leaks and replace any that are suspect. See *Freeze Plug Replacement* in this chapter. Remove any plugs that seal oil passages. Check oil and coolant passages for sludge, dirt and corrosion while cleaning. If the passages are very dirty, have the block boiled out by a machine shop. Blow out all passages with compressed air. Check the threads in the head bolt holes to be sure they are clean. If dirty, use a tap to true up the threads and remove any deposits.

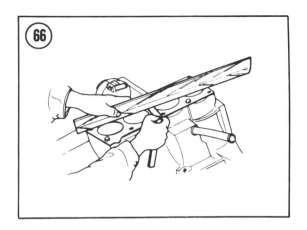

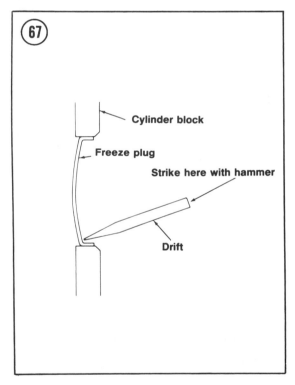

on the block. If there is any gap between the block and straightedge, measure it with a feeler gauge. See **Figure 66**. Measure from end to end and from corner to corner.

4. Measure the cylinder bores with a bore gauge as described in *Piston Clearance Check* in this chapter. If the cylinders exceed maximum tolerances, they must be rebored. Reboring is also necessary if the cylinder walls are badly scuffed or scored.

NOTE
Before boring, install all main bearing caps and tighten the cap bolts to specifications.

FLYWHEEL/DRIVE PLATE

Removal/Installation

1. Remove the engine as described in this chapter.
2. Remove the clutch from the flywheel on manual transmission models. See *Clutch Removal*, Chapter Nine.
3. Unbolt the flywheel from the crankshaft.
4. Installation is the reverse of removal. Tighten the bolts in a diagonal pattern to 45-55 ft.-lb. (61-75 N•m) on V6 engines or 60 ft.-lb. (82 N•m) on V8 engines.

FREEZE PLUG REPLACEMENT

The condition of all freeze plugs in the block should be checked whenever the engine is out of the car for service. If any sign of leakage or corrosion is found around one freeze plug, replace them all.

NOTE
Do not drive freeze plugs into the engine casting. It will be impossible to retrieve them and they can restrict coolant circulation, resulting in serious engine damage.

1. Tap the bottom edge of the freeze plug with a hammer and drift. Use several sharp blows to push the bottom of the plug inward, tilting the top out (**Figure 67**).

2. Examine the block for cracks. To confirm suspicions about possible leak areas, use a mixture of one part kerosene and 3 parts engine oil. Coat the suspected area with this solution, then wipe dry and immediately apply a solution of zinc oxide dissolved in wood alcohol. If any discoloration appears in the treated area, the block is cracked and should be replaced.

3. Check flatness of the cylinder block deck or top surface. Place an accurate straightedge

2. Grip the top of the plug firmly with pliers. Pull the plug from its bore (**Figure 68**) and discard.

3. Clean the plug bore thoroughly to remove all traces of the old sealer.

4. Apply a light coat of Loctite Stud N' Bearing Mount or equivalent to the plug bore.

5. Install the new core plug with an appropriate size driver or socket. The sharp edge of the plug should be at least 0.02 in. (0.5 mm) inside the lead-in chamfer.

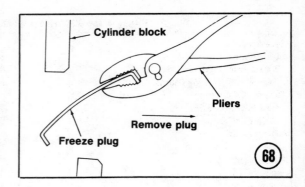

Table 1 V6 ENGINE SPECIFICATIONS

Type	60° V6
Displacement	173 cid (2.8 liter)
Bore	89 mm
Stroke	76 mm
Cylinder arrangement	
Right bank	1-3-5
Left bank	2-4-6
Firing order	1-2-3-4-5-6
Cylinder bore	
Diameter	88.992-89.070 mm
Out-of-round (maximum)	0.02 mm
Taper (thrust side, maximum)	0.02 mm
Piston	
Clearance	0.043-0.069 mm
Piston rings	
Ring groove clearance	
Top	0.030-0.070 mm
2nd	0.040-0.095 mm
Oil (maximum)	0.199 mm
Ring gap	
Top	0.25-0.50 mm
2nd	0.25-0.50 mm
Oil	0.51-1.40 mm
Piston pin	
Diameter	22.9937-23.0015 mm
Clearance	0.0065-0.0091 mm
Fit in rod	0.0187-0.515 mm press-fit
Camshaft	
Lift	
Intake	5.87 mm
Exhaust	6.67 mm
Journal diameter	47.44-47.49 mm
Journal clearance	0.026-0.101 mm
Crankshaft	
Main journal	
Diameter	63.340-63.364 mm
Taper (maximum)	0.005 mm
Out-of-round (maximum)	0.005 mm
Main bearing clearance	0.044-0.076 mm
End play	0.05-0.17 mm

(continued)

Table 1 V6 ENGINE SPECIFICATIONS (continued)

Crankpin	
Diameter	50.784-50.758 mm
Taper (maximum)	0.005 mm
Out-of-round (maximum)	0.005 mm
Connecting rod	
Bearing clearance	0.036-0.091 mm
Side clearance	0.16-0.44 mm
Valve system	
Lifter	Hydraulic (no adjustment needed)
Rocker arm ratio	1.5:1
Valve lash	1 1/2 turns from zero lash
Face angle	45°
Seat angle	46°
Seat runout	0.05 mm
Seat width	
Intake	1.25-1.50 mm
Exhaust	1.60-1.90 mm
Stem clearance	0.026-0.068 mm
Valve spring free length	48.5 mm
Valve spring load	
Closed	391 N @ 40 mm
Open	867 N @ 30 mm
Valve spring installed height	40 mm
Valve damper	
Free length	47.2 mm
Approximate number of coils	4

Table 2 V8 ENGINE SPECIFICATIONS

Type	90° V8
Displacement	305 cid (5.0 liter)
Bore	3.736 in.
Stroke	3.480 in.
Cylinder arrangement	
Left bank	1-3-5-7
Right bank	2-4-6-8
Firing order	1-8-4-3-6-5-7-2
Cylinder bore	
Out-of-round	0.0020 in.
Taper	
Thrust side	0.0005 in.
Relief side	0.0010 in.
Piston	
Clearance	0.0007-0.0017 in.
Piston	
Ring groove clearance	
Top	0.0012-0.0032 in.
Bottom	0.0012-0.0032 in.
Oil	0.002-0.007 in.
Gap	
Top	0.010-0.020 in.
Bottom	0.010-0.025 in.
Oil	0.015-0.055 in.
Piston pin	
Diameter	0.9270-0.9273 in.
Clearance (maximum)	0.001 in.
Fit in rod	0.0008-0.0016 in. interference

(continued)

5

Table 2 V8 ENGINE SPECIFICATIONS (continued)

Crankshaft	
Main journal diameter	
Front	2.4484-2.4493 in.
Intermediate	2.4481-2.4490 in.
Rear	2.4479-2.4488 in.
Main journal taper (maximum)	0.0010 in.
Main journal out-of-round (maximum)	0.0010 in.
Main bearing clearance	
Front	0.001-0.0015 in.
Intermediate	0.001-0.0020 in.
Rear	0.0025-0.0030 in.
End play	0.002-0.006 in.
Crankpin diameter	2.0986-2.0998 in.
Crankpin taper (maximum)	0.001 in.
Crankpin out-of-round (maximum)	0.001 in.
Rod bearing clearance	0.002-0.0030 in.
Rod side clearance	0.008-0.014 in.
Camshaft	
Journal diameter	1.8682-1.8692 in.
End play	0.004-0.012 in.
Valve system	
Lifter	Hydraulic
Rocker arm ratio	1.50:1
Valve lash	One turn down from zero lash
Face angle	45°
Seat angle	46°
Seat runout	0.002 in.
Seat width	
Intake	1/32-1/16 in.
Exhaust	1/16-1/32 in.
Stem clearance	0.0010-0.0027 in.
Valve spring free length	2.03 in.
Valve spring load	
Closed	76-84 lb. @ 1.70 in.
Open	194-206 lb. @ 1.25 in.
Valve damper	
Free length	1.86 in.
Approximate number of coils	4

Table 3 V6 TIGHTENING TORQUES

Fastener	ft.-lb.	N•m
Camshaft sprocket	15-20	20-27
Camshaft cover (rear)	6-9	8-12
Clutch cover to flywheel	13-18	18-24
Cylinder head	65-75	88-102
Connecting rod cap	34-40	46-54
Crankshaft pulley	20-30	27-41
Crankshaft pulley hub	66-84	90-115
Engine mounting bracket	70-92	95-125
Engine mounting torque strut bracket	30-40	40-54
Flex plate-to-torque converter	25-35	34-47
Flywheel	45-55	61-75
Front cover		
M8 x 1.25	13-18	18-24
M10 x 1.5	20-30	27-41
(continued)		

Table 3 V6 TIGHTENING TORQUES (continued)

Fastener	ft.-lb.	N•m
Intake manifold	20-25	27-34
Main bearing caps	63-74	85-100
Oil dipstick tube	20-30	27-41
Oil filter connector	24-34	32-46
Oil pan		
M6 x 1.0	6-9	8-12
M8 x 1.25	14-22	19-30
Oil pump	26-35	35-47
Oil pump cover	6-9	8-12
Oil pressure switch	4-5	5-7
Oil drain plug	15-20	20-27
Rear lifting bracket	20-30	27-41
Rocker arm cover	6-9	8-12
Rocker arm stud	43-49	58-66
Timing chain tensioner	13-18	18-24
Engine-to-transmission bolts	48-63	65-85
Water outlet	20-30	27-41
Water pump		
M6 x 1.0	6-9	8-12
M8 x 1.25	13-18	18-24
M10 x 1.5	20-30	27-41
Water pump pulley	13-18	18-24

Table 4 V8 TIGHTENING TORQUES

Fastener	ft.-lb.	N•m
Camshaft sprocket	20	27
Connecting rod cap	45	61
Crankcase front cover	8	11
Cylinder head	65	88
Exhaust manifold	20	27
Flywheel	60	81
Flywheel housing	30	40
Flywheel housing cover	8	11
Intake manifold	30	40
Main bearing cap	70	92
Oil pan-to-crankcase		
5/16 x 18	14	19
1/4 x 20	8	11
Oil pump	65	88
Oil pump cover	8	11
Rocker arm cover	5	7
Torsional damper	60	81
Water outlet	25	34
Water pump	30	40

5

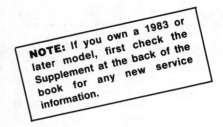
NOTE: If you own a 1983 or later model, first check the Supplement at the back of the book for any new service information.

CHAPTER SIX

FUEL, EXHAUST AND EMISSION CONTROL SYSTEMS

This chapter consists of service procedures for the air cleaner, carburetor, throttle body, fuel pump, fuel tank and lines, fuel-related emission controls and exhaust system.

THERMOSTATIC AIR CLEANER (THERMAC)

The air cleaner furnishes temperature-regulated air to the carburetor or throttle body to reduce emissions and improve driveability. The air cleaner snorkel is connected to a fresh air inlet duct and to a hot air hose/cover assembly surrounding the exhaust manifold. Air flow from these 2 sources is controlled by a control valve in the snorkel. This valve is operated by a vacuum motor mounted on the snorkel. The door and motor are connected by mechanical linkage inside the snorkel. A temperature sensor inside the air cleaner housing modulates vacuum to the motor according to air cleaner air temperature. **Figure 1** shows the major components in the air cleaner system.

When the engine is first started, the air cleaner draws hot air from near the exhaust manifold through the hot air hose (A, **Figure 2**). As the engine warms up, the control valve changes position to partially block off air from the hot air hose (B, **Figure 2**). When the air cleaner temperature reaches a specified value, the control valve closes off the hot air hose completely. This allows the air cleaner to draw intake air through the snorkel from the fresh air inlet duct (C, **Figure 2**).

Some engines use a check valve to keep the control valve closed during low temperature, low manifold vacuum operating conditions.

Filter Replacement

Remove the air cleaner cover wing nut(s). Remove the cover and lift out the old filter. **Figure 3** shows the V6 air cleaner; the 4-cylinder and V8 are similar. Wipe the inside of the air cleaner housing with a damp paper towel to remove dust, dirt and debris. Install a new filter. Reinstall the cover and tighten the wing nut(s) snugly.

Removal/Installation

NOTE
Leave the filter element inside the air cleaner housing during removal. This will prevent dirt and debris from dropping into the carburetor or throttle body.

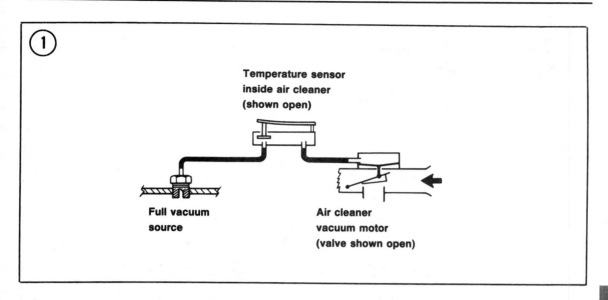

① Temperature sensor
inside air cleaner
(shown open)

Full vacuum
source

Air cleaner
vacuum motor
(valve shown open)

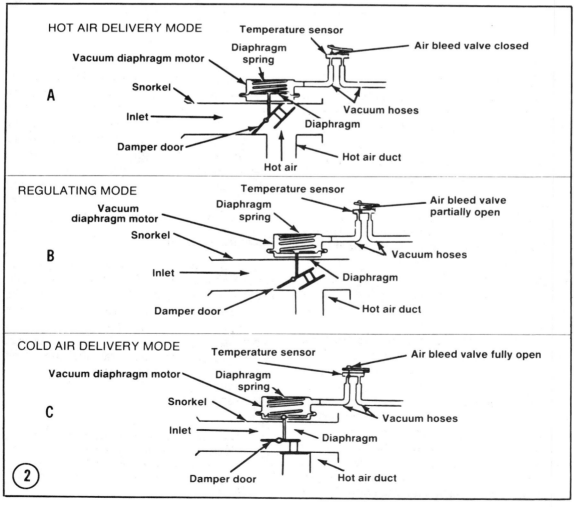

HOT AIR DELIVERY MODE

A

Temperature sensor

Diaphragm
spring

Vacuum diaphragm motor

Snorkel

Inlet

Damper door

Air bleed valve closed

Vacuum hoses

Diaphragm

Hot air duct

Hot air

REGULATING MODE

B

Vacuum
diaphragm motor

Snorkel

Inlet

Damper door

Temperature sensor

Diaphragm
spring

Air bleed valve
partially open

Vacuum hoses

Diaphragm

Hot air duct

COLD AIR DELIVERY MODE

C

Vacuum diaphragm motor

Snorkel

Inlet

Damper door

Temperature sensor

Diaphragm
spring

Air bleed valve fully open

Vacuum hoses

Diaphragm

Hot air duct

②

6

1. Unscrew and remove the air cleaner cover wing nut(s).

2. Unsnap the intake duct clamp (if so equipped) and remove the duct hose from the air cleaner snorkel.

3. Disconnect the hot air hose at the manifold heat cover.

4. Disconnect the PCV hose and any vacuum lines on the side of the air cleaner housing.

5. On 4-cylinder engines, remove the bolt from the snorkel support bracket (**Figure 4**).

6. Tilt the air cleaner housing and disconnect the line from the temperature sensor nipple on the underside (**Figure 5**). Disconnect any other vacuum lines on the underside of the housing.

7. Remove the air cleaner assembly and place on a clean flat surface.

8. Check the mounting gasket. If it is not found on the carburetor or throttle body air horn (**Figure 6**), it may be attached to the underside of the air cleaner housing.

9. Installation is the reverse of removal. If the old mounting gasket is damaged or missing, install a new gasket to prevent a vacuum leak. Tighten the wing nut(s) securely.

Control Valve Function Test

1. Unsnap the intake duct clamp (if so equipped) and remove the duct hose from the air cleaner snorkel.

2. Disconnect the vacuum line at the rear of the vacuum motor (**Figure 7**) and connect a hand vacuum pump to the nipple.

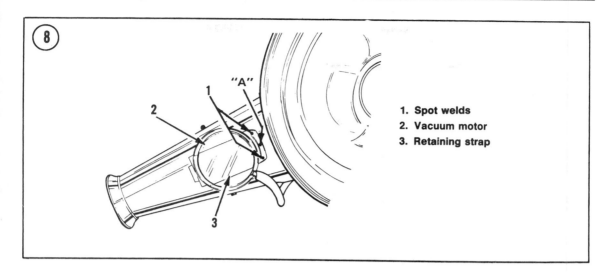

1. Spot welds
2. Vacuum motor
3. Retaining strap

3. Apply at least 7 in. Hg vacuum. The control valve should block off the snorkel passage completely.

4. Bend the vacuum pump hose to trap the vacuum. The control valve should remain closed. If it does not, check for binding linkage between the vacuum motor and valve. If the linkage is not corroded and does not bind, replace the vacuum motor assembly.

Vacuum Motor Replacement

1. Remove the air cleaner from the engine as described in this chapter.
2. Place the air cleaner on a clean flat surface. Remove the cover and filter element.
3. Disconnect the vacuum line at the vacuum motor.

NOTE
Support the air cleaner housing and snorkel in Step 4 to prevent damage to the snorkel during drilling.

4. Drill the 2 spot welds holding the motor retaining strap (1, **Figure 8**) with a 1/16 in. drill. Enlarge the drill hole as required to remove the retaining strap.
5. Lift the motor up and tilt it to unhook the linkage from the control valve. Remove the motor.
6. Drill a 7/64 in. hole in the snorkel at the center of the retaining strap (A, **Figure 8**).
7. Install the new vacuum motor, tilting it to connect the linkage to the control valve.

8. Install the new retaining strap with the sheet metal screw provided with the new motor.

NOTE
Make sure the sheet metal screw does not interfere with control valve operation when installed. If it does, cut off the end of the screw.

9. Reconnect the vacuum motor line. Install the filter element and the cover.

10. Install the air cleaner on the engine as described in this chapter.

Sensor Operational Check

NOTE
Perform this procedure with the engine off and cold.

1. Set the parking brake and block the front wheels.
2. Unscrew and remove the air cleaner cover wing nut(s). Remove the cover and filter element.
3. Check the hot air and intake duct hoses for cracks or other damage. Repair or replace as needed.
4. Disconnect the intake duct hose from the snorkel. Lift the air cleaner housing up enough to see into the snorkel.
5. Look inside the snorkel. The control valve should be in the open or full fresh air position (C, **Figure 2**).

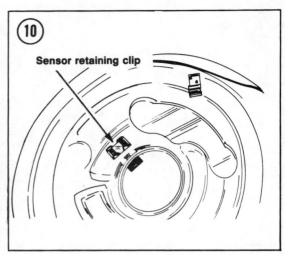

6. Depress the control valve with one finger and check for binding or sticking.

7. Tape a candy thermometer as close as possible to the temperature sensor (**Figure 9**) on the air inlet side of the sensor. Install the air cleaner cover without the wing nut(s).

8. Start the engine. The control valve should move to the closed or full heat position (A, **Figure 2**). If it does not, shut off the engine, cool the temperature sensor with an ice pack and retest. If the valve still does not close, check the vacuum lines for leakage.

NOTE
Some temperature sensors incorporate a check valve to delay control valve opening. The lower the temperature, the longer the delay.

9. If the control valve moves to the closed or full heat position, let the engine run for 5 minutes. Watch the control valve. When it starts to open, remove the air cleaner cover and note the thermometer reading. It should be approximately 123° F (46° C).

10. If the door does not move, remove the air cleaner cover and read the temperature. If the temperature is above 103° F (40° C), the sensor is defective.

11. A temperature of less than 103° F (40° C) is not sufficient to operate the valve. Install the air cleaner cover and let the engine continue to run. If the control valve still has not moved with the temperature above 103° F (40° C), replace the sensor.

Sensor Replacement

1. Disconnect the 2 vacuum lines at the sensor.

2. Pry the sensor retaining clip tabs open (**Figure 10**). Note position of the old sensor and remove it from the air cleaner housing.

3. Install a new sensor in the same relative position. Press down on the sensor edges and install the retaining clip on the hose connectors.

4. Reconnect the 2 vacuum lines to the sensor nipples from which they were removed.

CARBURETOR

The V6 engine uses a Rochester E2SE 2-barrel, 2-stage downdraft carburetor. The V8 engine uses a Rochester E4ME 4-barrel, 2-stage downdraft carburetor.

Both carburetors use an electrically operated mixture control solenoid (MCS) mounted on the air horn. This solenoid extends into the carburetor float bowl and controls air and fuel metered to the idle and main metering systems upon command from the Computer Command Control electronic control module (ECM). The ECM evaluates data from several sensors and cycles the solenoid plunger 10 times per second to control the air-fuel mixture for maximum performance and economy and minimum emissions.

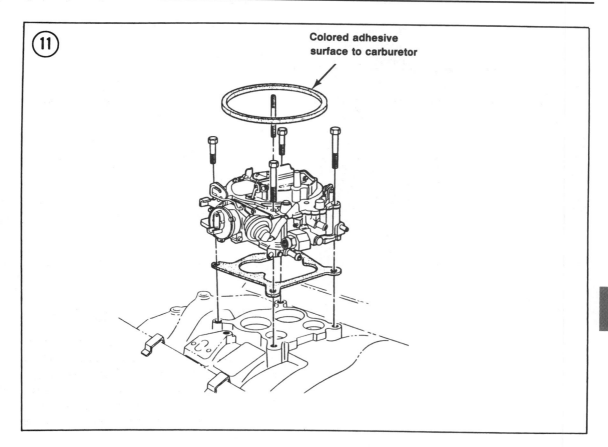

Colored adhesive surface to carburetor

A throttle position sensor (TPS) mounted on the carburetor signals the ECM whenever changes occur in the throttle position. The ECM holds the last-known air-fuel mixture ratio during throttle position changes.

An idle speed solenoid controls the carburetor idle speed on command from the ECM. Since the curb idle speed is programmed into the ECM, idle speed is automatic and cannot be adjusted.

NOTE
Do not try to adjust idle speed on either carburetor by adjusting the idle speed control screw.

The E4ME uses a single vacuum break to control choke operation. The E2SE uses a dual vacuum break system. The vacuum break rods are a non-bendable design and the choke cap is riveted to the housing. These tamper-resistant features are designed to prevent changes in the factory-adjusted choke setting.

The lean mixture screw in the float bowl requires the use of a special tool to turn it. The idle mixture screw in the throttle body and the TPS adjustment screw in the air horn are both recessed and sealed with a metal plug to prevent unauthorized changes in the factory adjustment.

WARNING
Tampering with the carburetor is a violation of Federal law. Choke, idle mixture and other sealed adjustments can legally be made only under specified circumstances. Adjustment of these systems should be left to a GM dealer.

Removal/Installation (Rochester E4ME)

Refer to **Figure 11** for this procedure.
1. Disconnect the negative battery cable.
2. Remove the air cleaner as described in this chapter.
3. Disconnect the throttle cable.

4. Disconnect the cruise control cable, if so equipped.

5. Disconnect the automatic transmission detent cable, if so equipped.

NOTE
Alphabetical code letters are cast into the carburetor vacuum fittings to assist in proper vacuum line installation.

6. Label and remove all vacuum lines at the carburetor. Disconnect all electrical connectors.

7. Disconnect the fuel line at the carburetor inlet (**Figure 12**). Plug the fuel line to prevent leakage.

8. Remove the 4 carburetor flange bolts. Remove the carburetor and insulator from the manifold.

9. Installation is the reverse of removal. Tighten flange nuts in a clockwise pattern to 12 ft.-lb. (16 N•m) to avoid warpage.

Removal/Installation
(Rochester E2SE)

1. Disconnect the negative battery cable.

2. Remove the air cleaner as described in this chapter.

NOTE
Alphabetical code letters are cast into the carburetor vacuum fittings to assist in proper vacuum line installation.

3. Label and disconnect all vacuum lines. Disconnect all electrical connectors.

4. Disconnect the fuel line at the inlet nut (**Figure 12**). Plug the fuel line to prevent leakage.

5. Disconnect the throttle cable.

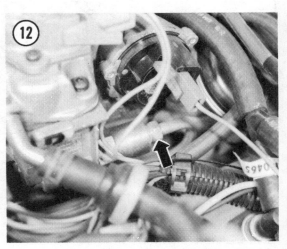

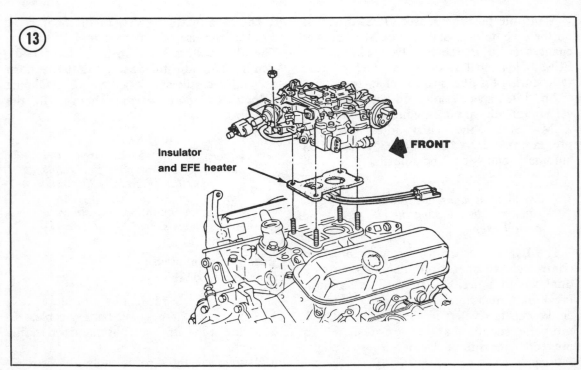

Insulator and EFE heater

FRONT

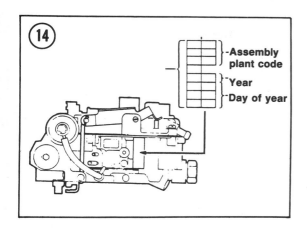

Assembly plant code
Year
Day of year

6. Disconnect the cruise control cable, if so equipped.

7. Disconnect the automatic transmission detent cable, if so equipped.

8. Remove the carburetor flange nuts. Remove the carburetor and EFE heater/insulator (**Figure 13**).

9. Installation is the reverse of removal. Tighten the attaching nuts in a diagonal pattern to 13 ft.-lb. (18 N•m).

Model Identification

The model identification on Rochester E4ME/E2SE carburetors is stamped vertically on the float bowl. **Figure 14** shows the E2SE carburetor; the E4ME is similar. The basic part number for all Rochester 2SE/E2SE carburetors is 170. The other letters and numbers identify the specific model year and calibration. To obtain the correct carburetor overhaul kit, write down all information on this identification pad and give it to the parts department of any GM dealer or auto parts store.

Disassembly (Rochester E4ME)

Refer to **Figure 15** for this procedure.

1. Use carburetor legs to prevent thottle plate damage while working on the carburetor. If legs are not available, thread a nut on each of four 2 1/4 in. bolts. Install each bolt in a flange hole and thread another nut on the bolt. This will hold the bolt securely to the carburetor and serve the same purpose as legs.

2. Remove the retaining screw holding the upper choke lever to the choke shaft. Rotate lever and remove rod from slot in lever.

3. Remove small screw in top of secondary metering rod hanger (**Figure 16**). Lift metering rod hanger up until rods clear air horn. Carefully place metering rod/hanger assembly to one side.

4. Press inner choke lever outward and hold with a small screwdriver. Twist choke rod counterclockwise and remove from inner choke lever.

5. Drive pump lever pivot pin inward until end of pin butts against air cleaner locating boss on air horn (**Figure 17**). Remove pump lever from pump link.

6. Remove primary vacuum break hose.

NOTE
The air horn screws have a Torx head. This is different than the usual Phillips head screw. Do not try to remove a Torx head screw with any tool other than a Torx head driver or the head will be damaged and require drilling out to remove the screw. T-20 and T-25 drivers are required on 1982 models for screw removal.

7. Remove 13 air horn attaching screws. Refer to **Figure 18** for location. Two countersunk screws are located next to the venturi and can easily be overlooked.

NOTE
Some carburetors may use a secondary air baffle deflector installed under the 2 center air horn screws marked "3" and "4" in Figure 18.

8. Lift air horn straight up and off float bowl to prevent damage to the MCS connector, TPS adjustment lever and small tubes protruding from air horn. Air horn gasket should remain on float bowl.

9. Remove vacuum break bracket. Remove vacuum break assembly from air valve rod. Remove air valve rod from air valve lever.

10. Push the TPS plunger up through the air horn seal with your fingers and remove from the air horn.

11. Invert the air horn and drive the lean mixture screw plug from the bottom of the air

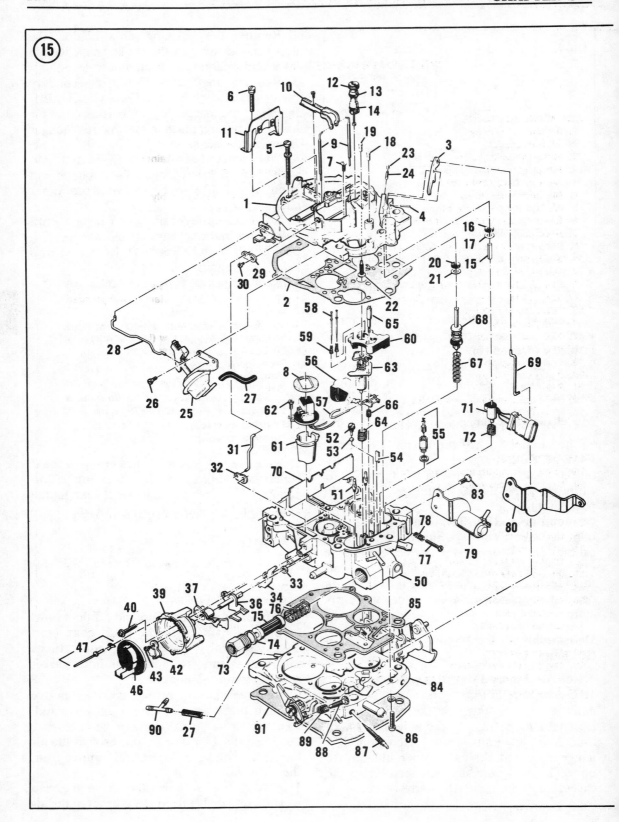

ROCHESTER E4ME CARBURETOR

AIR HORN PARTS:
1. Air horn assembly
2. Air horn gasket
3. Pump actuating lever
4. Pump lever hinge roll pin
5. Air horn long screw (2)
6. Air horn short screw
7. Air horn countersunk screw (2)
8. Solenoid connector to air horn gasket
9. Secondary metering rod (2)
10. Secondary metering rod holder and screw
11. Secondary air baffle
12. Idle air bleed valve
13. Idle air bleed valve O-ring (thick)
14. Idle air bleed valve O-ring (thin)
15. TPS actuator plunger
16. TPS plunger seal
17. TPS seal retainer
18. TPS adjusting screw
19. TPS screw plug
20. Pump plunger seal
21. Pump seal retainer
22. Solenoid plunger screw (rich stop)
23. Plunger stop screw plug (rich stop)
24. Solenoid adjusting plug (lean mixture)

CHOKE PARTS:
25. Front vacuum break control and bracket
26. Control attaching screw (2)
27. Vacuum hose
28. Air valve rod
29. Choke rod lever (upper)
30. Choke lever screw
31. Choke rod
32. Choke rod lever (lower)
33. Intermediate choke shaft seal
34. Secondary lockout lever
36. Int. choke shaft and lever
37. Fast idle cam
39. Choke housing kit
40. Choke housing to bowl screw
42. Choke coil lever
43. Choke coil lever screw
46. Stat cover and assembly (electric choke)
47. Stat cover attaching kit

FLOAT BOWL PARTS:
50. Float bowl assembly
51. Primary metering jet (2)
52. Pump discharge ball retainer
53. Pump discharge ball
54. Pump well baffle
55. Needle and seat assembly
56. Float assembly
57. Float assembly hinge pin
58. Primary metering rod (2)
59. Primary metering rod spring (2)
60. Float bowl insert
61. Bowl cavity insert
62. Connector attaching screw
63. Mixture control (M/C) solenoid and plunger assembly
64. Solenoid tension spring
65. Solenoid adjusting screw (lean mixture)
66. Solenoid adjusting screw spring
67. Pump return spring
68. Pump assembly
69. Pump link
70. Secondary bores baffle
71. Throttle position sensor TPS
72. TPS tension spring
73. Fuel inlet filter nut
74. Filter nut gasket
75. Fuel inlet filter
76. Fuel filter spring
77. Idle stop screw
78. Idle stop screw spring
79. Idle speed solenoid and bracket assembly
80. TRS bracket
83. Bracket attaching screw

THROTTLE BODY PARTS:
84. Throttle body assembly
85. Throttle body gasket
86. Throttle body screw
87. Idle needle and spring assembly (2)
88. Fast idle adjusting screw
89. Fast idle screw spring
90. Vacuum hose tee
91. Flange gasket

6

⑯

Secondary metering rods

Metering rod hanger

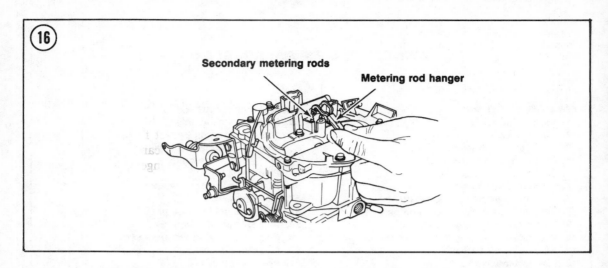

⑰

Pump lever

Pump lever roll pin

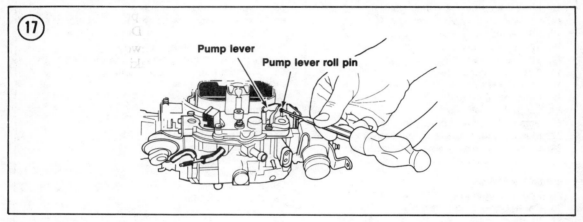

⑱

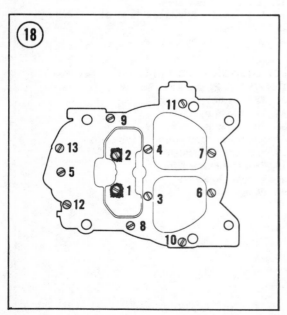

⑲

Lean mixture
screw plug

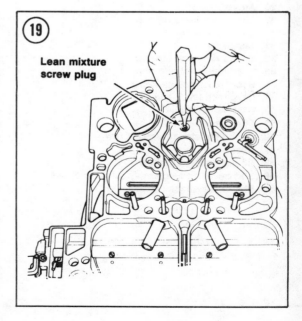

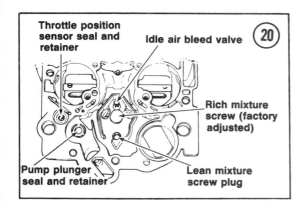

Throttle position sensor seal and retainer

Idle air bleed valve (20)

Rich mixture screw (factory adjusted)

Pump plunger seal and retainer

Lean mixture screw plug

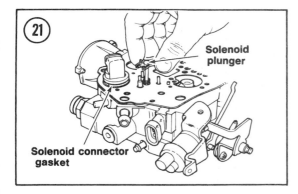

(21)

Solenoid plunger

Solenoid connector gasket

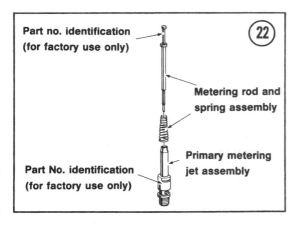

Part no. identification (for factory use only)

(22)

Metering rod and spring assembly

Primary metering jet assembly

Part No. identification (for factory use only)

horn with a punch (**Figure 19**). Discard the plug.

12. With air horn inverted, use a small screwdriver to remove staking holding TPS seal retainer. See **Figure 20**. Remove and discard retainer and seal.

13. Repeat Step 11 to remove the pump plunger retainer and seal (**Figure 20**). This completes air horn disassembly. Do not remove any other components or attempt

adjustment of the mixture screws or idle air bleed valve.

14. Lift solenoid/metering rod plunger straight up and out of the float bowl (**Figure 21**).

15. Remove the rubber seal from the mixture control solenoid connector.

16. Lift air horn gasket from dowel locating pins on float bowl. Discard gasket.

17. Remove pump plunger and return spring from pump well.

CAUTION
Use extreme care in Step 18 and Step 19 to prevent damage to the TPS and metering rod/spring assembly.

18. Place a flat tool or piece of metal across the float bowl casting. Depress and hold the TPS with a small screwdriver. Use a small chisel and remove staking holding TPS in place.

19. Push TPS and electrical connector assembly from the fuel bowl. Remove spring from TPS well.

20. Remove the plastic filler block over the float chamber.

21. Lift each primary metering rod from the guided metering jet. Make sure the return spring is removed with each rod, then slide spring off end rod. See **Figure 22**.

22. Remove screw holding MCS connector to the float bowl. *Do not* remove connector at this time.

23. Install tool part No. J-28696-10, BT-7928 or equivalent on upper end of lean mixture screw. Turn screw clockwise and count the number of turns required to lightly bottom the screw in the float bowl. Record the number of turns for reassembly reference.

24. Turn screw counterclockwise and remove from float bowl. Lift MCS and connector assembly from float bowl. *Do not* disassemble MCS.

25. Remove plastic insert from float bowl cavity under solenoid connector, if so equipped.

26. Remove solenoid screw tension spring located next to the float hanger pin.

27. Pull up on float assembly retaining pin and remove float assembly and needle.

6

Remove needle seat with tool part No. J-22769 or BT-3006M or a wide-blade screwdriver.

28. Remove large MCS tension spring from boss on bottom of float bowl.

CAUTION
It is not necessary to remove the primary metering jets for cleaning. The secondary metering jets are fixed in place and should not be removed or the float bowl may have to be replaced.

29. Remove pump discharge check ball retainer. Invert bowl and catch discharge ball in the palm of your hand. This completes disassembly of the float bowl. Do not remove the secondary air baffle or pump well fill slot baffle unless replacement is necessary.

30. Remove the fuel inlet nut, gasket, check valve filter and spring assembly.

31. Remove 3 screws and lockwashers holding the throttle body to the fuel bowl. Separate the throttle body and fuel bowl. Remove and discard the insulator gasket.

NOTE
Disassembly of the throttle body is not required for normal cleaning purposes. The throttle body is serviced as a complete assembly.

Disassembly
(Rochester E2SE)

The throttle shafts, secondary actuating lever and lockout lever are all coated with a special substance to reduce friction. The secondary throttle bore and valve are coated with a graphite compound to hold air leakage to a minimum. These coatings should not be damaged during overhaul.

NOTE
Do not remove external linkage screws or linkage for cleaning purposes. This will reduce the number of adjustments necessary after reassembly.

Refer to **Figure 23** for this procedure.

1. Use carburetor legs to prevent throttle plate damage while working on the carburetor. If legs are not available, thread a nut on each of four 2 1/4 in. bolts. Install each

ROCHESTER E2SE CARBURETOR

AIR HORN PARTS:
1. Mixture control solenoid
2. M/C solenoid screw (3)
3. M/C solenoid gasket
4. M/C solenoid spacer
5. M/C solenoid seal
6. M/C solenoid seal retainer
7. Air horn assembly
8. Air horn gasket
9. Air horn screw—short (2)
10. Air horn screw—long (3)
11. Air horn screw—large
12. Vent stack
13. Vent stack screw (2)
14. Seal pump plunger
15. Pump plunger seal retainer
16. TPS plunger seal
17. TPS plunger seal retainer
18. TPS plunger (throttle position sensor)

CHOKE PARTS:
19. Primary vacuum break and bracket assembly
20. Vacuum break connecting hose
21. Vacuum break connecting tee
22. Idle speed solenoid
23. Idle speed solenoid retainer
24. Idle speed solenoid nut
25. Vacuum break bracket attaching screw
26. Air valve link
27. Air valve link bushing
28. Air valve link retainer
29. Fast idle cam link
30. Vacuum break hose
31. Intermediate choke shaft/lever/link assembly
32. Intermediate choke link bushing
33. Intermediate choke link retainer
34. Secondary vacuum break and bracket assembly
35. Vacuum break attaching screw (2)
36. Choke cover and coil assembly
37. Choke lever attaching screw
38. Choke lever and contract assembly
39. Choke housing
40. Choke housing attaching screw (2)
41. Stat cover retainer kit

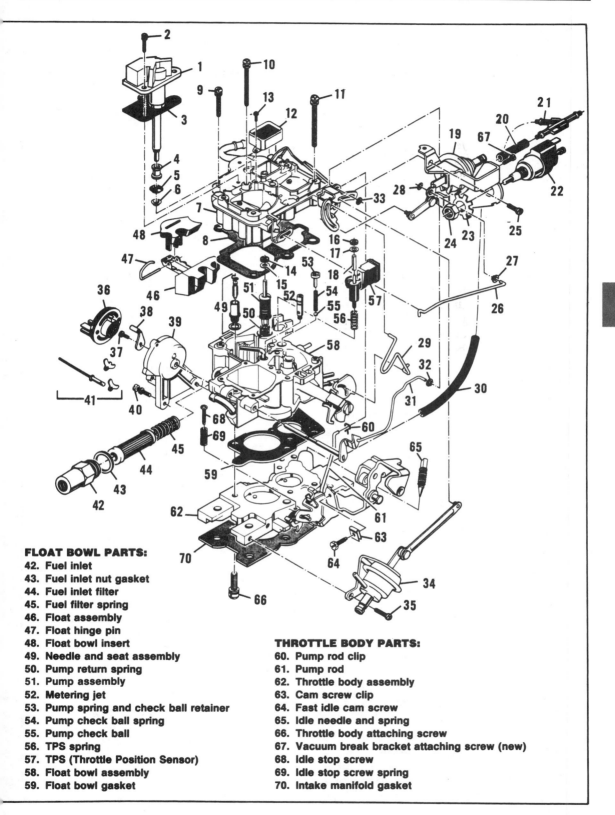

FLOAT BOWL PARTS:

42. Fuel inlet
43. Fuel inlet nut gasket
44. Fuel inlet filter
45. Fuel filter spring
46. Float assembly
47. Float hinge pin
48. Float bowl insert
49. Needle and seat assembly
50. Pump return spring
51. Pump assembly
52. Metering jet
53. Pump spring and check ball retainer
54. Pump check ball spring
55. Pump check ball
56. TPS spring
57. TPS (Throttle Position Sensor)
58. Float bowl assembly
59. Float bowl gasket

THROTTLE BODY PARTS:

60. Pump rod clip
61. Pump rod
62. Throttle body assembly
63. Cam screw clip
64. Fast idle cam screw
65. Idle needle and spring
66. Throttle body attaching screw
67. Vacuum break bracket attaching screw (new)
68. Idle stop screw
69. Idle stop screw spring
70. Intake manifold gasket

bolt in a flange hole and thread another nut to the bolt. This will hold the bolt securely to the carburetor and serve the same purpose as legs.

2. Remove the 3 screws holding the idle speed control and remove as an assembly.

3. Remove the secondary vacuum break diaphragm and bracket screws. Rotate assembly to disengage vacuum break link from choke lever slot.

4. Remove the pump rod retaining clip.

NOTE
Do not remove pump lever screw or lever from air horn.

5. Remove and discard the retaining clip holding the intermediate choke link at the choke lever. Remove link and plastic bushing from choke lever. Save the plastic bushing for reuse. See **Figure 24**.

6. Remove the 3 mixture control solenoid screws. Lift the solenoid from the air horn with a twisting motion. Remove and discard the solenoid gasket.

7. Remove and discard the solenoid stem seal and retainer (**Figure 25**). Keep spacer for reuse.

8. Rotate the fast idle cam and disconnect the fast idle cam link from the cam slot. See **Figure 26**.

NOTE
The air horn screws have a Torx head. This is different than the usual Phillips head screw. Do not try to remove a Torx head screw with any tool other than a Torx head driver or the head will be damaged and require drilling out to remove the screw. T-10, T-15, T-20, T-25 and T-30 drivers are required on 1982 models for screw removal.

9. Remove the 7 air horn attaching screws and lockwashers.

10. Separate the air horn from the main body. It may be necessary to tap the air horn gently with a rubber hammer to break the gasket seal.

11. Push the TPS plunger through the air horn seal and remove it.

12. Invert the air horn and use a small screwdriver to remove seal retainer staking.

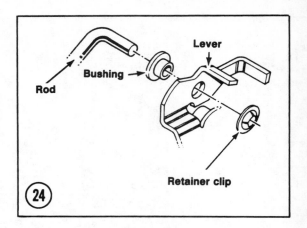

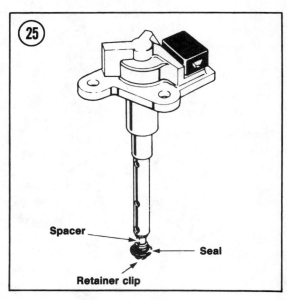

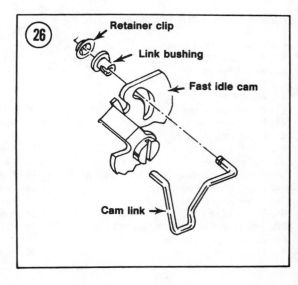

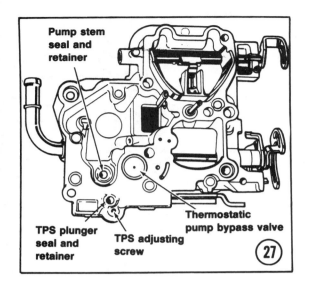

Pump stem seal and retainer

TPS plunger seal and retainer

TPS adjusting screw

Thermostatic pump bypass valve

(27)

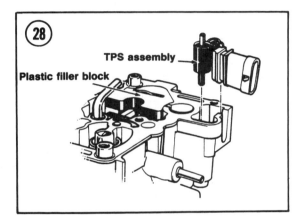

(28)

TPS assembly

Plastic filler block

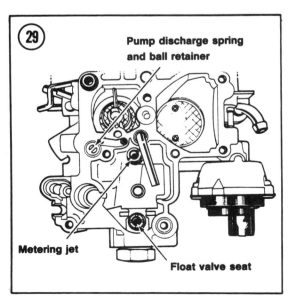

(29)

Pump discharge spring and ball retainer

Metering jet

Float valve seat

See **Figure 27**. Remove and discard retainer and seal.

NOTE
The accelerator pump plunger may remain in the air horn. If so, remove it before going on to the next step.

13. Repeat Step 12 to remove the pump plunger retainer. See **Figure 27**. Remove and discard retainer and seal.

NOTE
*The thermostatic pump bypass assembly (**Figure 27**) is permanently installed. Do not try to remove it. If defective, the entire air horn must be replaced.*

14. Remove the vent/screen assembly. This completes air horn disassembly.
15. Remove and discard the air horn-to-main body gasket.
16. Remove the pump plunger and spring from the pump well.
17. Carefully push up on the bottom of the TPS electrical connector under the float bowl and remove the TPS and spring from the main body well (**Figure 28**).
18. Remove the float valve filler block.
19. Hold the float valve clip in place and tilt the float to clear the vapor purge tube in the float bowl. Remove the float.
20. Remove the float valve seat and extended metering jet (**Figure 29**) with a wide-blade (10 mm minimum width) screwdriver.

NOTE
Do not remove or alter the adjustment of the calibration screw inside the metering jet. This is preset at the factory according to the ECM calibration.

21. Use needlenose pliers or a small slidehammer to remove the plastic retainer over the pump discharge spring and check ball (**Figure 30**).
22. Invert the main body and catch the discharge spring and check ball.
23. Remove the 4 throttle body attaching screws (**Figure 31**). Separate the throttle body from the main body. Remove and discard the gasket.

6

Inspection and Cleaning
(All Carburetors)

All parts provided in the carburetor overhaul kit (except the idle mixture needle) should be installed when overhauling the carburetor.

1. Check the choke and throttle plate shafts for grooving or wear. Make sure the choke and throttle plates can open and close freely.

NOTE
The choke and throttle plates are positioned during production and should not be removed unless damaged.

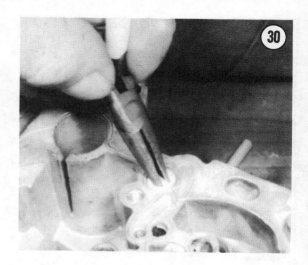

2. Clean all gasket residue from the air horn, main body and throttle body sealing surfaces with a putty knife. Work carefully to prevent casting damage.

CAUTION
All 3 carburetor castings are aluminum. Do not use a sharp instrument to clean the gasket residue or damage to the carburetor assemblies may result.

3. Lightly squeeze the float between a thumb and forefinger to check for fuel absorption. If moisture appears on the float surface, replace it.

NOTE
Some gasolines contain additives that will affect the Vitron tip of the fuel inlet needle. If carburetor problems develop which are the result of a deteriorated inlet needle tip, change brands of gasoline.

4. Check the Vitron tip of the fuel inlet needle for swelling or distortion. Discard the needle, as the overhaul kit contains a new needle for assembly.

5. Check the mixture control solenoid for sticking, binding or leakage. See *Mixture Control Solenoid Test* in this chapter.

6. Clean the main body, throttle body and air horn in a cold-immersion type carburetor cleaner. Suspend the air horn in the cleaner to prevent it from reaching the riveted choke cap and housing.

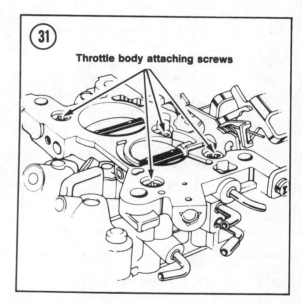

Throttle body attaching screws

7. Clean all solenoids, sensors, vacuum break diaphragms and other assist devices with a cloth lightly moistened in solvent, then wipe dry with a clean cloth.

CAUTION
Immersing these parts in carburetor cleaner will destroy them. The plastic bushing in the throttle lever, however, will not be damaged by carburetor cleaner.

Mixture Control Solenoid Test

Poor performance or poor fuel economy can result from a sticking, binding or leaking

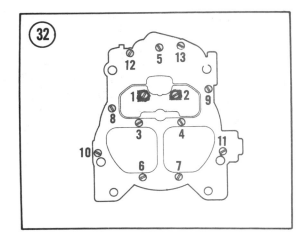

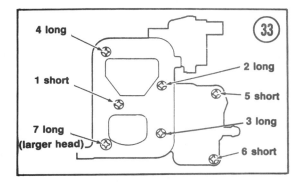

Assembly
(Rochester E4ME)

Assembly is the reverse of disassembly. All parts should fit together easily without forcing. Refer to **Figure 32** for air horn screw tightening sequence.

Assembly
(Rochester E2SE)

Assembly is the reverse of disassembly. All parts should fit together easily without forcing. If a new main body assembly is installed, stamp or engrave the model number on the float bowl. Refer to **Figure 33** for air horn screw tightening sequence.

Float Level Adjustment
(Rochester E4ME)

Refer to **Figure 34** and perform the numbered steps in sequence. All E4ME carburetors use an 11/32 in. (8.7 mm) float level. If the float level as measured varies more than ±1/16 in., adjust the float as follows:

1. If the level is too high, hold the retainer in place firmly and depress the center of the float pontoon until the correct setting is obtained.
2. If the level is too low, lift the metering rods out. Remove the solenoid connector screw. Turn the lean mixture solenoid screw clockwise and count number of turns required to lightly bottom the screw. Remove screw and lift solenoid and connector from float bowl. Remove float and bend float arm up. Reinstall parts, making sure lean mixture screw is backed out of float bowl the same number of turns required to seat it. Repeat Steps 1-3 shown in **Figure 34** to recheck float level.
3. If level is still incorrect after performing Step 2 above, repeat the step.

Float Level Adjustment
(Rochester E2SE)

Follow the procedure shown in **Figure 35** to make the float adjustment. All E2SE carburetors use a 13/32 in. (10.3 mm) float level setting.

MCS solenoid. The solenoid can be removed and tested with the carburetor on the engine.

1. Remove the 3 mixture control solenoid screws. Lift the solenoid from the carburetor air horn with a twisting motion. Remove and discard the solenoid gasket. Remove and discard the stem retainer and seal.
2. Connect a jumper wire between one of the solenoid terminals and the positive battery post.
3. Jumper the other solenoid terminal to a good ground.
4. Connect a hand vacuum pump to the solenoid stem and apply a minimum of 25 in. Hg vacuum.
5. Time the leak-down rate from 20 in. Hg to 15 in. Hg vacuum. If leakage exceeds 5 in. Hg in 5 seconds, replace the solenoid.
6. Remove the jumper wire from the positive battery post and note the vacuum pump reading. If it does not return to zero immediately (less than one second), replace the solenoid.

6

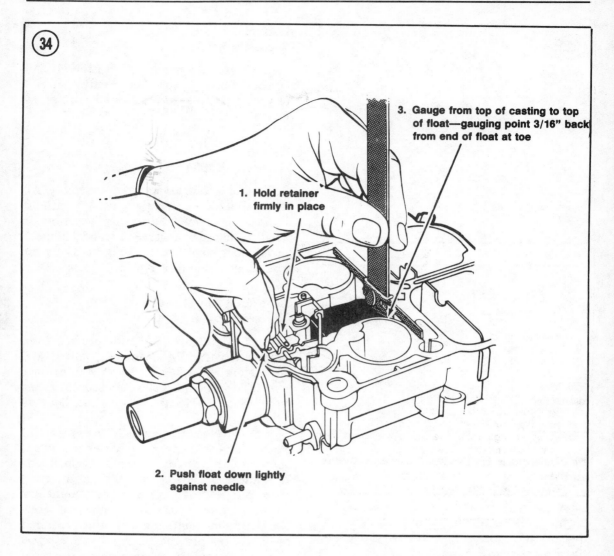

(34)

1. Hold retainer firmly in place

2. Push float down lightly against needle

3. Gauge from top of casting to top of float—gauging point 3/16" back from end of float at toe

THROTTLE BODY FUEL INJECTION

The 4-cylinder engine is equipped with a Rochester model 300 throttle body injection (TBI) unit (**Figure 36**). The V8 engine may be equipped with a Rochester model 400 TBI unit, also referred to as "Crossfire Fuel Injection." This system incorporates a pair of TBI injection units mounted independently on the intake manifold cover (**Figure 37**).

Model 300 TBI

The model 300 contains an electrically operated injector that meters fuel into the intake air stream under the direction of the electronic control module (ECM). The ECM receives electrical signals from various sensors, refers to its stored program memory and calculates the precise amount and timing of fuel required by the engine. Fuel delivery time of the injector is modified by the ECM to accomodate special engine conditions such as cranking, cold starts, altitude and acceleration or deceleration. The basic TBI assembly consists of 2 major aluminum castings:

 a. The throttle body contains a valve to control air flow.
 b. A fuel meter body assembly containing an integral fuel pressure regulator and injector.

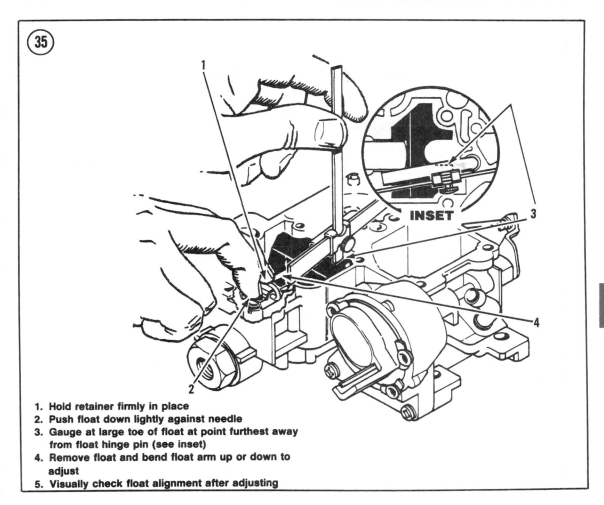

1. Hold retainer firmly in place
2. Push float down lightly against needle
3. Gauge at large toe of float at point furthest away from float hinge pin (see inset)
4. Remove float and bend float arm up or down to adjust
5. Visually check float alignment after adjusting

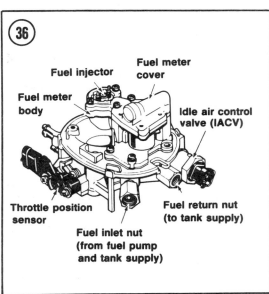

Fuel injector

Fuel meter cover

Fuel meter body

Idle air control valve (IACV)

Throttle position sensor

Fuel inlet nut (from fuel pump and tank supply)

Fuel return nut (to tank supply)

Model 400

The model 400 is essentially 2 model 300 TBI units mounted on a special intake manifold cover and connected by a common throttle rod and fuel line. This arrangement permits each TBI unit to supply the proper air-fuel mixture through long runners in the intake manifold to the cylinder bank on the opposite side of the engine, thus the name "Crossfire Fuel Injection." A special swirl plate is positioned directly below each throttle valve to improve mixture distribution.

System Operation

Filtered fuel is supplied to the TBI unit by an electric fuel pump mounted in the fuel tank. When the ignition switch is turned ON,

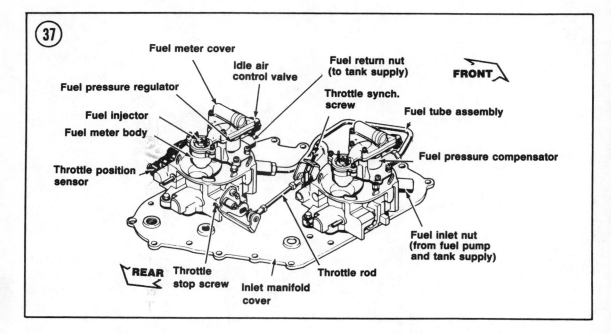

(37)

Fuel meter cover
Idle air control valve
Fuel return nut (to tank supply)
FRONT
Fuel pressure regulator
Throttle synch. screw
Fuel injector
Fuel tube assembly
Fuel meter body
Throttle position sensor
Fuel pressure compensator
Fuel inlet nut (from fuel pump and tank supply)
REAR Throttle stop screw
Throttle rod
Inlet manifold cover

a fuel pump relay activates the in-tank pump for 1.5-2 seconds to prime the injector. If the ECM does not receive a reference signal from the distributor within a certain time, it shuts down the fuel pump.

Fuel flow is controlled by varying the duration of injection according to signals from the ECM. Excess fuel passes through a pressure regulator and is then returned to the fuel tank. A throttle position sensor (TPI) informs the ECM of throttle valve position. An idle air control (IAC) assembly maintains a pre-programmed idle speed according to directions from the ECM.

Since the TBI system is electronically controlled, no attempt should be made to adjust the idle speed. Owner service should be limited to replacement only. If the TBI system is not working properly, take the car to a GM dealer for diagnosis and adjustment.

Relieving System Pressure

Before opening any fuel connection on a TBI system, the fuel pressure must be relieved.
1. Place transmission in NEUTRAL (manual) or PARK (automatic).
2. Set the parking brake and block the drive wheels.

3. Remove the fuel pump fuse from the fuse block.
4. Turn ignition key to START. The engine will start and run for a few seconds until it runs out of fuel. Turn ignition key to START position again and hold for 3 seconds. This will dissipate fuel pressure and permit safe disconnection of fuel lines.
5. Once service is completed, install fuel pump fuse and turn ignition key to ON but do not start the engine. Inspect for leaks and repair if necessary before starting the engine.

TBI Removal/Installation

4-cylinder engine

1. Relieve system pressure as described in this chapter.
2. Remove the air cleaner as described in this chapter.
3. Disconnect all electrical connectors at the throttle body.
4. Disconnect the throttle linkage, return spring and cruise control linkage (if so equipped).
5. Label and disconnect all vacuum lines from the throttle body.
6. Disconnect fuel supply and return lines at TBI assembly (**Figure 38**). Plug both lines to prevent leakage.

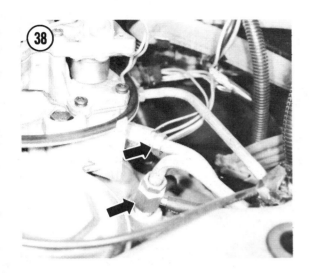

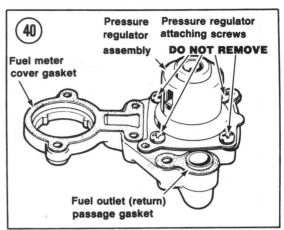

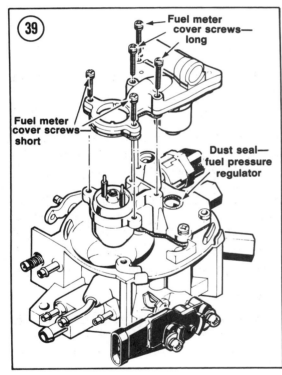

7. Remove 3 bolts holding throttle body to engine. Remove throttle body.

8. Installation is the reverse of removal. Tighten attaching bolts to 10-14 ft.-lb. (14-19 N•m).

V8 engine

Either TBI unit can be removed from the intake manifold cover by following the

procedure specified for the 4-cylinder engine and disconnecting the throttle rod between the TBI units. The procedure below is used to remove the entire TBI assembly and manifold cover.

1. Relieve system pressure as described in this chapter.

2. Remove air cleaner as described in this chapter.

3. Label and disconnect all vacuum lines at the TBI assembly.

4. Disconnect all electrical connectors at the TBI assembly.

5. Disconnect the throttle cable and transmission detent cable.

6. Disconnect cruise control cable, if so equipped.

7. Disconnect fuel supply and return lines at the TBI assembly. Plug both lines to prevent leakage.

8. Remove bolts and nuts from inlet manifold. Remove TBI assembly and manifold cover.

9. Installation is the reverse of removal. Tighten attaching bolts and nuts to 10-14 ft.-lb. (14-19 N•m).

Throttle Body Disassembly

1. Remove the air cleaner stud.

2. Remove the 5 fuel meter cover screws and lockwashers (**Figure 39**).

3. Lift fuel meter cover and pressure regulator assembly from the throttle body.

4. Remove and discard the fuel meter cover gaskets (**Figure 40**).

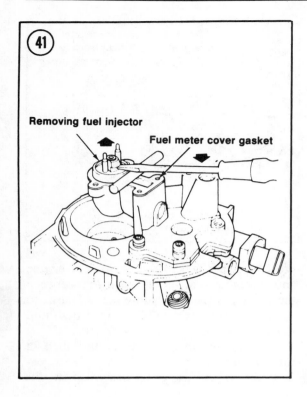

(41) Removing fuel injector

Fuel meter cover gasket

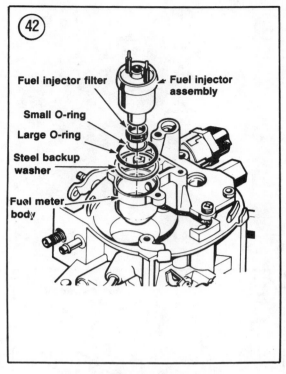

(42)

Fuel injector filter — Fuel injector assembly

Small O-ring

Large O-ring

Steel backup washer

Fuel meter body

beyond Step 7 and Step 8. Do not immerse injector in any type of cleaner.

7. Rotate injector fuel filter back and forth to remove from injector base.

8. Remove large O-ring and steel backup washer from top of fuel meter body injector cavity (**Figure 42**). Remove small O-ring from bottom of injector cavity.

9. Remove fuel inlet/outlet nuts and gaskets from fuel meter body.

10. Remove 3 fuel meter body screws and lockwashers (**Figure 43**). Remove fuel meter body and insulator gasket from throttle body assembly.

> *NOTE*
> *Under normal service conditions, the throttle body need not be immersed in cleaner. If such cleaning is required, the throttle position sensor (TPS) and idle air control (IAC) must be removed. This is a job for a GM dealer.*

Throttle Body Inspection

1. Clean all metal parts and blow dry with compressed air.

> *WARNING*
> *Do not remove the 4 screws holding the pressure regulator to the fuel meter cover. The regulator contains a large spring under considerable tension which could cause serious personal injury if released accidentally. The pressure regulator is preset at the factory and is serviced (with the fuel meter cover) only as a complete assembly.*

5. Remove the pressure regulator dust seal from the fuel meter body (**Figure 39**).

> *NOTE*
> *Do not immerse the fuel meter cover in carburetor cleaner, as it will damage the pressure regulator diaphragms and gaskets.*

6. With fuel meter gasket on fuel meter body, lift injector from body with a screwdriver as shown in **Figure 41**.

> *NOTE*
> *The fuel injector is serviced as a complete assembly. Do not disassemble*

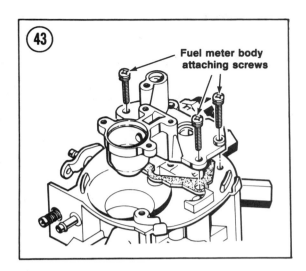

Fuel meter body attaching screws

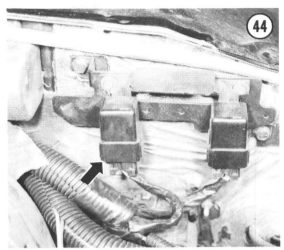

2. Inspect casting mating surfaces for damage that might affect gasket sealing.

3. Discard all O-rings.

4. Check injector fuel filter for plugging or damage. Clean or replace as required.

Throttle Body Assembly

Assembly is the reverse of disassembly. Apply the thread locking compound included in the overhaul kit to the fuel meter body attaching screws. Torque screws to 3.5 ft.-lb. (4 N•m). Lubricate injector O-rings with lithium grease or equivalent. Apply thread locking compound to fuel meter cover screws and tighten to 2.8 ft.-lb. (3 N•m).

FUEL PUMP

Carburetted engines use a non-serviceable mechanical fuel pump operated by a pushrod and camshaft eccentric. The fuel pump is located on the right front of the V6 engine and the left front of the V8 engine.

Fuel injected engines use an electric fuel pump located in the fuel tank. The pump is activated by a fuel pump relay in the engine compartment (**Figure 44**) when the ignition switch is turned ON.

The 2 most common fuel pump problems are incorrect pressure and low volume. Low pressure results in a too-lean mixture and too little fuel at high speeds. High pressure will cause carburetor flooding and result in poor

mileage. Low volume also results in too little fuel at high speeds.

If a fuel system problem is suspected, check the fuel filter first. See *Fuel Filter* in Chapter Three. If the filter is not clogged or dirty, test the fuel pump.

> *NOTE*
> *Incorrect fuel line pressure with TBI engines may be caused by a defective fuel pressure regulator or in-tank fuel pump. Because of the complexity of the system, fuel pump/pressure regulator testing is a job for a GM dealer.*

Pressure Test (Carburetted Engine)

1. Remove the air cleaner as described in this chapter.

2. Disconnect the fuel line at the carburetor fuel inlet.

3. Connect a pressure gauge and a flexible hose with a restrictor clamp between the fuel line and fuel inlet.

4. Start the engine and let it idle.

5. Let the pressure stabilize and read the gauge. It should read 5 1/2-6 1/2 psi.

6. Slowly increase the idle speed and watch the gauge. The pressure should not vary considerably at different engine speeds.

7. If the pump pressure is not within specifications in Step 5 or if it varies considerably in Step 6, replace the pump.

6

Flow Test
(Carburetted Engine)

1. Disconnect the fuel line at the carburetor inlet. Place the end of the line in a clean quart-size measuring container.

2. Run the engine at idle and time how long it takes to pump one pint of fuel into the container. If it takes more than 30 seconds, check for a restriction in the fuel line. If none is found, replace the pump.

Replacement
(Carburetted Engine)

Refer to **Figure 45** (V6 engine) or **Figure 46** (V8 engine).

1. Disconnect the negative battery cable.

2. Use 2 open-end wrenches to loosen the fuel line nut at the pump inlet fitting. Disconnect the outlet hose.

3. Remove the pump mounting bolts.

4. Remove the pump. Remove and discard the gasket/seal.

5. Clean any gasket residue from the engine mounting flange with a putty knife.

6. Lubricate the pushrod with engine oil and install. If the rod does not fit all the way down in the engine, rotate the engine until it does.

7. Install the fuel pump with a new gasket/seal. Tighten the V6 pump bolts to 15 ft.-lb. (20 N•m). Tighten the V8 pump bolts to 27 ft.-lb. (37 N•m).

8. Connect the fuel pump inlet pipe and outlet hose. Tighten the inlet fitting to 18 ft.-lb. (25 N•m).

9. Reconnect the negative battery cable.

10. Start the engine and let it run for 2 minutes. Check for fuel leaks at the pump base and inlet/outlet connections.

Replacement
(Fuel Injected Engine)

The electric fuel pump is an integral part of the fuel filter/vapor separator/fuel gauge sending unit in the fuel tank (**Figure 47**). To replace the pump, remove the fuel tank from the car as described in this chapter. Remove the cam ring holding the sending unit in the tank. Remove the sending unit assembly. Installation is the reverse of removal.

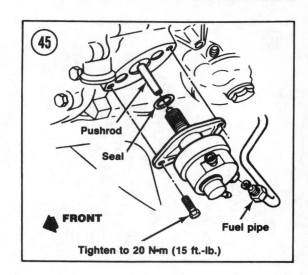

Pushrod
Seal
FRONT
Fuel pipe
Tighten to 20 N•m (15 ft.-lb.)

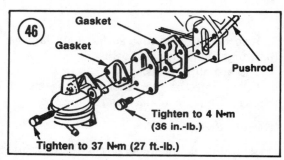

Gasket
Gasket
Pushrod
Tighten to 4 N•m (36 in.-lb.)
Tighten to 37 N•m (27 ft.-lb.)

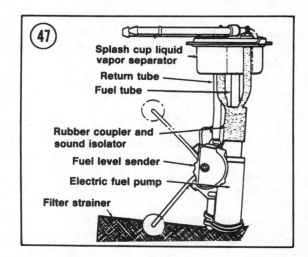

Splash cup liquid vapor separator
Return tube
Fuel tube
Rubber coupler and sound isolator
Fuel level sender
Electric fuel pump
Filter strainer

FUEL TANK AND LINES

The fuel tank is attached under the rear floorpan. Two metal straps hold the tank in place. One end of each strap is secured by a pin through the hinge. The other end is fastened with a bolt. See **Figure 48**.

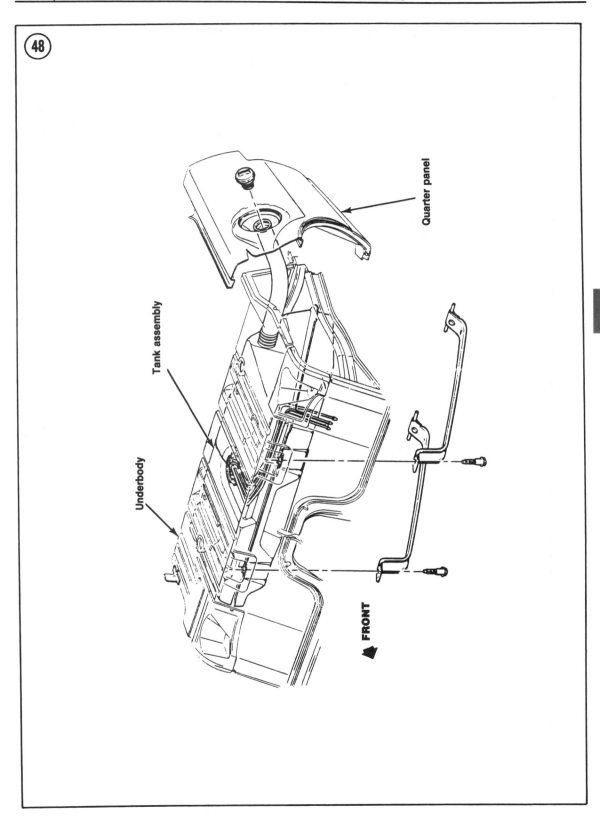

Fuel Tank Removal/Installation

1. Disconnect the negative battery cable.
2. Remove the fuel tank filler cap and siphon out the contents of tank.

> *WARNING*
> *Never store gasoline in an open container, since it is an extreme fire hazard. Store gasoline in a sealed metal container away from heat, sparks and flame.*

3. Raise the car with a jack and place it on jackstands.
4. Disconnect the exhaust pipe at the converter and rear hanger (**Figure 49**). Let exhaust system hang over axle assembly.
5. Remove tailpipe and muffler heat shields.
6. Remove fuel filler neck shield from behind the left rear tire. See **Figure 50**.
7. Remove rear suspension track bar and brace. See Chapter Eleven.

> *NOTE*
> *The fuel pump/gauge wiring harness is a permanent part of the sending assembly. Do not try to disconnect it at the pump in Step 8.*

8. Disconnect the fuel pump/gauge connector at the body harness.
9. Disconnect all sending assembly fuel pipes at their rubber hose connections to the vehicle fuel line system.
10. Remove the fuel pipe retaining bracket at the left rear side of the car. Remove the brake line clip from the bracket.
11. Support the axle assembly with a jack.
12. Disconnect the shock absorber lower ends. Lower the axle assembly and remove both coil springs. See *Axle Assembly Removal/Installation*, Chapter Eleven.
13. Remove tank strap bolts (**Figure 48**).
14. Rotate front of tank downward and slide to the right side. Use caution to avoid damage to the brake lines and cables. Remove the fuel tank.
15. If desired, remove the fuel pump/gauge sending unit cam ring. Remove the sending unit assembly.
16. Installation is the reverse of removal. Tighten fuel tank strap bolts to 25 ft.-lb. (34 N•m).

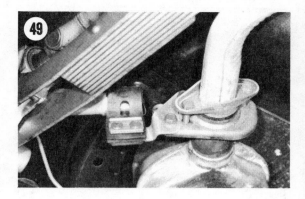

Repairing Fuel Tank Leaks

Fuel tank leaks can be repaired by soldering.

> *WARNING*
> *The fuel tank is capable of exploding and killing anyone nearby. Always observe the following precautions when repairing a tank.*

1. Have the tank steam-cleaned *inside* and *outside*.
2. Fill the tank with inert gas such as nitrogen or carbon dioxide or fill the tank *completely* with water. Gasoline residue on the tank walls can form a highly explosive vapor if allowed to mix with air.
3. Have a fire extinguisher close by.
4. After making the necessary repairs, pour the water out, put about one quart of gasoline in the tank and slosh it around. Pour the gasoline out, blow the tank dry and install it in the car.

EXHAUST SYSTEM

All models are fitted with a single muffler or resonator assembly, a single catalytic converter and connecting pipes. The exhaust manifold-to-crossover pipe connections on the 4-cylinder engine are a ball type and require no gasket.

The muffler inlet/outlet pipes are welded to the muffler. Replace the tailpipe whenever the muffler is replaced. Welded joints should be cut and the new connections clamped with U-bolts. Coat all slip joints (except at the converter) with an exhaust system sealer.

The exhaust system should be free of corrosion, leaks, binding, grounding or

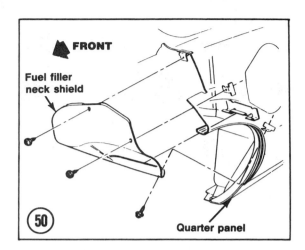

FRONT

Fuel filler
neck shield

(50)

Quarter panel

excessive vibration. Loose, broken or misaligned clamps, shields, brackets or pipes should be serviced as necessary to keep the exhaust system in a safe operating condition.

Removal/Installation

CAUTION
The exhaust system is extremely hot under normal operating conditions. To avoid the possibility of a bad burn, it is advisable to work on the system only when it is cool. Be especially careful around the catalytic converter. It reaches temperatures of 600° F or greater after only a brief period of engine operation.

1. Prior to removal, soak all bolts, nuts and pipe joints with a penetrating oil such as WD-40.
2. Undo the required clamps and hanger brackets.
3. Replace the worn, damaged or corroded components(s). Use new seals when installing a catalytic converter or crossover pipe.
4. Align the exhaust components. Start at the front of the system and tighten all nuts and bolts to specifications.

EMISSION CONTROL SYSTEMS

Computer Command Control (CCC) System

This electronically controlled system monitors up to 15 different engine/vehicle functions. It may control as many as 9 different operations through an electronic control module (ECM) and various sensors. **Figure 51** is a schematic of the CCC system showing the sensors and the functions controlled. Note that not all engines will use all of the components shown in **Figure 51**.

The ECM receives data signals concerning cooling system temperature, crankshaft and distributor rpm, throttle shaft position, manifold pressure and exhaust gas oxygen content. It processes this information and sends back signals to control the air-fuel mixture, distributor advance, canister purge, air management system and other functions.

If a problem develops in the CCC system, a "CHECK ENGINE" lamp will light on the instrument panel. When this happens, return the car to a GM dealer, who has the proper equipment and trained technicians to diagnose this complex system.

Evaporative Emission Control System

This system is used on all models to prevent gasoline vapors from escaping into the atmosphere. The ECM controls vacuum to a canister purge valve through a solenoid valve on 4-cylinder and V6 engines and through a canister control valve and thermo vacuum switch (TVS) on the V8 engine. If the purge valve on 4- and 6-cylinder engines does not operate properly, the entire canister must be replaced.

Some canisters draw purge air from the air cleaner. Others draw purge air through a filter in the bottom of the canister.

There is no scheduled maintenance of the system. Physical damage, leaks and missing components are the most common causes of evaporative system failures.

NOTE
General Motors has indicated that some fuel-injected Z-28 and Trans Am models may have a defective pressure and/or vent valve in the fuel system. Return the car to a dealer for inspection/correction if you have not already done so.

System inspection

1. Check the vapor lines for cracks or loose connections. Replace or tighten as necessary.

6

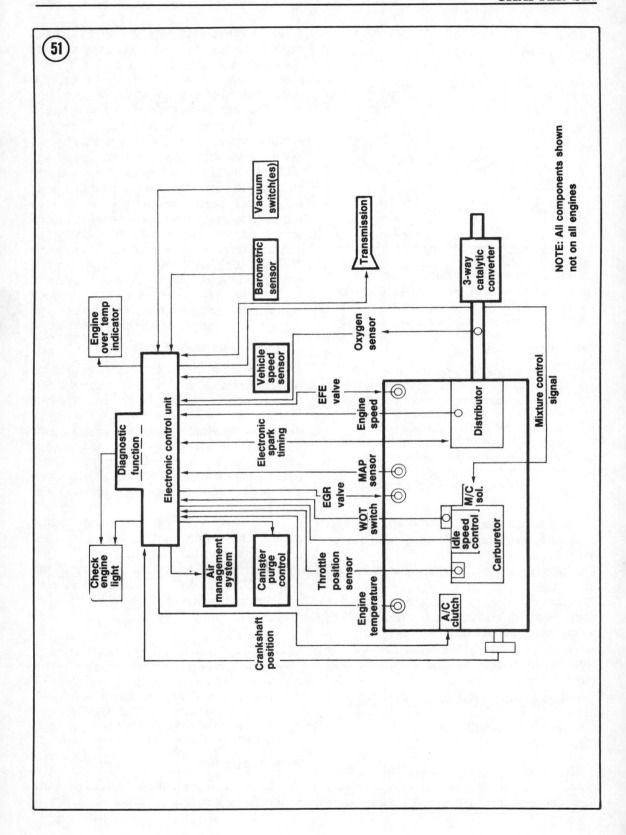

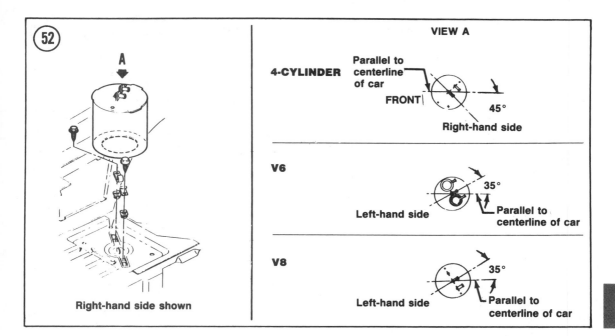

2. Check for a deformed fuel tank. Make sure the tank is not cracked and does not leak gasoline.

3. Inspect the carbon canister for cracks or other damage.

4. Check the vapor hoses and tubes to make sure they slope downhill from the carburetor on throttle body to the canister.

5. Check the fuel filler cap for a damaged gasket.

NOTE
Any damage or contamination which prevents the filler cap pressure-vacuum valve from working properly can result in deformation of the fuel tank.

Canister purge valve test

1. Disconnect the purge valve control vacuum line at the canister. There should be a vacuum signal from the line when the engine is operating above idle speed. If there is none, check the EGR system as described in this chapter.

2. Connect a hand vacuum pump to the purge valve control diaphragm. Apply 7-10 in. Hg vacuum.

3. If the valve does not hold the vacuum, the purge valve is defective. Replace the entire canister assembly.

4. If the valve holds vacuum, remove the purge line and check for vacuum. If there is none, check the PCV hoses and system.

Canister replacement

1. Note the position of the hoses attached to the canister.

2. Disconnect the hoses from the canister.

3. Loosen the canister bracket clamps. Remove canister.

4. Install the canister in the bracket. Position it according to engine as shown in **Figure 52**. Tighten the bracket screw.

5. Install the hoses to their correct canister fitting.

Crankcase Ventilation System

A crankcase ventilation system is used to recycle crankcase vapors into the combustion chambers for burning. A vent hose at the rear of the engine connects the crankcase to the valve cover. This provides a positive flow of air through the crankcase. Fresh air and crankcase vapors are drawn into the intake manifold through a PCV valve in the engine valve cover. **Figure 53** shows the PCV valve removed from the V6 engine valve cover; the 4-cylinder and V8 are similar.

The PCV system should be inspected and the PCV valve and air cleaner crankcase vent filter replaced at intervals specified in Chapter Three.

PCV system check

> *NOTE*
> *A clogged PCV valve or hose will result in a rough engine idle. Always check the PCV system before blaming a rough idle on the carburetor or ECM.*

1. Pull the PCV valve from the intake manifold or valve cover (**Figure 53**).
2. Start the engine and run at idle. Place a thumb over the end of the PCV valve. If no vacuum is felt, check for plugged hoses.
3. Shut the engine off and shake the PCV valve. If the check needle inside the valve does not rattle, replace the valve.
4. Check all system hoses for cracks, brittleness or loose connections. Tighten or replace as necessary.

Air Management System

The air management system shown in **Figure 54** consists of an air pump, air manifold, air switching valve and 2 check valves. The system reduces hydrocarbon and carbon monoxide emissions by pumping fresh air into the exhaust ports near the valves during cold engine operation. This allows the hot exhaust gases to burn for a longer time. When required by engine operating conditions, the ECM switches air injection from the exhaust ports to the catalytic converter or to the air cleaner.

The check valves prevent hot exhaust gases from reversing their flow in the system in case of a pump malfunction.

System test

1. Check and adjust the drive belt tension, if necessary. See *Drive Belts* in Chapter Three.
2. Inspect all system hoses for cracking, burning or loose connections. Replace hoses and tighten connections as necessary.
3. Start the engine. Disconnect the hoses at the air switching valve side of the check valve(s). There should be air flow to the

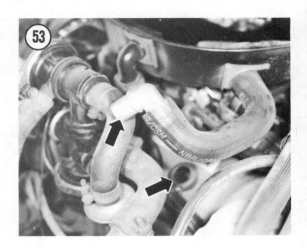

exhaust port outlet of the valve for several seconds, then the air flow should switch to the converter outlet side.
4. Increase engine speed to 1,500-2,000 rpm. Air flow should increase.
5. Reconnect the hoses. Increase engine speed to 2,000 rpm. Release the throttle quickly. If a backfire occurs, the air switching valve is not operating properly or the silencer is defective. Replace the air switching valve.
6. Disconnect the check valve line (**Figure 55**) and remove the check valve.
7. Blow through both ends of the valve. Suck air through both ends. The valve should pass air in only one direction (toward the exhaust manifold). If it passes air in both directions or does not pass air in the direction of the exhaust manifold, install a new check valve.

Further air management system testing should be left to a dealer. Correct system operation is dependent on the ECM and its testing is best left to a qualified technician.

Exhaust Gas Recirculation (EGR) System

This system recirculates a small amount of exhaust gas into the incoming air-fuel mixture through a negative backpressure EGR valve. This lowers the combustion temperature and reduces oxides of nitrogen (NOx) emissions.

The EGR valve is located at the right side of the TBI assembly (**Figure 56**); behind the carburetor on V6 engines (**Figure 57**); and to the left of the carburetor on V8 engines (**Figure 58**).

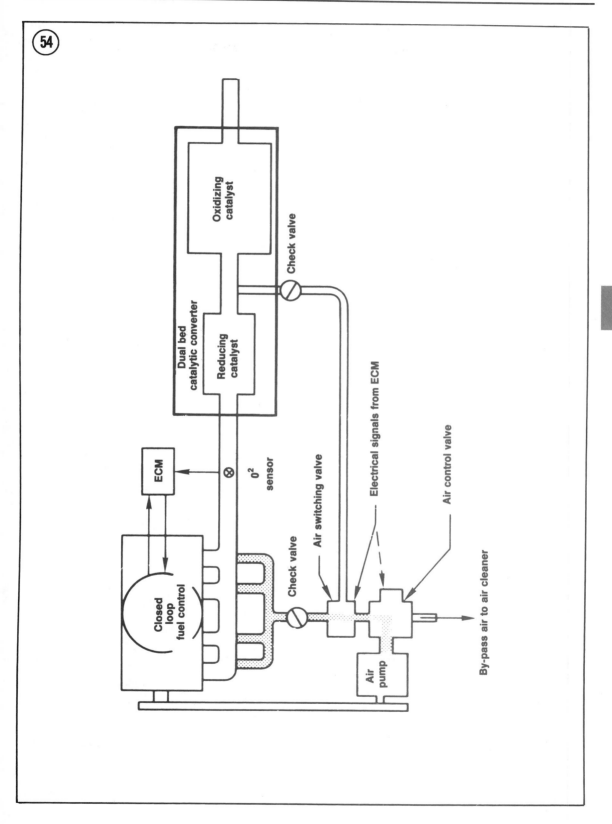

Valve operation is controlled by vacuum received from a carburetor or throttle body port and the amount of backpressure in the exhaust system.

System operational check

> **CAUTION**
> *If checking the EGR system on a hot engine, wear gloves to avoid a bad burn.*

1. Reach under the EGR valve and push on the diaphragm plate with an index finger. If the diaphragm does not move freely from open to closed position, replace the EGR valve.

2. Tee a vacuum gauge between the EGR valve and its vacuum line.
3. Place transmission in NEUTRAL (manual) or PARK (automatic). Start the engine and warm to normal operating temperature (upper radiator hose hot).
4. Open the throttle until the vacuum gauge reads at least 8 in. Hg of vacuum.
5. Remove the vacuum line from the EGR valve. The diaphragm plate should move downward and engine speed should increase.
6. Reconnect the vacuum line. The diaphragm plate should move upward and engine speed should decrease.

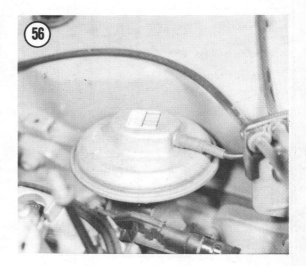

> **NOTE**
> *The diaphragm plate may vibrate during this procedure. This is normal and does not indicate a defective valve.*

7. If the diaphragm plate and engine speed do not react as specified in Step 5 and Step 6, take the car to your GM dealer for further testing and diagnosis.

Cleaning and inspection

1. Remove the air cleaner as described in this chapter.
2. Remove the EGR valve from the intake manifold or manifold adapter.

> **NOTE**
> *Do not sandblast the valve or wash it in solvent.*

3. Check the valve passages for carbon buildup. Light deposits may be cleaned with

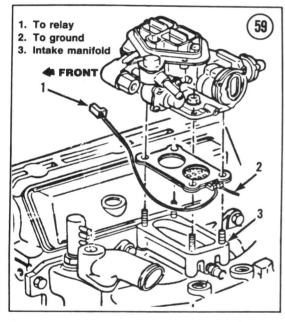

1. To relay
2. To ground
3. Intake manifold

FRONT

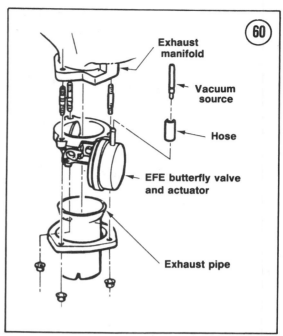

Exhaust manifold

Vacuum source

Hose

EFE butterfly valve and actuator

Exhaust pipe

careful use of a wire brush. If the deposits are heavy, replace the valve. Be sure to use a new gasket when installing the EGR valve.

Catalytic Converter

The catalytic converter is mounted in the exhaust system between the exhaust manifold pipe and the muffler/resonator. Carbon monoxide and unburned hydrocarbons in the exhaust gas are oxidized as they pass through the converter. This process changes the harmful pollutants into harmless carbon dioxide and water. The converter's catalysts also reduce NOx to pure nitrogen and oxygen. The converter requires no maintenance other than replacement of the heat shield, if damaged.

Early Fuel Evaporation (EFE) System

The EFE system is used on some engines to improve cold engine driveability. The system used on V6 engines consists of a ceramic heater grid contained within the rubber isolator between the carburetor and intake manifold (**Figure 59**). With the ignition ON and the coolant temperature low, voltage is applied to the EFE heater through an ECM-controlled relay. As engine coolant reaches a specified temperature, the ECM turns off the relay, shutting off the heater.

Other engines use a vacuum-operated EFE system (**Figure 60**). During cold engine operation, the butterfly valve diverts exhaust gas flow, heating the intake manifold more rapidly. Valve operation is controlled by a thermal vacuum valve (TVV) according to engine coolant temperature.

EFE system diagnosis should be left to your GM dealer. No system maintenance is required.

Table 1 TIGHTENING TORQUES

Fastener	ft.-lb.	N•m
Carburetor mounting nuts		
E2SE	13	18
E4ME	12	16
Throttle body bolt/nut	15	20
Fuel inlet nut	25	34
Fuel line to fuel inlet	18	24
Fuel pump (carburetted engines)		
V6	15	20
V8	27	37
EGR valve		
4-cylinder	10	14
V6	13-18	18-24
V8	15-22	20-30
Exhaust pipe-to-manifold	15	20
Exhaust system		
U-bolts	22	30
Brackets	10-12	15-17

NOTE: If you own a 1983 or later model, first check the Supplement at the back of the book for any new service information.

CHAPTER SEVEN

COOLING, HEATING AND AIR CONDITIONING

The pressurized cooling system used on Camaro and Firebird models consists of a radiator, water pump, cooling fan, thermostat, coolant recovery tank, temperature sensors and connecting hoses. The crossflow radiator is mounted on the engine compartment front body support panel. The water pump on all engines is mounted to the block and coupled directly with the cooling fan.

The heater is a hot water type which circulates coolant through a small radiator (heater core) under the instrument panel.

The air conditioning system is a cycling clutch (intermittent) orifice type and uses outside air at all times, except during MAX A/C operation.

This chapter includes service procedures for the radiator, water pump, thermostat, heater and air conditioner. Cooling system flushing procedures are also described. Torque values are provided in **Table 1** at the end of the chapter.

COOLING SYSTEM FLUSHING

The recommended coolant is a 50/50 mixture of water and ethylene glycol antifreeze. The radiator should be drained, flushed and refilled at the intervals specified in Chapter Three.

NOTE
Under no circumstances should a chemical flushing agent be used. Flush the cooling system with clear water only.

1. Coolant can stain concrete and harm plants. Park the car over a gutter or similar area.
2. Place the heater temperature lever on the instrument panel in the HOT position.
3. Open the drain valve at the bottom of the outlet tank. See **Figure 1**.
4. Let the cooling system drain. Close the drain valve.
5. Remove the thermostat as described in this chapter. Temporarily reinstall the thermostat housing.
6. Disconnect the top radiator hose from the radiator. Disconnect the bottom hose from the water pump inlet.
7. Disconnect the heater hoses at the engine.
8. Connect a garden hose to the heater hose nearest the front of the engine. This does not have to be a positive fit, as long as most of the water enters the heater hose. Run water into

the heater hose until clear water flows from the other heater hose.

9. Insert the garden hose into the top radiator hose. Run water into the top hose until clear water flows from the bottom hose.

10. Insert the garden hose into the hose fitting at the bottom of the radiator. Run water into the radiator until clear water flows from the top fitting. Turn off the water.

11. Disconnect the coolant recovery tank hoses (**Figure 2**). Remove and empty the tank. Flush the recovery tank first with soapy water, then clean water. Drain the tank and reinstall. Connect the hoses.

12. Connect the hoses to the water pump inlet and the radiator. Open the heater coolant control valve.

13. Pour 5 quarts of Prestone II or equivalent antifreeze into the radiator. Add sufficient water to bring the coolant level to the base of the filler neck. Do not install the radiator cap.

14. Add enough coolant to the recovery tank to bring its level up to the "FULL" mark. Install the recovery tank cap.

15. Start the engine and run at fast idle until the upper radiator hose is hot. Return the engine to normal idle.

16. Add sufficient coolant to bring the level up to the base of the radiator filler neck. Install the radiator cap with the cap arrow aligned with the overflow tube (**Figure 3**).

THERMOSTAT

The thermostat blocks coolant flow to the radiator when the engine is cold. As the engine warms up, the thermostat gradually opens, allowing coolant to circulate through the radiator. The 195° thermostat used with all engines (except altitude) should start to open at approximately 188° F and be fully open at 206° F. Some altitude engines use a 180° thermostat which should start to open at about 160° F and be fully open at 190° F. Check the thermostat when removed to determine its opening point; the heat range should be stamped on the thermostat flange.

Removal and Testing

1. Make sure the engine is cool. Disconnect the negative battery cable.

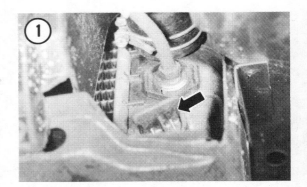

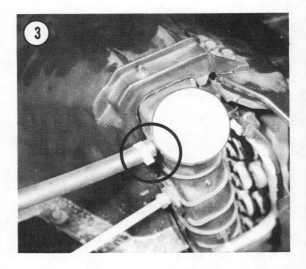

2. Place a clean container under the radiator drain valve. Remove the radiator cap and open the drain valve. Drain about one quart of coolant from the radiator. If the coolant is clean, save it for reuse.

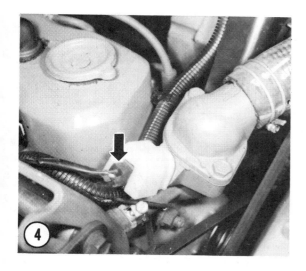

3A. 4-cylinder engine—Disconnect the upper radiator hose from the thermostat housing.

3B. V6 and V8 engine—Remove the air cleaner. See Chapter Six.

4. Disconnect the electrical connector(s) at the thermostat housing. See **Figure 4** (4-cylinder engine), **Figure 5** (V6 engine) or **Figure 6** (V8 engine).

5. Remove the 2 bolts holding the thermostat housing. Remove the thermostat housing with the coolant hose attached.

6. Remove the thermostat from the cylinder head (4-cylinder) or manifold (V6 and V8). Remove and discard the gasket.

7. Pour some of the coolant into a container that can be heated. Submerge the thermostat in this coolant and suspend a thermometer as shown in **Figure 7**.

NOTE
Support the thermostat with wire so it does not touch the sides or bottom of the pan.

8. Heat the coolant until the thermostat has opened fully. Check the coolant temperature. It should be approximately 206° F (190° F for altitude thermometers). If the thermostat is not fully open at this temperature, replace it.

9. Let the thermostat cool to room temperature. Hold it close to a light bulb and check for leakage. If light can be seen around the valve, the thermostat is defective.

In-car Testing

Thermostat operation (except on altitude models) can be tested without removing it from the car. This procedure requires the use

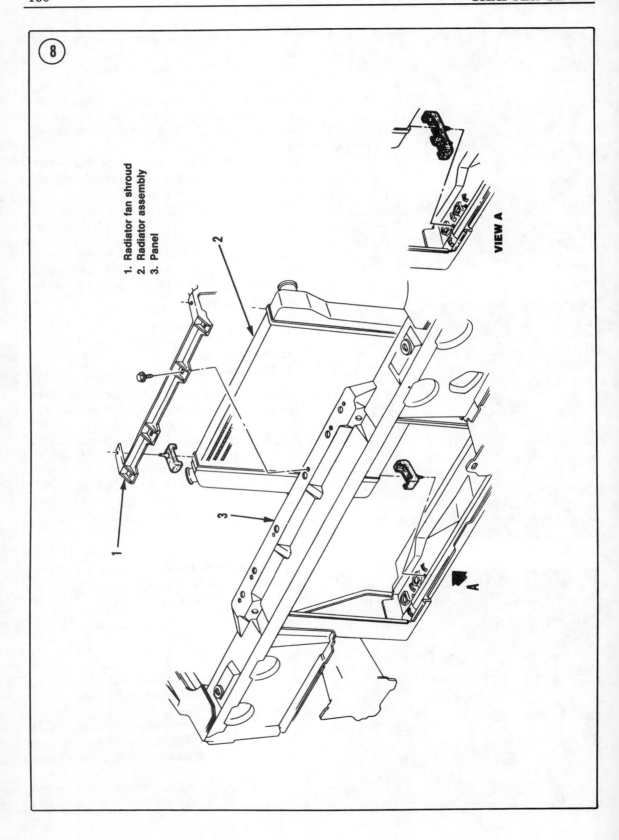

8

1. Radiator fan shroud
2. Radiator assembly
3. Panel

VIEW A

of 2 thermostat sticks available from GM dealers. A thermostat stick looks like a pencil and is made of a chemically impregnated wax material which melts at a specific temperature.

This technique can be used to determine the thermostat's operation by marking the thermostat housing with 188° F or 206° F sticks, depending upon the problem. As the coolant reaches 188° F, the mark made by that stick will melt. The mark made by the 206° F stick will not melt until the coolant increases to that temperature.

Overheated engine

1. Relieve the cooling system pressure. Carefully remove the radiator cap.
2. Rub the 206° F stick on the thermostat housing.
3. Start the engine and run at a fast idle.
4. If no coolant flows through the upper radiator hose by the time the mark starts to melt, replace the thermostat.

Slow engine warmup

1. Relieve the cooling system pressure. Carefully remove the radiator cap.
2. Rub the 188° F stick on the thermostat housing.
3. Start the engine and run at a fast idle.
4. If coolant flows through the upper radiator hose before the mark starts to melt, replace the thermostat.

Installation

1. If a new thermostat is being installed, test it as described in this chapter.
2. Clean the thermostat housing and manifold mating surfaces to remove all gasket or RTV sealant residue.
3. Install the thermostat in the manifold.
4A. 4-cylinder engine—Install a new gasket to the thermostat housing with gasket adhesive.
4B. V6 and V8 engine—Run a 3 mm (1/8 in.) bead of RTV sealant along the thermostat housing sealing surface on the intake manifold.
5. Install the housing to the cylinder head (4-cylinder) or manifold (V6 and V8). Tighten

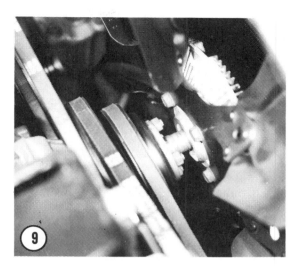

the 4-cylinder housing bolts to 20 ft.-lb. (27 N•m). Tighten the V6 and V8 housing bolts to 30 ft.-lb. (41 N•m).
6. V6 and V8 engine—Install the air cleaner. See Chapter Six.
7. Refill the cooling system to the specified level as described in this chapter.
8. Connect the negative battery cable.

RADIATOR

An aluminum and plastic radiator is used on some models. It can be identified by a note on the outlet tank about 5 in. below the filler neck. If so equipped, use care in hose and radiator replacement to avoid damage to the plastic tank fittings.

Removal/Installation

Refer to **Figure 8** for this procedure.
1. Make sure that the engine is cool enough to touch comfortably.
2. Coolant can stain concrete and harm plants. Park the car over a gutter or similar area. Place a clean container under the draincock.
3. Open the drain valve at the lower side of the outlet tank (**Figure 1**).
4. When the coolant reserve tank is empty, remove the radiator cap (**Figure 3**) to promote faster draining.
5. Unbolt and remove the fan (**Figure 9**). If equipped with a fan clutch, place the clutch in

an upright position to prevent fluid leakage.

6. Disconnect the upper and lower radiator hoses at the radiator.

7. Remove the overflow hose from the radiator nipple. See **Figure 10**.

8. If equipped with automatic transmission, disconnect and plug the oil cooler lines at the radiator.

9. Remove the fan shield, if so equipped.

10. Remove the upper and lower shroud retaining screws.

11. Lift the radiator and shroud assembly straight up.

> *NOTE*
> *The radiator is held in place at the bottom by 2 cradles fastened to the radiator support.*

12. Installation is the reverse of removal. Make sure the radiator lower cradles are properly positioned in the radiator recess and engage the radiator as it is lowered into place.

Radiator Hose Replacement

Replace any hoses that are cracked, brittle, mildewed or very soft and spongy. If a hose is in doubtful condition, but not definitely bad, replace it to be on the safe side. This will avoid the necessity of a roadside repair.

> *NOTE*
> *Be sure to use a molded replacement hose. Plain or pleated rubber hoses do not have the same strength as reinforced molded hoses.*

1. Partially drain the cooling system when replacing an upper hose. Completely drain it to replace a lower hose.

2. To replace a hose, loosen its clamp nut at each end. Twist the hose to break it free of the fitting and take it off.

> *CAUTION*
> *Do not use oil or grease as a lubricant to assist in hose replacement. It may cause the rubber to deteriorate.*

3. New hoses can be installed easily by smearing dishwasher liquid on the fitting and the inside diameter of the hose.

> *CAUTION*
> *To prevent hose or clamp damage, do not overtighten.*

4. Tighten the hose clamps snugly. Recheck them for tightness after operating the car for a few days.

WATER PUMP

A water pump may warn of impending failure by making noise. If the seal is defective, coolant may leak from behind the pump pulley. The water pump can be replaced on all models without discharging the air conditioning system. The pump is serviced as an assembly.

Removal/Installation
(4-cylinder Engine)

1. Disconnect the negative battery cable.

2. Drain the cooling system as described in this chapter.

3. Loosen accessory units as required and remove the drive belts.

4. Remove the fan and pump pulley.

> *NOTE*
> *It may be necessary to remove the alternator and/or air conditioning compressor on some models to provide access for Step 5 and Step 6. Do not disconnect any air conditioning system lines.*

5. Disconnect the heater hose and lower radiator hose at the water pump.

6. Remove the water pump bolts. Remove the water pump.

7. Installation is the reverse of removal. Use a new gasket and coat the pump bolt threads with RTV sealant. Tighten bolts to 15 ft.-lb. (20 N•m). Adjust drive belt tension as described in Chapter Three. Refill the cooling system and check for leaks.

Removal/Installation (V6 and V8 Engine)

1. Disconnect the negative battery cable.

2. Drain the cooling system as described in this chapter.

3. Remove the fan shroud or radiator upper support.

4. Loosen accessory units as required and remove drive belts.

5. Remove the fan and pulley from water pump hub.

6. Remove upper and lower alternator brackets and air pump brace/bracket.

7. Remove the power steering pump lower bracket from the water pump, if so equipped. Swing pump to one side out of the way.

8. Disconnect the lower radiator hose and heater hose at the water pump.

9. Remove the water pump bolts. Remove the water pump.

10. Installation is the reverse of removal. Use new water pump gaskets. Tighten radiator and heater hose clamps to 20 in.-lb. (2 N•m). Tighten accessory bracket bolts to 30 ft.-lb. (41 N•m). Adjust drive belt tension as described in Chapter Three. Refill cooling system and check for leaks.

HEATER

The heater system consists of a blower air inlet and a heater/defroster assembly. Ram air vent, heat and defrost functions are controlled by the heater/defroster assembly. The blower air inlet is connected to the front of the dash in the engine compartment. The heater/defroster is fastened to the rear of the dash in the passenger compartment. Mounting gaskets on both components prevent air, water and noise from entering the passenger compartment. **Figure 11** shows the heater system air flow.

Troubleshooting

1. If the heater does not produce heat, make sure the engine will warm up in a reasonable amount of time. If the thermostat sticks in the open position, the engine will not completely warm up. Since hot engine coolant provides heat for the heater, a defective thermostat may be the problem.

2. If the heater blower does not work, check the 25 amp fuse in the HTR-AC cavity of the fuse block.

3. If the fuse is good, test the blower switch, resistor block and motor as described in this chapter.

Blower Motor and Switch Testing

Power to the blower motor is provided through the ignition switch and a 25 amp fuse in the HTR-AC cavity of the fuse block. Blower motor speed is controlled by the switch on the control assembly.

1. Remove the control assembly as described in this chapter.

2. If the problem is in the blower speed, check for continuity between the terminals of the fan switch at all switch positions with a test lamp. See **Figure 12**.

3. The lamp should light for each connected pair of terminals. There should be no continuity (lamp should not light) between the switch case and any terminal.

Blower Switch Replacement

1. Remove the control assembly as described in this chapter.

2. Pry the switch knob off carefully with a screwdriver.

3. Remove the fasteners holding the switch to the control assembly.

4. Align the pin on the new switch with the hole in the mounting bracket and install the fasteners securely.

5. Push the knob onto the switch shaft as far as it will go. Reinstall the control assembly.

Resistor Block Test

The resistor block is mounted on the heater housing in the engine compartment.

7

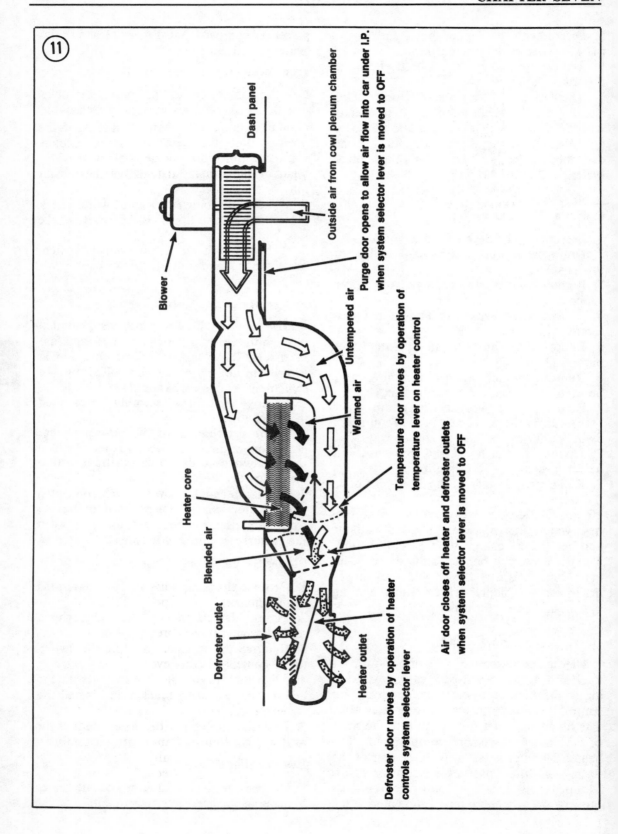

⑪

Dash panel

Blower

Outside air from cowl plenum chamber

Purge door opens to allow air flow into car under I.P. when system selector lever is moved to OFF

Untempered air

Warmed air

Temperature door moves by operation of temperature lever on heater control

Heater core

Blended air

Defroster outlet

Heater outlet

Defroster door moves by operation of heater controls system selector lever

Air door closes off heater and defroster outlets when system selector lever is moved to OFF

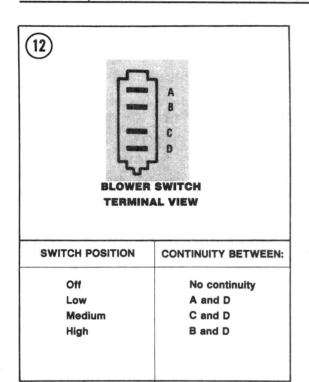

**BLOWER SWITCH
TERMINAL VIEW**

SWITCH POSITION	CONTINUITY BETWEEN:
Off	No continuity
Low	A and D
Medium	C and D
High	B and D

1. Disconnect the resistor block electrical connector.
2. Remove the resistor block retaining screws. Remove the resistor block.
3. Test the resistors for an open circuit with a self-powered test lamp. Replace if open.

Control Assembly Removal/Installation

Refer to **Figure 13** for this procedure.
1. Disconnect the negative battery cable.
2. Remove the control/radio console trim plate.
3. Remove 3 control assembly screws. Pull the assembly out.
4. Disconnect the control cables and electrical connections.
5. Remove the control assembly.
6. Installation is the reverse of removal. Install the lower right control assembly screw first to correctly align assembly in console.

Control Cables

The control cables connect to the control assembly and heater crank arms by snap-in retaining tabs (**Figure 13**).

Cable Adjustment

The temperature cable has a slider-type self-adjustment feature. As the temperature lever is moved through its full range of travel, the cable clip assumes a position to seat the temperature valve in both extreme positions. The vent/defrost cable requires no adjustment.

Blower Motor Removal/Installation

1. Disconnect the negative battery cable.
2. Disconnect the wiring connectors at the blower motor and resistor block. Remove the radio capacitor, if so equipped.
3. Remove the blower motor cooling tube.
4. Remove the blower motor attaching screws. Remove the blower motor/cage assembly from the case.
5. Hold the blower motor cage and remove the screw holding the cage to the motor shaft. Slide the cage from the motor shaft.
6. Installation is the reverse of removal. Reinstall radio capacitor, if so equipped.

Heater Core Removal/Installation

1. Drain the cooling system as described in this chapter.
2. Disconnect heater inlet/outlet hoses at heater core.
3. Remove the right lower hush panel.
4. Remove the right lower instrument panel trim panel.
5. Remove the ESC module on fuel injected V8 models.
6. Remove 4 heater case cover screws. Remove heater case cover.
7. Remove core support plate and baffle screws.
8. Remove heater core, support plate and baffle from heater case.
9. Installation is the reverse of removal.

AIR CONDITIONING

This section covers the maintenance and minor repairs that can prevent or correct common air conditioning problems. Major repairs require special training and equipment and should be left to a dealer or air conditioning expert.

7

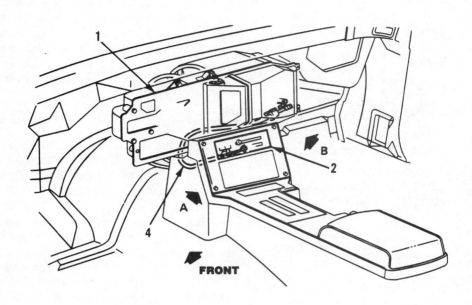

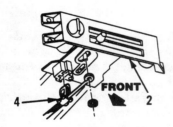

FRONT

Cable adjustment: After installation, adjust by
pushing lever to full hot position.
1. Heater and blower case
2. Control assembly
3. Bracket and lever
4. Cable assembly

VIEW A

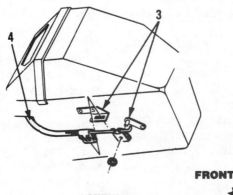

FRONT

VIEW B

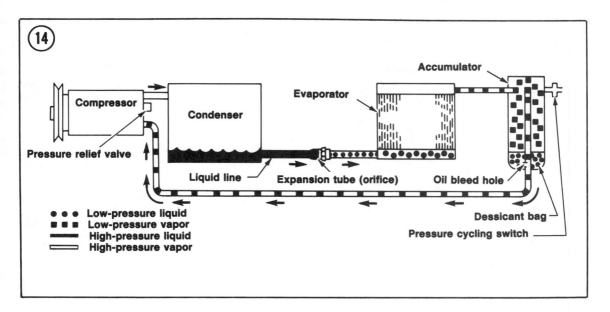

(14)

Accumulator

Compressor

Condenser

Evaporator

Pressure relief valve

Liquid line   Expansion tube (orifice)   Oil bleed hole

● ● ● Low-pressure liquid
■ ■ ■ Low-pressure vapor
━━━━ High-pressure liquid
▭▭▭ High-pressure vapor

Dessicant bag
Pressure cycling switch

System Operation

There are 5 basic components common to the air conditioning system used with all engines.
   a. Compressor.
   b. Condenser.
   c. Accumulator/dehydrator.
   d. Orifice tube.
   e. Evaporator.

For practical purposes, the cycle begins at the compressor (**Figure 14**). The refrigerant enters the low-pressure side of the compressor in a warm low-pressure vapor state. It is compressed to a high-pressure hot vapor and pumped out of the high-pressure side to the condenser.

Air flow through the condenser removes heat from the refrigerant and transfers the heat to the outside air. As the heat is removed, the refrigerant condenses to a warm high-pressure liquid.

The refrigerant then flows through the plastic expansion tube with its mesh screen and orifice to the evaporator, where it removes heat from the passenger compartment air that is blown across the evaporator's fins and tubes. Refrigerant flow continues to the accumulator/dehydrator, where moisture is removed and impurities are filtered out. The refrigerant is stored in the accumulator/dehydrator until it is needed.

From the accumulator/dehydrator, the refrigerant then returns to the compressor as a warm low-pressure liquid.

GET TO KNOW YOUR VEHICLE'S SYSTEM

Figure 14 shows the major components of the Camaro/Firebird air conditioning system. Refer to it to locate each of the following components in turn.
   a. Compressor.
   b. Condenser.
   c. Accumulator/dehydrator.
   d. Orifice tube.
   e. Evaporator.
   f. Vacuum tank (see **Figure 15**).

Compressor

The compressor is located on the front of the engine, like the alternator, and is driven by a V-belt (**Figure 16**). The large pulley on the front of the compressor contains an electromagnetic clutch. This activates and operates the compressor when the air conditioning is switched on. A pressure relief valve opens to discharge refrigerant if operating pressure exceeds 430 psi (2,760 kPa). Some systems may use a muffler to reduce compressor noise and high-pressure line vibrations.

7

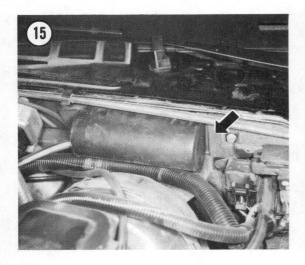

Condenser

The condenser (**Figure 17**) is mounted in front of the radiator. Air passing through the condenser tubes and fins removes heat from the refrigerant in the same manner it removes heat from the engine coolant as it passes through the radiator. The radiator cooling fan also pulls air through the condenser.

Accumulator/dehydrator

The accumulator/dehydrator is a small tank-like unit (**Figure 18**) connected to the evaporator outlet tube.

Orifice Tube

The plastic orifice tube is located inside the evaporator inlet pipe at the liquid line connection. It meters refrigerant into the evaporator.

Evaporator

The evaporator (**Figure 19**) is located in the passenger compartment cooling unit as a part of the blower motor assembly. Warm air is blown across the fins and tubes, where it is cooled and dried and then ducted into the passenger compartment by the blower.

Vacuum Tank

The air conditioning system fitted to Camaro/Firebird models uses a vacuum supply tank to store vacuum for use whenever

inlet manifold vacuum decreases, as during heavy acceleration. See **Figure 15**. The vacuum tank contains a check valve.

Pressure Sensing Switch

This switch is located on a Schrader valve type low-side fitting and cycles on and off to prevent an evaporator freeze-up. Cycling of the compressor will cause occasional slight changes in engine speed and power under certain operating conditions, but this should be considered normal.

ROUTINE MAINTENANCE

Basic maintenance of the air conditioning system is easy; at least once a month, even in cold weather, start your engine, turn on the air conditioner and operate it at each of the control settings. Operate the air conditioner

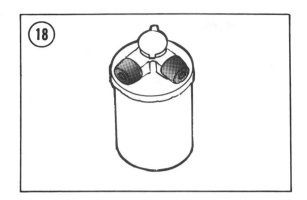

for about 10 minutes, with the engine running at about 1,500 rpm. This will ensure that the compressor seal does not deform from sitting in the same position for a long period of time. If deformation occurs, the seal is likely to leak.

The efficiency of the air conditioning system also depends in great part on the efficiency of the cooling system. If the cooling system is dirty or low on coolant, it may be impossible to operate the air conditioner without overheating. Inspect the coolant. If necessary, flush and refill the cooling system as described in this chapter.

Use an air hose and a soft brush to clean the radiator and condenser fins and tubes. Remove any bugs, leaves or other imbedded debris.

Check drive belt tension as described under *Drive Belts*, Chapter Three.

If the condition of the cooling system thermostat is in doubt, test it as described in this chapter.

Inspection

1. Clean all lines, fittings and system components with solvent and a clean rag. Pay particular attention to the fittings; oily dirt around connections almost certainly indicates a leak. Oil from the compressor will migrate through the system to the leak. Carefully tighten the connection, but do not overtighten and strip the threads. If the leak persists, it will soon be apparent once again as oily dirt accumulates.

2. Clean the condenser fins and tubes with a soft brush and an air hose or with a high-pressure stream of water from a garden hose. Remove any bugs, leaves or other imbedded debris. Carefully straighten any bent fins with a screwdriver, taking care not to puncture or dent the tubes.

3. Start the engine and check the operation of the blower motor and the compressor clutch by turning the controls on and off. If either the blower or clutch fails to operate, shut off the engine and check the HTR-A/C fuse in the fuse block. See *Fuses and Fusible Links*, Chapter Eight. If the fuse (or fusible link) is blown, replace it. If not, remove and clean the fuse holder contacts. Then check the clutch and blower operation again. If they still will not operate, take the car to a dealer or air conditioning specialist.

REFRIGERANT

The air conditioning system uses a refrigerant called dichlorodifluoromethane or R-12.

> *WARNING*
> *Refrigerant creates freezing temperatures when it evaporates. This can cause frostbite if it touches skin and blindness if it touches the eyes. If discharged near an open flame, R-12 creates poisonous gas. If the refrigerant can is hooked up to the pressure side of the compressor, it may explode. Always wear safety goggles and gloves when working with R-12.*

Charging

This section applies to partially discharged or empty air conditioning systems. If a hose has been disconnected or any internal part of the system exposed to air, the system should be evacuated and recharged by a dealer or air conditioning shop. Recharge kits are available from auto parts stores. Be sure the kit includes a gauge set. Refer to **Figure 20** for this procedure.

NOTE
This procedure is used with the GM part No. J-5725-04 Manifold Gauge Set. Another gauge set may require a slightly different procedure. Carefully read and understand the gauge manufacturer's instructions before charging the system.

1. Connect the low pressure gauge of manifold gauge set part No. J-5725-04 to the accumulator fitting.
2. Connect the center gauge set hose to the R-12 can.
3. Start the engine and run at normal idle with the choke wide open.
4. Turn the A/C control lever OFF.
5. Open the R-12 source valve. Let one 14-oz. can of R-12 flow into the system through the accumulator fitting. Immediately engage the compressor by returning the A/C control lever to NORM and turning the blower on HI. This will draw the rest of the R-12 charge into the system. The total R-12 charge for Camaro/Firebird air conditioning systems is 48 fl. oz. (1,362 ml).
6. Shut the R-12 source valve off. Run the engine for 30 seconds to clear the lines and gauges.

WARNING
Never remove a gauge line from its adapter with the line connected to the air conditioning system. Disconnect the line at the service fitting. Removing the charging hose at the gauge set while still connected to the accumulator can cause serious personal injury.

7. Remove the hose adapter at the accumulator quickly to prevent excessive R-12 loss. Install the protective cap on the accumulator fitting.

8. Check the system for leaks. Shut the engine off.

TROUBLESHOOTING

If the air conditioner fails to blow cold air, the following steps will help locate the problem.

1. Stop the car and look at the control settings. One of the most common air conditioning problems occurs when the temperature is set for maximum cold and the blower is set on LOW. This promotes ice buildup on the evaporator fins and tubes, particularly in humid weather. Eventually, the evaporator will ice over completely and restrict air flow. Turn the blower on HIGH and place a hand over an air outlet. If the blower is running but there is little or no air flowing through the outlet, the evaporator is probably iced up. Leave the blower on HIGH. Turn the temperature control OFF or to its warmest setting and wait. It will take 10-15 minutes for the ice to start melting.
2. If the blower does not run at any speed, the fuse may be blown, there may be a loose wiring connection or the motor may be burned out. Check the fuse block for a blown or incorrectly seated fuse, then check the wiring for loose connections.
3. If the blower runs but not on high speed, check for a blown fuse in the electrical wiring between the junction terminal and the air conditioner relay.
4. Shut off the engine and inspect the compressor drive belt. If loose or worn, tighten or replace. See *Drive Belts* in Chapter Three.
5. Start the engine. Check the compressor clutch by turning the air conditioner ON and OFF. If the clutch does not activate, have the system checked by a GM dealer or air conditioning shop.
6. If the system appears to be operating as it should, but air flow into the passenger compartment is not cold, check the condenser for debris that could block air flow. Recheck the cooling system as described under *Routine Maintenance* in this chapter. If the preceding steps have not solved the problem, take the car to a GM dealer or an air conditioning shop for service.

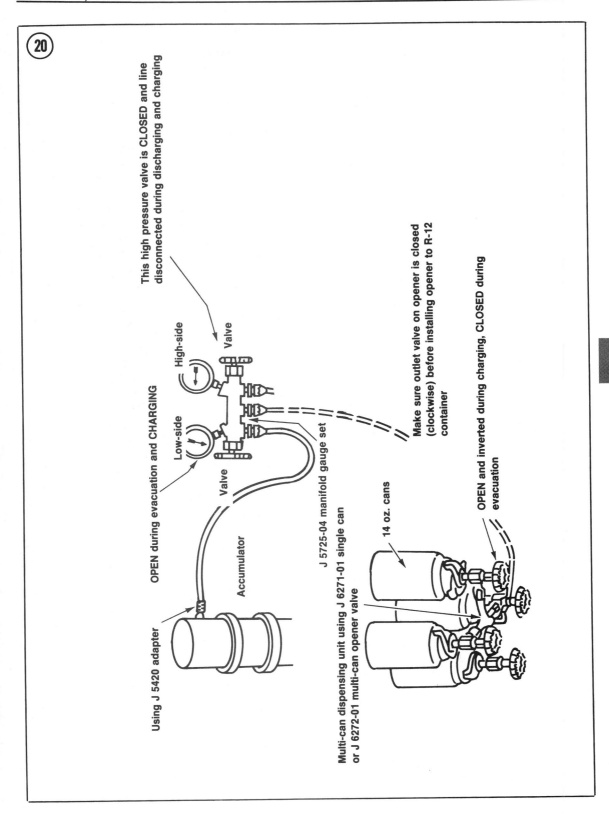

20

This high pressure valve is CLOSED and line disconnected during discharging and charging

High-side

Valve

OPEN during evacuation and CHARGING

Low-side

Valve

J 5725-04 manifold gauge set

Accumulator

Using J 5420 adapter

Multi-can dispensing unit using J 6271-01 single can or J 6272-01 multi-can opener valve

14 oz. cans

Make sure outlet valve on opener is closed (clockwise) before installing opener to R-12 container

OPEN and inverted during charging, CLOSED during evacuation

7

Table 1 TIGHTENING TORQUES

Fastener	ft.-lb.	N·m
Coolant recovery tank	27 in.-lb.	3
Thermostat housing		
4-cylinder	25	34
V6, V8	30	41
Water pump (4-cylinder)	15	20
Water pump (V6)		
M6 x 1.0	6-9	8-12
M8 x 1.25	13-18	18-24
M10 x 1.25	20-30	27-41
Water pump (V8)	30	40
Water pump pulley	13-18	18-24
Water outlet		
4-cylinder	20	27
V6	13-18	18-24
V8	25	34
Alternator		
Bracket-to-head	30-40	40-54
Brace-to-cover	20-30	27-41
Pivot bolt	20-30	27-41
Adjusting bolt	20-25	27-34
Air conditioning		
Bracket-to-cover	25-35	35-50
Compressor attachment	30-40	40-54

NOTE: If you own a 1983 or later model, first check the Supplement at the back of the book for any new service information.

CHAPTER EIGHT

ELECTRICAL SYSTEMS

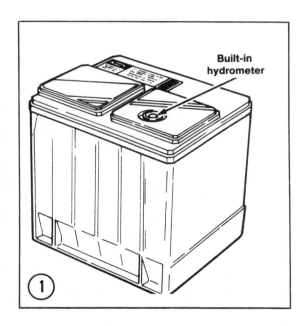

This chapter provides service procedures for the battery, charging system, starter, ignition system, lights, switches, turn indicators, horn, windshield wipers and washers, fuses and fusible links. **Table 1** and **Table 2** are at the end of the chapter.

8

BATTERY

All Camaro/Firebird models are equipped with a Freedom II maintenance-free battery which incorporates a visual test indicator (**Figure 1**). This test indicator is a built-in hydrometer in one cell. It provides visual information of battery condition for testing only and should not be used as a basis of determining whether the battery is properly charged or discharged, good or bad.

Using the Test Indicator

Refer to **Figure 2**. Make sure the battery is level and the test indicator sight glass is clean. A penlight is useful under dim lighting conditions to determine the indicator color. Look down into the sight glass. If the dot appears green in color, the battery has a sufficient charge for testing. If it appears dark or black, charge the battery before testing. A clear or light yellow appearance indicates that the battery should be replaced and the charging system checked.

Care and Inspection

1. Disconnect both battery cables (**Figure 3**), negative first, then positive. Remove the battery hold-down clamp.

2. Attach a battery carry strap to the terminal posts. Remove the battery from the engine compartment.

3. Check the entire battery case for cracks. If the battery has removable filler caps, cover the vent holes in each cap with a small piece of masking tape.

> *NOTE*
> *Keep cleaning solution out of the battery cells in Step 4 or the electrolyte will be seriously weakened.*

4. Clean the top of the battery with a stiff bristle brush using baking soda and water solution (**Figure 4**). Rinse the battery case with clear water and wipe dry with a clean cloth or paper towel.

5. Inspect the battery tray in the engine compartment for corrosion and clean if necessary with the baking soda/water solution.

6. Remove the masking tape from the filler cap vent holes. Position the battery on the battery tray and install the hold-down clamp. Tighten the clamp bolt to 6 ft.-lb. (8 N•m).

7. Clean the battery cable clamps with a stiff wire brush or one of the many tools made for this purpose (**Figure 5**). The same tool is used for cleaning the battery posts (**Figure 6**).

8. Reconnect the positive battery cable, then the negative cable.

> *CAUTION*
> *Be sure the battery cables are connected to their proper terminals. Connecting the battery backwards will reverse the polarity and can damage the alternator.*

9. Tighten the battery connections and coat with a petroleum jelly such as Vaseline or a light mineral grease.

10. If the battery has removable filler caps, check the electrolyte level. Top up with distilled water, if necessary.

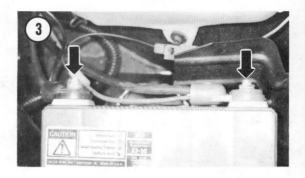

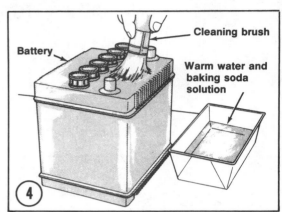

Cleaning brush

Battery

Warm water and baking soda solution

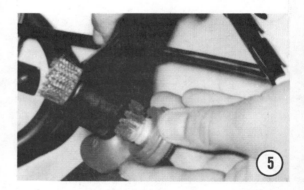

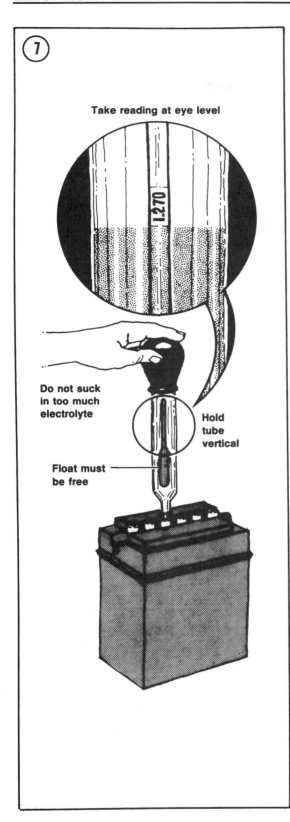

⑦

Take reading at eye level

1.270

Do not suck
in too much
electrolyte

Hold
tube
vertical

Float must
be free

Testing

This procedure applies to batteries with removable filler caps. Testing Freedom II batteries requires special equipment, but any good service station or your GM dealer can make the test for a nominal fee.

Hydrometer testing is the best way to check battery condition. Use a hydrometer with numbered gradations from 1.100-1.300 rather than one with just color-coded bands. To use the hydrometer, squeeze the rubber ball, insert the tip in a cell and release the ball (**Figure 7**).

Draw enough electrolyte to float the weighted float inside the hydrometer. Note the number in line with the surface of the electrolyte. This is the specific gravity for the cell. Return the electrolyte to the cell from which it came.

The specific gravity of the electrolyte in each battery cell is an excellent indicator of that cell's condition. A fully charged cell will read 1.260 or more at 20° C (68° F). If the cells test below 1.200, the battery must be recharged. Charging is also necessary if the specific gravity varies more than 0.025 from cell to cell.

NOTE
If a temperature-compensated hydrometer is not used, add 0.004 to the specific gravity reading for every 10° above 80° F (25° C). For every 10° below 80° F (25° C), subtract 0.004.

Charging

The battery does not have to be removed from the car for charging. Just make certain that the area is well-ventilated and that there is no chance of sparks or flames occuring near the battery.

WARNING
Charging batteries give off highly explosive hydrogen gas. If this explodes, it may spray battery acid over a wide area.

Disconnect the negative battery cable first, then the positive cable. Install a pair of screw-in battery charging posts or a charging adapter strap (**Figure 8**) to provide an

8

adequate conductive surface for the charger leads. On unsealed batteries, make sure the electrolyte is fully topped up. Remove the vent caps and place a folded paper towel over the vent openings to catch any electrolyte that may spew as the battery charges.

Connect the charger to the battery— negative to negative, positive to positive. If the charger output is variable, select a low setting (5-10 amps), set the voltage regulator to 12 volts and plug the charger in. If the battery is severely discharged, allow it to charge for at least 8 hours. Batteries that are not as badly discharged require less charging time. **Table 1** gives approximate charge rates. On unsealed batteries, check charging progress with the hydrometer.

Jump Starting

If the battery becomes severely discharged on the road, it is possible to start and run a vehicle by jump starting it from another battery. If the proper procedure is not followed, jump starting can be dangerous. Check the electrolyte level before jump starting any battery. If it is not visible or if it appears to be frozen, do not attempt to jump start the battery. Do not jump start Freedom II batteries when the temperature is 32° F (0° C) or lower.

> *WARNING*
> *Use extreme caution when connecting a booster battery to one that is discharged to avoid personal injury or damage to the vehicle.*

1. Position the 2 cars so that the jumper cables will reach between the batteries, but the cars do not touch.
2. Connect the jumper cables in the order and sequence shown in **Figure 9**.

> *WARNING*
> *An electrical arc may occur when the final connection is made. This could cause an explosion if it occurs near the battery. For this reason, the final connection should be made to the alternator mounting bracket and not the battery itself.*

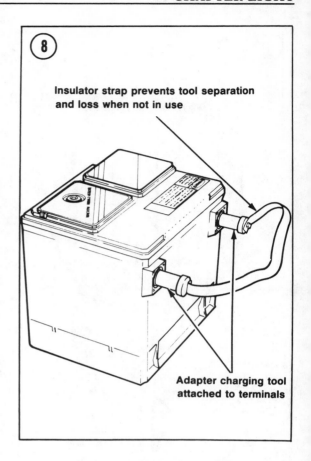

Insulator strap prevents tool separation and loss when not in use

Adapter charging tool attached to terminals

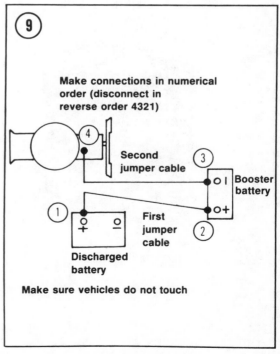

Make connections in numerical order (disconnect in reverse order 4321)

Second jumper cable

Booster battery

First jumper cable

Discharged battery

Make sure vehicles do not touch

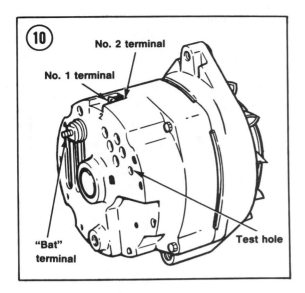

No. 2 terminal

No. 1 terminal

"Bat" terminal

Test hole

3. Check that all jumper cables are out of the way of moving parts on both engines.

4. Start the car with the good battery and run the engine at a moderate speed.

5. Start the car with the discharged battery. Once the engine starts, run it at a moderate speed.

CAUTION
Racing the engine may cause damage to the electrical system.

6. Remove the jumper cables in the exact reverse order shown in **Figure 9**. Begin at point No. 4, then 3, 2 and 1.

CHARGING SYSTEM

The charging system consists of the battery, alternator, voltage regulator, charge indicator light and wiring. Two Delcotron alternators are used: the 10-SI and the 15-SI. They differ primarily in output rating. The output rating is stamped on the alternator frame.

Both alternator models use an integral solid-state voltage regulator. The regulator is serviced only by replacement.

Charging System Test

A voltmeter with a 0-20 volt scale and an engine tachometer are required for an accurate charging system test.

1. Check the alternator belt tension. See *Drive Belts*, Chapter Three.

2. Check the battery terminals and cables for corrosion and/or loose connections. Clean and tighten as necessary.

3. Check all wiring connections between the alternator and engine.

4. Connect the positive voltmeter lead to the positive battery cable clamp. Connect the negative voltmeter lead to the negative battery cable clamp. Make sure the ignition and all accessories are off.

5. Record the battery voltage displayed on the voltmeter scale. This is the base voltage.

6. Connect a tachometer to the engine according to the manufacturer's instructions.

7. Start the engine and bring its speed up to about 1,500 rpm. The voltmeter reading should increase from that recorded in Step 5, but not by more than 2 volts.

8. If the voltage does not increase, perform the *Undercharge Test*. If the voltage increase is greater than 2 volts, remove the alternator and have it checked by a dealer or an automotive electrical shop for grounded or shorted field windings.

Undercharge Test

A voltmeter with a 0-20 volt scale, an ammeter and a carbon pile are required for this procedure. Refer to **Figure 10** for test points.

1. Turn the ignition switch ON. Make sure all electrical harness leads are properly connected.

2. Connect the negative voltmeter lead to a good engine ground. Connect the positive voltmeter lead between a good engine ground and the following alternator terminals (see **Figure 10**):

   a. BAT terminal.
   b. No. 1 terminal.
   c. No. 2 terminal.

3. Read the voltmeter as each connection in Step 2 is made. A zero reading at any of the connections indicates an open circuit.

4. Disconnect the voltmeter. Disconnect the negative battery cable.

5. Disconnect the alternator wiring connector at the BAT terminal. Connect an ammeter between the BAT terminal and the wiring connector.

8

6. Reconnect the negative battery cable. Turn on all accessories.

7. Connect a carbon pile across the battery posts.

8. Start the engine and run at 2,000 rpm. Adjust the carbon pile to obtain the maximum current output.

9. If the ammeter reading is within 10 amps of the alternator's rated output, the unit is satisfactory.

10. If the ammeter reading is not within 10 amps of the rated output, remove the alternator and have it checked by your GM dealer or an automotive electrical shop.

Regulator Test

An approved regulator tester (GM part No. CTW-1170 or equivalent) is required to determine whether the regulator is functioning properly. Since this test may require disassembly of the alternator and does require the use of special test equipment, have it performed by your dealer or an automotive electrical shop.

Alternator Removal/Installation

1. Disconnect the negative battery cable.

2. Remove the electrical connectors from the rear of the alternator (**Figure 11**).

3. Loosen the alternator adjusting bolt (A, **Figure 12**).

4. Move the alternator toward the engine and remove the drive belt from the pulley.

5. Remove the bracket pivot bolt (B, **Figure 12**). Remove the alternator.

6. Installation is the reverse of removal. Tighten the pivot bolt to 25 ft.-lb. (34 N•m). Adjust the belt tension as described under *Drive Belts*, Chapter Three. Tighten the adjusting bolt to 20 ft.-lb. (27 N•m).

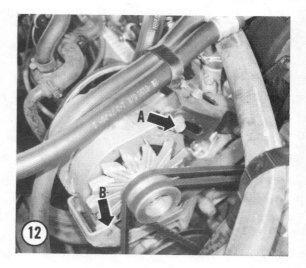

STARTER

The Delco 5MT starter is used with all engines. **Figure 13** shows the 4-cylinder engine starter. The starter solenoid is enclosed in the drive housing to protect it from exposure to dirt and adverse weather conditions.

This section includes on-car testing of the starter, starter and solenoid replacement and

starter brush replacement. Complete starter overhaul is not practical nor is it possible. The field coils and pole shoes in the 5MT are permanently bonded to the motor frame. If the coils or shoes are defective, the motor must be replaced as an assembly. Starter brushes, however, can be replaced.

It is possible that the armature of the 5MT starter may disintegrate if the ignition switch fails. If the starter drive overruns but the solenoid does not disengage when the engine is started, the 5MT will run freely at a very high rpm, causing the armature to self-destruct. If this happens, check the ignition switch prior to installing a new motor or it may also self-destruct.

On-car Testing

Two of these procedures require a fully charged 12 volt battery to be used as a booster and a pair of jumper cables. Use the jumper cables as outlined in *Jump Starting* in this chapter, following all of the precautions noted.

Slow cranking starter

1. Connect the jumper cables. Listen to the starter cranking speed as the engine is started. If the cranking speed sounds normal, check the battery for loose or corroded connections or a low charge. Clean and tighten the connections as required. Recharge the battery if necessary.
2. If cranking speed does not sound normal, clean and tighten all starter solenoid connections and the battery ground on the engine.
3. Repeat Step 1. If the cranking speed is still too slow, replace the starter.

Starter solenoid clicks, starter does not crank

1. Clean and tighten all starter and solenoid connections. Make sure the terminal eyelets are securely fastened to the wire strands and are not corroded.
2. Connect the jumper cables. If the starter still does not crank, replace it.

Starter solenoid chatters (no click), starter does not crank

1. Place the transmission in NEUTRAL or PARK.
2. Remove the purple wire at the solenoid. Connect a jumper wire between this solenoid connector and the positive battery post.
3. Try starting the engine. If it starts, check the ignition switch, neutral switch or starting circuit wiring for loose connections. If the engine does not start, replace the solenoid.

Starter spins but does not crank

Remove the starter. Check the armature shaft for corrosion. If there is none, the starter drive mechanism is slipping. Replace the starter with a new or rebuilt unit.

Starter Solenoid Replacement

1. Disconnect the negative battery cable.
2. Remove the plastic protective cover from the solenoid electrical connectors, if so equipped.
3. Disconnect the field strap at the starter from the motor terminal.
4. Remove the solenoid-to-drive housing screws and the motor terminal bolt.
5. Rotate the solenoid 90° and remove from the drive housing with the plunger return or torsion spring.
6. Installation is the reverse of removal.

Starter Removal/Installation

Refer to **Figure 14** (V8 engine), **Figure 15** (V6 engine) or **Figure 16** (4-cylinder engine) for this procedure.
1. Disconnect the negative battery cable.
2. Set the parking brake and place the transmission in PARK or 1st gear. Jack up the front of the car and place it on jackstands.
3. Remove the plastic protective cover from the solenoid electrical connectors. Disconnect the starter cable and solenoid wires.
4. Remove the starter braces, shields and brackets as necessary.
5. Remove the starter mounting bolts. Remove the starter.
6. Installation is the reverse of removal. Reinstall any shims that were removed to

8

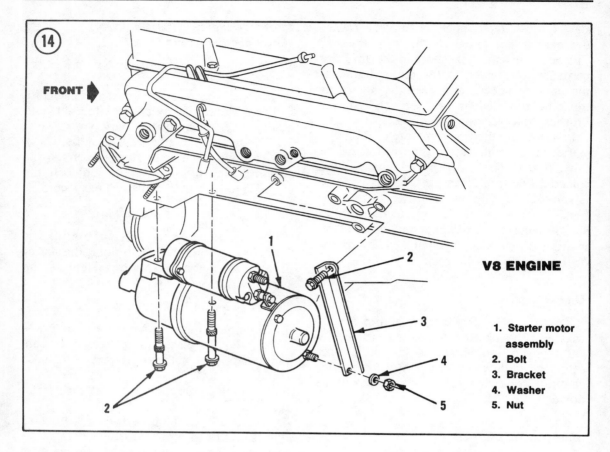

(14)

FRONT ▶

V8 ENGINE

1. Starter motor
   assembly
2. Bolt
3. Bracket
4. Washer
5. Nut

assure proper pinion-to-flywheel mesh. Tighten the mounting bolts to 26-37 ft.-lb. (36-50 N•m).

Starter Brush Replacement

Brush replacement requires partial disassembly of the starter. Refer to **Figure 17** for this procedure.

1. Remove the 2 through bolts, commutator end frame and insulator washer.
2. Separate the field frame from the drive housing. Remove the armature and washer.
3. Remove the brush holder from the brush support.
4. Remove the brush holder screw. Separate the brush and holder.
5. Inspect the plastic brush holder for cracks or broken mounting pads.
6. Check the brushes for length and condition. Replace all if any are worn to 1/4 in. or less in length.
7. Reverse Steps 1-4 to assemble the starter.

IGNITION SYSTEM

The ignition system consists of the battery, a breakerless distributor, ignition coil, ignition switch, ignition module, spark plugs and connecting primary and secondary wiring.

All engines use a High Energy Ignition (HEI) distributor with Electronic Spark Timing (EST). All changes in ignition timing are controlled by an electronic control module (ECM) based on data received from various engine sensors. A backup spark advance system is used to signal the ignition module in the distributor if the ECM should fail.

Some engines also use Electronic Spark Control (ESC). ESC retards spark advance when an electronic controller senses engine detonation. The retard mode is held for 20 seconds, then spark control returns to EST.

A magnetic pickup assembly in the HEI distributor contains a permanent magnet, a

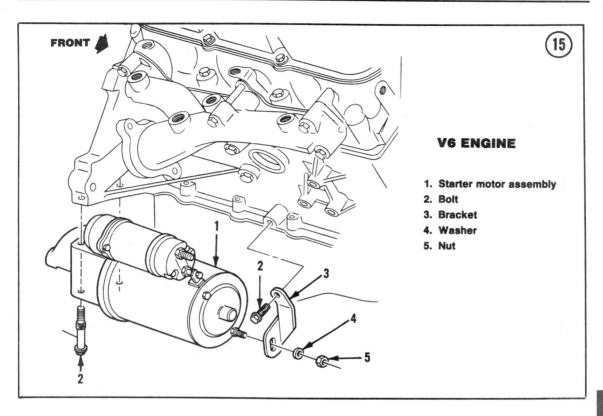

V6 ENGINE

1. Starter motor assembly
2. Bolt
3. Bracket
4. Washer
5. Nut

8

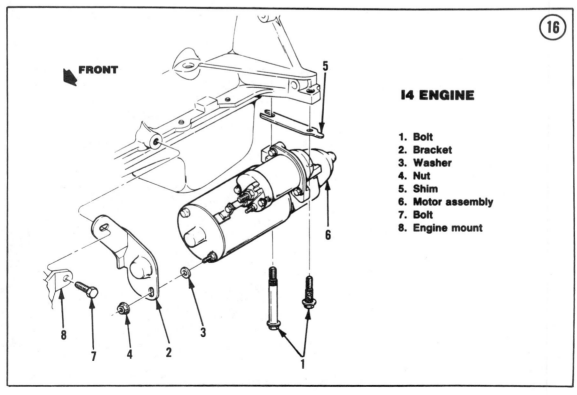

I4 ENGINE

1. Bolt
2. Bracket
3. Washer
4. Nut
5. Shim
6. Motor assembly
7. Bolt
8. Engine mount

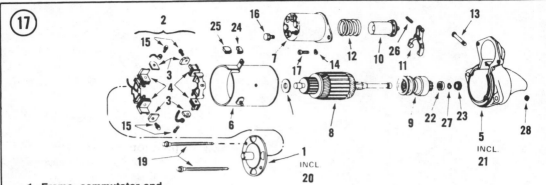

1. Frame, commutator end
2. Brush and holder package
3. Brush
4. Brush holder
5. Housing, drive end
6. Frame and field assembly
7. Solenoid switch
8. Armature
9. Drive assembly
10. Plunger
11. Shift lever
12. Plunger return springer
13. Shift lever shaft
14. Lockwasher
15. Screw, brush attaching
16. Screw, field lead to switch
17. Screw, switch attaching
18. Washer, brake
19. Through bolt
20. Bushing, commutator end
21. Bushing, drive end
22. Pinion stop collar
23. Thrust collar
24. Grommet
25. Grommet
26. Plunger pin
27. Pinion stop retainer ring
28. Lever shaft retaining ring

pole piece with internal teeth and a pickup coil. A timer core with external teeth rotates inside the pole piece. When the timer core teeth align with the pole piece teeth, a voltage is induced in the pickup coil. This voltage signal is sent to an electronic module in the distributor. The module breaks the coil primary circuit, inducing a high voltage in the ignition coil secondary windings. This high voltage is sent to the distributor where it is directed to the appropriate spark plug by the rotor.

A radio noise suppression capacitor is located in the distributor.

Distributor Removal/Installation

The V6 (**Figure 18**) and V8 (**Figure 19**) distributors are mounted vertically at the rear of the engine block.

The 4-cylinder distributor is mounted at the rear of the engine block on the passenger's side.

The V6 and V8 distributors can be removed without difficulty, but the 4-cylinder distributor can only be removed from under the vehicle. On Camaro and Firebird models with the 4-cylinder engine, it will be necessary to jack up the front of the car, place it on

4. Release the coil connectors from the distributor cap.

5. Rotate the distributor cap latches counterclockwise with a screwdriver. The V8 distributor uses 4 latches; the V6 and 4-cylinder distributors use 2 latches. Remove the cap and set it to one side out of the way.

6. Disconnect the 4-terminal ECM harness at the distributor.

7. Mark the position of the distributor housing and block. Note the rotor position.

8. Remove the distributor clamp screw and clamp. See **Figure 21** (V8 distributor shown). It may be necessary to retrieve the screw and clamp with a magnetic tool on the V6 engine.

NOTE
The oil pump drive shaft may come out with the distributor. Be sure to reinstall it when you reinstall the distributor.

9. Pull upward on the distributor with a rotating motion. As the drive gear disengages from the camshaft drive gear, the rotor will move slightly.

10. Installation is the reverse of removal. If the engine has been turned over with the distributor out, repeat Step 2. Align the distributor and block marks made in Step 7. When the distributor engages the camshaft drive gear, the rotor will turn slightly and the distributor will seat fully.

8

jackstands and remove the right front wheel to provide access to the distributor. On V6 and V8 engines, you may find it more convenient to remove the air cleaner before attempting distributor removal.

1. Disconnect the negative battery cable.

2. Turn the engine over by hand until the No. 1 cylinder is at top dead center on its compression stroke. The 0 degree mark on the timing tab will align with the notch scribed on the pulley and the distributor rotor will point to the No. 1 terminal in the distributor cap.

3. Disconnect the wiring harness at the distributor. See **Figure 20** (V8 distributor shown).

**Ignition Coil Replacement
(4-cylinder and V6 Engine)**

The V6 coil is bracket-mounted on the right-hand side of the engine. The 4-cylinder coil is bracket-mounted to the inner right-hand fender behind the battery.

1. Disconnect the negative battery cable.

2. Disconnect the electrical connector and coil wire.

3A. V6 coil—Remove the 4 screws holding the coil to the bracket. Remove the coil.

3B. 4-cylinder coil—Remove the 2 bolts holding the coil bracket. Remove the coil and bracket.

4. Installation is the reverse of removal.

Ignition Coil Replacement
(V8 Engine)

The coil is mounted in the distributor cap. Remove the cap. Remove the coil cover attaching screws and cover. Remove the coil attaching screws. Lift coil and leads from distributor cap. See **Figure 22**.

Ignition Module Replacement

The module is located inside the distributor. See **Figure 23**. Replacement can be made with the distributor in the engine, but it will be far easier to remove the distributor for module replacement.

1. Disconnect the negative battery cable.
2. Remove the distributor as described in this chapter.
3. Remove the distributor rotor attaching screws. Remove the rotor.
4. Disconnect the wiring connectors at each end of the module. Remove the 2 module screws. Remove the module.

NOTE
The module base which mates against the distributor base is covered with silicone grease to protect the module from heat. Apply the packet of grease accompanying the new module to its base before installation.

5. Wipe the distributor base and the module with a clean, dry cloth. Apply silicone grease to the distributor and module base before installing the new module.
6. Installation is the reverse of removal.

LIGHTING SYSTEM

Headlights

Rectangular combination high/low halogen lamps are standard equipment on all Firebird models. Individual rectangular high and low sealed-beam lamps are standard on all Camaro models, with a halogen inboard lamp optional. Always replace a burned-out headlight with another of the same type. While halogen and ordinary sealed-beam lamps are physically interchangeable, the wiring circuitry is different.

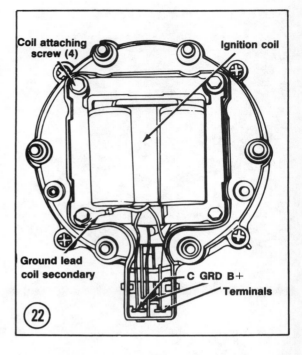

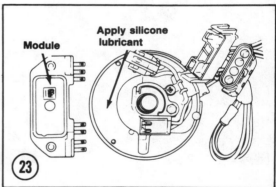

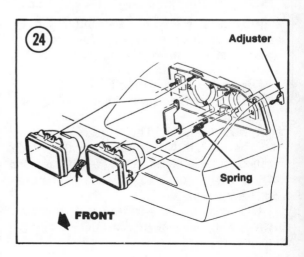

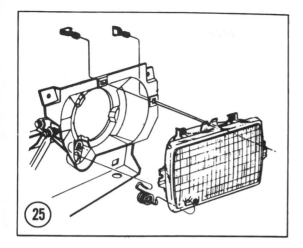

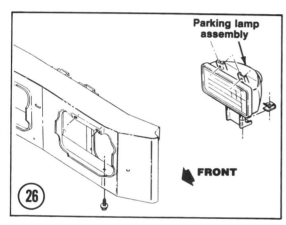

Parking lamp assembly

FRONT

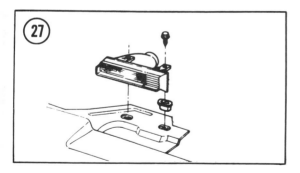

3. Remove the retaining ring. Disconnect the lamp at the wiring connector. Remove the lamp.

NOTE
The inboard lamp has a dual connector plug; the outboard lamp has a triple plug.

4. Attach the wiring connector to the new lamp. Place the lamp in position with the number molded into the lens face at the top.
5. Install the retaining ring. Expand the spring with the cotter pin tool and connect it to the retaining ring.
6. Install the headlamp bezel.
7. Check operation of the lights. Have headlight aim checked by a dealer or official lamp adjusting station.

Replacement
(Firebird)

Refer to **Figure 25** for this procedure.
1. Turn the light switch to bring the headlights into position. Do not turn lights on.
2. Remove the 4 headlight bezel screws and bezel.
3. Pull the retaining spring to one side with a cotter pin removal tool and disengage the spring from the headlight.
4A. Rotate the right headlight clockwise to release it from the aiming pins.
4B. Rotate the left headlight counterclockwise to release it from the aiming pins.
5. Disconnect the wiring connector from the back of the bulb.
6. Remove the retaining ring.
7. Installation is the reverse of removal.

Front Park/Turn Signal Lamp

Refer to **Figure 26** (Camaro) or **Figure 27** (Firebird) for this procedure.
To replace the bulb, turn the socket at the rear of the housing a partial turn and remove from the housing. Depress the bulb in the socket, rotate counterclockwise and remove. Installation is the reverse of removal.
To replace the housing, remove the headlamp bezel. Remove 2 screws inside the

Replacement
(Camaro)

Refer to **Figure 24** for this procedure.
1. Open the hood. Remove the headlamp bezel retaining screws and bezel.
2. Use a cotter pin removal tool to disengage the retaining ring spring. Remove the 2 attaching screws.

8

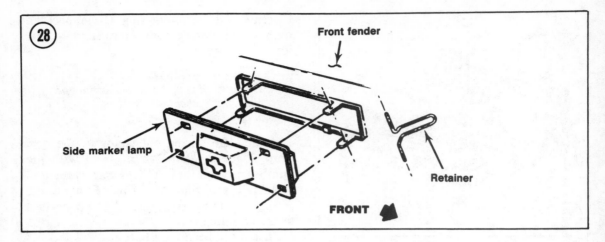

headlamp housing. Remove the housing. Installation is the reverse of removal.

Side Marker Lamp and Lens

Refer to **Figure 28** for this procedure.
1. Reach up under the front fender and turn the bulb socket counterclockwise 90° to remove from the housing.
2. Depress bulb in socket, rotate counterclockwise and remove.
3. Reverse Step 1 and Step 2 to install new bulb.
4. If housing removal is required, remove the retainer clips and remove housing.
5. To install the housing, position against the fender and install the retainer clips.

Rear Lamp Assembly Service

Refer to **Figure 29** for this procedure. All rear lamp bulbs are replaced by removing the rear trim panel screws and removing the panel. Remove the 5 wing nuts at the lamp assembly and remove the assembly. Depress and turn the individual sockets counterclockwise to remove them from the lamp assembly. Depress bulb in socket, rotate counterclockwise and remove. Replacement is the reverse of removal.

Dome Lamp Replacement

1. Grasp the dome lamp lens and squeeze it as you pull downward.
2. Remove the bulb from the terminal clips.
3. If lamp housing is to be removed, remove the stud retainers. Disconnect the wiring

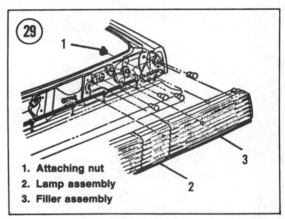

1. Attaching nut
2. Lamp assembly
3. Filler assembly

harness from the housing and remove the housing.
4. Installation is the reverse of removal.

Instrument Lights

The instrument cluster must be removed to replace any lamp. See *Instruments* in this chapter.

IGNITION SWITCH

A blade-type terminal switch with one multiple connector is used. The switch is attached to the steering column with a stud and a screw. The dimmer light switch is attached in such a way that it must be removed in order to remove the ignition switch.

Removal

1. Disconnect the negative battery cable.

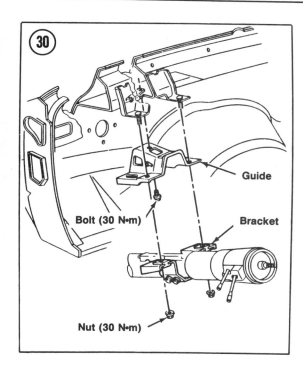

Guide

Bolt (30 N•m)

Bracket

Nut (30 N•m)

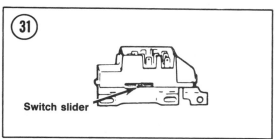

Switch slider

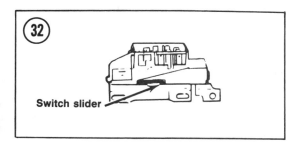

Switch slider

2. Remove the steering column trim panel cover screws and cover.

3. Remove the support bracket bolts (**Figure 30**). Lower the steering column.

4. Disconnect the ignition switch connector.

5. Remove the dimmer switch fasteners. Disengage the switch from its actuator rod and remove.

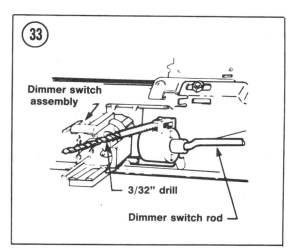

Dimmer switch assembly

3/32" drill

Dimmer switch rod

6. Remove the ignition switch fasteners. Disengage the switch from its actuator rod and remove from the steering column.

Installation

1A. Standard column—If equipped with key release feature, position the ignition switch slider to the extreme left as shown in **Figure 31**, then move it 2 detents to the right.

1B. Tilt column—Position the switch slider to the extreme right (**Figure 32**), then move it 2 detents to the left.

2. Install the actuator rod in the switch slider hole.

3. Install the switch to the steering column and tighten the lower stud to 35 in.-lb. (3.9 N•m).

4. Install the dimmer switch and depress it sufficiently to insert a 3/32 in. drill as shown in **Figure 33**.

5. Move the dimmer switch upward to remove all lash, then tighten the attaching screws and nut to 35 in.-lb. (3.9 N•m).

6. Reverse Steps 1-4 of *Removal* procedure.

Testing

1. Perform Steps 1-4 of *Ignition Switch Removal* in this chapter.

2. Identify the switch terminals according to **Figure 34**.

3. Test the switch with an ohmmeter or a self-powered test lamp. There should be continuity in each switch position as shown in **Table 2**.

8

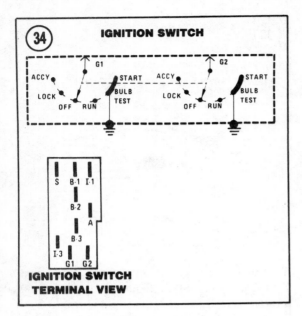

IGNITION SWITCH

IGNITION SWITCH
TERMINAL VIEW

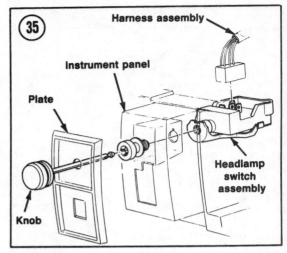

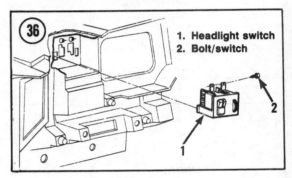

1. Headlight switch
2. Bolt/switch

HEADLIGHT SWITCH

The combination 3-position headlight switch is mounted in the lower left of the instrument panel on Camaros. It controls circuits to the headlights, parking/marker and tail lights, license plate, interior and instrument panel lights.

The rocker-type light switch used on Firebirds is mounted at the upper left of the instrument panel. It controls the same circuits as the Camaro switch, as well as the headlight retractors.

The switch must be removed on either car for continuity testing.

Removal/Installation
(Camaro)

Refer to **Figure 35** for this procedure.
1. Disconnect the negative battery cable.
2. Remove the upper instrument panel pad. See Chapter Thirteen.
3. On air conditioned vehicles, remove the instrument panel cluster bezel and cluster as described in this chapter.
4. Remove speaker bracket.
5. Remove knob and shaft at switch. Remove switch bezel.
6. Disconnect electrical connector. Remove the switch.
7. Installation is the reverse of removal.

Removal/Installation
(Firebird)

Refer to **Figure 36** for this procedure.
1. Disconnect the negative battery cable.
2. Remove the right and left lower trim plates.
3. Remove the instrument panel cluster trim plate.
4. Remove 2 switch assembly retaining screws.
5. Depress the side tangs and pull the switch assembly from the instrument panel. Disconnect the wiring connector at the switch. Remove the switch from the switch assembly.
6. Installation is the reverse of removal.

Testing

1. With the switch removed, identify the terminals according to **Figure 37** (Camaro) or **Figure 38** (Firebird).

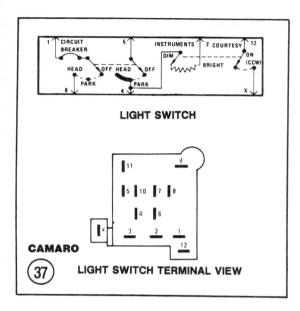

LIGHT SWITCH

CAMARO

LIGHT SWITCH TERMINAL VIEW

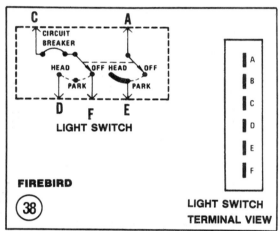

LIGHT SWITCH

FIREBIRD

(38)

LIGHT SWITCH
TERMINAL VIEW

2. Test the switch with an ohmmeter or self-powered test lamp.

Wiper/Washer Switch Testing

1. Remove multi-function lever wiring harness from the 3-terminal connector at the wiper motor. Turn the ignition ON.

2. Ground one lead of a 12-volt test lamp and probe the center terminal of the multi-function lever harness with the other lead. The lamp should light.

3. Move the multi-function lever to the low-speed position. Connect the probe lead of the test lamp to the positive battery terminal with a jumper wire.

4. Probe each outer harness terminal. The test lamp should light at either terminal.

5. Move the multi-function lever to the high-speed position. Probe each outer harness terminal as in Step 4. The test lamp should light at only one outer terminal.

6. Move the multi-function lever to the OFF position. Repeat Step 5. The test lamp should light at the opposite outer terminal.

7. If the test lamp does not light as specified in Steps 2-6, replace the multi-function switch.

Removal/Installation

1. Remove the ignition and dimmer switches as described in this chapter.

2. Disconnect the switch wiring connector.

3. Remove the switch actuator rack assembly.

4. Remove the pivot and switch assembly.

5. Installation is the reverse of removal. Assemble the rack with its first tooth between the first and second teeth of the sector.

COOLANT TEMPERATURE SWITCH

Vehicles with a standard cluster use a temperature warning lamp in the instrument panel. Those equipped with the optional gauge cluster have a temperature gauge. Both types are controlled by a thermal switch in the thermostat housing which senses coolant temperature. See **Figure 39**.

8

Testing

1. Remove the temperature switch as described in this chapter. See **Figure 40** (4-cylinder engine), **Figure 41** (V6 engine) or **Figure 42** (V8 engine) for switch location.

2. Measure the resistance across the terminals with an ohmmeter. The resistance should be approximately 350 ohms at a temperature of 100° F.

3. Place the switch in a pan of coolant and heat the pan until the coolant comes to a rapid boil.

4. Repeat Step 2. The resistance should drop considerably at a temperature of about 260° F, indicating that the switch has closed.

5. Replace the switch if it does not meet the specifications in Step 2 and Step 4.

Replacement

> *NOTE*
> *Remove the radiator cap to relieve any pressure when installing a new coolant temperature switch.*

Refer to **Figure 40** (4-cylinder engine), **Figure 41** (V6 engine) or **Figure 42** (V8 engine) for this procedure.

1. Disconnect the electrical lead at the switch. Remove the switch.

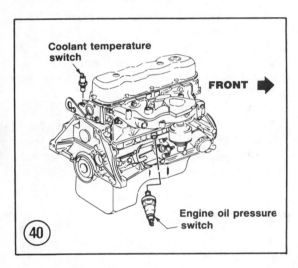

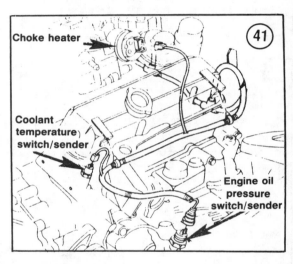

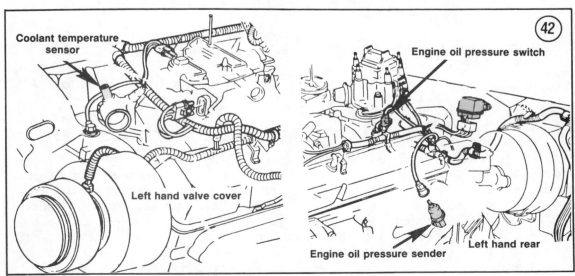

2. Wrap a piece of Teflon tape around the threads of the new switch. Teflon paste or other electrically conductive water-resistant sealers can also be used.

3. Install the new switch and torque to 72 in.-lb. (7 N•m).

4. Reconnect the electrical lead to the switch terminal.

OIL PRESSURE SWITCH

Refer to **Figure 40** (4-cylinder engine), **Figure 41** (V6 engine) or **Figure 42** (V8 engine) for oil pressure switch location.

If the oil pressure warning light does not come on when the ignition is turned to START and the engine is not running, disconnect the wiring connector and ground it to the engine block. If the warning light comes on, replace the oil pressure switch. If the warning light still does not come on, check for a burned-out bulb or an open in the wiring between the bulb and the oil pressure switch.

If the oil pressure warning light remains on with the engine running, check the oil level in the crankcase. If the level is satisfactory, check the switch wiring for a short. If none is found, replace the oil pressure switch.

INSTRUMENTS

Current is supplied to the instrument cluster gauges and lamps by a printed circuit. This is made of copper foil bonded to a polyester base such as Mylar. There is no approved procedure for in-vehicle testing of the printed circuit. Using a probe may pierce the printed circuit or burn the copper conductor. If no damage seems apparent, check each circuit with a test light or ohmmeter. If an open or short circuit is found, replace the printed circuit board.

Instrument Cluster Removal/Installation

Camaro

Refer to **Figure 43** for this procedure.

1. Disconnect the negative battery cable.

2. Remove the bezel attaching screws and bezel.

3. Remove 6 cluster attaching screws. Pull cluster forward and disconnect the speedometer cable and electrical connectors.

4. Remove the cluster lens to provide access to individual gauges for service.

5. Installation is the reverse of removal.

Firebird

Refer to **Figure 44** and **Figure 45** for this procedure.

1. Remove the right and left lower trim plates. Remove instrument cluster trim plate.

2. Remove 6 cluster attaching screws. Pull cluster forward and disconnect the speedometer cable and electrical connectors.

3. Remove the trip odometer and reset knob (if so equipped). Remove the cluster lens to provide access to individual gauges for service.

4. Installation is the reverse of removal.

Cluster Printed Circuit Board Replacement

1. Remove the instrument cluster as described in this chapter.

8

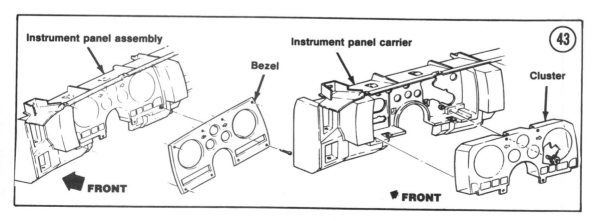

Instrument panel assembly   Instrument panel carrier   **43**

Bezel   Cluster

FRONT   **FRONT**

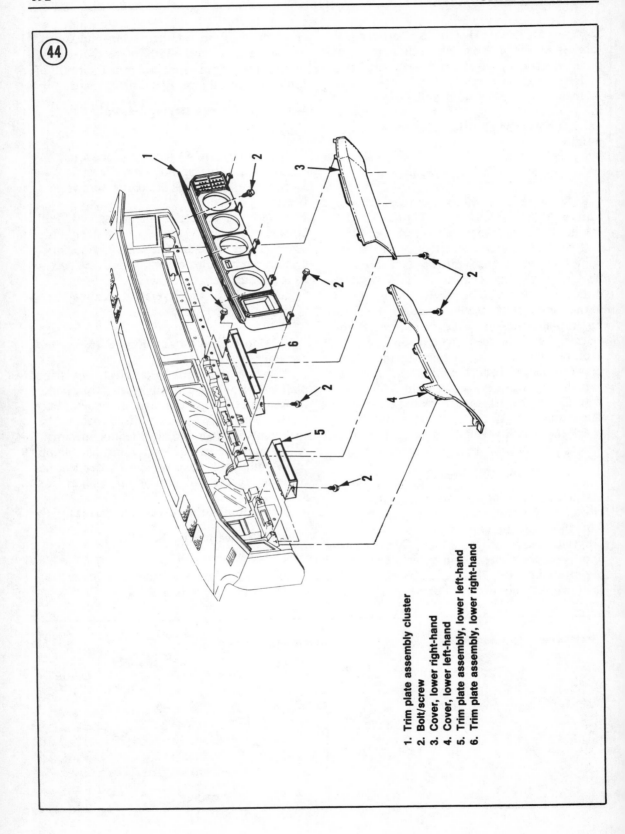

44

1. Trim plate assembly cluster
2. Bolt/screw
3. Cover, lower right-hand
4. Cover, lower left-hand
5. Trim plate assembly, lower left-hand
6. Trim plate assembly, lower right-hand

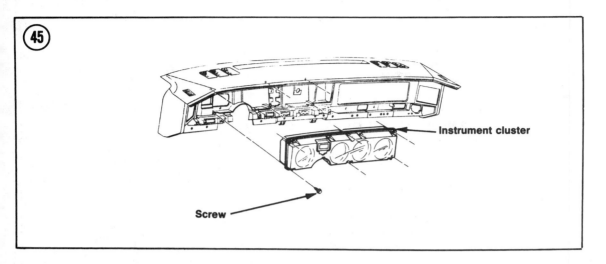

45

Instrument cluster

Screw

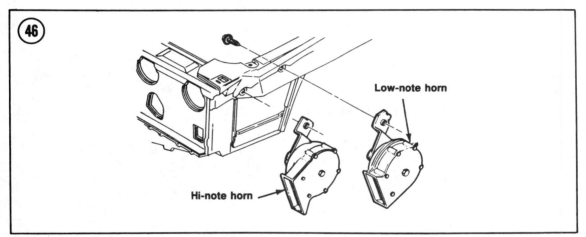

46

Low-note horn

Hi-note horn

8

2. Remove all bulbs and retaining nuts from the cluster housing.

3. Remove the printed circuit.

4. Installation is the reverse of removal.

HORN

Single or dual horns are used, depending on the model. A relay in the circuit reduces the length of heavy gauge wire required to operate the horn(s) and provides higher voltage at the horn(s). Horn location is shown in **Figure 46**.

Testing

Voltage is applied to the horn relay at all times. Depressing the horn pad grounds the relay coil and closes its contacts. If the horn does not sound, check the 20A fuse in the fuse block cavity marked CSTY, then check the horn mounting screw. The screw provides a ground for the horn circuit. If corroded or loose, clean or tighten as required.

If the horn still does not sound, disconnect the green wire at the horn. Connect a jumper wire between the positive battery terminal and the horn. The horn should sound if its ground is good. If this does not locate the problem, connect a 12-volt test lamp to the green wire and press the horn pad on the steering wheel. If the horn still does not work, the problem is either a defective horn relay or a disconnected wire under the horn pad. Remove the horn pad and check for bent metal contacts or a disconnected wire. If none are found, test the relay.

Relay Testing

1. Ground the horn relay coil. The relay is located in the convenience center on the left-hand side of the dash panel near the fuse box. See **Figure 47**.

2. If the horn sounds, disconnect the black relay lead. If the horn stops sounding with the lead disconnected, the horn switch is faulty. If the horn continues to sound, isolate the relay from the circuit.

3. Use a self-powered test lamp and check to see if the relay contacts are open. If they are, look for a short in the black wire. If they are not open, replace the relay.

Horn Replacement

1. Disconnect the horn wire from the horn terminal.

2. Remove the horn bracket screws.

3. Remove the horn and bracket from the engine compartment.

4. Remove the horn from the bracket.

5. Installation is the reverse of removal.

WINDSHIELD WIPERS AND WASHERS

Camaro/Firebird models use a 2-speed wiper motor with attached washer pump mounted in the center of the bulkhead (**Figure 48**). An optional pulse wiper system uses a depressed park motor. The wiper arms and blades park above the windshield lower molding. The washer reservoir (**Figure 49**) is connected to the pump by a rubber hose.

> *NOTE*
> *The wiper motor uses locking-type connectors. Disconnect these carefully when wiper testing or replacement is necessary.*

Wiper Troubleshooting

1. If the wipers do not work, check the 25 amp fuse in the fuse block cavity marked **WIPER**. See *Fuses and Fusible Links* in this chapter.

2. If the wipers do not work with a good fuse, connect a jumper wire from the wiper motor housing to the car body and test for ground. Ground is supplied by a ground strap and the

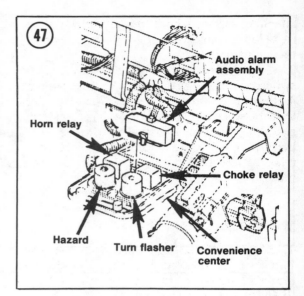

attaching screws. Check the screws and strap for a loose connection or corrosion. Clean or tighten as necessary.

3. If the wipers still do not work, check wiper switch continuity as described in this chapter.

4. If switch continuity is good, run a jumper wire between the positive battery terminal and the motor terminal accepting the black/pink wire. If the motor runs, replace the relay switch. If it does not run, replace the motor.

Wiper Motor Current Draw Test

1. Remove the 25 amp fuse from the fuse block cavity marked WIPER. Connect an ammeter across the fuse cavity terminals.

2. Turn the ignition switch ON. Run the wipers at high speed with the windshield dry. The normal current draw is a maximum 5 amps.

3. A current draw of less than 5 amps indicates a weak internal circuit breaker, open armature or bad brushes.

4. A current draw in excess of 5 amps indicates a shorted armature, defective gearbox relay or binding in the motor.

Wiper Motor Replacement

NOTE
Wiper motors contain ceramic permanent magnets. Handle the motor carefully and do not tap with a hammer or the magnets may be damaged.

1. Disconnect the negative battery cable.

2. Remove the cowl vent screen. See Chapter Thirteen.

3. Remove drive link(s) from motor crank arm.

4. Disconnect wiring and washer hoses.

5. Remove 3 motor attaching screws.

6. Remove motor while guiding crank arm through the hole.

7. Installation is the reverse of removal. Be sure motor is in park position before connecting crank arm to drive link(s). Tighten the attaching screws to 30-45 in.-lb. (4-5 N•m).

Washer Reservoir Replacement

Figure 49 shows the washer reservoir. To remove, disconnect the fluid hose. Remove the retaining screws and lift the assembly from the bulkhead. Installation is the reverse of removal.

CAUTION
Do not operate the washer pump without fluid in the reservoir.

Washer Pump Replacement

1. Remove the washer hoses from the pump.

2. Disconnect the wires from the pump relay.

3. Remove the plastic pump cover.

4. Remove the attaching screws holding the pump frame to the motor gearbox. Remove the pump and frame.

FUSES AND FUSIBLE LINKS

Camaro/Firebird models use a single fuse block containing mini-fuses and circuit breakers. In addition, a convenience center contains the audio alarm (headlight buzzer) assembly, horn relay, choke relay, turn signal and hazard flashers.

The fuse block is a swing-down unit mounted on the underside of the instrument panel to the left of the steering column and is protected by a plastic cover. To gain access to the fuse block, rotate the knob at the rear of the plastic cover a partial turn in either direction, swing the rear of the cover downward and remove. Fuse and circuit breaker identification is shown in **Figure 50**.

The convenience center is a swing-down unit mounted on the underside of the instrument panel to the right of the steering column (**Figure 51**). This provides a central access to buzzers, relays and flasher units. All are plug-in units.

Mini-fuses are identified by a numbered ampere value and a color code. Some colors make it difficult to determine whether the fuse is good or bad. Terminals on each side permit testing with a test light or volt/ohmmeter without removing the fuse from the fuse block. **Figure 52** shows a blown fuse, test points and mini-fuse color codes.

8

⑤⓪

* (30) on Camaro

No.	Name	Color/Size (amps)	Circuit Protected	Cavity Protected/Cavity Connector Color
1.	Ecm ign	Red (10)	Computer command control	
2.	Fuel pump	Yellow (20)	Electronic fuel injection	
3.	Radio	Red (10)	Radio, cruise control	Radio
4.	Stop haz.	Yellow (20)	Audio alarm system (chime/buzzer) Lights: stop, turn	
5.	Tail	Yellow (20)	Lights: Front park/front marker Lights: Tail/rear marker License, radio	
6.	C-h	Yellow (20)	Choke heater	
7.	Htr a/c	White (25)	Air conditioning, heater	
8.	CSTY	Yellow (20)	Cargo compartment light Electronic fuel injection (V8 only) Hatch release, horn, cigar lighter Interior lights, power antenna Power remote mirrors, radio/digital clock	BAT (black)
9.	Wdo Circuit breaker	(35)*	Power windows	Wdo (orange)
10.	Pwr acc Circuit breaker	(35)*	Defogger, power door locks, power seats	Pwr acc (green)
11.	Crank	Purple (3)	Charging system Electronic fuel injection	
12.	Wiper	White (25)	Wiper-washer	
13.	Inst	Tan (5)	Audio alarm system (chime/buzzer) Lights: instrument panel	Lp
14.	Gauges	Red (10)	Audio alarm system (chime/buzzer) Computer command control Charging system, choke heater Electronic fuel injection, gauges Rear window defogger, warning indicators	Ign (white)
15.	Turn b/u	Yellow (20)	Back-up lights, turn lights	
16.	Tbi inj 1	Purple (3)	Electronic fuel injection (V8 only)	
17.	Tbi inj 2	Purple (3)	Electronic fuel injection (V8 only)	

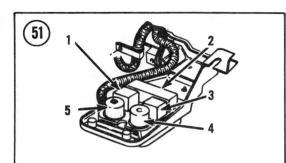

1. Horn relay
2. Seat belt, ignition key, headlight buzzer
3. Choke relay (not used with EFI)
4. Hazard flash
5. Signal flash

To test for blown mini fuse:

1. Pull fuse out and check visually.
2. With the circuit activated, use a test light across the points shown.

MINI FUSE COLOR CODE	
Rating	Color
5 amp	Tan
10 amp	Red
20 amp	Yellow
25 amp	White

To replace, pull out the old mini-fuse. Be sure to install a new one of the same color. Whenever a fuse blows, find out the cause before replacing it. Usually, the trouble is a short circuit in the wiring. This may be caused by worn-through insulation or by a wire that works its way loose and touches metal. Carry several spare fuses of the proper amperage values in the glove compartment.

Fusible Links

These are short lengths of wire smaller in gauge than the wire in the circuit. They are covered with a thick non-flammable insulation and are intended to burn out if an overload occurs, thus protecting the wiring harness and accessories. All models use 5 fusible links. A 14 gauge red wire/molded splice is installed at the starter solenoid BAT terminal. A 16 gauge red wire is located at the junction block to protect all unfused 12 gauge or larger wiring. A 20 gauge red wire/molded splice installed at the junction block protects the alternator warning light and field circuitry. Two 20 gauge red wire/molded splices are installed at the junction block to protect the battery-to-starter circuit.

> *CAUTION*
> *Always replace a burned fusible link with a replacement bearing the same color code or wire gauge. Never use ordinary wire, as this can cause an overload, an electrical fire and complete loss of the vehicle.*

Burned-out fusible links can usually be detected by melted or burned insulation. When the link appears to be good but the starter does not work, check the circuit for continuity with an ohmmeter or a self-powered test lamp.

TURN SIGNALS

> *NOTE*
> *The turn signal flasher is located in the convenience center.*

Testing

1. *One side flashes later than the other or only one side operates:* Check for a burned-out

8

bulb. Clean socket of any corrosion. Check for a badly grounded bulb. Check for breaks in the wiring.

2. *Turn signals do not work at all:* Check the 20 amp fuse in the fuse block cavity marked TURN B/U by operating the backup lights. If the fuse is good, check the wiring for a break or poor connection. If the wiring is good, install a new flasher unit.

3. *Lights flash slowly or stay on:* Make sure the battery is fully charged. Check the fuse in the TURN B/U cavity for a poor contact. Check for a break or poor connection in the wiring. If none of these problems are found, replace the flasher.

4. *Lights flash too quickly:* Check for a burned-out bulb or disconnected wire. If none are found, replace the flasher.

HAZARD FLASHER

The hazard flasher is identical in appearance to the turn signal flasher. It is located in the convenience center.

Testing

1. Check the 20 amp fuse in the fuse block cavity marked STOP/HAZ by operating the stoplights.
2. If the fuse is good and the turn signals operate on both sides, replace the hazard flasher.

Table 1 STATE OF BATTERY CHARGE

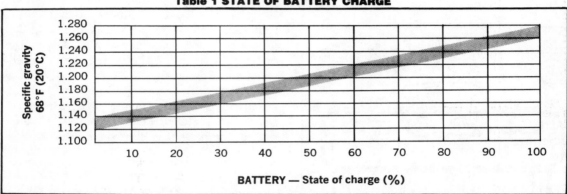

Table 2 IGNITION SWITCH CHECK

Switch Position	Terminals
OFF	All open
START	GRD 1 and GRD 2—grounded
	IGN 1, BAT 1 and SOL—connected
RUN	IGN 1, BAT 1 and ACC—connected
	BAT 2, BAT 3 and IGN 3—connected
ACCESSORY	ACC and BAT 2—connected
(BAT 1, 2 and 3 terminals are common).	

NOTE: If you own a 1983 or later model, first check the Supplement at the back of the book for any new service information.

CHAPTER NINE

CLUTCH AND TRANSMISSION

All vehicles with the 4-cylinder or V6 engine use a Muncie 4-speed manual transmission as standard equipment. Those equipped with the V8 engine use a Borg-Warner 4-speed manual transmission as standard equipment. The 3-speed Turbo Hydramatic 200C automatic transmission is optional.

Power is transmitted from the engine to the transmission, then to the differential where it is sent to the axle shafts which turn the wheel hubs. Manual transmissions are connected to the engine by the clutch; automatic transmissions are connected to the engine by a torque converter.

This chapter provides inspection, repair and replacement procedures for the clutch and manual transmission, as well as inspection and replacement procedures for the automatic transmission. Automatic transmission repair requires special skills and tools and should be left to a dealer or other qualified shop. The inspection procedures will tell you if repairs are necessary. Tightening torques are provided in **Table 1** at the end of the chapter.

CLUTCH

Major clutch components are the flywheel, driven plate or disc, pressure plate/cover assembly, clutch fork and clutch release bearing (**Figure 1**). The clutch operating system consists of the pedal/bracket assembly, clutch linkage and clutch lever.

The linkage transmits pedal pressure to the clutch lever assembly. As the clutch fork pivots on its shaft, the inner end pushes against the release bearing. The bearing pushes against the release levers in the pressure plate/cover assembly, releasing the clutch.

Parts Identification

Some clutch parts have 2 or more names. To prevent confusion, the following list gives part names used in this chapter and common synonyms.

    a. Clutch fork—Release fork, throw-out arm, withdrawal lever.
    b. Pressure plate—Pressure plate assembly, clutch cover.
    c. Disc—Driven plate.
    d. Release bearing—Throw-out bearing.

9

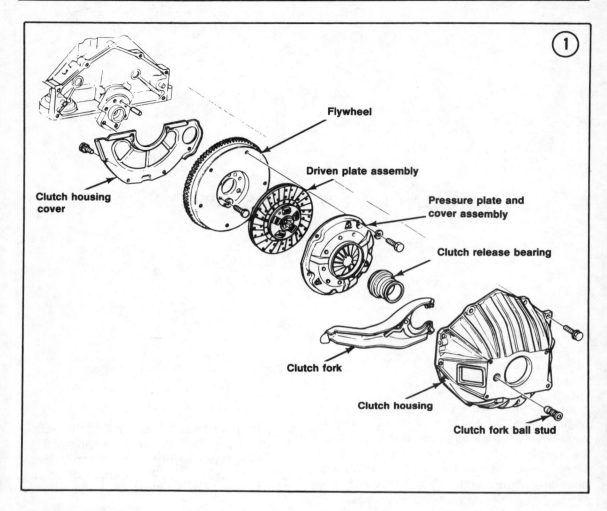

Flywheel

Driven plate assembly

Clutch housing cover

Pressure plate and cover assembly

Clutch release bearing

Clutch fork

Clutch housing

Clutch fork ball stud

Linkage Inspection

1. Start the engine and run at idle. Apply the footbrake and hold the clutch pedal approximately 1/2 in. (12 mm) from the floor mat. Shift the transmission from 1st to REVERSE several times. If this can be done smoothly, the clutch is releasing fully. If the shift is not smooth, adjust the clutch.

2. Shut the engine off and check the clutch pedal bushings for excessive wear or sticking.

3. Raise the vehicle with a jack and place it on jackstands. Check the clutch fork for proper installation on the ball stud. Insufficient fork lubrication can cause the fork to separate from the ball.

4. Check the cross shaft levers and support bracket for bending, cracking or other damage. Replace as necessary.

5. Check engine mounts. If loose or damaged, they can let the engine shift its position. This will cause binding on the clutch linkage at the cross shaft. Make sure there is clearance between the cross shaft and both mount brackets.

Pedal Free Travel Adjustment

One linkage adjustment compensates for all normal clutch wear. Refer to **Figure 2** for this procedure.

1. Disconnect the return spring at the clutch fork.

2. Rotate the clutch lever/shaft assembly to position clutch pedal firmly against dash brace rubber bumper.

3. Push outer end of clutch fork to the rear until the release bearing lightly touches the pressure plate fingers.

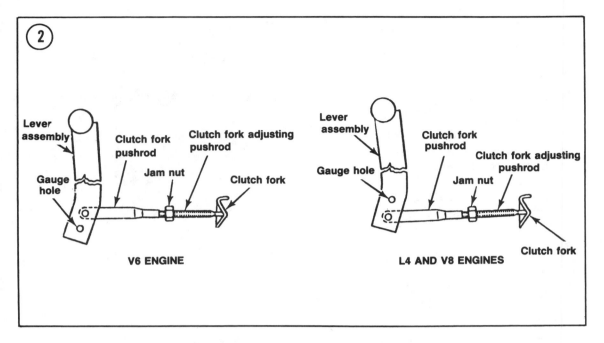

V6 ENGINE

L4 AND V8 ENGINES

4. Remove the pushrod retainer. Remove the pushrod from its hole in the lever and install in the gauge hole. Loosen the jam nut and increase the rod length until all lash is removed.

5. Remove the pushrod from the gage hole and return to its original position. Install retainer and tighten jam nut. Do not change rod length while tightening the nut.

6. Reinstall return spring. Check pedal free travel. It should be 0.875 ± 0.30 in.

Post-adjustment Check

A clutch that has been slipping may continue to slip after free play adjustment because of previous heat damage. Wait at least 12 hours after free travel adjustment to assure that clutch has adequately cooled, then perform the following procedure:

1. Drive in high gear at 20-25 mph.
2. Depress clutch pedal to the floor. Increase engine speed to 2,500-3,500 rpm.
3. Engage the clutch quickly by snapping your foot off the pedal. Depress the throttle pedal for full acceleration.

NOTE
Repeating this procedure more than once may cause the clutch to overheat and should be avoided.

4. If the clutch is working properly, engine speed should drop noticeably in Step 3, then increase with vehicle speed. If engine speed does not decrease, the clutch requires service.

Clutch Removal

1. Support the engine and remove the transmission as described in this chapter.
2. Disconnect the clutch fork pushrod and return spring.
3. Remove the flywheel housing. Slide the clutch fork off the ball stud and remove fork from dust boot.
4. Make alignment marks on the clutch cover and flywheel for reference during reassembly.
5. Insert GM tool part No. J-5824 or a dummy shaft made from an old input shaft through the clutch disc hub.

NOTE
An input shaft from a junk transmission can be used to make a dummy shaft. Inexpensive aligning bars can also be purchased from some auto parts stores. Some tool rental dealers and parts stores rent universal aligning bars which can be adapted.

6. Unbolt the clutch cover from the flywheel (**Figure 3**). Loosen the bolts in several stages

using a diagonal pattern to prevent warping the cover.

7. Remove the pressure plate and disc from the flywheel (**Figure 4**).

Clutch Disc Inspection

Check the clutch disc for the following:
a. Oil or grease on the facings.
b. Glazed or warped facings.
c. Loose or missing rivets.
d. Broken springs.
e. Loose fit or rough movement on the transmission input shaft splines.

Small amounts of oil or grease may be removed with aerosol brake cleaner and the facings dressed with a wire brush. However, if the facings are soaked with oil or grease, the clutch disc must be replaced. The disc must also be replaced if any of the other defects is present or if the facings are partially worn and a new pressure plate is being installed.

Pressure Plate Inspection

1. Check the pressure plate for:
a. Scoring.
b. Burn marks.
c. Cracks.

2. Check the diaphragm spring (**Figure 5**) for wear or damage at the release bearing contact surface. Check for bent or broken spring fingers and replace the pressure plate if found.

If the clutch trouble still is not apparent, take the pressure plate and disc to a competent machine shop. Have the disc and pressure plate checked for runout and the diaphragm spring checked for correct finger height. Do not attempt to dismantle the pressure plate or readjust the fingers yourself without the proper tools and experience.

Clutch Installation

1. Be sure your hands are clean and free of oil or grease.

2. Make sure the disc facings, pressure plate and flywheel are free of oil, grease and other foreign material.

3. Place the clutch disc and pressure plate in position on the flywheel. The side of the disc stamped "FLYWHEEL" should face the flywheel when assembled.

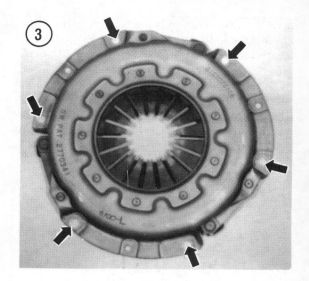

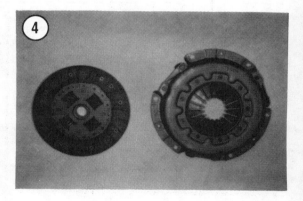

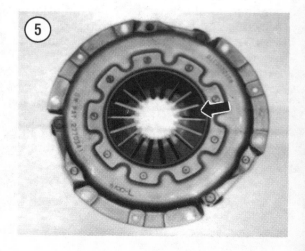

4. If the old pressure plate is being reinstalled, be sure the alignment marks on the clutch cover and flywheel are lined up.

5. Start but do not tighten the cover bolts. Center the disc and pressure plate with GM tool part No. J-5824. A dummy shaft can also be used for alignment.

6. Tighten the cover bolts gradually in a diagonal pattern to specifications. Remove alignment tool.

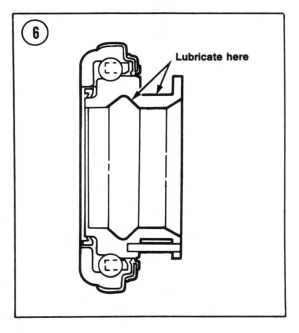

7. Lubricate the clutch fork fingers and ball socket at the release bearing end with graphite grease and install the fork on the ball stud.

8. Lubricate release bearing collar and clutch fork groove with graphite grease, as shown in **Figure 6**.

9. Install the clutch fork and dust boot in the clutch housing.

10. Install release bearing on clutch fork. Install flywheel housing and tighten bolts to specifications.

11. Install transmission as described in this chapter.

12. Connect the clutch fork pushrod and return spring. Lubricate spring and pushrod ends.

13. Adjust pedal free travel.

Clutch Pedal
Removal/Installation

Refer to **Figure 7** for this procedure.

1. Disconnect the negative battery cable.

2. Disconnect the clutch pedal return spring.

3. Remove the hush pad from underneath the dash.

4. Remove the cruise control switch at the clutch pedal, if so equipped.

5. Disconnect the clutch pedal rod from the pedal. Remove the pedal pivot bolt nut. Pull the bolt out far enough to remove the pedal.

6. Installation is the reverse of removal.

9

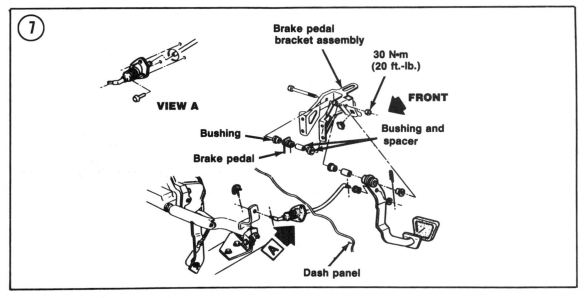

Clutch Cross Shaft
Removal/Installation

Refer to **Figure 8** for this procedure.

1. Remove return spring. Disconnect clutch pedal and fork pushrods from their respective cross shaft levers.

2. Loosen outboard ball stud nut. Slide stud from bracket slot.

3. Move cross shaft outward to clear the inboard ball stud, then lift out and remove from the vehicle.

4. Check cross shaft nylon ball stud seats for wear or damage.

5. Installation is the reverse of removal. Adjust clutch linkage as described in this chapter.

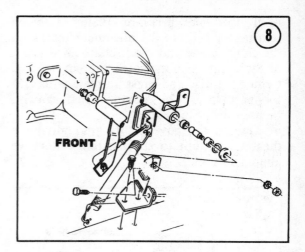

MANUAL TRANSMISSION

Two 4-speed manual transmissions are used: the light-duty Muncie 76 mm and the heavy-duty Borg-Warner 83 mm gearbox. The transmission designation in millimeters refers to the measured distance between the main shaft and countergear centerlines.

Both use external rod-type floor shifters and are fully synchronized transmissions with blocker ring synchronizers and a sliding mesh type reverse gear. The gearshift lever assembly is mounted on top of the transmission extension housing and requires no adjustment.

Transmission overhaul is not the best starting point for a beginning mechanic. However, it does not require special training or much special equipment. Overhaul does require patience and the ability to concentrate. The work area must be clean, free of distractions and inaccessible to pets and small children.

Before starting work, read this entire section. Obtain any special tools necessary or appropriate substitutes. Check parts availability with local suppliers.

Shift Lever
Removal/Installation

Refer to **Figure 9** for this procedure.

1. Raise the car with a jack and place it on jackstands.

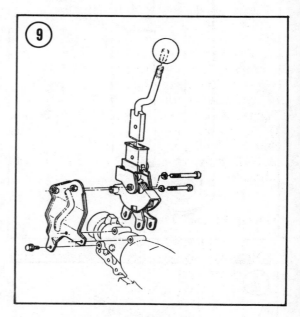

2. Disconnect the shift rods from the control levers.

3. Remove the jackstands and lower the car to the ground.

4. Remove the shift lever knob and parking brake lever grip.

5. Remove the console cover screws, raise console cover and disconnect the electrical connectors. Remove the console cover.

6. Remove the shift boot bolts and boot.

7. Remove the shift lever mounting bolts. Remove shift lever.

8. Installation is the reverse of removal. Tighten attaching bolts to 25 ft.-lb. (35 N•m).

Transmission Removal/Installation

1. Raise the car with a jack and place it on jackstands.
2. Drain the transmission lubricant.
3. Remove torque arm. See Chapter Eleven.
4. Remove the drive shaft. See Chapter Eleven.
5. Disconnect the speedometer cable and all electrical connectors at the transmission.
6. Remove the exhaust brace.
7. Remove shifter support attaching bolts at the transmission.
8. Disconnect the shift linkage from the shift lever.
9. Support the transmission with a jack. Remove the crossmember attaching bolts.
10. Remove transmission mount attaching bolt. Remove mount and crossmember.
11. Remove the transmission-to-engine bolts. Slide the transmission away from the engine and remove from under the car.
12. Installation is the reverse of removal. Tighten all fasteners to specifications (**Table 1**). Adjust shift linkage as described in this chapter. Refill transmission with 3 1/2 pints of SAE 80W or SAE 80W-90 GL-5 gear lubricant.

Muncie 4-Speed Transmission Disassembly

Refer to **Figure 10** for this procedure.
1. Remove side cover bolts. Remove side cover assembly.
2. Remove drive gear bearing retainer bolts, retainer and gasket.
3. Remove snap ring. Pull outward on drive gear and insert a screwdriver between the bearing, large snap ring and case. Carefully pry bearing off drive gear. See **Figure 11**.
4. Remove extension housing bolts. Remove drive gear, main shaft and extension housing from case (**Figure 12**).
5. Expand main shaft rear bearing snap ring at extension housing (**Figure 13**) and remove extension housing.
6. Insert tool part No. J-22246 or a dummy shaft at the front of the countershaft. Drive the shaft and Woodruff key from rear of case. Tool part No. J-22246 or dummy shaft will keep roller bearings in place inside the countergear bore. Remove the gear and bearings.
7. Remove reverse idler gear stop ring. Drive the reverse idler shaft and Woodruff key through the rear of the case with a long drift or punch (**Figure 14**).

Assembly

1. Insert tool part No. J-22246 or a dummy shaft in the countergear. Wipe the roller bearings with heavy grease. Load 27 bearings and a bearing thrust washer at each end of the countergear. See **Figure 15**.
2. Install countergear assembly through the rear of the case with a tanged thrust washer at each end. Washer tangs should face away from gear and align with case recesses.
3. Install reverse idler gear and Woodruff key from rear of case.
4. Fit extension housing over rear of main shaft. Expand snap ring and slide housing in place. Seat snap ring in rear bearing groove.
5. Load 14 main shaft bearings into drive gear cavity. Fit 4th speed blocker ring onto drive gear clutching surface with clutching teeth toward the gear.
6. Install the drive gear assembly over the front of the main shaft. Make sure the blocker ring notches align with the keys in the 3-4 synchronizer assembly.
7. Install new gasket on extension housing and install case over drive gear and main shaft.
8. Install extension housing bolts. Use seal on bottom bolt.
9. Install front bearing outer snap ring to bearing. Position bearing over drive gear stem and fit into front case bore.
10. Install drive gear stem snap ring.
11. Install drive gear bearing retainer with a new gasket. Retainer oil hole must be at the bottom.
12. Move synchronizer sleeves to neutral positions. Install cover, gasket and fork assembly to case. Forks must align with their synchronizer sleeve grooves.

Main Shaft Disassembly/Assembly

Refer to **Figure 16** for this procedure.
1. Remove 3-4 synchronizer hub snap ring from main shaft (**Figure 17**).

9

⑩

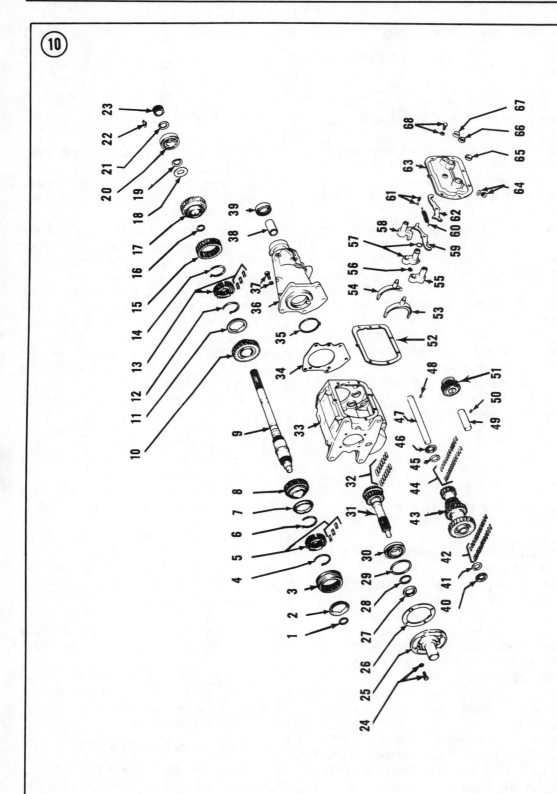

MUNCIE 4-SPEED TRANSMISSION

1. Snap ring, hub to shaft
2. Synch. ring
3. 3-4 synch. sleeve
4. Synch. key spring
5. Synch. hub and keys
6. Synch. key spring
7. Synch. ring
8. Third gear
9. Main shaft
10. Second gear
11. Synch. ring
12. Synch. key spring
13. Synch. hub and keys
14. Synch. key spring
15. 1-2 synch. sleeve and reverse gear
16. Snap ring, hub to shaft
17. First gear
18. Thrust washer
19. Waved washer
20. Ring bearing
21. Snap ring, bearing to shaft
22. Speedo gear clip
23. Speedo drive gear
24. Bearing retainer bolts and washers (4)
25. Front bearing retainer
26. Bearing retainer gasket
27. Bearing retainer oil seal
28. Snap ring
29. Bearing snap ring
30. Front bearing
31. Drive gear
32. Pilot bearings
33. Case
34. Extension to case gasket
35. Rear bearing to extension retaining ring
36. Rear extension
37. Extension to case retaining bolts and washers
38. Rear extension bushing
39. Rear seal
40. Thrust washer
41. Spacer
42. Countergear shaft roller bearings
43. Countergear
44. Countergear shaft roller bearings
45. Spacer
46. Thrust washer
47. Countergear shaft
48. Countergear shaft key
49. Reverse idler shaft
50. Idler shaft key
51. Reverse idler gear
52. Side cover gasket
53. 3-4 shift fork
54. 1-2 shift fork
55. 3-4 shifter shaft
56. Retaining E-ring
57. 1-2 shifter shaft with O-rings
58. Reverse shifter shaft
59. 3-4 detent cam
60. Detent cam spring
61. Reverse detent ball and spring
62. 1-2 detent cam
63. Shift cover
64. Plug and gasket
65. Shifter shaft seal
66. Shifter shaft seal
67. Shift cover bolts and washers
68. Shift cover attaching bolts and lockwashers

9

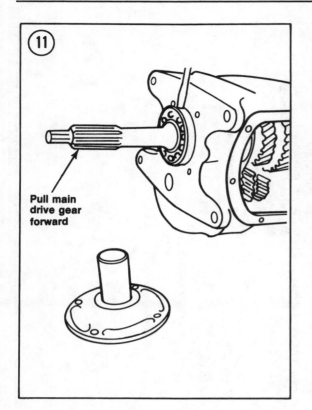

Pull main
drive gear
forward

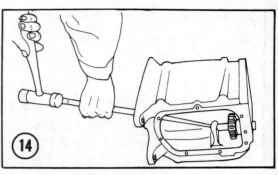

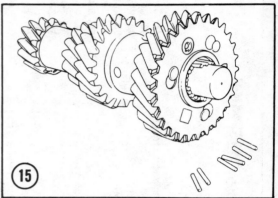

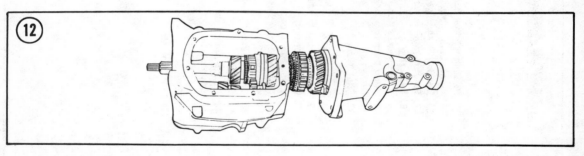

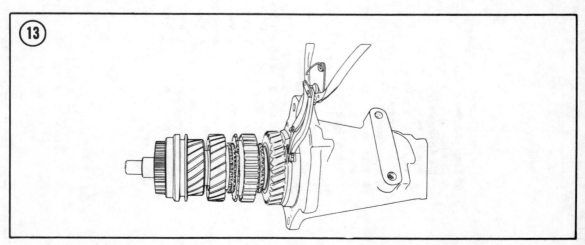

MUNCIE TRANSMISSION MAIN SHAFT

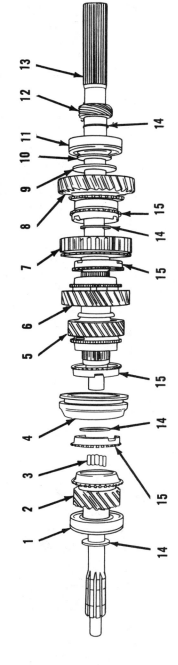

1. Drive gear bearing
2. Drive gear
3. Main shaft pilot bearings
4. 3-4 synchronizer assembly
5. Third speed gear
6. Second speed gear
7. 1-2 synchronizer and
   reverse gear assembly

8. First speed gear
9. Thrust washer
10. Spring washer
11. Rear bearing
12. Speedo drive gear
13. Main shaft
14. Snap ring
15. Synchronizing
    "blocker" ring

9

2. Remove 3-4 synchronizer assembly, 3rd gear blocker ring and 3rd gear from front of main shaft.

3. Depress speedometer retaining clip. Slide speedometer gear off main shaft.

4. Remove rear bearing snap ring from main shaft groove (**Figure 18**).

5. Support 1st gear with press plates. Press on rear of main shaft to remove 1st gear, thrust washer, spring washer and rear bearing from rear of main shaft.

6. Remove 1-2 synchronizer hub snap ring. Remove 1-2 synchronizer, 2nd speed blocker ring and 2nd gear from rear of main shaft.

7. Assembly is the reverse of disassembly.

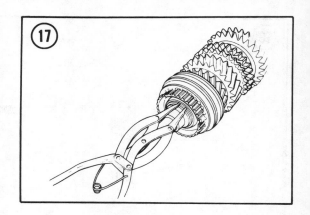

Cleaning and Inspection

1. Wash the transmission case and components in clean solvent.

2. Inspect the case for cracks. Check front and rear faces for burrs and dress off with a fine mill file, if necessary.

3. Check all gear teeth for signs of wear or damage.

4. Inspect all roller bearings for excessive wear.

5. Inspect countershaft and reverse idler shaft for wear. Replace if necessary.

6. Check all washers for wear or distortion. Replace as necessary.

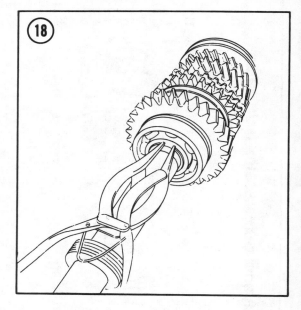

Drive Gear Bearing Replacement

The use of a hydraulic press and a universal bearing remover is required for this procedure.

1. Remove the snap ring from the drive gear.

2. Install the universal bearing remover and press the bearing from the shaft.

3. Press the new bearing on the shaft with its snap ring groove facing away from the gear.

4. Install the snap ring.

Drive Gear Bearing Retainer Oil Seal Replacement

1. Pry the old seal out with a screwdriver (**Figure 19**).

2. Install the new seal with an appropriate driver. The lip of the seal must face the rear of the retainer.

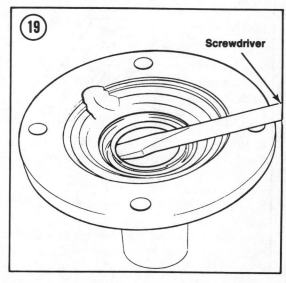

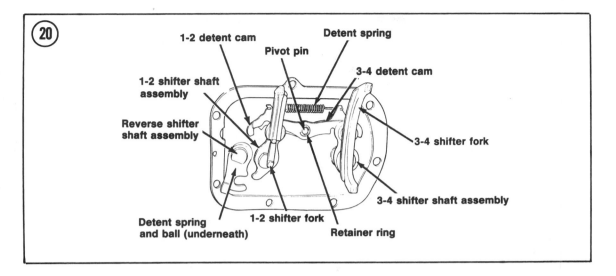

(20)

1-2 detent cam

Pivot pin

Detent spring

3-4 detent cam

1-2 shifter shaft assembly

Reverse shifter shaft assembly

3-4 shifter fork

3-4 shifter shaft assembly

Detent spring and ball (underneath)

1-2 shifter fork

Retainer ring

Extension Housing Oil Seal/Bushing Replacement

1. Pry the old seal out with a screwdriver. Drive old bushing into the extension housing with an appropriate driver.
2. Coat inner diameter of new bushing and seal with transmission lubricant.
3. Install new bushing with an appropriate driver, then install new oil seal.

Reverse Idler Gear Bushing

The reverse idler gear bushing is pressed into the gear and finish bored in place. If defective, replace the reverse idler gear.

Transmission Cover Disassembly/Assembly

Refer to **Figure 20** for this procedure.
1. Remove shift levers. Remove both shift forks from shift shaft assemblies.
2. Remove all 3 shift shaft assemblies from cover.
3. Pry lip seal from cover. Pry O-ring seal from 1-2 and reverse shafts, if necessary.
4. Remove detent cam spring and pivot retainer circlip.
5. Mark detent cams for reassembly reference and remove.
6. Install 1-2 detent cam on pivot pin. Detent spring tang must project up over the 3-4 shift shaft cover opening.

7. Install 3-4 detent cam on pivot pin. Detent spring tang must project up over the 1-2 shift shaft cover opening.
8. Install pivot retainer circlip. Hook detent cam spring into cam notches.
9. Install 1-2 and 3-4 shift shaft assemblies in cover.
10. Install shift forks to respective shift shaft assemblies. Seat forks fully by lifting up on detent cam.
11. Install reverse detent ball and spring to cover. Install reverse shift shaft assembly to cover.

Borg-Warner 4-Speed Transmission Disassembly

Refer to **Figure 21** for this procedure.
1. Shift transmission into 2nd gear.
2. Remove shift cover bolts, cover and gasket. Remove both shift forks.
3. Remove drive gear bearing retainer bolts, retainer and gasket.
4. Remove lock pin from reverse shifter lever boss with a punch (**Figure 22**). Pull shift shaft out far enough to disengage reverse shift fork from reverse gear.
5. Remove extension housing bolts. Tap housing to the rear with a plastic mallet. Slide extension to the rear until reverse idler shaft clears reverse idler gears.
6. Rotate extension to the left to free shift fork from reverse gear collar. Remove extension housing and discard gasket.

9

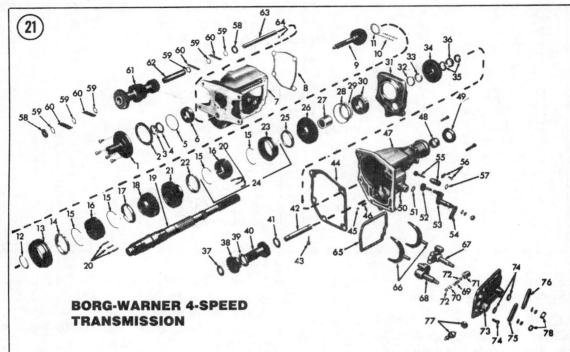

BORG-WARNER 4-SPEED TRANSMISSION

1. Bearing retainer
2. Gasket
3. Selective fit snap ring
4. Spacer washer
5. Bearing snap ring
6. Main drive gear bearing
7. Transmission case
8. Rear bearing retainer gasket
9. Main drive gear
10. Bearing rollers (16)
11. Washer
12. Snap ring
13. Third and fourth speed clutch sliding sleeve
14. Fourth speed gear synchronizing ring
15. Clutch key spring
16. Clutch hub
17. Third speed gear synchronizing ring
18. Third speed gear
19. Main shaft
20. Clutch keys (3)
21. Second speed gear
22. Second speed gear synchronizing ring
23. First and second speed clutch sliding sleeve
24. First and second speed clutch assembly
25. First speed gear synchronizing ring
26. First speed gear

27. First speed gear sleeve
28. Rear bearing snap ring
29. Thrust washer
30. Rear bearing
31. Rear bearing retainer
32. Washer
33. Selective fit snap ring
34. Reverse gear
35. Snap ring
36. Speedometer drive gear
37. Reverse idler front thrust washer (flat)
38. Reverse idler gear (front)
39. Snap ring
40. Reverse idler gear (rear)
41. Thrust bearing (needle)
42. Reverse idler shaft
43. Reverse idler shaft lock pin and welch plug
44. Rear bearing retainer to case extension gasket
45. Reverse shifter shaft detent ball
46. Reverse shifter shaft ball detent spring
47. Case extension
48. Extension bushing
49. Rear oil seal
50. Reverse shifter shaft lock pin
51. Reverse shifter shaft O-ring seal

52. Reverse shift fork
53. Reverse shifter shaft and detent plate
54. Reverse shifter lever
55. Speedometer driven gear and fitting
56. Retainer and bolt
57. O-ring seal
58. Washer (tanged)
59. Spacer
60. Bearing rollers (28)
61. Countergear
62. Countergear roller spacer
63. Countershaft
64. Countershaft Woodruff key
65. Gasket
66. Forward speed shift forks
67. First and second speed gear shifter shaft and detent plate
68. Third and fourth speed gear shifter shaft and detent plate
69. Poppet spring
70. Interlock pin
71. Interlock sleeve
72. Detent balls
73. Transmission side cover
74. Lip seals
75. Third and fourth speed shifter lever
76. First and second speed shifter lever
77. TCS switch and gasket
78. Lever attaching nuts

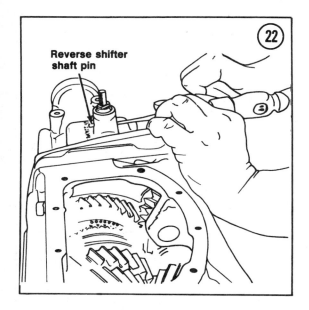

Reverse shifter shaft pin

㉒

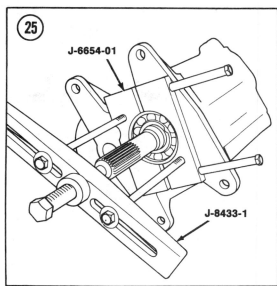

㉕

J-6654-01

J-8433-1

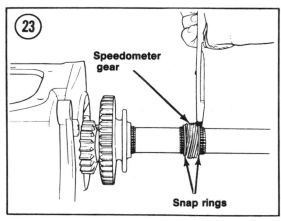

㉓

Speedometer gear

Snap rings

㉔

Lock bolt

Reverse idler gear

Reverse gear

9

7. Remove speedometer gear outer snap ring (**Figure 23**). Remove speedometer gear from main shaft. Remove inner snap ring.

8. Remove reverse gear from main shaft (**Figure 24**). Slide rear portion of reverse idler gear from transmission case.

9. Remove front bearing snap ring. Remove selective fit snap ring and spacer.

10. Install puller part Nos. J-6654-01 and J-8433-1 or equivalent as shown in **Figure 25** and remove main drive gear bearing.

11. Remove rear retainer lock bolt.

12. Move 1-2 and 3-4 synchronizer sleeves forward to provide clearance for main shaft removal. Remove main shaft and rear bearing retainer from transmission case.

13. Remove front reverse idler gear and thrust washer.

14. Install tool part No. J-24658 or a dummy shaft as shown in **Figure 26**. Drive countergear shaft from countergear. Remove countergear and tanged thrust washers. Check case for loose pilot bearings.

Assembly

Refer to **Figure 21** for this procedure.

1. Install countergear tanged thrust washers in case recesses with heavy grease to hold them in place.

2. Install countergear in case. Slide dummy shaft or tool part No. J-24658 to the front of

the case. Install countergear shaft from rear of case.

3. Install countergear shaft Woodruff key. Tap shaft into gear until flush with transmission case rear face.

4. Install front reverse idler gear with its teeth facing forward. Install thrust washer with heavy grease to hold it in place.

5. Install 16 roller bearings and washer in main drive gear. Attach drive gear to main shaft assembly.

6. Move 3-4 synchronizer sliding sleeve forward.

7. Fit a new rear bearing retainer-to-case gasket on rear of case. Install main shaft and drive gear assembly in case.

8. Align rear bearing retainer with transmission case. Install locating pin and retainer locking bolt.

9. Install bearing snap ring on front main bearing. Install bearing with an appropriate driver (**Figure 27**).

10. Install spacer and selective fit snap ring to hold main drive bearing.

11. Install front bearing retainer with a new gasket. Apply sealer to bolts and torque to specifications (**Table 1**).

12. Install rear reverse idler gear to engage splines with part of gear in case.

13. Position bearing retainer-to-extension housing gasket on rear face of bearing retainer. Slide reverse gear on shaft.

14. Install speedometer gear with both selective snap rings.

15. Install idler shaft into extension housing to align shaft hole with hole in boss.

16. Install reverse idler shaft lock pin. Install new welch plug with sealer in boss opening.

17. Install reverse shift shaft and detent plate in extension housing. Use heavy grease to hold reverse shift fork in place and install in reverse shift shaft.

18. Install reverse shift shaft O-ring on reverse shift shaft.

19. Install tanged thrust washer on reverse idler shaft. Washer tang must fit in notch of idler thrust face.

20. Move 1-2 and 3-4 synchronizer sleeve into neutral position. Pull reverse shift shaft partially out of extension housing. Push reverse shift fork forward as far as possible.

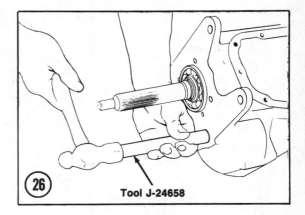

(26) Tool J-24658

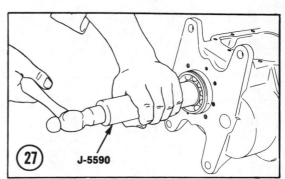

(27) J-5590

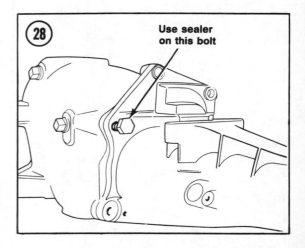

(28) Use sealer on this bolt

21. Fit extension housing onto main shaft. Push in on shift shaft to engage shift fork with reverse gear shift collar. Rotate shift shaft to move reverse gear to the rear and slide extension housing up against transmission case.

22. Install reverse shift shaft lock pin. Install extension housing bolts. Use sealer on the bolt shown in **Figure 28**.

23. Install rear bearing retainer bolts.
24. Move 1-2 synchronizer to 2nd gear position. Move 3-4 synchronizer to neutral. Fit forward shift forks in sliding sleeves.
25. Move 1-2 shift shaft and detent plate into 2nd gear position.
26. Install cover gasket with sealer. Install cover to transmission. Check transmission operation.

Main Shaft Disassembly/Assembly

Refer to **Figure 29** for this procedure.
1. Remove 3-4 synchronizer snap ring at front of main shaft. Slide washer, synchronizer assembly and 3rd gear from main shaft.
2. Expand rear bearing retainer snap ring (**Figure 30**) and remove retainer.
3. Remove rear bearing-to-main shaft snap ring (**Figure 31**).
4. Support main shaft under 2nd gear as shown in **Figure 32**. Press main shaft from rear bearing, 1st gear, 1-2 synchronizer assembly and 2nd gear.
5. Assembly is the reverse of removal. Install new selective fit snap rings. The correct size is the thickest that will assemble properly.

Cleaning and Inspection

1. Wash the transmission case and components in clean solvent.
2. Inspect case for cracks.
3. Check case faces for burrs. Dress any burrs with a fine mill file.
4. Check all gear teeth for signs of wear or damage.
5. Inspect all roller bearings for excessive wear.
6. Replace all worn spacers or thrust washers.

Drive Gear Bearing Retainer Oil Seal Replacement

1. Pry out old seal with a screwdriver.
2. Lubricate the inner diameter of new seal with transmission lubricant.
3. Install new seal with an appropriate driver until it bottoms in retainer bore.

Extension Housing Oil Seal/Bushing Replacement

1. Pry old seal from rear of extension housing.
2. Drive bushing into housing with an appropriate driver.
3. Press new bushing into rear of extension housing with an appropriate driver.
4. Lubricate the inner diameter of the bushing and a new seal. Install new seal with an appropriate driver.

AUTOMATIC TRANSMISSION

Checking Procedure

1. Park the car on a level surface.
2. Make sure the engine starts only when the shift lever is in NEUTRAL or PARK. If it will start in any other position, check the neutral start/backup light switch as described in this chapter.
3. Make sure the backup lights go on when the transmission is shifted to REVERSE.
4. Make sure the car moves forward in DRIVE and backward in REVERSE.
5. Make sure the shift selector indicator points to the correct range. If the indicator is out of alignment, adjust the shift linkage as described in this chapter.
6. Check fluid level as described in this chapter.
7. Shut off the engine. Check the throttle lever and cable bracket on the side of the carburetor or throttle body (**Figure 33**) for damage. Replace as necessary.

Neutral Start/Backup Lamp Switch Adjustment

Refer to **Figure 34** for this procedure.
1. Remove the shift knob. Remove the console. See Chapter Thirteen.
2. Move shifter assembly into neutral notch in detent plate.
3. Loosen switch attaching screws.
4. Rotate switch on shifter assembly until service adjustment hole is aligned with carrier tang hole.
5. Insert a gauge pin to a depth of 15 mm.
6. Tighten attaching screws to 1.5 ft.-lb. (2 N•m).

9

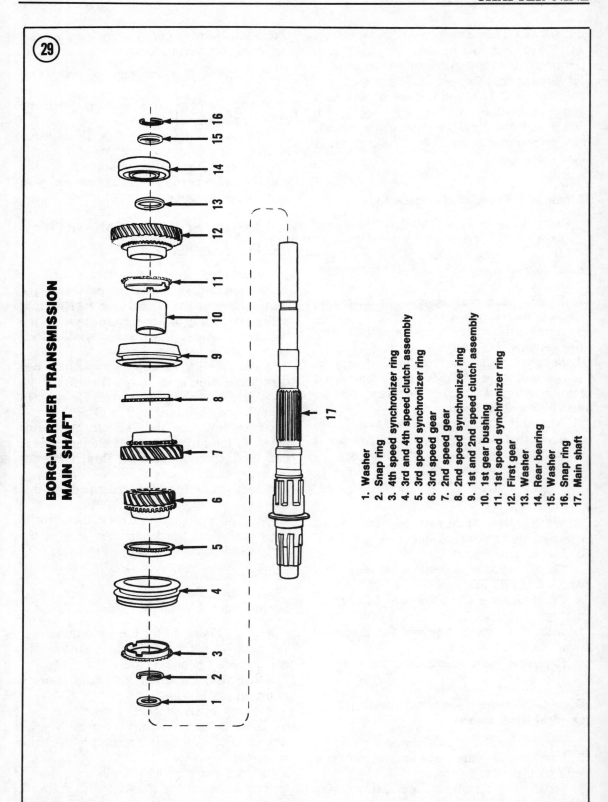

**BORG-WARNER TRANSMISSION
MAIN SHAFT**

1. Washer
2. Snap ring
3. 4th speed synchronizer ring
4. 3rd and 4th speed clutch assembly
5. 3rd speed synchronizer ring
6. 3rd speed gear
7. 2nd speed gear
8. 2nd speed synchronizer ring
9. 1st and 2nd speed clutch assembly
10. 1st gear bushing
11. 1st speed synchronizer ring
12. First gear
13. Washer
14. Rear bearing
15. Washer
16. Snap ring
17. Main shaft

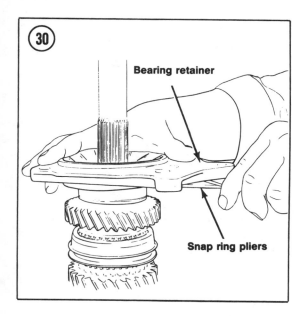

Bearing retainer

Snap ring pliers

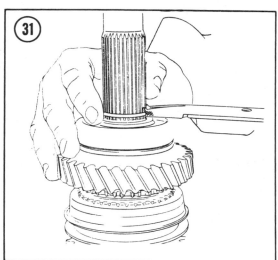

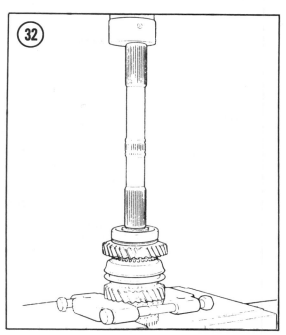

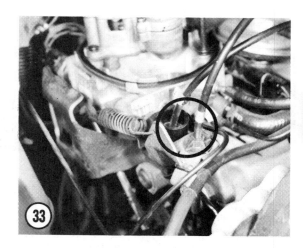

7. Remove gauge pin.

8. Install console (Chapter Thirteen) and shift knob.

Fluid Level Check

1. With the engine idling, shift from PARK to each of the other gear positions, then shift back to PARK.

2. Pull out the dipstick, wipe it off, reinsert it, then pull it back out.

3. Note the fluid level. If the engine is warm, it should be within the crosshatch section on the dipstick (**Figure 35**).

4. If the fluid level is low, add DEXRON II transmission fluid through the dipstick filler tube to bring the level to the middle of the crosshatch section on the dipstick. Use only DEXRON II fluid.

Shift Linkage Adjustment

The automatic transmission uses a cable park lock system between the shifter linkage and the ignition switch (**Figure 36**). If shift linkage adjustment is necessary, be sure the lock cable system functions properly. When the shift lever is placed in PARK with the

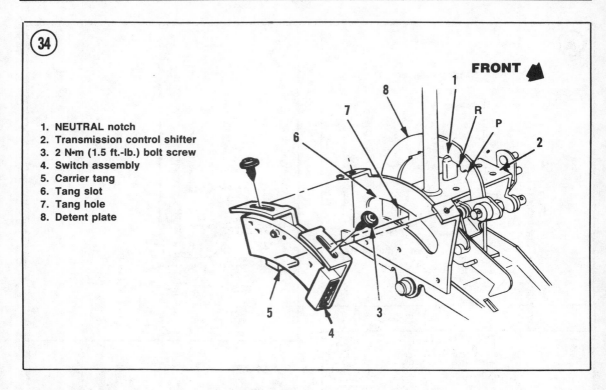

34

1. NEUTRAL notch
2. Transmission control shifter
3. 2 N•m (1.5 ft.-lb.) bolt screw
4. Switch assembly
5. Carrier tang
6. Tang slot
7. Tang hole
8. Detent plate

FRONT

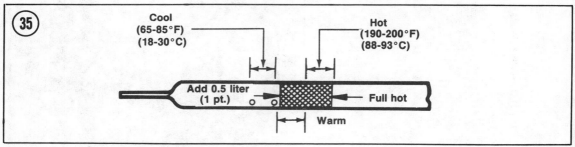

35

Cool
(65-85°F)
(18-30°C)

Hot
(190-200°F)
(88-93°C)

Add 0.5 liter
(1 pt.)

Full hot

Warm

ignition OFF, the column cable controls a block-up on the lock pawl lever (B, **Figure 36**). Refer to **Figure 37** for linkage adjustment.

1. Move the shift lever to NEUTRAL.
2. Place lever A in the neutral detent position.
3. Assemble the clamp spring washer and screw to lever B and the control rod.
4. Hold the clamp tightly against lever B and tighten the clamp screw against the rod.
5. Tighten the clamp screw snugly.
6. Move the shift lever through the gearshift range. The pointer will align properly if the adjustment is correct. If it does not align, repeat Steps 1-5.

TV Cable Adjustment

Refer to **Figure 38** for this procedure.

1. Depress re-adjust tab (**Figure 39**). Move slider back through fitting in direction away from carburetor or throttle body lever until slider stops against the fitting. Release re-adjust tab.

2A. With V6 or V8 engine, manually open the carburetor or throttle body lever to its full throttle stop position. The cable will automatically adjust itself by ratcheting through its slider. Release the carburetor or throttle body lever to complete the adjustment. **Figure 40** shows the TV cable at the carburetor when properly adjusted.

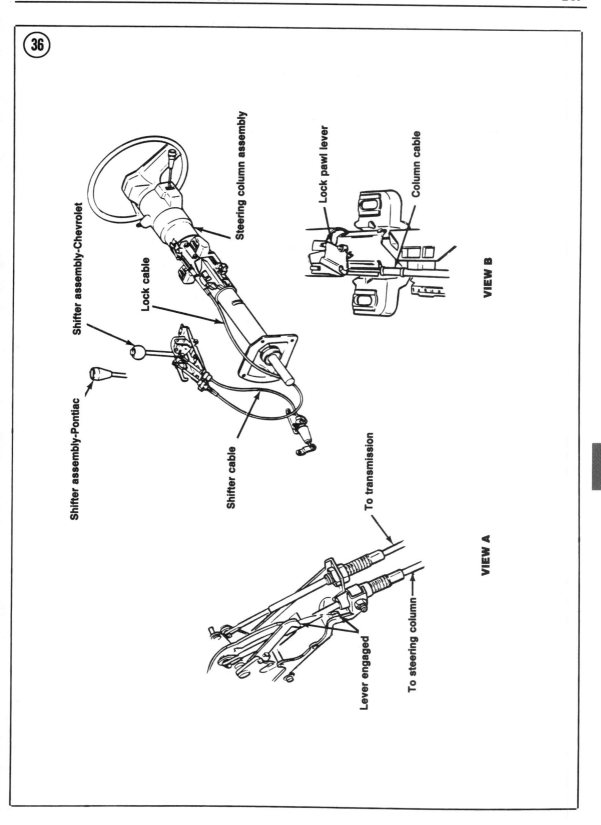

36

Steering column assembly

Lock pawl lever

Column cable

VIEW B

Shifter assembly-Chevrolet

Lock cable

Shifter assembly-Pontiac

Shifter cable

To transmission

9

Lever engaged

To steering column

VIEW A

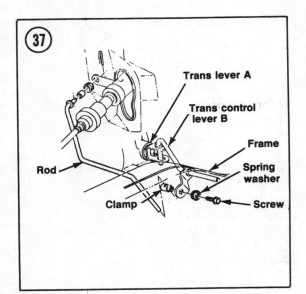

(37)

Trans lever A

Trans control lever B

Frame

Rod

Spring washer

Clamp

Screw

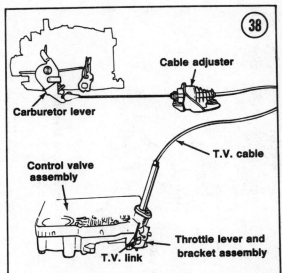

(38)

Cable adjuster

Carburetor lever

Control valve assembly

T.V. cable

T.V. link

Throttle lever and bracket assembly

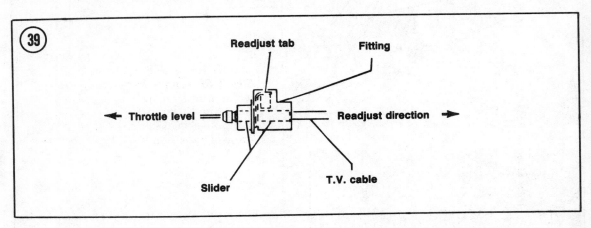

(39)

Readjust tab

Fitting

Throttle level

Readjust direction

Slider

T.V. cable

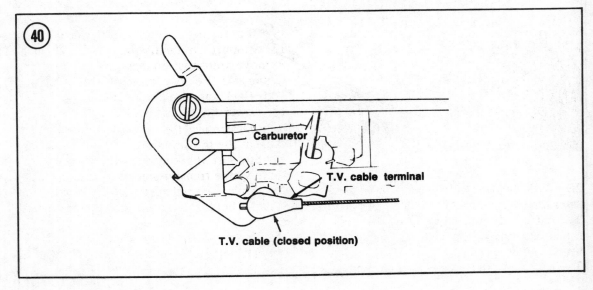

(40)

Carburetor

T.V. cable terminal

T.V. cable (closed position)

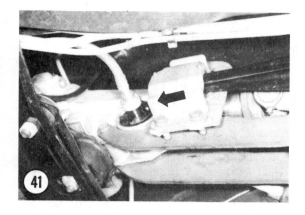

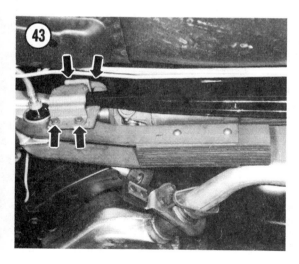

Transmission Removal

1. Disconnect the negative battery cable.
2. Remove the air cleaner assembly. See Chapter Six.
3. Disconnect the TV cable at the carburetor or throttle body.
4. Raise the front of the car with a jack and place it on jackstands.
5. Remove transmission oil dipstick. Remove upper bolt on dipstick tube. Remove tube.
6. Disconnect and remove the drive shaft. See Chapter Eleven.
7. Disconnect the speedometer cable (**Figure 41**) and shift cable (A, **Figure 42**) at the transmission.
8. Disconnect the TCC electrical connector (B, **Figure 42**) at the transmission.

> *WARNING*
> *Place a piece of wood between the floor pan and torque arm before performing Step 9. Rear spring force will cause the torque arm to move toward the floor pan when the arm is disconnected. This can damage the floor pan and possibly cause physical injury.*

9. Remove the torque arm-to-transmission bolts (**Figure 43**).
10. Remove converter cover. Mark the flywheel and torque converter for reassembly reference.
11. Remove the converter-to-flywheel bolts.
12. Support transmission with a jack. Remove transmission rear mount bolts (A, **Figure 44**). Remove crossmember attaching bolts (B, **Figure 44**) and crossmember.
13. Lower the transmission slightly with the jack. Disconnect the oil cooler lines and TV cable at the transmission.
14. Support the engine with another jack. Remove the transmission-to-engine bolts.
15. Move the transmission back slightly and install a holding fixture to prevent the torque converter from falling out.
16. Lower the transmission carefully to prevent damage to cooler lines, TV cable or shift linkage. Remove the transmission.

2B. With 4-cylinder engines, rotate the idler lever to its maximum travel stop position. The cable will automatically adjust itself by ratcheting through its slider. Release the throttle idler lever.
3. Check TV cable for sticking or binding.

Transmission Installation

Installation is the reverse of removal, plus the following:

1. Make sure the converter weld nuts are flush with the flex plate before installing the flex plate-to-converter bolts. The converter should rotate freely in this position.

2. Tighten the flex plate-to-converter bolts by hand, then tighten to specifications to ensure proper converter alignment.

3. Install a new oil seal on the oil filler tube.

4. Adjust the shift linkage and TV cable as described in this chapter.

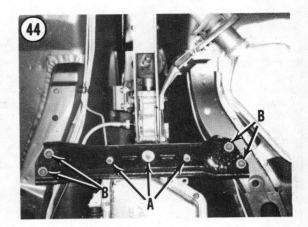

Table 1 TIGHTENING TORQUES

Fastener	ft.-lb.	N•m
Clutch		
Pedal bumper stop	10	15
Pedal-to-mounting bracket	20	30
Cross shaft		
Bolt	25	35
Nut	20	30
Bracket screw	15	20
Cross shaft nut	20	30
Flywheel-to-crankshaft		
4-cylinder	44	60
V6	45-55	61-75
V8	60	90
Flex plate-to-converter	25-35	34-47
Flywheel housing	30	40
Flywheel housing cover	9	13
Borg-Warner 4-speed manual transmission		
Drive gear retainer	15	20
Cover-to-case bolt	15	20
Extension housing bolts	45	60
Filler plug	15	20
Transmission-to-clutch housing bolts	55	75
Crossmember-to-body bolts	35	47
Crossmember-to-mount bolts	35	47
Transmission-to-mount bolts	35	47
Shift lever-to-shift shaft bolt	25	30
Muncie 4-speed manual transmission		
Drive gear retainer	18	25
Side cover-to-case bolts	18	25
Extension housing	40	55
Shift lever-to-shift shaft bolt	18	25
Filler plug	15	20
Drain plug	18	25
Rear bearing retainer	25	35
Extension-to-rear bearing bolts	25	35
Retainer-to-case bolt	35	47
Crossmember-to-body bolts	35	47
Crossmember-to-mount bolt	35	47
Transmission-to-mount bolt	35	47
Automatic transmission		
Oil pan bolts	10-13	14-18
Flywheel-to-converter	35	47
Converter cover		
V6	25	30
4-cylinder	7	10
Transmission-to-engine bolts	35	47
Converter housing cover screws	8	10
Transmission support-to-frame	40	55
Mount-to-transmission support	25	34
TV cable-to-case	8	10
Oil cooler pipes		
At radiator	10	14
At transmission	12	16

9

CHAPTER TEN

FRONT SUSPENSION AND STEERING

Camaro and Firebird models use an independent front suspension with lower control arms, ball-joint assemblies and cast steering knuckles. Front wheel relationship is maintained by 2 tie rods connected to a relay rod and steering arms on knuckles.

Coil springs are mounted between the lower control arms and spring housings on the front crossmember. Direct acting strut assemblies provide ride control. The upper end of each strut extends through the fender well and is attached to the upper mount with a nut. The lower strut end is attached to the steering knuckle.

A spring steel stabilizer shaft controls front suspension side roll. The stabilizer ends are connected to the lower control arms by link bolts and isolated by rubber grommets.

The lower control arm is connected to the suspension crossmember. The control arm ball-joint is a press-fit in the arm and is connected to the steering knuckle.

Figure 1 shows the major components of the front suspension, including the brake caliper, hub and disc assembly and wheel bearings.

Tightening torques (**Table 1**) and alignment specifications (**Table 2**) are provided at the end of the chapter.

FRONT SUSPENSION

Strut Removal/Installation

1. Set the parking brake. Place the transmission in NEUTRAL or PARK.
2. Loosen the front wheel lug nuts.
3. Raise the front of the car with a jack and place it on jackstands. Support the lower control arm with a jack.
4. Remove the brake hose bracket (A, **Figure 2**).
5. Remove the 2 strut mounting bolts (B, **Figure 2**).
6. Remove the upper mount assembly cover (**Figure 3**). Remove the upper strut nut.
7. Remove the strut and shield.
8. Installation is the reverse of removal. Tighten fasteners to specifications (**Table 1**).

Coil Spring Removal/Installation

An adapter (GM tool part No. J-23028) and hydraulic jack are required to protect the inner bushings. See **Figure 4**.

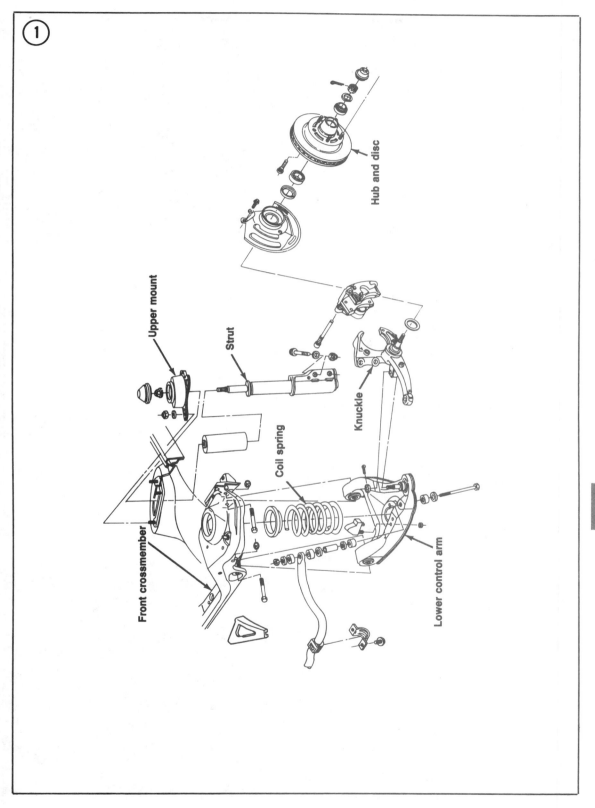

1

Hub and disc

Upper mount

Strut

Knuckle

Coil spring

Lower control arm

Front crossmember

10

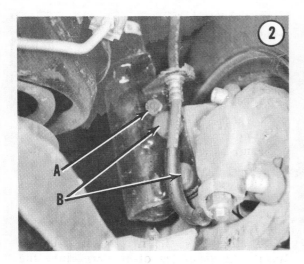

1. Loosen the front wheel lug nuts.
2. Raise the front of the car with a jack and place it on jackstands.
3. Remove the stabilizer shaft and bushings at the lower control arm (**Figure 5**).
4. Remove the pivot bolt nuts, but do not remove the bolts at this time.
5. Install tool part No. J-23028 to the hydraulic jack and position it as shown in **Figure 4**.
6. Place a jackstand under the outside frame rail on the opposite side of the car.
7. Raise the hydraulic jack with tool part No. J-23038 attached to relieve tension on control arm pivot bolts. Remove the bolts.
8. Lower the jack carefully and remove spring with insulator. Tape insulator to spring.
9. Installation is the reverse of removal. Install the spring with the tape at the lowest position (A, **Figure 6**). The end of the spring must cover all or part of one inspection drain hole (B, **Figure 6**) when properly installed.

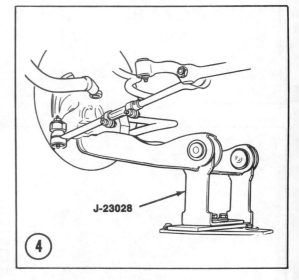

Stabilizer Shaft Removal/Installation

1. Raise the front of the car with a jack and place it on jackstands.
2. Remove the link bolt holding each end of the stabilizer bar to the lower control arm (**Figure 7**). Remove the spacer, retainers and grommets.
3. Remove the bracket mounting bolts at each side of the frame (**Figure 8**). Remove the brackets, rubber bushings and stabilizer shaft.

4. Installation is the reverse of removal. Align the rubber bushings in the brackets with the bushing slit facing the front of the car. Tighten the link nut to 15 ft.-lb. (20 N•m). Hold the stabilizer shaft about 55 mm from the bottom of the side rail (**Figure 9**) and tighten insulator bracket bolts to 25 ft.-lb. (35 N•m).

Lower Control Arm
Removal/Installation

1. Loosen the front wheel lug nuts.
2. Raise the front of the car with a jack and place it on jackstands. Position the jackstands under the frame jack pads to the rear of the front wheels.
3. Remove the front wheel/tire assembly.
4. Remove the coil spring as described in this chapter.
5. Separate the lower ball-joint stud from the steering knuckle with a puller or fork-type separator.
6. Remove the control arm.
7. Installation is the reverse of removal. Install the front leg of the arm into the crossmember before installing the rear leg. Position control arm to obtain proper trim height dimensions when pivot bolts are tightened. See *Trim Height Measurement* in this chapter. Install both pivot bolts with their head facing the front of the car and tighten to 65 ft.-lb. (90 N•m).

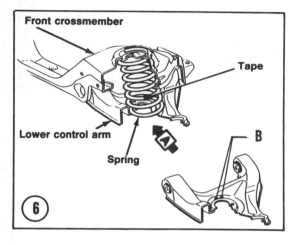

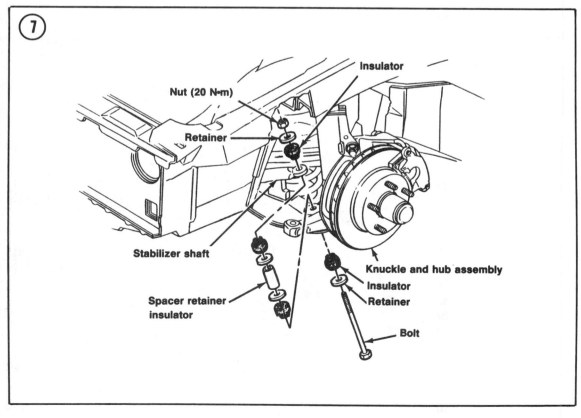

Lower Ball-joint Inspection

The lower front suspension ball-joint is pressed into the lower control arm. The ball-joint contains a visual wear indicator (**Figure 10**). Ball-joint inspection is done with the car on the ground so that its weight will load the ball-joints properly.

Ball-joint wear is indicated by the position of the grease fitting nipple. On a new ball-joint, this nipple will project 0.050 in. (1.27 mm) below the surface of the ball-joint cover. As normal wear occurs, the nipple will gradually move up into the cover.

To inspect the ball-joint, clean the grease fitting and nipple to remove all dirt and

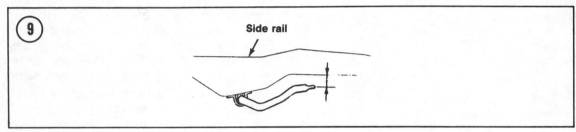

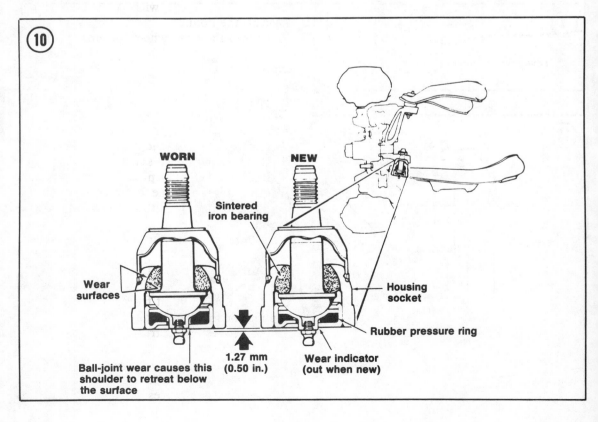

grease. Scrape the cover with a screwdriver. If the nipple is flush with or inside the cover surface, replace the ball-joint.

Lower Ball-joint Replacement

1. Remove the lower control arm as described in this chapter.
2. Remove the grease fitting.

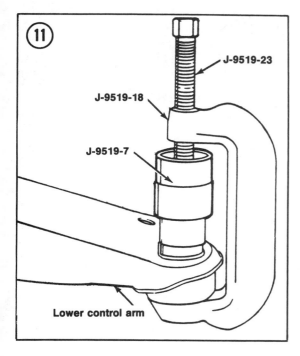

Lower control arm

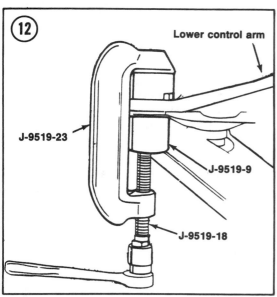

3. Install a C-clamp with appropriate receivers as shown in **Figure 11** and press the ball-joint from the control arm.
4. Press a new ball-joint into the control arm as shown in **Figure 12**.
5. Install the control arm as described in this chapter. Tighten the ball stud nut to 90 ft.-lb. (120 N•m), then tighten enough more to align nut slot with stud hole. Install a new cotter pin and lubricate the ball-joint fitting.

Control Arm Bushing Replacement

Bushing replacement requires the use of special tools and should be done by a GM dealer or qualified specialist.

Knuckle, Hub and Disc Removal/Installation

Refer to **Figure 13** for this procedure.
1. Remove the master cylinder cover and siphon about two-thirds of the brake fluid from the reservoir with a clean syringe. Discard the fluid.
2. Loosen the front wheel lug nuts.
3. Raise the front of the car with a jack and place it on jackstands.
4. Remove the wheel/tire assemblies.
5. Remove the brake hose bracket at the strut.
6. Remove the caliper support.
7. Remove the hub and disc assembly.
8. Remove the splash shield.
9. Remove the cotter pin and castellated nut from the tie rod at the knuckle. Separate the tie rod and knuckle with a puller or fork-type separator.
10. Support the lower control arm with a jack.
11. Remove the cotter pin and castellated nut from the lower control arm ball-joint. Separate the ball-joint from the knuckle with a puller or fork-type separator.
12. Remove the strut mounting bolts. Remove the knuckle.
13. Installation is the reverse of removal. Tighten all fasteners to specifications (**Table 1**) and bleed the brakes (Chapter Twelve).

10

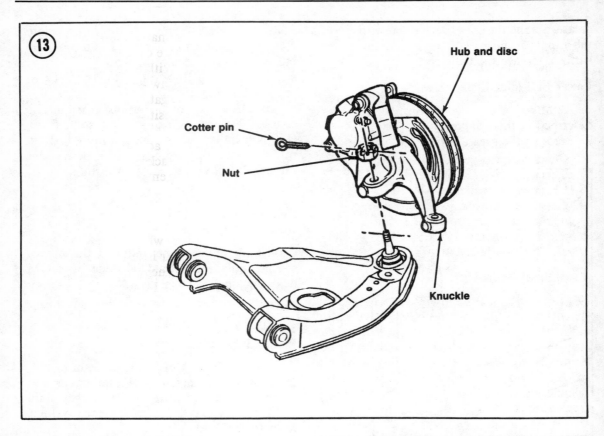

⑬

Hub and disc

Cotter pin

Nut

Knuckle

Trim Height Measurement

Front trim height differs according to tire size. If adjustment is necessary, it is best to have your GM dealer perform the service.

1. Lift the front bumper up about 1 1/2 in. and release it. The car will settle on its own. Repeat this a total of 3 times.

2. Push the front bumper down about 1 1/2 in. and release it. The car will settle on its own. Repeat this a total of 3 times.

3. Measure from the center of the lower control arm front bushing bolt head to the lowest point of the ball stud assembly (excluding the grease fitting). This is shown in **Figure 14** as dimension Z:

   a. With P195/75 tires, dimension Z should be 32-52 mm.

   b. With P205/70 tires, dimension Z should be 35-55 mm.

   c. With P215/60 tires, dimension Z should be 26-46 mm.

4. Adjustment is made at the lower control arm bolt, if necessary.

WHEEL ALIGNMENT

Several suspension angles affect the running and steering of the front wheels. These angles must be properly aligned to prevent excessive wear, as well as to maintain directional stability and ease of steering. The angles are:

   a. Caster.

   b. Camber.

   c. Toe.

   d. Steering axis inclination.

   e. Steering lock angle.

Steering axis inclination and steering lock angles are built in and cannot be adjusted. These angles are measured to check for bent suspension parts. Caster and camber should not be adjusted without a front-end rack. Toe can be adjusted as described in this section.

Pre-alignment Check

Adjustment of the steering and various suspension angles is affected by several factors. Perform the following steps before any adjustments are attempted.

1. Check tire pressure and wear. See *Tire Wear Analysis*, Chapter Two.
2. Check ball-joint play as described in this chapter.
3. Check for broken or sagging front/rear springs.
4. Remove any excessive load.
5. Check shock absorber action.
6. Check steering gear for wear or damage.
7. Check steering linkage play.
8. Check wheel balance.
9. Check rear suspension for looseness.

Front tire wear problems can indicate alignment problems. These are covered under *Tire Wear Analysis*, Chapter Two.

Caster and Camber

Caster is the inclination from vertical of the line through the ball-joints. Positive caster shifts the wheel forward; negative caster shifts the wheel rearward. Caster causes the wheels to return to a straight-ahead position after a turn. It also prevents the wheels from wandering due to wind, potholes or uneven road surfaces.

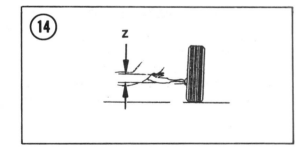

Camber is the inclination of the wheel from vertical. With positive camber, the top of the tire leans outward. With negative camber, the top of the tire leans inward. Excessive camber causes tire wear. Negative camber wears the inside of the tire; positive camber wears the outside.

Caster and camber adjustment requires the use of a front-end rack and special tools. It should not be attempted by the home mechanic.

Toe

Since the front wheels tend to point outward when the car is moving in a forward direction, the distance between the front edges of the tire (A, **Figure 15**) is generally slightly less than the distance between the rear edges (B, **Figure 15**) when the car is at rest.

NOTE
This is less true of radial tires than of bias ply or bias belted tires. The toe setting for radial tires may be quite small; in some cases, it may be zero.

Toe Adjustment

Although toe adjustment requires only a simple homemade tool, it usually is not worth the trouble for home mechanics. Alignment shops include toe adjustment as part of the alignment procedure, so you probably will not save any money by doing it yourself. The procedure described here can be used for an initial toe setting after control arm or ball-joint replacement.

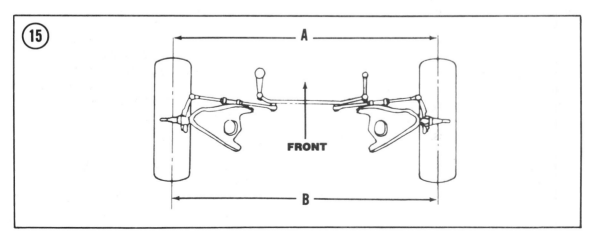

1. With the steering wheel centered, roll the car forward about 15 ft. on a smooth, level surface.

2. Mark the center of the tread at the front and rear of each tire.

3. Measure the distance between the forward chalk marks (A, **Figure 15**). Use 2 pieces of telescoping aluminum tubing. Telescope the tubing so each end contacts a chalk mark. Using a sharp scribe, mark the small diameter tubing where it enters the large diameter tubing.

4. Measure between the rear chalk marks with the telescoping tubes. Make another mark on the small tube where it enters the large one. The distance between the 2 scribe marks is the toe-in and must be divided in half to determine the amount of toe at each wheel.

5. If toe-in is incorrect, loosen the 2 clamp bolts on the tie rod adjustable sleeve (**Figure 16**) at each wheel.

6. Rotate the tie rod adjuster until the wheel has 1/2 of the desired total toe specification. Repeat the procedure with the other tie rod.

7. When toe-out is set correctly, make sure the number of threads showing on each end of the adjusting sleeve are equal. Tie rod end housings must be at right angles to the steering arm. Tighten the clamp bolts to 15 ft.-lb. (20 N•m).

Steering Axis Inclination

Steering axis inclination is the inward or outward lean of the line through the ball-joints. It is not adjustable on Camaro or Firebird models.

Steering Lock Angles

When a vehicle turns, the inside wheel makes a smaller circle than the outside wheel. Because of this, the inside wheel turns at a greater angle than the outside wheel. These angles are not adjustable, but are measured to check for bent suspension and steering parts.

Axle Housing Alignment

If rear tire wear indicates a bent axle housing, have your dealer or front-end shop check the axle housing alignment on an

alignment machine. Camber reading should be minus 3° to plus 5°. Toe-out should range between zero-1/16 in. If either reading is out of specification, frame straightening equipment can be used to realign the axle housing without removing it from the car.

WHEEL BEARINGS

The front wheels use taper roller bearings which must be correctly adjusted. The cones are a slip-fit on the spindle and their inside diameter must be properly lubricated to allow the cones to creep. The spindle nut must be a free-running fit on the threads.

Adjustment

1. Raise the front of the car with a jack and place it on jackstands.

2. Remove the dust cap from the hub. Remove and discard the cotter pin in the spindle nut.

3. Rotate the wheel in a forward direction while tightening the spindle nut to 12 ft.-lb. (16 N•m).

4. Back the spindle nut off until it reaches the "just loose" position.

5. Tighten the spindle nut by hand. If necessary, loosen it just enough to align either hole in the spindle with a slot in the nut.

6. Install a new cotter pin and bend the ends over.

7. Install a dial indicator and measure the hub assembly end play. If properly adjusted,

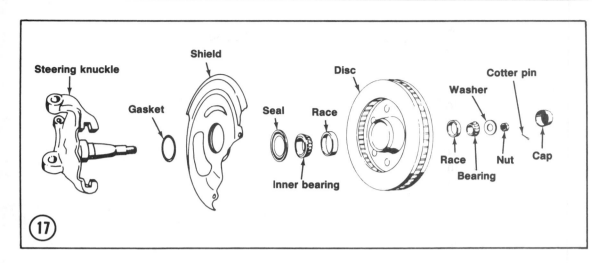

Steering knuckle   Shield   Disc   Cotter pin
Gasket   Seal   Race   Washer   Race   Nut   Cap
Inner bearing   Bearing

(17)

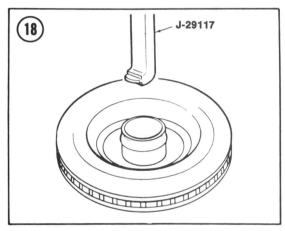

J-29117

(18)

there should be 0.001-0.005 in. (0.03-0.13 mm) end play.

8. Install the dust cap. Remove the jackstands and lower the car to the ground.

Hub and Disc Replacement

1. Loosen the front wheel lug nuts.

2. Raise the front of the car with a jack and place it on jackstands.

3. Remove the wheel/tire assembly.

4. Remove the dust cap from the hub. Remove and discard the cotter pin. Remove the hub nut and washer from the spindle.

5. Remove the brake caliper. See Chapter Twelve.

6. Pull the hub and disc assembly straight off the spindle to prevent damage to the bearings or spindle.

7. Installation is the reverse of removal.

Hub Assembly Bearing and Seal Replacement

Refer to **Figure 17** for this procedure.

1. Remove the hub assembly as described above.

2. Remove the inner roller bearing from the hub.

3. Pry the inner bearing lip seal from the hub and discard it.

4. Insert tool part No. J-29117 or equivalent behind the bearing races in the hub assembly (**Figure 18**) and drive the races out.

5. Install new races in the hub assembly with an appropriate driver.

6. Lightly grease the spindle at the outer and inner bearing seats, shoulder and seal seat with a good quality, high-temperature wheel bearing grease.

7. Install the inner bearing cone and roller assembly in the hub. Wipe an extra quantity of grease on the outside of the bearing with your finger.

8. Place a new grease seal in position. Cover with a flat plate or block of wood and tap into place until the seal is flush with the hub. Wipe a thin coat of grease across the seal lip.

9. Install the hub to the spindle carefully to prevent damage to the spindle or bearing.

10. Install the outer wheel bearing assembly. Install the washer and hub nut. Tighten the nut to 12 ft.-lb. (16 N•m) while rotating the wheel in a forward direction.

11. Adjust the wheel bearings as described in this chapter.

10

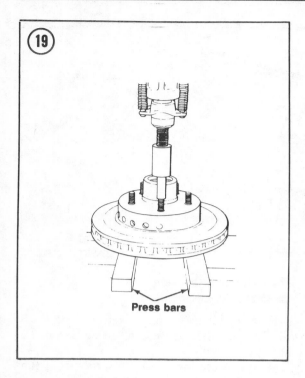

Press bars

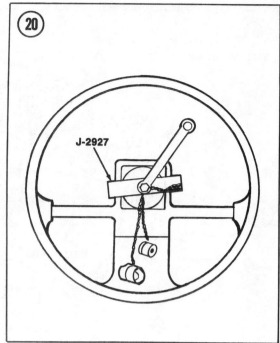

J-2927

Front Wheel Stud
Removal/Installation

This procedure requires the use of a hydraulic press.

1. Loosen the front wheel nuts.
2. Raise the front of the car with a jack and place it on jackstands.
3. Remove the wheel/tire assembly.
4. Remove the brake caliper. See Chapter Twelve.
5. Remove the hub and disc assembly as described in this chapter.
6. Support the hub assembly on press bars and press the damaged stud from the hub (**Figure 19**).
7. Install a new stud in the hub. Tap the stud lightly with a hammer to start the bolt serrations in the hole. Make sure the bolt is square with the hub flange.
8. Support the hub assembly on press bars and press the new stud into the hub.
9. Install the hub and rotor assembly as described in this chapter.
10. Install the brake caliper. See Chapter Twelve.
11. Install the wheel/tire assembly. Tighten the lug nuts to specifications (**Table 1**).

STEERING

Steering Wheel Removal/Installation

WARNING
Use of a wheel puller other than GM part No. J-2927 or equivalent can shear or loosen the plastic fasteners used to maintain steering column rigidity.

1. Disconnect the negative battery cable.
2. Remove the steering wheel shroud screws from the underside of the wheel.
3. Remove shroud and horn contact lead assembly from the steering wheel.
4. Remove the snap ring. Remove and discard the steering wheel nut.

WARNING
Do not use a knock-off wheel puller for Step 5 or it will damage the steering column.

5. Install wheel puller part No. J-2927 or equivalent as shown in **Figure 20** and remove the steering wheel.
6. Installation is the reverse of removal. Align the wheel and shaft marks to assure that the straight-ahead wheel position corresponds to the straight-ahead position of the front wheels.

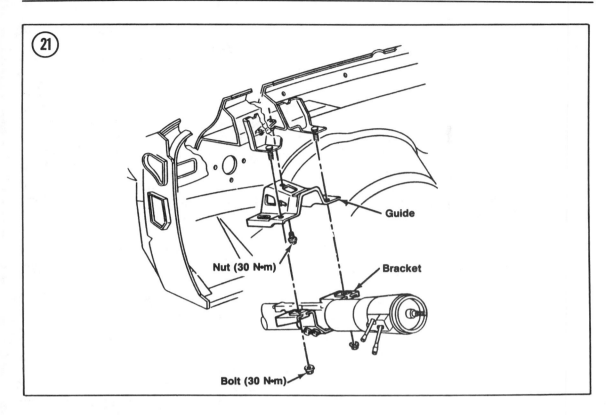

Guide

Nut (30 N•m)

Bracket

Bolt (30 N•m)

7. Install a new wheel nut and tighten to 30 ft.-lb. (40 N•m).

Steering Column
Removal/Installation

WARNING
The steering column is very susceptible to damage during and after removal from the car. Hammering, dropping or leaning on the column can damage internal plastic injections used to maintain rigidity.

This procedure can be used with both standard and tilt columns.
1. Disconnect the negative battery cable.
2. Remove the nut and bolt from the upper intermediate shaft coupling.
3. Separate the upper intermediate shaft coupling from the lower end of the steering column.
4. Disconnect the shift linkage at the lower shift lever.
5. Disconnect all electrical harness connectors from the steering column.

6. Remove the screws holding the toe pan to the floorboard.
7. Remove the nuts holding the bracket to the instrument panel (**Figure 21**).
8. Disconnect the shift position indicator pointer, if so equipped.
9. Remove the steering column.
10. Installation is the reverse of removal.

Steering Linkage

The steering linkage is a parallelogram type which connects both front wheels to the steering gear by a pitman arm. The 2 tie rods are connected to the steering arms and relay rod by ball studs. The left end of the relay rod is supported by the pitman arm, which is driven by the steering gear pitman shaft. The right end of the relay rod is supported by an idler arm, which pivots on a support connected to the frame rail. **Figure 22** shows the major steering linkage components.

Steering Linkage/Suspension Check

1. Raise the car on one side with a jack positioned at the frame torque box (directly

10

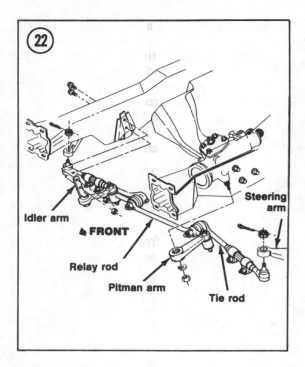

Idler arm

▲ **FRONT**

Relay rod

Pitman arm

Steering arm

Tie rod

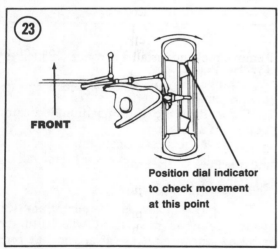

FRONT

Position dial indicator
to check movement
at this point

behind the front wheel) until the tire is about one inch off the ground.

2. Install a dial indicator as shown in **Figure 23**.

3. Place the steering wheel in the locked position.

4. Grasp the front wheel at each side and move the wheel in and out at the back.

5. The dial indicator should read 0.108 in. (2.74 mm) or less. If the reading exceeds this specification, inspect all linkage pivots and ball studs for looseness. Replace as necessary.

Tie Rod Replacement

Refer to **Figure 24** for this procedure.

1. Raise the front of the car with a jack and place it on jackstands.

2. Remove and discard the ball stud cotter pins.

3. Remove the ball stud nuts. Separate the ball studs from the steering knuckle and relay rod as required with tool part No. J-6627 or equivalent. See **Figure 25**.

4. Loosen the tie rod adjusting clamp bolts. If the torque required to remove the nut from

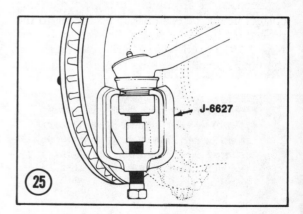

J-6627

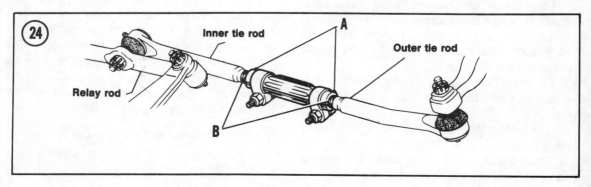

Inner tie rod

Outer tie rod

Relay rod

A

B

the clamp bolt exceeds 7 ft.-lb. (9 N•m) after breakaway, discard the nut and bolt and install new ones at reassembly.

5. Unscrew the tie rod ends.

6. Installation is the reverse of removal. The sleeve clamp must be positioned between the locating dimples at either end of the sleeve (A, **Figure 24**). The distance at each end of the sleeve must be equal within 3 threads (B, **Figure 24**).

Relay Rod Removal/Installation

The installed position of the relay rod is critical. The left and right ends of the rod *must* be kept at the same height. Side-to-side height of the rod is controlled by adjusting the position of the idler arm.

Before disconnecting the relay rod, scribe the position of the idler arm-to-frame to assure that the idler arm is reinstalled in the same position. Make sure the idler support does not turn in the bushing, as such motion can cause incorrect relay rod height when reinstalled.

If the relay rod, idler arm or pitman arm is replaced, it is absolutely necessary that the correct height be established according to the procedure in this chapter. Special tools part Nos. J-29193 and J-29194 are required to seat the tapers when installing the relay rod.

26

1. Raise the car with a jack and place it on jackstands.

2. Remove the inner tie rod ends (A, **Figure 26**) from the relay rod as described in this chapter.

3. Remove the relay rod ball stud nut at the pitman arm (B, **Figure 26**).

4. Separate the relay rod from the pitman arm with an appropriate puller.

NOTE
It may be necessary to move the linkage back and forth to free the pitman arm from the relay rod.

5. Remove the nut from the idler arm (C, **Figure 26**). Remove the relay rod.

NOTE
*If a new relay rod is to be installed, proceed to **Relay Rod Height Adjustment** before continuing with Step 6.*

6. Connect relay rod to idler arm. Make sure idler stud seal is in place. Seat tapers with tool part No. J-29193 or part No. J-29194 as required with 15 ft.-lb. (20 N•m) torque. Remove tool and install a new nut. Tighten to 40 ft.-lb. (54 N•m).

7. Repeat Step 6 to connect the relay rod to the pitman arm.

8. Install the tie rod ends as described in this chapter.

9. Lower the car to the floor. Adjust toe-in and align the steering wheel.

Relay Rod Height Adjustment

The following procedure *must* be performed whenever the relay rod, idler arm or pitman arm is installed.

1. Clean both flats on the relay rod (**Figure 27**) carefully with a wire brush.

10

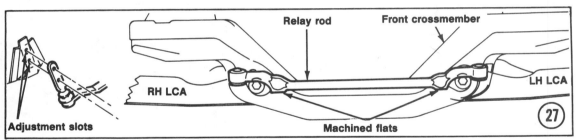

Adjustment slots | Relay rod | Front crossmember | RH LCA | LH LCA | Machined flats | 27

2. Install tool part No. J-33093 on the flat near the pitman arm.

3. Install a socket on the head of the front pivot bolt of the lower control arm on the driver's side of the car.

4. Measure and record dimension A shown in **Figure 28**.

5. Remove tool part No. J-33093 and the socket and install on the idler arm end of the relay rod. Check dimension B shown in **Figure 29**.

6. If dimension A and dimension B are not within ±1 mm of each other, loosen the idler arm attaching bolts. Adjust the idler arm position until the 2 dimensions are within specifications. Tighten the idler arm attaching bolts and remove the socket and tool part No. J-33093.

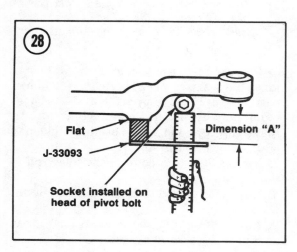

Flat

J-33093

Dimension "A"

Socket installed on head of pivot bolt

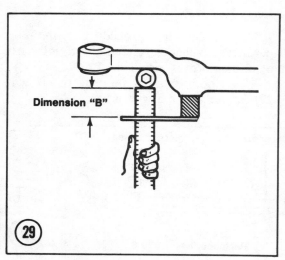

Dimension "B"

Pitman Arm Removal/Installation

1. Raise the front of the car with a jack and place it on jackstands.

2. Remove the nut from the pitman arm ball stud (A, **Figure 30**).

3. Separate the relay rod from the pitman arm with a puller. Pull down on the relay rod to remove it from the stud.

4. Remove the pitman arm nut from the pitman shaft (B, **Figure 30**). Scribe marks on arm and shaft for reassembly.

CAUTION
Do not hammer on the puller in Step 5 to separate the pitman arm from the shaft. This can cause internal damage to the steering gearbox.

5. Mark the pitman arm-to-shaft relationship. Separate the pitman arm from the pitman shaft with a puller as shown in **Figure 31**. Remove the pitman arm.

6. Install the pitman arm to the pitman shaft, aligning the marks made in Step 4.

7. Install pitman shaft nut and tighten to 180 ft.-lb. (250 N•m).

8. Install relay rod to pitman arm. Seat the tapers with tool part No. J-29193 or part No. J-29194 as required using a 15 ft.-lb. (20 N•m) torque. Remove the tool and install a new nut. Tighten to 40 ft.-lb (54 N•m).

9. Adjust relay rod height as described in this chapter.

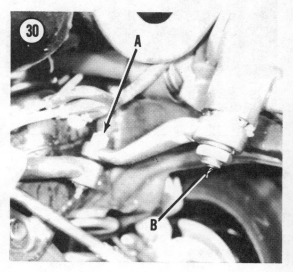

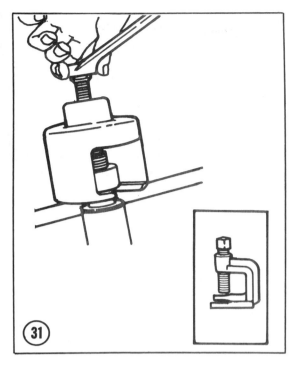

(31)

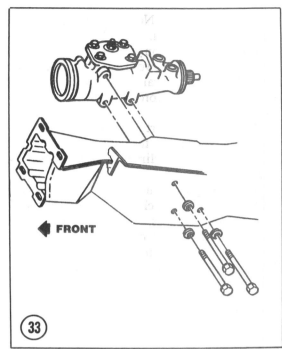

◀ FRONT

(33)

(32)

Idler Arm Replacement

1. Raise the front of the car with a jack and place it on jackstands.

2. Remove the nuts, washers and bolts holding the idler arm to the frame.

3. Remove the idler arm-to-relay rod ball stud nut (**Figure 32**).

4. Separate the idler arm from the relay rod with a puller.

5. Remove the idler arm.

6. Install the idler arm to the frame but do not tighten the mounting bolts, washers and nuts.

7. Connect the relay rod to the idler arm. Make sure the seal is on the stud. Seat the tapers with tool part No. J-29193 or part No. J-29194 as required using a 15 ft.-lb. (20 N•m) torque. Remove the tool and install a new nut. Tighten to 40 ft.-lb. (54 N•m).

8. Adjust the relay rod height as described in this chapter.

Power Steering Gearbox
Removal/Installation

1. Disconnect and cap the pressure and return hoses at the steering gearbox.

2. Remove the coupling shield.

3. Remove the coupling-to-steering shaft flange bolts.

4. Raise the car with a jack and place it on jackstands.

5. Remove the pitman arm from the pitman shaft as described in this chapter.

6. Remove the bolts holding the steering gearbox to the frame (**Figure 33**). Remove the gearbox.

7. Installation is the reverse of removal. Tighten all fasteners to specifications (**Table 1**).

10

Table 1 TIGHTENING TORQUES

Fastener	ft.-lb.	N•m
Strut assembly		
Strut-to-knuckle bolt	195	265
Strut-to-upper mount nut	50	70
Upper mount-to-wheelhouse tower	28	20
Lower control arm		
Pivot bolt nuts	65	90
Bumper-to-control arm	20	28
Control arm ball-joint to knuckle	90	120
Knuckle		
Strut-to-knuckle bolts	195	265
Control arm ball-joint to knuckle	90	120
Steering linkage		
Knuckle-to-tie rod end nut	40	54
Tie rod clamp nuts	14	19
Tie rod-to-intermediate rod nut	40	54
Pitman arm-to-intermediate rod nut	40	54
Pitman arm-to-steering gear nut	180	250
Idler arm-to-intermediate rod nut	40	54
Idler arm-to-frame nut	50	70
Power steering pump		
Reservoir bolt	35	48
Flow control fitting	35	48
Pressure hose	20	27
Power steering gear		
Gear-to-frame bolts	80	110
Pressure/return line fittings	20	27
Pitman shaft nut	185	240
Coupling flange bolt	30	40
Steering wheel		
Wheel-to-shaft nut	30	40
Bracket-to-column support nuts	25	34
Bracket-to-column bolt	30	40
Toe pan-to-dash screw	45 in.-lb.	5
Toe pan clamp screws	60 in.-lb.	7
Clamp-to-steering shaft nut	55	70
Flex coupling nuts	20	27
Flex coupling-to-shaft bolt	30	40

Table 2 ALIGNMENT SPECIFICATIONS

Caster	+3° ±0.5°
Camber	+1° ±0.5°
Toe-in (degrees per wheel)	
Z28	+0.2° ±0.05°
Others	+0.15° ±0.05°

REAR SUSPENSION, DIFFERENTIAL AND DRIVE SHAFT

Camaro and Firebird models use a link-type rear suspension. The axle housing is connected to the body by 2 lower control arms and a track bar. A single torque arm is used instead of upper control arms. The torque arm is rigidly mounted to the rear axle housing at the rear and to the transmission at the front with a rubber bushing. Coil springs support the car's weight, with ride control provided by tubular shock absorbers at the rear of the axle housing. A stabilizer bar is optional. **Figure 1** shows the major components of the rear suspension.

A semi-floating rear axle is used with an open drive line. Five different axle ratios are used, depending upon engine/transmission usage. A limited slip differential is also available as an option in all 5 ratios.

This chapter provides service procedures for the rear suspension, the rear axle assembly and the drive shaft. Tightening torques are listed in **Table 1** at the end of the chapter.

REAR SUSPENSION

Shock Absorber Replacement

Refer to **Figure 2** for this procedure.
1. Raise the rear of the car with a jack and place it on jackstands to support the rear axle.
2. Pull back the carpeting in the rear of the car and remove the shock absorber mounting nut.
3. Remove the nut and washer from the lower shock absorber mount (**Figure 3**).
4. Remove the shock absorber.
5. Installation is the reverse of removal. Tighten the upper nut to 13 ft.-lb. (17 N•m). Tighten the lower nut to 70 ft.-lb. (95 N•m).

Coil Spring Replacement

Refer to **Figure 4** for this procedure.
1. Raise the car with a jack and place it on jackstands to support the rear axle.
2. Remove the track bar mounting bolt at the axle (A, **Figure 5**). Loosen the track bar bolt at the body brace (B, **Figure 5**).
3. Disconnect the rear brake hose clip at the underbody (**Figure 6**).
4. Remove the lower nut from the shock absorber on each side of the car.
5. If equipped with a 4-cylinder engine, disconnect and remove the drive shaft as described in this chapter.
6. Carefully lower rear axle. Remove spring(s) and insulator(s).
7. Installation is the reverse of removal. Tighten all fasteners to specifications.

11

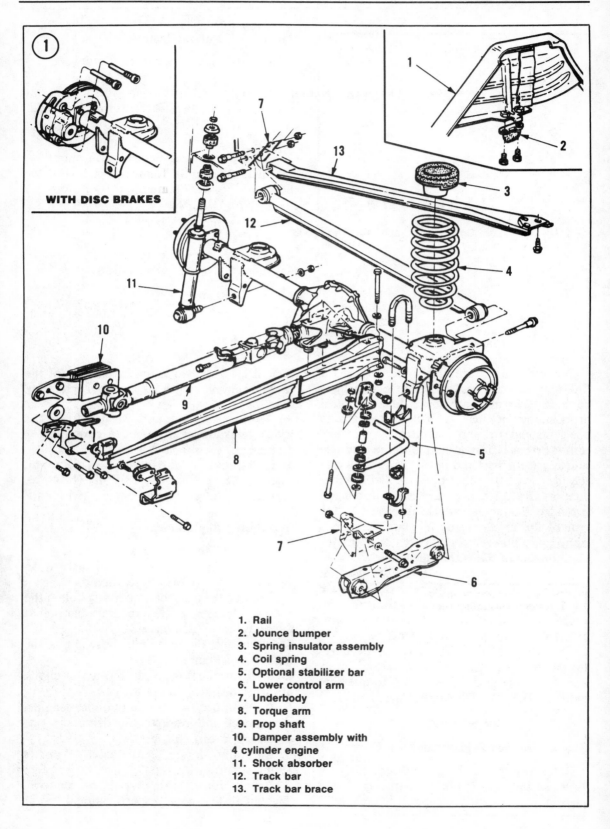

1. Rail
2. Jounce bumper
3. Spring insulator assembly
4. Coil spring
5. Optional stabilizer bar
6. Lower control arm
7. Underbody
8. Torque arm
9. Prop shaft
10. Damper assembly with
4 cylinder engine
11. Shock absorber
12. Track bar
13. Track bar brace

WITH DISC BRAKES

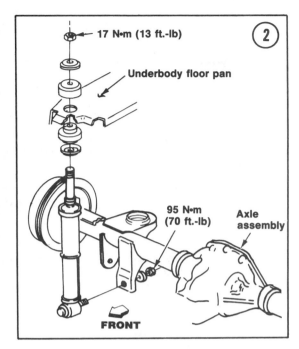

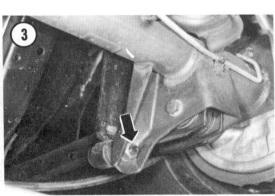

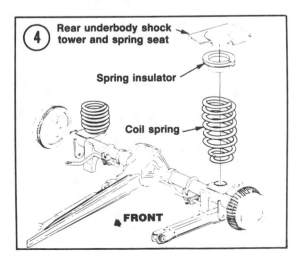

Track Bar Removal/Installation

Refer to **Figure 7** for this procedure.

1. Raise the rear of the car with a jack and place it on jackstands. Support the rear axle at curb height position.

2. Remove the track bar bolt and nut at the rear axle (**Figure 8**). Remove the bolt at the body bracket (A, **Figure 5**).

3. Remove the track bar.

4. Installation is the reverse of removal. Tighten all fasteners to specifications.

11

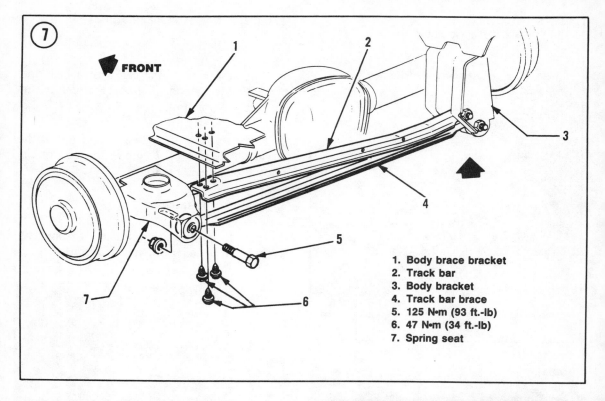

FRONT

1. Body brace bracket
2. Track bar
3. Body bracket
4. Track bar brace
5. 125 N•m (93 ft.-lb)
6. 47 N•m (34 ft.-lb)
7. Spring seat

Track Bar Brace Removal/Installation

Refer to **Figure 7** for this procedure.

1. Raise the rear of the car with a jack and place it on jackstands. Support the rear axle at curb height position.
2. Remove the heat shield screws from the track bar brace.
3. Remove the 3 track bar brace-to-body brace screws (**Figure 9**).
4. Remove the body bracket nut and bolt (B, **Figure 5**). Remove the track bar brace.
5. Installation is the reverse of removal. Tighten all fasteners to specifications.

Rear Lower Control Arm Removal/Installation

When necessary to remove both control arms, remove and install them one at a time to prevent the axle from rolling or slipping sideways.

1. Raise the rear of the car with a jack and place it on jackstands. Support the rear axle at curb height position.
2. Remove the bolt holding the lower control arm to the axle housing (**Figure 10**).

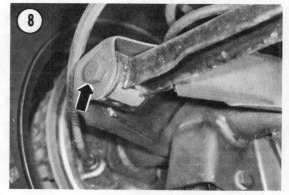

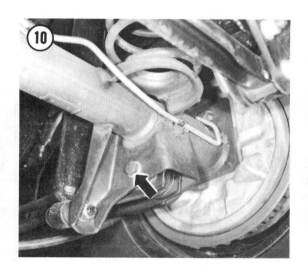

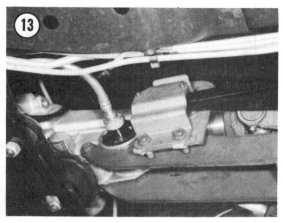

3. Remove the bolt holding the control arm to the underbody (**Figure 11**).

4. Remove the control arm.

5. Installation is the reverse of removal. Tighten all fasteners to specifications.

Rear Lower Control Arm Bushing Replacement

1. Remove the control arm as described in this chapter.

2. Press the old bushing out with an arbor press using an appropriate size receiver and driver.

3. Press the new bushing in place.

4. Install the control arm as described in this chapter.

Torque Arm Removal/Installation

CAUTION
Remove the coil springs before attempting to remove the torque arm. Failure to do so will result in the rear axle twisting forward, possibly damaging the vehicle.

1. Raise the car with a jack and place it on jackstands. Support the rear axle with a hydraulic jack.

2. Remove the coil springs as described in this chapter.

3. Remove the torque arm attaching bolts at the rear axle (**Figure 12**).

4. Remove the torque arm attaching bracket at the transmission (**Figure 13**). Remove the torque arm.

11

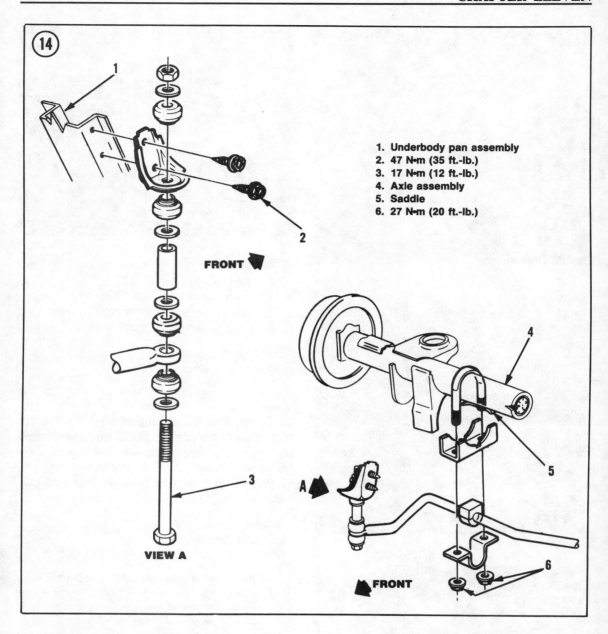

(14)

1. Underbody pan assembly
2. 47 N•m (35 ft.-lb.)
3. 17 N•m (12 ft.-lb.)
4. Axle assembly
5. Saddle
6. 27 N•m (20 ft.-lb.)

FRONT

VIEW A

FRONT

5. Installation is the reverse of removal. Tighten all fasteners to specifications.

Rear Stabilizer
Removal/Installation

Refer to **Figure 14** for this procedure.
1. Remove the bolt holding the stabilizer bar to the underbody pan bracket at each side of the car.
2. Remove the U-bolt nuts holding the stabilizer bar to each side of the axle.

3. Remove the stabilizer bar and bushings.
4. Inspect the bushings carefully. Replace any that are worn or deteriorated.
5. Installation is the reverse of removal. Tighten all fasteners to specifications.

DRIVE SHAFT

All Camaro/Firebird models use a one-piece drive shaft. A universal joint and splined slip yoke is used at the transmission end of the shaft. A second universal joint

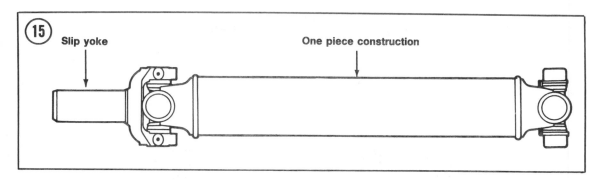

Slip yoke | One piece construction

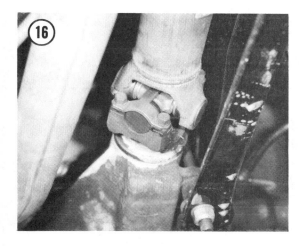

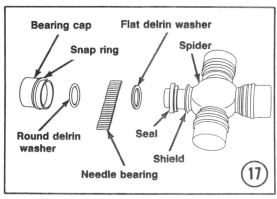

connects the drive shaft with the pinion flange at the rear.

The universal joints are factory-lubricated and cannot be lubricated while on the car. Universal joint bearings installed at the factory have a nylon injection ring. A repair kit is available containing a new spider with bearing assemblies and snap rings to overhaul worn universal joints.

Figure 15 shows the drive shaft design.

Drive Shaft Removal

NOTE
Do not pound on the yoke ears while removing or installing the drive shaft, as this can fracture the nylon injection rings in the factory-installed universal joints.

1. Raise the car with a jack and place it on jackstands.
2. Scribe or chalk alignment marks on the shaft and pinion flange for reassembly reference.
3. Disconnect the rear universal joint from the companion flange (**Figure 16**).
4. Support the drive shaft and tape the bearing cups together to prevent loss of the bearing rollers.
5. Move the drive shaft to the rear and pass it under the axle housing to disengage it from the transmission.
6. Remove the drive shaft from the vehicle.

Installation

1. Slide the drive shaft into the transmission.
2. Align the rear universal joint with the rear axle pinion flange. Make sure the bearings are properly seated in the pinion flange yoke and that the alignment marks scribed during removal are aligned.
3. Install the retaining bolts (**Figure 16**) and tighten evenly to 15 ft.-lb. (20 N•m).

UNIVERSAL JOINTS

The single cardan joint consists of a single spider and 4 sets of needle bearings, bearing seals, caps and cap retainers. Replacement universal joint kits are the internal snap ring type. See **Figure 17**.

11

Factory Installed Universal Joint Disassembly

Production universal joints are retained by nylon injected rings. Removal of the universal joint destroys the nylon ring and the universal joint must be discarded.

1. Support the lower ear of the drive shaft yoke with a 1 1/8 in. socket on the base plate of a hydraulic press.
2. Install a cross press such as tool part No. J-9522-3 over the open horizontal bearing cup (**Figure 18**) and press the cup from the yoke ear.
3. Rotate the drive shaft 180° and repeat Step 1 and Step 2 to press the opposite bearing cup from the yoke.
4. Remove the spider from the yoke.

Service Replacement Universal Joint Disassembly

1. Paint alignment marks on the drive shaft and slip yoke for reassembly reference. Remove slip yoke from drive shaft.
2. Remove the loose bearing caps from the spider. Apply liberal quantities of penetrating oil to the bearing caps in the shaft yoke.

> *CAUTION*
> *Clamp only the forged portion of the slip yoke or drive shaft yoke in the vise in Step 3. Clamping the drive shaft tube in a vise can distort the tube and result in drive line vibration after installation.*

3. Clamp the drive shaft yoke or slip yoke in a vise.
4. Remove the bearing cap retaining clips. If necessary, tap the ends of the bearing caps with a hammer to relieve any pressure on the clips.
5. Unclamp and reposition the yoke in the vise so it is supported on the vise jaws.
6. Tap the end of one bearing cap with a hammer and drive the opposite cap from the yoke.
7. Unclamp and reposition the yoke in the vise, then remove the remaining bearing cap.
8. Remove the spider from the yoke.

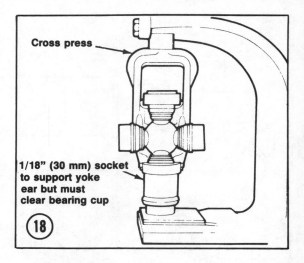

Cross press

1/18" (30 mm) socket to support yoke ear but must clear bearing cup

18

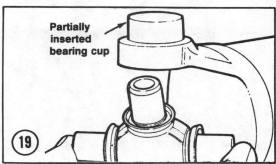

Partially inserted bearing cup

19

Cleaning and Inspection

1. Clean the yoke bearing cap bores with solvent and a wire brush.
2. Wash the bearing caps, bearings and spider in solvent. Wipe dry with a clean shop cloth.
3. Check the caps, bearings and spider for brinneling, flat spots, scoring, cracks or excessive wear. Replace the entire assembly if any part(s) shows such conditions.

Universal Joint Assembly

1. If replacing original universal joints that had nylon injected retaining rings, remove any remaining sheared plastic from the yoke grooves.
2. Lubricate all components with chassis grease. Wipe the outside of the bearing caps with a thin film of chassis grease.
3. Install the bearing cap seals on the spider.
4. Partially install a bearing and needle bearing assembly in the shaft yoke (**Figure 19**).

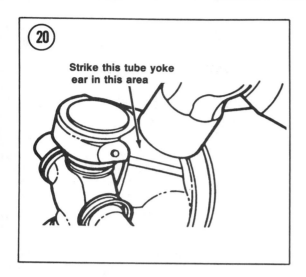

Strike this tube yoke ear in this area

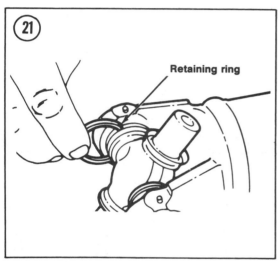

Retaining ring

5. Place the spider in the shaft yoke. Install the opposite bearing cap and needle bearing assembly in the yoke.

6. Support the yoke on the vise jaws. Seat both caps in the yoke by tapping lightly with a hammer (**Figure 20**).

7. Install the bearing cap retaining clips (**Figure 21**).

8. Install the remaining 2 bearing cap and needle bearing assemblies in the spider.

9. Tape the caps on the spider to hold them in place until the drive shaft is reinstalled.

REAR AXLE AND AXLE SHAFTS

This section includes removal, installation and inspection procedures for the standard rear axle, and axle shafts. Rear axle repair requires special skills and many expensive special tools. The inspection procedures will tell you if repairs are necessary.

Limited slip rear axles contain a clutch pack with guides, shims and preload springs. Refer all service on such axles to a dealer or other qualified mechanic.

Carrier Cover
Gasket Replacement

1. Raise the car with a jack and place it on jackstands.

2. Place a clean container underneath the carrier housing.

3. Remove the cover bolts (**Figure 22**).

4. Pry the cover loose with a screwdriver and let the lubricant drain.

5. Remove the cover. Remove and discard the gasket.

6. Clean the gasket sealing surfaces on the cover and carrier.

7. Install the cover with a new gasket.

8. Install the cover bolts and tighten to 20 ft.-lb. (27 N•m) in a crisscross pattern to assure a uniform draw on the gasket.

9. Fill the carrier with lubricant to within 3/8 in. of the filler plug hole.

Axle Shaft
Removal/Installation

1. Raise the car with a jack and place it on jackstands.

11

2. Remove the wheel/tire assembly and brake drum. See *Drum Brakes*, Chapter Twelve.

3. Remove the carrier cover and drain the lubricant.

4. Remove the rear axle pinion shaft lock screw and pinion shaft (**Figure 23**).

5. Push the flanged end of the axle shaft in toward the center of the car. Remove the C-lock from the shaft (**Figure 23**).

6. Carefully withdraw the axle shaft from the carrier housing to prevent damage to the oil seal.

7. Installation is the reverse of removal.

Axle Shaft Oil
Seal/Bearing Replacement

1. Remove the axle shaft as described in this chapter.

2. Pry the seal from the housing.

3. Install a bearing removal tool to a slide hammer, as shown in **Figure 24**.

4. Insert the tool into the bore and engage its tangs with the bearing outer race. Remove the bearing.

5. Lubricate a new bearing with gear lubricant.

6. Install the bearing with an installer tool as shown in **Figure 25**. The tool must bottom against the housing shoulder to properly seat the bearing.

7. Lubricate the seal lips with gear lubricant.

8. Fit the seal in the housing bore and tap in place with a seal installer until it is flush with the axle tube.

Rear Axle
Removal/Installation

1. Raise the car with a jack. Support the car with jackstands placed at the frame. Install the jack under the rear axle housing.

2. Disconnect the shock absorbers as described in this chapter.

3. Remove the bolt holding the left side of the track bar to the axle.

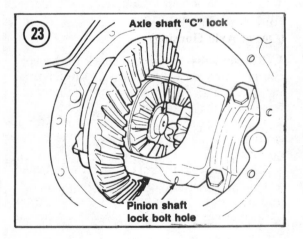

(23) Axle shaft "C" lock

Pinion shaft
lock bolt hole

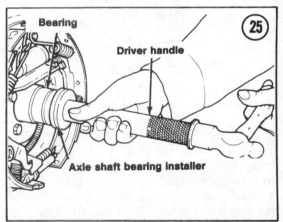

(25) Bearing

Driver handle

Axle shaft bearing installer

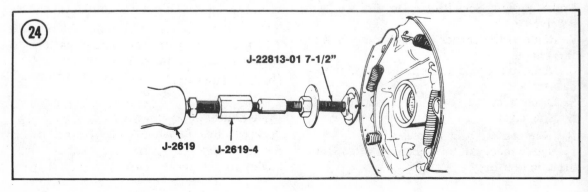

(24) J-22813-01 7-1/2"

J-2619   J-2619-4

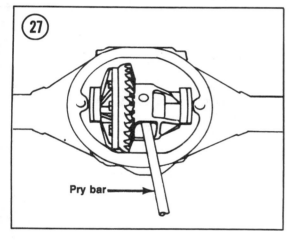

Pry bar ——→

4. Remove the brake line junction block bolt at the axle housing (**Figure 26**). Disconnect brake lines from junction block and cap lines to prevent leakage.

5. Lower the rear axle assembly and remove the springs as described in this chapter.

6. Remove the rear wheel/tire assemblies and brake drums. See *Brake Drums*, Chapter Twelve.

7. Remove the carrier cover as described in this chapter.

8. Remove the axle shafts as described in this chapter.

9. Disconnect the brake lines from the axle housing clips.

10. Remove the backing plates.

11. Disconnect the lower control arms from the axle housing.

12. Disconnect the torque arm at the axle.

13. Mark the drive shaft and companion flange relationship. Remove the drive shaft as described in this chapter.

14. Remove the rear axle housing.

15. Installation is the reverse of removal. Fill the rear axle to within 3/8 in. of the filler plug hole. Bleed the brakes; see Chapter Twelve.

Differential
Removal/Installation

1. Remove the axle as described in this chapter.

2. Mark the differential bearing caps with a centerpunch for reassembly alignment reference.

3. Remove the differential bearing cap bolts.

4. Pry the rear axle case from the carrier as shown in **Figure 27**. Work carefully to prevent damage to the gasket sealing surface.

5. Tie the left and right bearing shims and outer races in sets for proper reinstallation.

6. Installation is the reverse of removal. Tighten all fasteners to specifications.

Differential Inspection
(Out of Axle Housing)

1. Rotate the ring gear and check for broken, chipped or worn teeth. Check the differential for rough movement. Have the differential repaired if these conditions are found.

2. Inspect all bearings and cups for pitting, galling, flat spots or cracks. Replace as necessary.

3. Check the differential case for an elongated or enlarged pinion mate shaft bore.

4. Inspect the machined thrust washer surface areas for nicks, gouges, cracks or burrs.

5. Check the case for cracks or other damage. Replace the case if any of these conditions are found.

Differential Inspection
(In Axle Housing)

1. Mount a dial indicator on the housing as shown in **Figure 28** to measure ring gear backlash. The indicator plunger should touch the drive side of a ring gear tooth at right angles to the tooth. Hold the pinion from

11

turning with one hand and rotate the ring gear against the dial indicator with the other.

2. Check at 4 points around the ring gear. Backlash should be 0.005-0.009 in. (0.13-0.23 mm) for all new gears, with less than 0.002 in. (0.05 mm) variation between points checked. If it does not meet these specifications, have the differential disassembled and adjusted.

3. Measure ring gear runout. It should not exceed 0.002 in. (0.05 mm). If it does, have the differential repaired.

Tooth Contact Pattern Test

1. Wipe all oil from the axle housing. Clean each ring gear tooth carefully.

2. Apply a light coat of gear marking compound to the drive side of the ring gear teeth.

3. Rotate the ring gear slowly in both directions. Compare the contact pattern pressed into the marking compound with those shown in **Figure 29**.

4. The desired tooth contact pattern under a light load is shown in **Figure 30**. If the pattern is not correct, have the differential disassembled and adjusted.

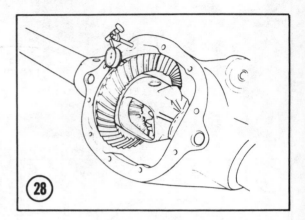

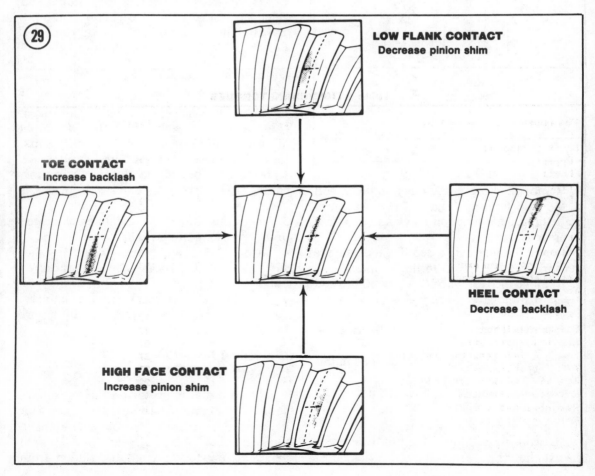

LOW FLANK CONTACT
Decrease pinion shim

TOE CONTACT
Increase backlash

HEEL CONTACT
Decrease backlash

HIGH FACE CONTACT
Increase pinion shim

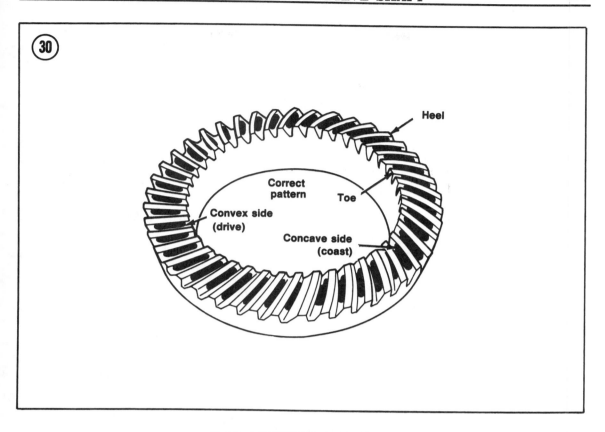

Table 1 TIGHTENING TORQUES

Fastener	ft.-lb.	N·m
Shock absorber nut		
Upper	13	17
Lower	70	95
Track bar		
Bolt	93	125
Nut	58	78
Track bar brace		
Nut	58	78
Screws	34	47
Control arm-to-rear axle	68	93
Control arm-to-underbody	68	93
Torque arm		
Bolt	20	27
Nut	100	135
Stabilizer shaft bolt	12	17
Stabilizer bracket screw	35	47
Stabilizer shaft clamp to U-bolt nut	20	27
Axle bumper bracket bolt	20	27
Rear universal joint-to-pinion flange	15	20
Rear axle housing cover	30	41
Rear wheel-to-axle shaft	80	108
Rear axle filler plug	20	17
Steel wheel lug nuts	80	110
Aluminum wheel lug nuts	100	140

CHAPTER TWELVE

BRAKES

Camaro and Firebird models use a dual hydraulic power brake system with disc brakes at the front and drum brakes at the rear. Rear disc brakes are optional. A dual reservoir master cylinder (**Figure 1**) is used, with the smaller front reservoir connected to the front disc brakes. The larger rear reservoir is connected to the rear brakes.

A combination valve is bracket-mounted to the master cylinder (**Figure 2**) and contains a metering and proportioning section. The pressure differential warning switch in the combination valve compares front and rear brake pressure. If a pressure loss occurs in either brake system, a warning light on the instrument panel comes on to alert the driver.

Power brakes are standard, with vacuum boost provided by a power booster unit.

A ratchet-type hand-operated parking brake lever is mounted in the console between the front seats and is connected to the rear wheel brakes through a series of cables underneath the floor pan.

Tightening torques are provided in **Table 1** at the end of the chapter.

FRONT DISC BRAKES

The front disc brake assembly uses a single piston, pin slider caliper. The caliper operates on a damped iron rotor retained on the hub assembly by the wheel studs and wheel nuts.

Pad Inspection

1. Loosen the front wheel lug nuts.
2. Raise the front of the car with a jack and place it on jackstands.

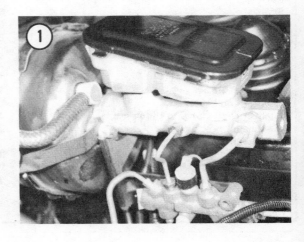

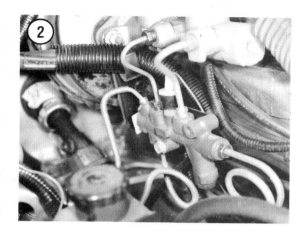

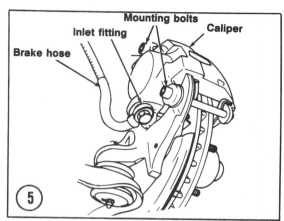

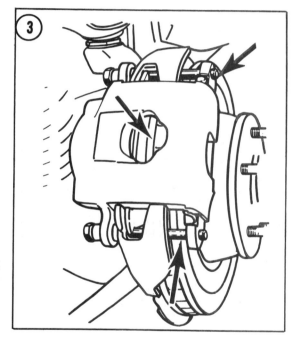

3. Remove the wheel/tire assemblies.

4. Look through the inspection hole in the caliper and check the lining wear at each end of the pad (**Figure 3**). Check lining thickness visually.

5. If any lining is worn to within 1/32 in. of the metal shoe at any point, replace all pads.

6. Install the wheel/tire assemblies. Lower the car to the ground.

7. Tighten wheel lug nuts to specifications (**Table 1**).

Pad Replacement

1. Set the parking brake. Place the transmission is 1st gear (manual) or PARK (automatic).

2. Loosen the front wheel lug nuts.

3. Remove the master cylinder cover and use a large syringe to remove about two-thirds of the brake fluid in each reservoir.

NOTE
Discard this brake fluid. Do not reuse.

4. Raise the front of the car with a jack and place it on jackstands.

5. Install a C-clamp as shown in **Figure 4** and tighten until the piston bottoms in the bore.

6. Remove the C-clamp. Remove the bolt holding the inlet fitting, as shown in **Figure 5**.

7. Remove the 2 Allen head mounting bolts (**Figure 5**).

NOTE
If the bolts are corroded, discard and install new ones when the caliper is reinstalled.

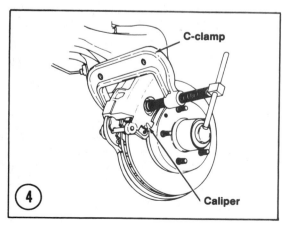

12

8. Remove the caliper. Suspend it from the front frame with a wire hook. See **Figure 6**.

9. Remove the pads from the caliper (**Figure 7**).

10. Remove the sleeves from the caliper bolt holes. Remove the bushings from the bolt hole grooves. See **Figure 7**.

11. Inspect the pads. Light surface dirt, oil or grease stains may be sanded off. If oil or grease has penetrated the surface, replace the pads. Since brake fluid will ruin the friction material, pads must be replaced if any brake fluid has touched them.

12. Check the caliper piston seal and boot area for brake fluid leaks. If brake fluid has leaked from the caliper housing, replace the caliper. If the leak appears to come from the seal area, rebuild the caliper as described in this chapter.

13. Inspect the brake rotor as described in this chapter.

14. Install new bushings in the caliper bolt hole grooves. Install new sleeves in the bolt holes.

15. Install the retainer spring on the inner pad (**Figure 8**) with a rotating motion.

16. Install the inner pad carefully (**Figure 9**). If the inner pad retainer clip is bent during installation, the brakes may rattle.

17. Install the outer pad. Install the caliper to the rotor with a rotating motion. Install the mounting bolts and tighten to 35 ft.-lb. (47 N•m).

18. Install the inlet fitting attachment bolt and tighten to 32 ft.-lb. (44 N•m).

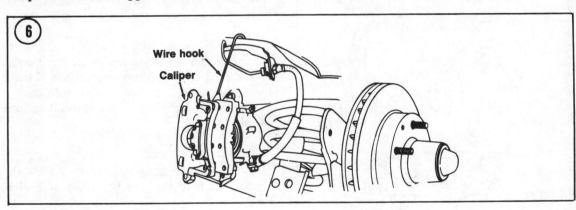

⑥

Wire hook

Caliper

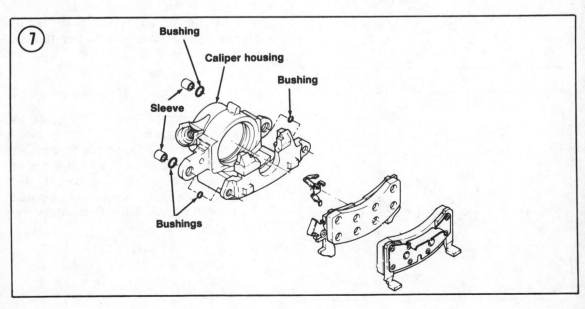

⑦

Bushing

Caliper housing

Bushing

Sleeve

Bushings

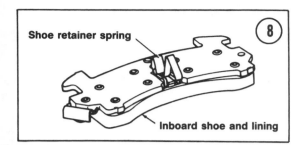

Shoe retainer spring

Inboard shoe and lining

⑧

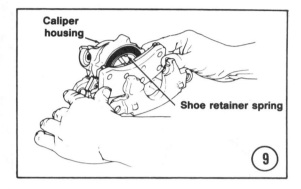

Caliper housing

Shoe retainer spring

⑨

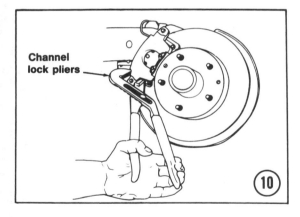

Channel lock pliers

⑩

19. Use a pair of channel-lock pliers to tightly cinch the outer pad ears to the caliper. See **Figure 10**.

20. Install the wheel/tire assemblies and lower the car to the ground. Tighten wheel lug nuts to specifications (**Table 1**).

21. Fill the master cylinder to within 1/4 in. of the divider in the reservoir. Use fresh DOT 3 or DOT 4 brake fluid from an unopened container.

CAUTION
Do not use brake fluid from a previously opened container. Brake fluid absorbs moisture from the air.

Moisture in the hydraulic lines can result in erratic or slow braking.

22. Pump the brake pedal several times to seat the new pads and road test the car to make sure the brakes operate properly.

Caliper Removal

1. Perform Steps 1-7 of *Pad Replacement* in this chapter.
2. Remove the brake line inlet fitting. Remove the caliper.
3. Mark the left and right calipers for identification if both are removed.

Caliper Overhaul

Refer to **Figure 11** for this procedure.
1. Remove the pads from the caliper. Remove the sleeves from the caliper bolt holes. Remove the bushings from the bolt hole grooves.
2. Pad the inside of the caliper with shop cloths and direct a stream of low-pressure compressed air into the caliper inlet hole (**Figure 12**) to remove the piston.
3. Remove and discard the caliper dust boot (**Figure 13**).

NOTE
Use a plastic or wooden dowel for seal removal in Step 4. Do not pry seal out with a screwdriver or other metal tool. This can scratch the piston bore or burr the seal groove edge.

4. Remove and discard the piston seal. Remove the bleed screw.
5. Clean the caliper and piston with rubbing alcohol. Make sure all grooves and passages are clean, then blow dry with compressed air.
6. Inspect the caliper bore and piston for pitting or scoring. Replace the piston if pitted or scored. Replace the caliper if bore corrosion cannot be removed with crocus cloth.
7. Coat a new piston seal with clean brake fluid and install it in the caliper bore. The seal should be seated firmly in the groove without twisting it.
8. Lubricate the new dust boot with clean brake fluid and install it over the piston as shown in **Figure 14**.

12

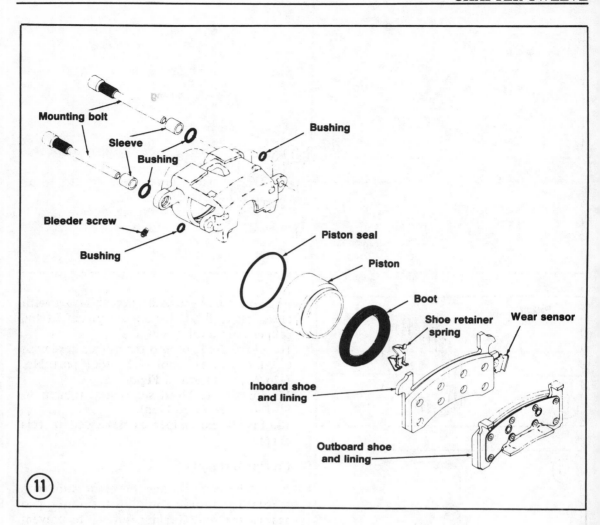

Mounting bolt

Sleeve

Bushing

Bleeder screw

Bushing

Bushing

Piston seal

Piston

Boot

Shoe retainer
spring

Wear sensor

Inboard shoe
and lining

Outboard shoe
and lining

⑪

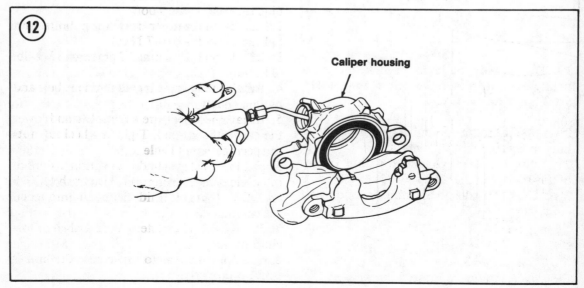

⑫

Caliper housing

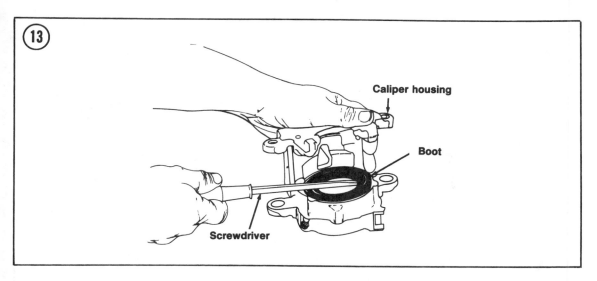

⑬

Caliper housing

Boot

Screwdriver

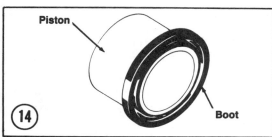

Piston

⑭

Boot

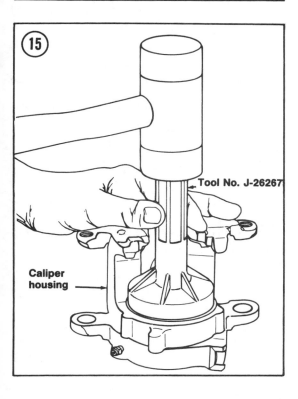

⑮

Tool No. J-26267

Caliper
housing

9. Lubricate the caliper bore housing with clean brake fluid. Install the piston in the caliper bore until it bottoms.

10. Drive the boot into the caliper bore with a boot installer tool (GM tool part No. J-26267) as shown in **Figure 15**.

11. Install the bleed screw and tighten to 80-140 in.-lb. (9-16 N•m).

12. Install the caliper as described in this chapter.

Caliper Installation

1. Install the caliper over the brake rotor with a rotating motion, holding the outer pad against the rotor braking surface to prevent pinching the piston boot.

2. Install the caliper mounting bolts and tighten to 35 ft.-lb. (47 N•m).

3. Install the inlet fitting. Tighten to 32 ft.-lb. (44 N•m).

4. Install the inlet fitting attachment bolt and tighten snugly.

5. Install the wheel/tire assemblies and lower the car to the ground. Tighten wheel lug nuts to specifications (**Table 1**).

6. Fill the master cylinder to within 1/4 in. of the divider in the reservoir. Use fresh DOT 3 or DOT 4 brake fluid from an unopened container.

7. Bleed the brake system as described in this chapter.

8. Road test the car to make sure the brakes operate properly.

12

Rotor Removal/Installation

1. Raise the front of the car with a jack and place it on jackstands.
2. Remove the caliper as described in this chapter.
3. Remove the brake rotor from the drive flange studs.
4. Installation is the reverse of removal.

Rotor Inspection

1. Inspect the rotor for cracks, rust or scratches. Replace the rotor if cracked. Light rust can be removed with crocus cloth or medium emery paper. Heavy rust or deep scratches should be removed by resurfacing the rotor. This can be done by a dealer or a machine shop.

NOTE
If the rotor is resurfaced, its finished thickness should not be less than 0.980 in. (24.84 mm). This minimum dimension is cast on the rotor.

2. Check the rotor thickness with a micrometer at 4 equal points. Take each reading with the micrometer positioned one inch from the edge of the rotor. If the measurements vary more than 0.0005 in. (0.0127 mm), resurface or replace the rotor as required.

REAR DISC BRAKES

The optional rear disc brake assembly uses a single piston, pin slider caliper. The caliper piston contains a self-adjusting mechanism for the parking brake.

Pad Inspection

See *Front Disc Brakes, Pad Inspection* in this chapter.

Pad Replacement

1. Remove the master cylinder cover. Use a large syringe to remove about two-thirds of the brake fluid in each reservoir.
2. Loosen the rear wheel lug nuts. Raise the rear of the car with a jack and place it on jackstands.

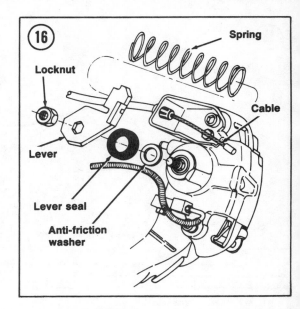

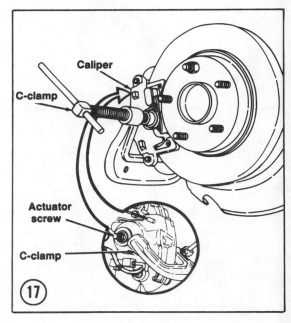

3. Remove the rear wheels. Reinstall one lug nut with its flat side facing the rotor to keep the rotor in place.
4. Loosen the equalizer locknut. Loosen the adjusting nut to remove tension on the parking brake cable.
5. Remove the parking brake cable and spring at the caliper lever. Hold the lever and remove the locknut. Remove lever, lever seal and anti-friction washer. See **Figure 16**.

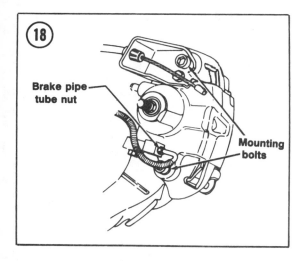

Brake pipe tube nut

Mounting bolts

(18)

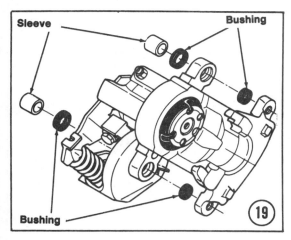

Sleeve

Bushing

Bushing

(19)

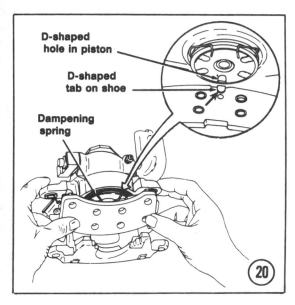

D-shaped hole in piston

D-shaped tab on shoe

Dampening spring

(20)

CAUTION
Do not let the C-clamp touch the actuator screw in Step 6.

6. Install a C-clamp as shown in **Figure 17** and tighten until the piston bottoms in its bore.

7. Remove the C-clamp. Reinstall the anti-friction washer, lever seal, lever and nut. See **Figure 16**. Lever seal bead must face the caliper housing.

8. Loosen the brake pipe nut (**Figure 18**) and disconnect from the caliper. Cap the brake pipe and plug the caliper fitting.

9. Remove caliper mounting bolts (**Figure 18**). Remove the caliper assembly.

10. Remove the pads from the caliper.

11. Remove the mounting bolt sleeves. Remove the 2 large and 2 small bushings. See **Figure 19**.

12. Carefully pry the flexible 2-way check valve from the end of the piston with a small screwdriver.

13. Inspect the pads. Light surface dirt, oil or grease stains may be sanded off. If oil or grease has penetrated the surface, replace the pads. Since brake fluid will ruin the friction material, pads must be replaced if any brake fluid has touched them.

14. Check the caliper piston seal and boot area for brake fluid leaks. If brake fluid has leaked from the caliper housing, replace the caliper.

15. Inspect the brake rotor as described under *Front Disc Brakes*.

16. Lubricate the bushings with part No. 5459912 silicone grease or equivalent and install in caliper with new sleeves.

17. Lubricate a new 2-way check valve with part No. 5459912 silicone grease or equivalent and press into the end of the piston.

18. Install the inboard pad in the caliper. The D-shaped tab on the pad must engage the piston hole, as shown in **Figure 20**. If tab and hole do not align, rotate piston until they do.

19. Install the outboard pad in the caliper. Install the caliper and tighten mounting bolts to 30-45 ft.-lb. (41-61 N•m).

12

20. Remove cap from brake pipe. Install pipe in caliper fitting. Tighten to 15 ft.-lb. (20 N•m).

> *NOTE*
> *If the brass block and bolt were removed with the brake pipe, install the block and bolt using 2 new copper washers. Tighten to 18-30 ft.-lb. (25-41 N•m).*

21. Apply heavy force to brake pedal to set caliper. Cinch outboard pad ears to caliper as shown in **Figure 21** with 12 in. channel lock pliers.

22. Clean all grease and oil from caliper seal area. Lubricate with silicone brake lubricant. Install a new anti-friction washer.

23. Lubricate a new lever seal with silicone brake lubricant. Install seal with bead against caliper housing.

24. Install lever on actuator screw hex. Lever must point downward.

25. Rotate lever toward front of car and hold. Install nut and tighten to 30-40 ft.-lb. (40-54 N•m). Rotate lever back until it reaches the caliper stop.

26. Install return spring and connect the parking brake cable. Tighten cable equalizer until the lever starts to move off the caliper. Loosen adjustment until the lever moves back to the stop.

27. Remove the wheel nut holding the rotor in place. Install the wheel on each side.

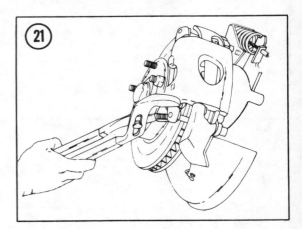

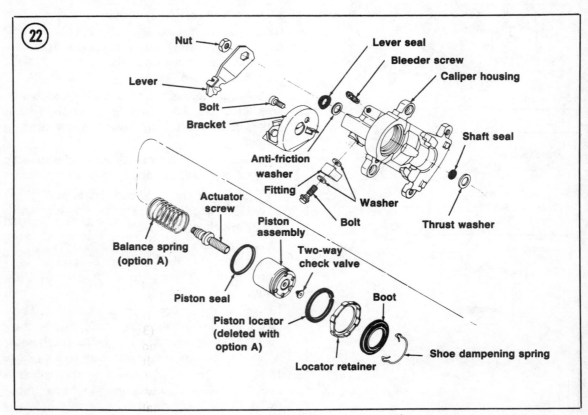

28. Remove the jackstands and lower the car to the ground. Tighten wheel lug nuts to specifications (**Table 1**).

29. Fill the master cylinder to within 1/4 in. of the divider in the reservoir. Use clean DOT 3 or DOT 4 brake fluid from an unopened container.

CAUTION
Do not use brake fluid from a previously opened container. Brake fluid absorbs moisture from the air. Moisture in the hydraulic lines can result in erratic or slow braking.

30. Bleed the brakes as described in this chapter. Road test the car to make sure the brakes operate properly.

Caliper Removal

1. Perform Steps 1-9 of *Rear Disc Brakes, Pad Replacement* in this chapter.
2. Mark the right and left calipers for reassembly if both are removed.

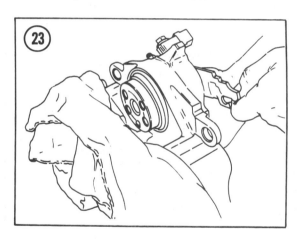

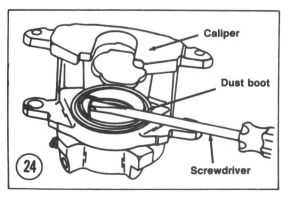

Caliper Overhaul

Refer to **Figure 22** for this procedure.
1. Remove the pad dampening spring from the piston end.
2. Support the caliper in a vise with protective jaws. Pad the inside of the caliper with shop cloths.
3. Move the parking brake lever back and forth (**Figure 23**) and work the piston from the caliper bore. If this does not work, remove the lever and rotate the adjusting screw with a wrench.
4. Remove balance spring, if so equipped.
5. Remove nut, lever, lever seal and anti-friction washer.
6. Depress threaded end of actuator screw and remove from the caliper.
7. Remove dust boot with a screwdriver as shown in **Figure 24**.
8. Carefully pry locator retainer from caliper. Remove piston locator, if so equipped.

NOTE
Use a plastic or wooden dowel for seal removal in Step 9. Do not pry seal out with a screwdriver or other metal tool. This can scratch the piston bore or burr the seal groove edge.

9. Remove and discard the piston seal. Remove the bleed screw, bolt, fitting and copper washers. Do not remove bracket unless damaged.
10. Clean the caliper and piston with rubbing alcohol. Make sure all grooves and passages are clean, then blow dry with compressed air.
11. Inspect the caliper bore and piston for pitting or scoring. Replace the piston if pitted or scored. Replace the caliper if bore corrosion cannot be removed with crocus cloth.
12. Install bleeder screw and tighten to 80-140 in.-lb. (9-16 N•m).
13. Install bracket, if removed, and tighten bolt to 24-38 ft.-lb. (33-52 N•m).
14. Install fitting and bolt with new copper washers. Tighten bolt to 18-30 ft.-lb. (25-40 N•m).
15. Lubricate a new piston seal with clean brake fluid and install it in the caliper bore.

12

The seal must be seated firmly in the groove with no twists in it.

16. Install actuator screw thrust washer with bearing surface facing the caliper. Lubricate the shaft seal with clean brake fluid and install on actuator screw.

17. Lubricate the actuator screw with clean brake fluid and install in the piston.

NOTE
If equipped with a balance spring, fit the spring in the piston recess.

18. Dip the piston, piston installer part No. J-33077 and piston locator in clean brake fluid. Place piston on clean workbench with check valve end facing down. Position installer tool on piston. Install locator about 3/4 in. on installer tool. See **Figure 25**.

19. Lubricate caliper bore with clean brake fluid. Start piston in caliper and press in with installer tool part No. J-23072 or equivalent until piston extends about 3/8 in. See **Figure 26**.

20. Install locator retainer over piston end with flat side facing inward. Use tool part No. J-33078 as shown in **Figure 27** to seat piston in caliper bore.

21. Install piston boot with inside lip in piston groove and boot fold toward end of piston that acts on the inboard pad.

22. Reinstall tool part No. J-33078 (**Figure 25**) and push piston in until it bottoms.

23. Lubricate anti-friction washer and lever seal with silicone brake lubricant. Install over actuator screw with seal bead against caliper.

24. Install lever on actuator screw. Rotate lever away from stop and hold. Install and tighten nut to 30-40 ft.-lb. (41-54 N•m), then move lever back to stop position.

25. Fit outer diameter of boot in caliper recess. Use tool part No. J-28678 to seat boot as shown in **Figure 28**.

NOTE
Parking brake lever may have to be moved off the stop to extend the piston slightly before installing spring in Step 26. If so, be sure to push piston back in bore before installing caliper.

26. Install dampening spring in piston end groove as shown in **Figure 29**.

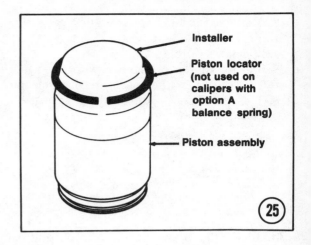

Installer

Piston locator (not used on calipers with option A balance spring)

Piston assembly

㉕

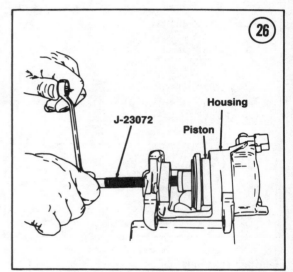

㉖

J-23072

Housing

Piston

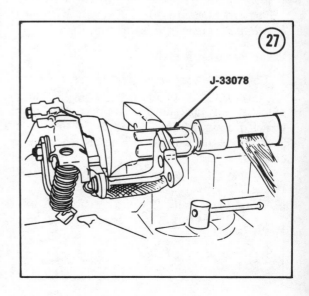

㉗

J-33078

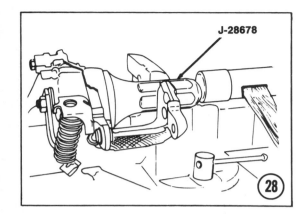

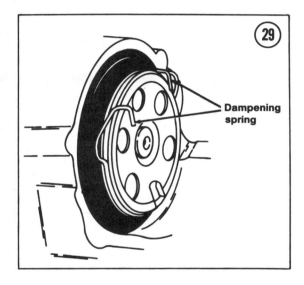

Dampening spring

Caliper Installation

Perform Steps 16-30 of *Rear Disc Brakes, Pad Replacement* in this chapter.

Rotor Removal/Installation

1. Loosen the rear wheel lug nuts.
2. Raise the rear of the car with a jack and place it on jackstands. Remove the rear wheel/tire assemblies.
3. Remove the calipers as described in this chapter.
4. Remove the brake rotor from the wheel flange.
5. Installation is the reverse of removal.

Rotor Inspection

See *Front Disc Brakes, Rotor Inspection* in this chapter.

REAR DRUM BRAKES

The rear drum brakes are a self-adjusting duo-servo design. The drums fit over the rear wheel hub studs and are retained by the wheel/tire lug nuts.

Shoe Removal

Refer to **Figure 30** for this procedure.
1. Raise the rear of the car with a jack and place it on jackstands.
2. Mark the wheel and the axle relationship. Remove the wheel.
3. Mark the drum and the axle relationship. Remove the drum.
4. Remove the brake return springs. Depress the shoe hold-down springs and remove from the hold-down pins along with the lever pivot. Remove the hold-down pins. See **Figure 31**.
5. Lift the actuator lever up. Remove the actuator link, lever, pivot and return spring (**Figure 32**).
6. Spread the brake shoes to disconnect the parking brake strut and spring (**Figure 33**).
7. Expand the shoes until they clear the axle flange. Disconnect the parking brake cable and remove the shoes. Note the adjuster spring position and remove the spring and the adjuster screw (**Figure 34**).
8. Remove the circlip holding the parking brake lever to the secondary shoe. Remove the parking brake lever.

Inspection

> *WARNING*
> *Do not inhale brake dust. It contains asbestos, which can cause lung cancer.*

1. Clean all parts except the linings with aerosol brake cleaner or new brake fluid. Do not clean with gasoline, kerosene or solvents.

> *CAUTION*
> *If cleaning with brake fluid, keep it off the lining surfaces. Brake fluid will ruin the linings and they will have to be replaced.*

2. Check drums for visible scoring, excessive or uneven wear and corrosion. If you have precision measuring equipment, measure the

12

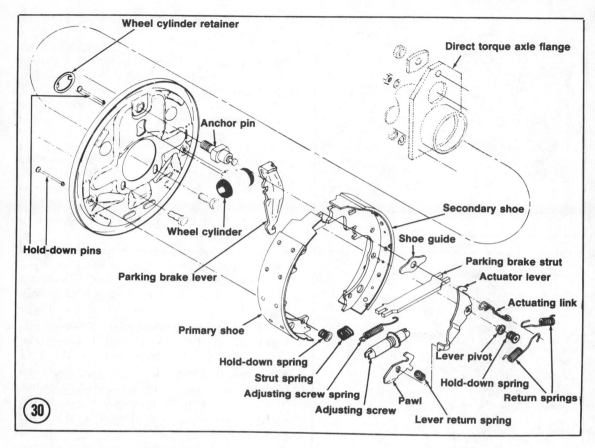

30

Wheel cylinder retainer

Direct torque axle flange

Anchor pin

Secondary shoe

Wheel cylinder

Shoe guide

Hold-down pins

Parking brake strut

Actuator lever

Parking brake lever

Actuating link

Primary shoe

Lever pivot

Hold-down spring

Hold-down spring

Strut spring

Return springs

Adjusting screw spring

Pawl

Adjusting screw

Lever return spring

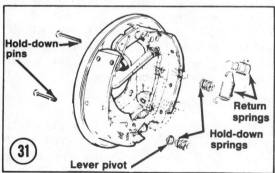

31

Hold-down pins

Return springs

Hold-down springs

Lever pivot

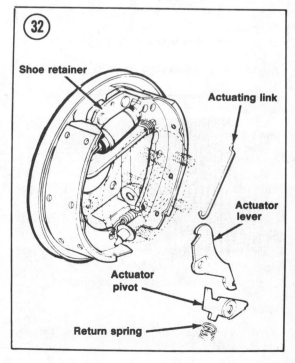

32

Shoe retainer

Actuating link

Actuator lever

Actuator pivot

Return spring

drum for wear. If you do not have the equipment, this can be done by a dealer or a machine shop. If the drum has surface damage or excessive runout, it can be resurfaced by a machine shop. However, the inside diameter must not exceed the maximum wear specification of 243.6 mm stamped on the drum. If the drum would have to be cut larger than this to correct it, it must be replaced.

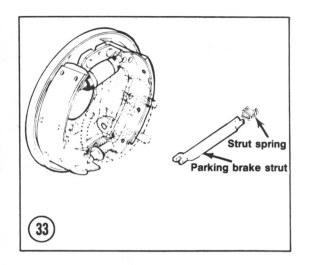

Strut spring

Parking brake strut

(33)

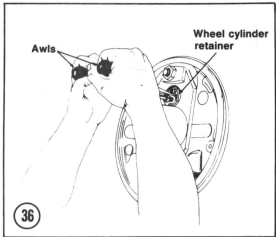

Awls

Wheel cylinder retainer

(36)

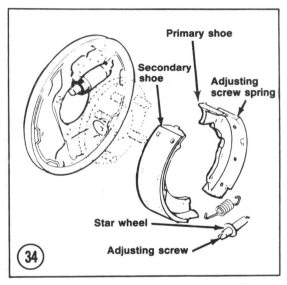

Primary shoe

Secondary shoe

Adjusting screw spring

Star wheel

Adjusting screw

(34)

(35)

3. Inspect the lining material on the brake shoes. Make sure it is not cracked, unevenly worn or separated from the shoes. Light surface oil or grease stains may be sanded off. If oil or grease has soaked beneath the surface, replace the shoes. Since brake fluid will ruin the linings, the shoes must be replaced if brake fluid has touched them. Shoes must also be replaced if the lining material has worn to within 1/32 in. of the shoe rivets.

4. Check all springs for overheating, weakness or deformation.

5. Inspect the wheel cylinders for signs of leakage or boot damage. If wet areas are found near the cylinder boots, the wheel cylinder should be overhauled.

Wheel Cylinder Overhaul

1. Disconnect the inlet tube from the wheel cylinder at the rear of the support plate (**Figure 35**). Remove the bleeder screw above the inlet.

2. Pry the wheel cylinder retainer from the support plate with 2 awls as shown in **Figure 36**. Remove the wheel cylinder.

3. Remove the boots, piston cups, expanders and spring from the wheel cylinder bore (**Figure 37**).

4. Discard all rubber parts. Clean the cylinder and pistons with rubbing alcohol. Do not use gasoline, kerosene or solvents. These leave a residue which can cause rubber parts to soften and swell.

12

5. Check the pistons for scratches, scoring or other damage. Replace if necessary.

6. Inspect the cylinder bore for scoring or corrosion. Light scoring or corrosion can be removed with crocus cloth. If the bore is badly scored or pitted, replace the wheel cylinder.

7. If the cylinder bore is resurfaced with crocus cloth, clean it a second time with rubbing alcohol and blow dry with compressed air.

8. Coat the piston cups with clean brake fluid and install the return spring/expander, cups and pistons in the cylinder bore.

9. Install a boot over each end of the cylinder and thread the bleed screw into the cylinder. Tighten the screw to 30-70 in.-lb. (3.4-7.9 N•m).

10. Install the wheel cylinder to the support plate. Place a wooden block between the cylinder and the axle flange.

11. Position a new retainer over the wheel cylinder stud and install by pressing in place with a 1 1/8 in. 12-point socket and extension (**Figure 38**).

12. Tighten the inlet tube nut to 120-280 in.-lb. (13.6-20.3 N•m).

Shoe Installation

Refer to **Figure 30** for this procedure.

1. Apply a light coat of brake grease to the support plate at the points shown in **Figure 39**.

2. Install the parking brake lever to the secondary shoe. Install the circlip retainer. See **Figure 40**.

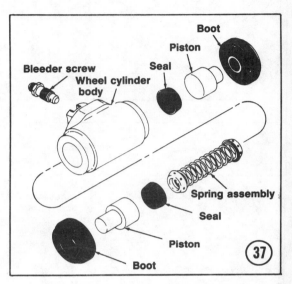

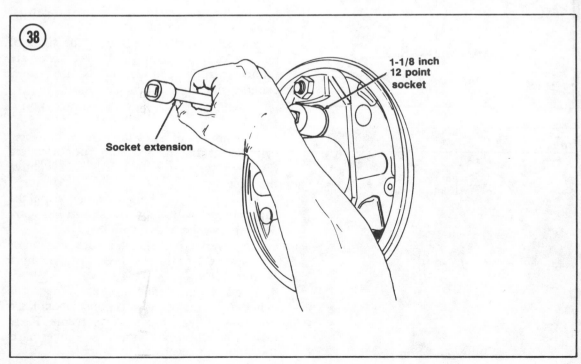

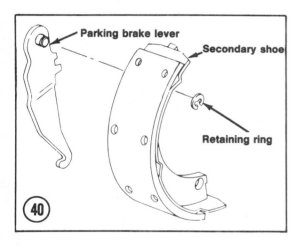

(39)

* **Shoe contact surfaces (6)**

(40)

Parking brake lever

Secondary shoe

Retaining ring

3. Lubricate the adjuster screw threads with clean brake fluid.

NOTE
Adjuster screw spring coils must not be positioned over the starwheel in Step 4. Left- and right-hand adjuster springs differ and should not be interchanged.

4. Position the brake shoes to the support plate. Install the adjuster screw and spring as shown in **Figure 41**.
5. Spread the shoes enough to install the parking brake strut and spring. The spring end of the strut should engage the primary shoe.
6. Install the actuator pivot, lever and return spring.
7. Install the actuator link in the shoe retainer. Lift up on the lever and connect the link and lever.
8. Install the hold-down pins, lever pivot and hold-down springs.
9. Install the shoe return springs.
10. Install the wheel/tire assemblies.
11. Adjust the parking brake as described in this chapter.
12. Make sure that both rear wheels rotate freely.
13. Bleed the brakes as described in this chapter.
14. Drive the car backward and forward about 10 feet several times, applying the brakes to adjust them.
15. Readjust the parking brake linkage cable at the equalizer to prevent possible rear brake drag.

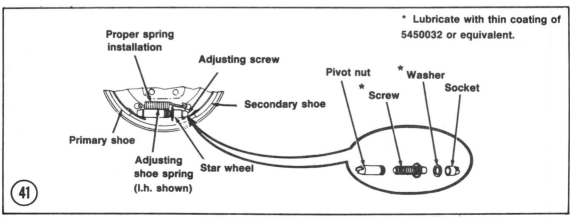

(41)

Proper spring installation

Adjusting screw

* **Lubricate with thin coating of 5450032 or equivalent.**

Pivot nut

* **Washer**

* **Screw**

Socket

Secondary shoe

Primary shoe

Adjusting shoe spring (l.h. shown)

Star wheel

12

MASTER CYLINDER

The aluminum master cylinder uses a plastic reservoir with a single reservoir cover. The master cylinder is attached to the power brake booster on all vehicles. See **Figure 42**.

A quick take-up feature is incorporated to provide a large volume of fluid to the front disc brakes at low pressure when the brake pedal is applied. This low-pressure fluid accomodates caliper seal and spring retraction requirements during initial braking effort.

Removal

Refer to **Figure 43** for this procedure.
1. Disconnect the negative battery cable.
2. Disconnect and plug the hydraulic lines at the master cylinder.

> *CAUTION*
> *Brake fluid will damage paint. Wipe up any spilled fluid immediately, then wash the area with soap and water.*

3. Remove the 2 attaching nuts from the booster unit studs.
4. Remove the master cylinder.

Overhaul

Refer to **Figure 44** for this procedure.
1. Clean the outside of the master cylinder with clean brake fluid or rubbing alcohol.
2. Remove the reservoir cover and diaphragm. Drain the reservoir and discard the fluid.
3. Clamp the master cylinder by one mounting flange in a vise equipped with protective jaws. If protective jaws are not available, wrap the cylinder in shop cloths.
4. Depress and hold the primary piston. Remove the lock ring.
5. Withdraw the primary piston from the bore. Cover the bore with a shop cloth and used compressed air to remove the secondary piston. See **Figure 45**.

> *NOTE*
> *Do not disassemble the primary piston. This is factory-set and if defective must be replaced.*

6. Use a pry bar as shown in **Figure 46** to remove the reservoir.

7. Remove the 2 reservoir grommets.

> *NOTE*
> *Do not try to remove the quick take-up valve from the reservoir bore. The valve is not serviceable. If defective, the master cylinder must be replaced as an assembly.*

8. Clean all metal parts in brake fluid. Do not clean with gasoline, kerosene or solvents. These leave a residue which can cause rubber parts to soften and swell.
9. If the rebuild kit includes piston assemblies, discard the old ones. If not, remove the old piston cups and install new ones. Be sure the new cups face in the same direction as the old ones.

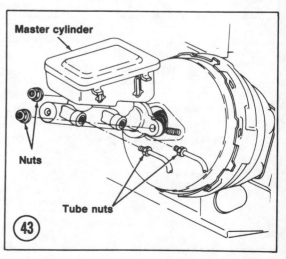

Master cylinder

Nuts

Tube nuts

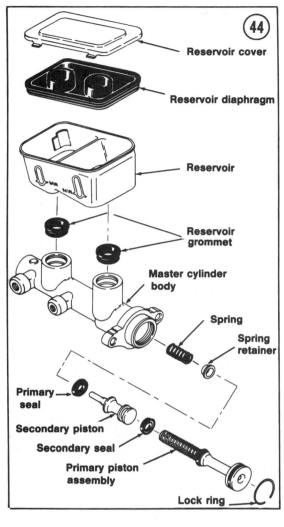

(44)

Reservoir cover

Reservoir diaphragm

Reservoir

Reservoir grommet

Master cylinder body

Spring

Spring retainer

Primary seal

Secondary piston

Secondary seal

Primary piston assembly

Lock ring

10. Check the cylinder bore for wear, scoring, pitting or corrosion. Since the master cylinder is aluminum and the bore is anodized, it cannot be honed. If any defect is found, replace the master cylinder.

11. Lubricate all parts in clean brake fluid and insert the secondary piston and return spring assembly in the cylinder bore.

12. Install the primary piston assembly.

13. Depress and hold the primary piston while installing the lock ring in the cylinder bore groove. Make sure the snap ring is completely seated.

14. Install the reservoir grommets.

15. Remove the master cylinder from the vise and install the reservoir with a downward rocking motion until the bottom of the reservoir touches the top of each grommet. See **Figure 47**.

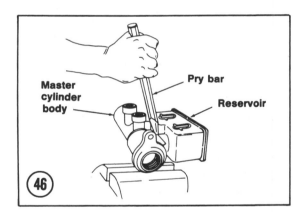

Master cylinder body

Pry bar

Reservoir

(46)

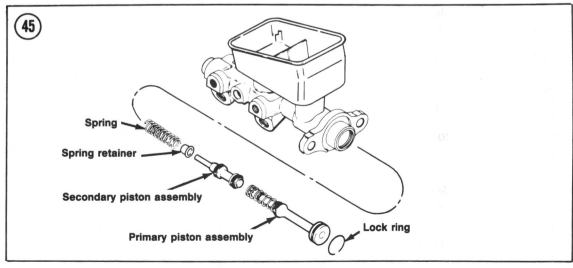

(45)

Spring

Spring retainer

Secondary piston assembly

Primary piston assembly

Lock ring

12

Installation

Installation is the reverse of removal. Tighten booster attaching nuts to 22-30 ft.-lb. (30-45 N•m). Tighten hydraulic line fittings to 120-280 in.-lb. (14-20 N•m). Fill the master cylinder reservoir to within 1/4 in. of the divider with clean DOT 3 or DOT 4 brake fluid. Bleed the brakes as described in this chapter. Start the engine and depress the brake pedal to set the warning light switch in position. Check for external hydraulic leaks.

COMBINATION VALVE

The combination valve is not serviceable and must be replaced if any of its 3 functions do not work properly.

Electrical Circuit Testing

1. Squeeze the plastic locking ring on the electrical connector at the pressure differential switch and pull the connector off.
2. Connect the electrical connector to ground with a jumper lead.
3. Turn the ignition ON; the warning lamp should light. If the lamp does not light, check for a burned-out bulb or a short in the circuit wiring.

Warning Light Switch Testing

1. Connect a suitable length of hose to a rear brake bleed screw. Place the other end of the hose in a container partially filled with clean brake fluid.
2. Remove the master cylinder cover and make sure the 2 reservoirs are full. If not, top up as required with clean DOT 3 or DOT 4 brake fluid.
3. Turn the ignition ON. Open the bleed screw while an assistant applies moderate pressure to the pedal. The warning lamp on the instrument panel should light.
4. Close the bleed screw. Have the assistant apply moderate-to-heavy pressure on the pedal. The instrument panel light should go out.
5. Repeat Steps 1-4 with a front brake bleed screw and look for the same results.

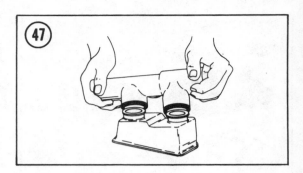

6. If the warning lamp does not light during Step 3 and Step 4, connect the switch terminal to ground with a jumper lead. If the lamp lights, the warning light switch in the combination valve is defective. Replace the combination valve.

Combination Valve Replacement

1. Disconnect the electrical connector at the combination valve.
2. Disconnect and plug the hydraulic lines at the combination valve.
3. Remove the 2 screws holding the valve to its mounting bracket. Remove the valve.
4. Installation is the reverse of removal. Tighten the mounting screws to 15 ft.-lb. (21 N•m). Bleed the brakes as described in this chapter.

POWER BOOSTER

The power booster can be serviced if defective. Since the procedure is complex and requires the use of many special tools, it is best left to a GM dealer.

Testing

1. Check the brake system for hydraulic leaks. Make sure the master cylinder reservoirs are filled to within 1/4 in. of the divider.
2. Start the engine and let it idle for about 2 minutes, then shut it off. Place the transmission in NEUTRAL and set the parking brake.
3. Depress the brake pedal several times to exhaust any vacuum remaining in the system.
4. When the vacuum is exhausted, depress and hold the pedal. Start the engine. If the

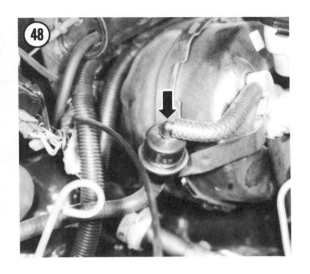

pedal does not start to fall away under foot pressure (requiring less pressure to hold it in place), the power booster unit is not working properly.

5. Disconnect the vacuum line at the booster. If vacuum can be felt at the line with the engine running, reconnect it and repeat Step 4. If the brake pedal does not move downward, replace the booster unit.

6. Run the engine for at least 10 minutes at fast idle. Shut the engine off and let it stand for 10 minutes. Depress the brake pedal with about 20 lb. of force. If the pedal feel is not the same as it was with the engine running, replace the booster unit.

Vacuum Hose and Filter Inspection

1. Check the vacuum hose between the filter and booster unit for leaks or loose connections.
2. Remove the charcoal filter in the outlet hose. See **Figure 48** for the 4-cylinder filter; the V6 and V8 filters are similar. It should be possible to blow air into the booster end of the filter, but not into the carburetor end. If air flows both ways or neither way, replace the filter.

Removal/Installation

1. Disconnect the negative battery cable.
2. Remove the master cylinder attaching nuts. Slide the master cylinder from the

booster mounting studs and move it to one side out of the way.
3. Disconnect the booster pushrod from the brake pedal. Remove the booster attaching nuts and booster unit from the cowl.
4. Installation is the reverse of removal. Since the master cylinder lines are not disconnected during this procedure, it is not necessary to bleed the brake system.

STOPLIGHT SWITCH

The stoplight switch is mounted on the brake pedal arm with a tubular clip (**Figure 49**).

Switch Replacement

1. Disconnect the wiring harness connector at the switch.
2. Rotate the switch and tubular clip to align the clip tang with the bracket slot.
3. Remove the switch.
4. Installation is the reverse of removal.

Switch Adjustment

1. Depress the brake pedal and push the switch into the tubular clip until it seats.
2. Pull the brake pedal up until it is firmly against the pedal stop. This automatically adjusts the switch.
3. Rotate the switch 1/2 turn counterclockwise to prevent it from holding the brake pedal on after adjustment.
4. Check for free play between the pedal and switch by pulling the pedal upward. Electrical contact should be made when the pedal is depressed 0.53 in. (13.5 mm) from its fully released position.
5. If further adjustment is required, rotate or pull the switch in its clip until contact is made as specified in Step 4.

BRAKE BLEEDING

The hydraulic system should be bled whenever air enters it. Air in the brake lines will compress, rather than transmit pedal pressure to the brake operating parts. If the pedal feels spongy or if pedal travel increases considerably, brake bleeding is usually called for. Bleeding is also necessary whenever a brake line is disconnected.

12

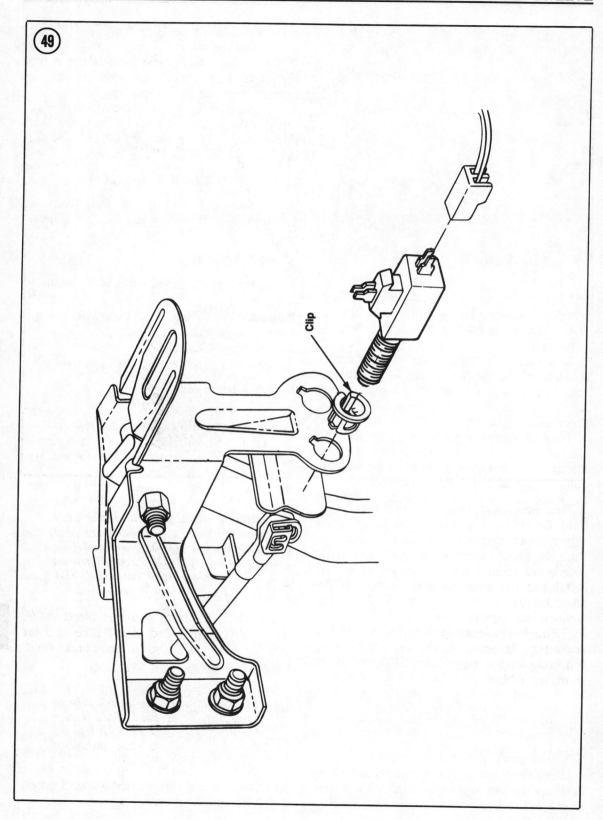

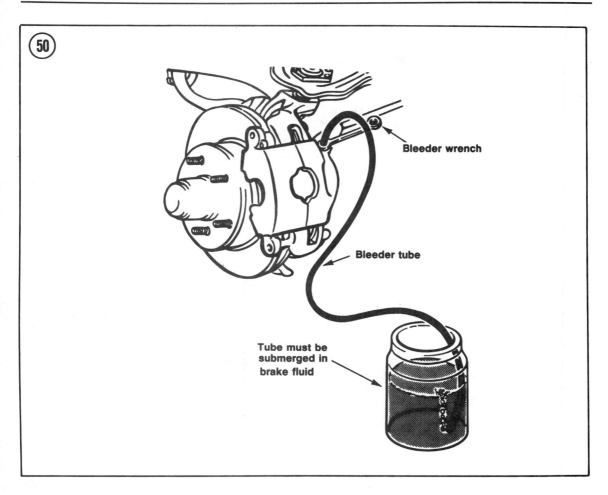

Bleeder wrench

Bleeder tube

Tube must be
submerged in
brake fluid

This procedure requires handling brake fluid. Be careful not to get any fluid on brake rotors, shoes, drums or linings. Clean all dirt from the bleed valves before beginning. Two people are needed; one to operate the brake pedal and the other to open and close the bleed valves.

Since the brake system consists of 2 individual systems, each system is bled separately. Bleeding should be done in the following order: right rear, left rear, right front, left front.

NOTE
Do not allow the master cylinder reservoirs to run dry during bleeding.

1. Clean away any dirt around the master cylinder reservoir cover. Remove the cover and top up the master cylinder with brake fluid marked DOT 3 or DOT 4.

NOTE
DOT 3 means that the brake fluid meets current Department of Transportation quality standards. If the fluid does not say DOT 3 somewhere on the label, buy a brand that does. DOT 4 brake fluid can also be safely used.

2. Attach a plastic tube to the bleed valve. Immerse the other end of the tube in a jar containing several inches of clean brake fluid. See **Figure 50**.

NOTE
Do not allow the end of the tube to come out of the brake fluid during bleeding. This could allow air into the system and the bleeding procedure would have to be done over.

3. Slowly press the brake pedal 2 or 3 times, then hold it down.

12

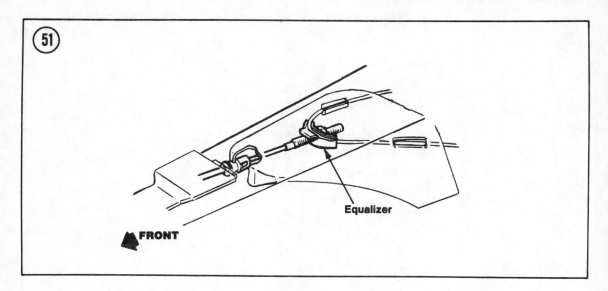

(51)

Equalizer

FRONT

4. With the brake pedal down, open the bleed valve 3/4 turn. Let the brake pedal sink to the floor, then close the bleed valve. Do not let the pedal up until the bleed valve is closed.

5. Let the pedal back up slowly. Wait 15 seconds.

6. Repeat Steps 3-5 (including the 15 second wait) until the fluid entering the jar is free of air bubbles.

7. Repeat the process for the other bleed valves.

> *NOTE*
> *Keep an eye on the brake fluid level in the master cylinder during bleeding. If the fluid level is allowed to drop too low, air will enter the brake lines and the entire bleeding procedure will have to be repeated.*

PARKING BRAKE

Adjustment
(Rear Drum Brakes)

Adjustment is recommended when lever travel is greater than 17 ratchet clicks or less than 13 clicks.

1. Pull the parking brake pedal exactly 2 ratchet clicks.

2. Raise the car with a jack and place it on jackstands.

3. Clean the equalizer connector nut and threads (**Figure 51**) with a wire brush. Lubricate the threads with brake fluid.

4. Tighten adjusting nut until left rear wheel can barely be turned forward with both hands, but cannot be turned to the rear.

5. Disengage the parking brake. Both rear wheels should rotate freely in either direction without drag.

6. Remove the jackstands and lower the car to the ground.

Brake Adjustment
(Rear Disc Brakes)

1. Set parking brake in fully released position.

2. Raise the rear of the car with a jack and place it on jackstands.

3. Hold the brake cable stud from rotating and tighten equalizer nut to remove all cable slack.

4. Make sure caliper levers contact housing stops. If not, loosen the cable until they return to the stops.

5. Operate parking brake several times and check adjustment. Parking brake lever should travel 13 notches if adjustment is correct.

6. Make sure the levers are on the caliper stops. Remove the jackstands and lower the vehicle to the ground.

Front Cable Replacement

Refer to **Figure 52** for this procedure.

1. Raise the front of the car with a jack and place it on jackstands.

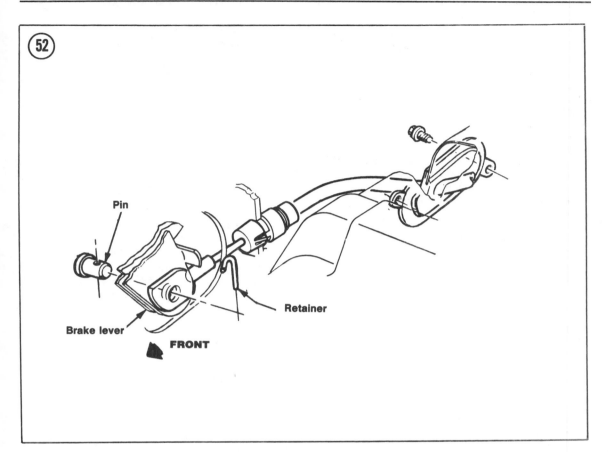

(52)

Pin

Brake lever

Retainer

FRONT

2. Remove the equalizer adjusting nut. Remove the spring retainer clip from the bracket.

3. Lower the car and remove the upper console cover and lower console screws. See *Console Removal/Installation*, Chapter Thirteen.

4. Lift rear of lower console and remove cable retainer pin, retainer and cable.

5. Installation is the reverse of removal. Adjust the parking brake as described in this chapter.

Rear Cable Replacement

1. Raise the rear of the car with a jack and place it on jackstands.
2. Loosen equalizer adjusting nut. Disconnect rear cable at connector.
3A. Drum brakes—Mark wheel-to-axle flange relationship. Remove wheel and brake drum. Bend retainer fingers and remove cable from brake shoe operating lever.
3B. Disc brakes—Push caliper apply lever forward, remove cable from tang in lever and release lever.
4. Installation is the reverse of removal. Adjust the parking brake as described in this chapter.

BRAKE PEDAL

The pedal height and travel is fixed and cannot be adjusted. If pedal travel exceeds 1.92 in. (49 mm) with rear drum brakes or 2.52 in. (64 mm) with rear disc brakes, drive the car backward and forward to activate the brake adjuster. If this does not bring the pedal travel within specifications, bleed the brakes. See *Brake Bleeding* in this chapter. Adjust the parking brake as described in this chapter. Check for hydraulic fluid leaks and correct if found. Inspect the front and rear brake linings and replace if excessively worn.

12

Table 1 TIGHTENING TORQUES

Fastener	ft.-lb.	N•m
Pedal-to-bracket nut	22	30
Pedal bracket-to-dash	18	25
Parking brake-to-console	9	12
Combination valve screw	15	21
Brake pipe-to-master cylinder nut	18	24
Brake pipe-to-combination valve nut	17	24
Brake pipe-to-hose nut	18	24
Junction block-to-axle housing screw	20	27
Backing plate-to-axle flange	10	14
Master cylinder-to-power booster nuts	20	27
Power booster-to-dash nuts	15	20
Caliper bleed screw	11	15
Front brake hose-to-caliper	32	44
Splash shield bolt	10	14
Caliper mounting bolt	35	48

CHAPTER THIRTEEN

BODY

This chapter provides service procedures for the front end panel, bumpers, hood, fenders, doors, door handles, door windows, rear compartment lift window, seats, glove box, instrument panel and console. A few special tools are required for some of these procedures. Other body repairs require many special skills and tools and should be left to a dealer or body shop.

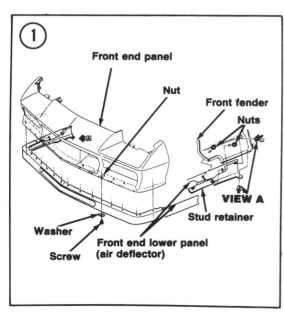

FRONT END PANEL AND BUMPER ASSEMBLY

Removal/Installation (Camaro)

Refer to **Figure 1** and **Figure 2** for this procedure.

1. Open the hood. Remove the air deflector.
2. Remove the side and bottom fasteners holding the left- and right-hand front end panel covers in place.
3. Remove the horn.
4. Disconnect the side marker lamp wiring harness.
5. Remove the right- and left-side upper fasteners.
6. Remove the outer bracket bolts.
7. Remove the center bracket bolts.
8. Remove the front end panel.
9. Remove the upper reinforcement assembly and headlamps.
10. Remove the right- and left-hand grille assemblies.
11. Remove the bolts holding the impact bar to the engine compartment rail.

NOTE
Perform Step 12 only if the vehicle has been in an accident. If not, impact bar disassembly is an unnecessary step.

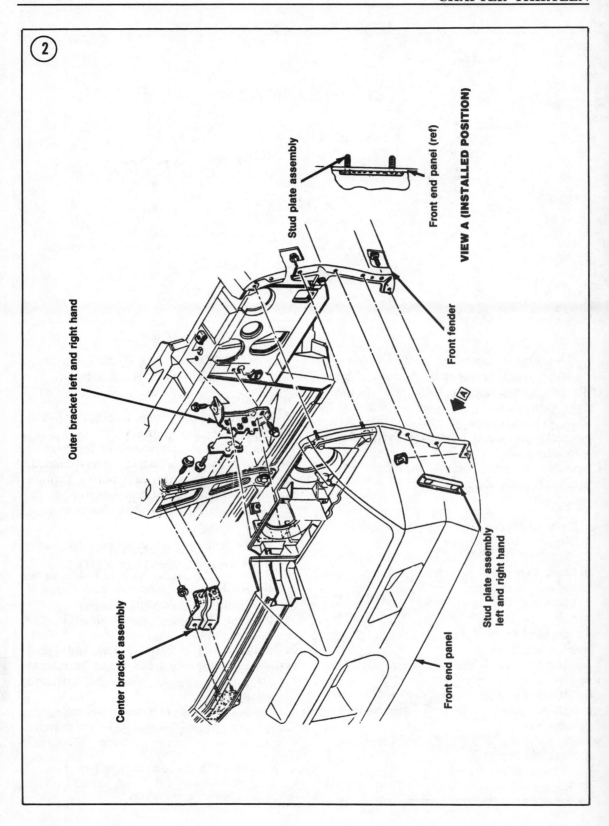

②

Stud plate assembly

Front end panel (ref)

VIEW A (INSTALLED POSITION)

Front fender

Outer bracket left and right hand

Center bracket assembly

Stud plate assembly left and right hand

Front end panel

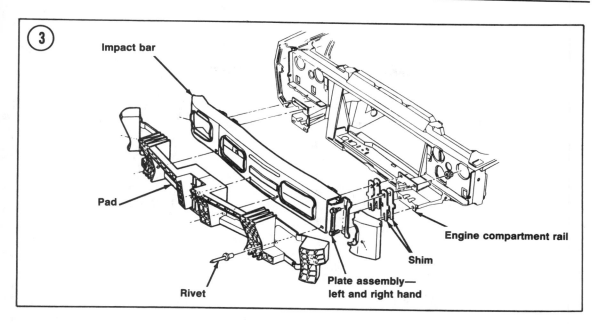

Figure 3 labels: ③ Impact bar · Pad · Rivet · Plate assembly—left and right hand · Shim · Engine compartment rail

12. Remove the pop rivets holding the pad to the impact bar. See **Figure 3**.

13. Installation is the reverse of removal. If the impact bar and pad are disassembled, reassemble with nuts and bolts. Tighten impact bar-to-frame rail fasteners to 20 ft.-lb. (27 N•m) and front end panel fasteners to 8 ft.-lb. (10 N•m).

Removal/Installation (Firebird)

Refer to **Figure 4** for this procedure.

1. Remove the lower air deflector.

2. Remove the side and bottom fasteners holding the right- and left-hand front end panel covers in place.

3. Remove the fascia-to-fender attaching nuts.

4. Remove the fascia-to-reinforcement push-in retainers.

5. Remove the parking lamp attaching screws.

6. Remove the upper reinforcement attaching screws. Remove the front end panel.

7. Remove the left- and right-hand grilles.

8. Remove the front end panel reinforcement screws and fasteners from the fascia.

9. Remove the bolts holding the impact bar to the engine compartment rail.

NOTE
Perform Step 10 only if the vehicle has been in an accident. If not, impact bar disassembly is an unnecessary step.

10. Remove the pop rivets holding the pad to the impact rail. See **Figure 5**.

11. Installation is the reverse of removal. If the impact bar and pad are disassembled, reassemble with nuts and bolts. Tighten impact bar-to-frame rail fasteners to 20 ft.-lb. (27 N•m) and front end panel fasteners to 8 ft.-lb. (10 N•m).

REAR BUMPER REMOVAL/INSTALLATION

Refer to **Figure 6** (Camaro) and **Figure 7** (Firebird) for this procedure.

1. Remove the spare tire from the rear compartment.

2. Remove the right and left tail lamp assemblies. Disconnect the wiring harness at the body and place with the taillamp assemblies.

3. Remove the bumper cover lower retainers.

4. Remove the right- and left-side bumper cover retainers from inside the rear compartment.

5. Remove the license plate bracket.

6. Remove the cover upper retainers. Remove the cover.

13

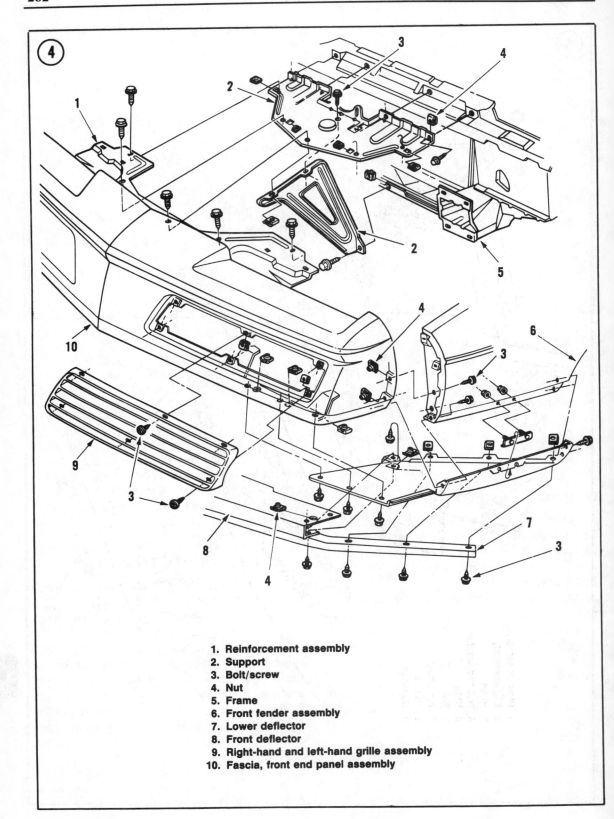

1. Reinforcement assembly
2. Support
3. Bolt/screw
4. Nut
5. Frame
6. Front fender assembly
7. Lower deflector
8. Front deflector
9. Right-hand and left-hand grille assembly
10. Fascia, front end panel assembly

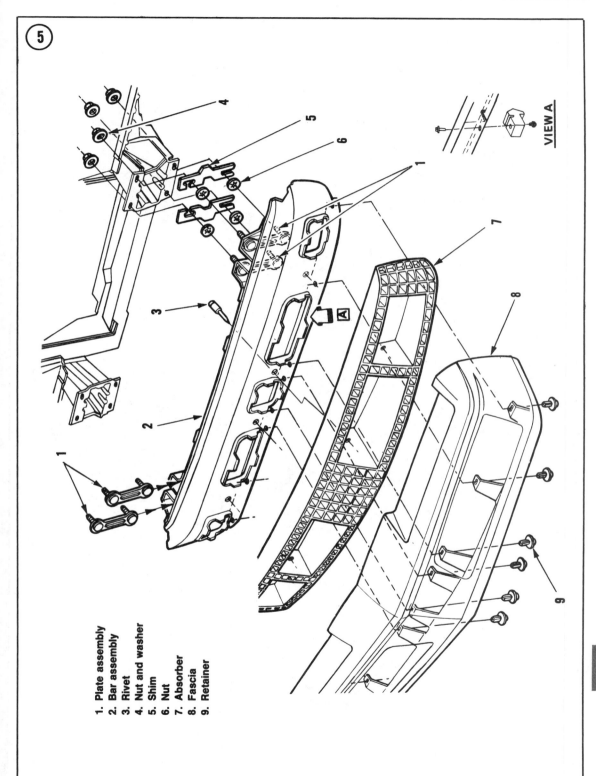

(5)

VIEW A

A

1. Plate assembly
2. Bar assembly
3. Rivet
4. Nut and washer
5. Shim
6. Nut
7. Absorber
8. Fascia
9. Retainer

13

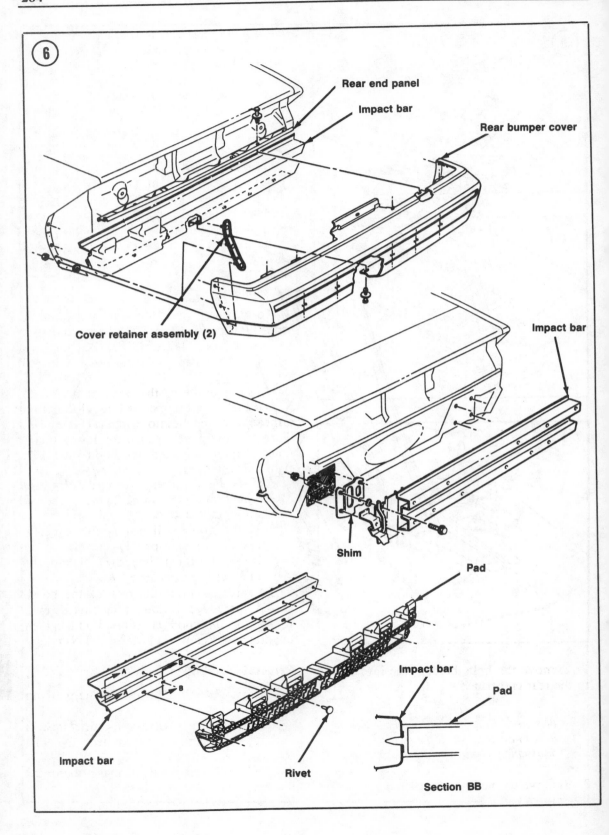

⑥

Rear end panel

Impact bar

Rear bumper cover

Cover retainer assembly (2)

Impact bar

Shim

Pad

Impact bar

Impact bar

Pad

Impact bar

Rivet

Section BB

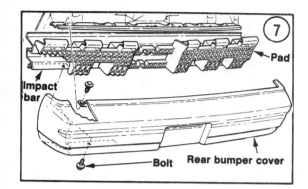

Pad

Impact bar

Bolt   Rear bumper cover

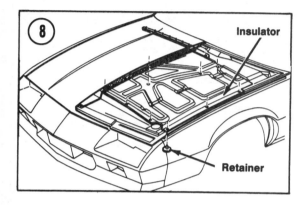

⑧

Insulator

Retainer

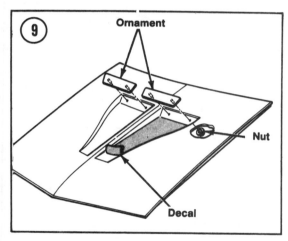

⑨

Ornament

Nut

Decal

7. Remove the bolts holding the impact bar to the rear end panel.

NOTE
Perform Step 8 only if the vehicle has been in an accident. If not, impact bar disassembly is an unnecessary step.

8. Remove the pop rivets holding the pad to the impact bar.

9. Installation is the reverse of removal. If the pad is disassembled from the impact bar, reinstall with nuts and bolts. Tighten the impact bar fasteners to 20 ft.-lb. (27 N•m) and the rear bumper cover fasteners to 8 ft.-lb. (10 N•m).

HOOD

The hood used with carburetted engines (**Figure 8**) differs from that used with fuel injected engines (**Figure 9**). Hood hinges are fastened to the fender panel with a gas strut used at each hinge. When replacing struts, make certain both have the same color coding.

Adjustment

1. To move the hood forward, to the rear or from side to side, loosen the hinge-to-fender screws at each side. Align the hood as necessary, then tighten the bolts to 8 ft.-lb. (10 N•m).
2. To raise or lower the front of the hood, loosen the hood bumper locknuts located on either side of the radiator support (**Figure 10**). Turn the bumpers to raise or lower them. Once properly adjusted, the hood should be tight when latched.
    a. If the hood rattles or moves downward when hand pressure is applied, readjust the bumpers higher.
    b. If the hood will not latch properly, readjust the bumpers lower.
    c. Once adjustment is correct, tighten the bumper locknuts.
3. To raise or lower the rear of the hood, loosen the hinge-to-hood attaching screws. Reposition the hood as required and tighten the attaching screws to 8 ft.-lb. (10 N•m).

Removal/Installation

This procedure requires the help of an assistant.
1. Disconnect the underhood lamp wire. On fuel injected models, disconnect the TBI solenoid lead.
2. Use a soft lead pencil to make alignment marks around the hinges directly on the hood. The marks will make installation easier.

13

3. Place a thick layer of rags beneath the trailing edge of the hood to protect the paint.

4. Place a protective cover over the windshield. Install a block of wood between the hood and windshield to prevent a sudden rearward movement of the hood.

5. While an assistant supports one side of the hood, remove the hinge-to-hood screws. See **Figure 11**.

6. Support your side of the hood while the assistant removes the other hinge-to-hood screws. Lift the hood off and place it out of the way.

NOTE
Do not place the hood flat on the floor or ground. Lean it up against a wall or other solid object to prevent the possibility of damage.

7. Installation is the reverse of removal. Line up the alignment marks made before removal. If necessary, adjust the hood as described in this chapter.

FENDER
REMOVAL/INSTALLATION

Refer to **Figure 12** for this procedure.

1. Open and support the hood.

2. Remove the fender skirt-to-fender screws.

3. Remove the lower air deflector.

4. Remove the fascia-to-fender fasteners.

5. Z-28 only—Remove the body rocker side molding and lower front end panel-to-fender screws.

6. Remove the horn. Disconnect side marker wire harness.

7. Remove the lower fender brace screws. Remove the lower fender rear screw.

8. Remove the antenna escutcheon from the fender, if so equipped.

9. Remove the hood hinge-to-fender fasteners.

10. Remove the upper fender fasteners.

11. Slide fender to the rear while pulling outward on it. Remove the fender.

12. If installing a new fender, transfer the side marker lamp, fender wheelhouse, fasteners and molding to the new fender.

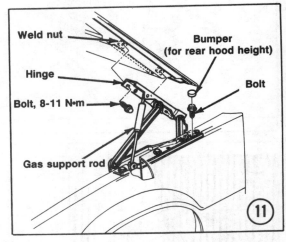

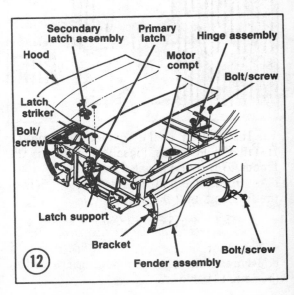

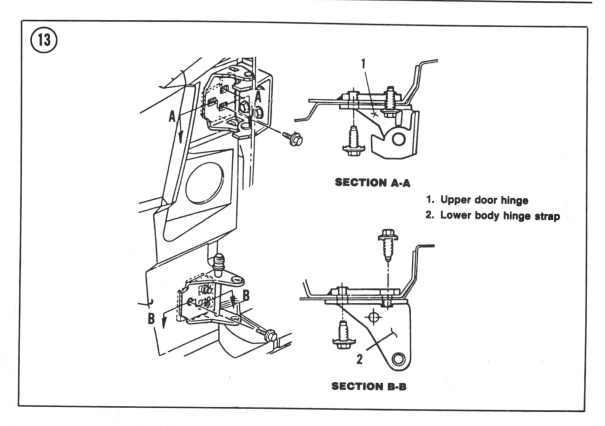

SECTION A-A

1. Upper door hinge
2. Lower body hinge strap

SECTION B-B

13. Installation is the reverse of removal. Install the fasteners loosely and adjust the fender to provide equal spacing at the cowl, door front edge and door top edge. Tighten the fasteners to 7 ft.-lb. (10 N•m).

FRONT DOORS

The door hinges are welded to the door panel and bolted to the body hinge pillars (**Figure 13**). No adjustment is possible. A removable hinge pin allows the door to be removed from the body, if necessary.

Removal

1. If the door contains power-operated components, remove the trim panel, insulator pad and water deflector as described in this chapter. Disconnect the wire harnesses inside the door. Remove the wire harnesses and rubber conduit from the door.
2. Tape the door and body pillars above the lower hinge with cloth-backed body tape.

CAUTION
*Cover the door spring (**Figure 14**) with a towel to prevent it from snapping out and causing injury during Step 3. Do not apply pressure to the hold-down link.*

3. Insert a long screwdriver blade under the hold-down link pivot point and over the top of the spring. Cover the spring with a towel and lift the screwdriver to disengage the spring.

13

4. Spread the hinge pin barrel clip (**Figure 15**) with 2 small screwdrivers and move the clip above the pin recess.

NOTE
The clip will fall free when the hinge pin is removed.

5. Have an assistant support the door. Remove the lower hinge pin with locking pliers and a plastic hammer.

6. When the lower hinge pin is removed, install a bolt in its place to maintain door position while removing the upper hinge.

7. Remove the upper hinge bolts at the pillar. Remove the lower hinge bolt. Remove the door.

Installation

A special spring compressor tool (GM tool part No. J-28625) is required for this procedure. Refer to **Figure 13**.

1. Have an assistant position the door to the body. Install a bolt in the lower hinge pin hole.

2. Bolt the upper hinge to the pillar. Install the lower hinge pin with its pointed end facing down.

3. Insert the door spring in the spring compressor tool part No. J-28625. Compress the spring and tool in a vise and install the tool bolt to hold the spring compressed. See **Figure 16**.

4. Remove the tool and spring from the vise. Install the tool and spring in the door lower hinge. The slot in one tool jaw fits over the hold-down link. The hole on the other jaw fits over the bubble.

5. Remove the tool bolt and tool. Open and close the door to check proper spring operation.

6. If the door contains power-operated components, install the wire harnesses and conduit. Connect the wire harnesses and install the door trim panel as described in this section.

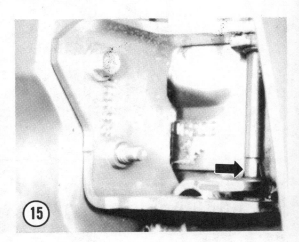

(15)

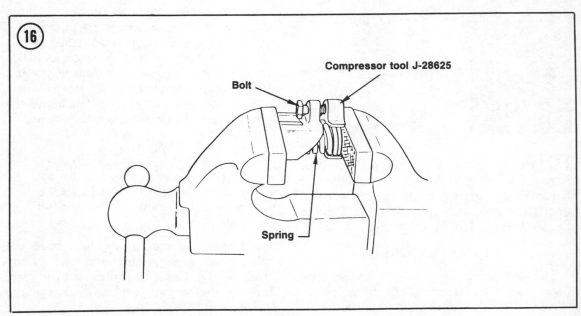

(16)

Bolt

Compressor tool J-28625

Spring

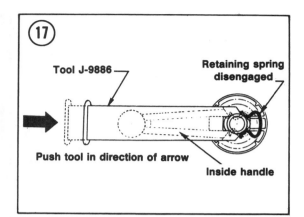

Tool J-9886

Retaining spring disengaged

Push tool in direction of arrow

Inside handle

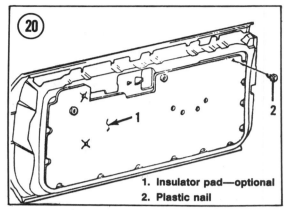

1. Insulator pad—optional
2. Plastic nail

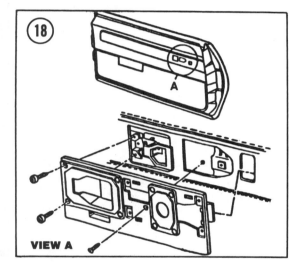

A

VIEW A

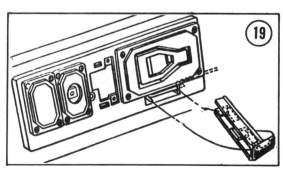

Trim Panel
Removal/Installation

The one-piece trim panel hangs over the door inner panel at the top and is fastened in place by side and bottom clips. The armrest and pull handle assembly is fastened in place with screws after the trim panel is installed.

1. If equipped with window regulator handles, insert a door clip remover tool behind the regulator (**Figure 17**) and push the retaining clip off the spindle. Remove the handle.

2. If equipped with pull cup opener (**Figure 18**), remove the bezel retaining screws. Pry the lock knob off the lock rod. Slide the knob forward and remove. See **Figure 19**.

3. If equipped with remote control mirror, disconnect the cable end from the bezel.

4. Pry power switches from the trim panel and disconnect the wire harnesses.

5. Remove all armrest-to-inner panel screws.

6. Use a putty knife, a wide-blade screwdriver or a door panel trim stick to pry the trim panel retaining pins from the edge of the inner door panel.

NOTE
Some vehicles may have an insulator pad installed between the trim panel and the inner panel water deflector. This insulator pad is retained in place with plastic nails.

7. Carefully remove the insulator pad with a putty knife, if so equipped. See **Figure 20**.

8. Carefully remove the water deflector with a putty knife. See **Figure 21**.

9. Installation is the reverse of removal. Make sure the armrest retaining clips are properly positioned on the inner door panel before installing the watershield. Use a silicone gasket sealer to attach the water deflector and repair any tears with duct tape.

13

Window Removal

The glass is retained to the window regulator sash with rivets which must be drilled out for glass removal. Installation of the glass requires rivet tool part No. J-29022 and a supply of rivets (part No. 20184399 or equivalent). Refer to **Figure 22** for this procedure.

1. Raise the window glass to a half-up position.
2. Remove the door trim panel, insulator pad (if so equipped) and water deflector as described in this chapter.
3. Punch out the center of the rivets holding the glass to the regulator sash and front up-stop (4, **Figure 22**).
4. Unbolt and remove the rear guide channel through the access hole.
5. Unbolt and remove the up-stop and support on the inner panel.
6. Use a 1/4 in. drill bit to drill out the attaching rivets in Step 3.
7. Raise the glass up to remove it from the sash channel. Remove the glass from the door.

Window Installation

Refer to **Figure 22** for this procedure.

1. Blow out drillings and shavings from the bottom of the door with compressed air.
2. If reinstalling the old glass, inspect the rivet bushings and retainers for damage. If necessary to replace, use a flat-bladed screwdriver with the blade covered with cloth body tape. Pry out old bushing and snap new bushing and retainer in place.
3. Lower glass into the door. Position glass on sash channel and align sash holes with glass bushings.
4. Install new rivets with tool J-29022.
5. Align up-stop to glass and install new rivets with tool part No. J-29022.
6. Install rear guide channel.
7. Install front up-stop and support on inner door panel.
8. Check window operation. Install water deflector, insulator pad (if so equipped) and trim panel.

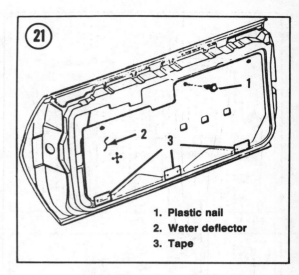

1. Plastic nail
2. Water deflector
3. Tape

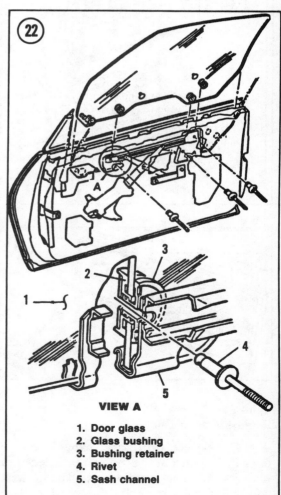

VIEW A

1. Door glass
2. Glass bushing
3. Bushing retainer
4. Rivet
5. Sash channel

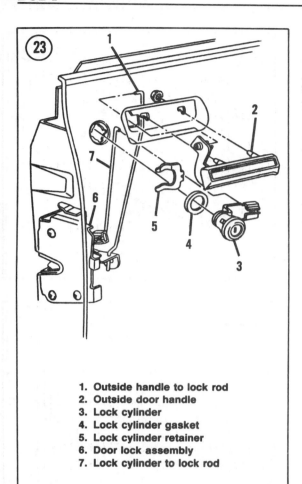

1. Outside handle to lock rod
2. Outside door handle
3. Lock cylinder
4. Lock cylinder gasket
5. Lock cylinder retainer
6. Door lock assembly
7. Lock cylinder to lock rod

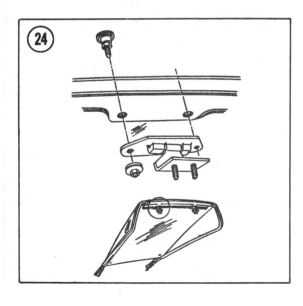

DOOR LOCK REPLACEMENT

1. Raise the window glass to its full up position.
2. Remove the door trim panel as described in this chapter.
3. Pull back the water deflector enough to expose the lock access hole.
4. Disconnect the lock rod at the lock cylinder. See **Figure 23**.

CAUTION
Wear gloves to prevent injury when removing the cylinder retainer by hand in Step 5.

5. Slide the cylinder retainer forward to disengage it from the cylinder body. Remove the lock cylinder and gasket.
6. Installation is the reverse of removal. Lubricate with WD-40 or equivalent spray lubricant.

REAR COMPARTMENT LIFT WINDOW

The lift window consists of a solid formed glass with 2-piece urethane-attached moldings and a finishing panel bolted to the bottom of the glass. Tubular gas supports are mounted on each side of the window and attached to the body.

Removal/Installation

This procedure requires the help of an assistant.
1. Support the lift window in the fully open position.
2. Place a blanket or several towels between the upper edge of the lift window and the roof to prevent accidental paint damage.
3. Remove the nuts holding the glass to the hinge (**Figure 24**).
4. While an assistant supports the center of the lift window, remove the bolt connecting each gas support to the window.
5. Disconnect the electric window defogger wiring connector, if so equipped.
6. Remove the lift window from the body and place on a blanket or other protective covering out of the way where it will not be damaged.

13

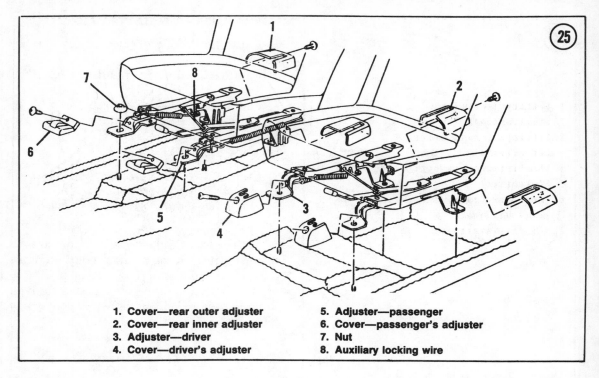

1. Cover—rear outer adjuster
2. Cover—rear inner adjuster
3. Adjuster—driver
4. Cover—driver's adjuster
5. Adjuster—passenger
6. Cover—passenger's adjuster
7. Nut
8. Auxiliary locking wire

7. Installation is the reverse of removal. Tighten the gas support bolts to 3.5-5 ft.-lb. (5-7 N•m). Wear safety glasses and tighten the glass-to-hinge bolts to 11 ft.-lb. (16 N•m).

WARNING
Overtorquing these bolts may cause the glass to break.

FRONT SEATS

Seats are secured to adjuster mechanisms. The adjuster/seat assembly fits over studs welded to the floor pan anchor plates and is retained by nuts. See **Figure 25** for manual seats and **Figure 26** for power seats.

Removal/Installation

1. Draw the seat to its full-forward and full-up position. Power seats should be as high as the adjustment will permit.
2. Remove the rear foot covers and/or carpet retainers to provide access to the attaching nuts. Remove the rear attaching nuts.
3. Return the seat to its full-rearward position.
4. Remove the front foot or track covers, as necessary. Remove the front attachings nuts.

5. Tilt power seats back and disconnect all electrical connectors (**Figure 27**). Remove the seat(s).
6. Installation is the reverse of removal. Tighten attaching nuts to 15-21 ft.-lb. (20-28 N•m). Check seat operation for smooth and complete travel.

REAR SEAT

Cushion Removal/Installation

Push the lower forward seat edge to the rear (**Figure 28**). Lift the seat up and pull on the cushion frame to disengage the frame wires from the seat pan retainers. Installation is the reverse of removal.

Folding Seat Back
Removal/Installation

Refer to **Figure 29** for this procedure.
1. Remove the rear seat cushion as described in this chapter.
2. Remove the pivot support bracket nut on each side of the seat back.
3. Remove the rear seat back.
4. Installation is the reverse of removal.

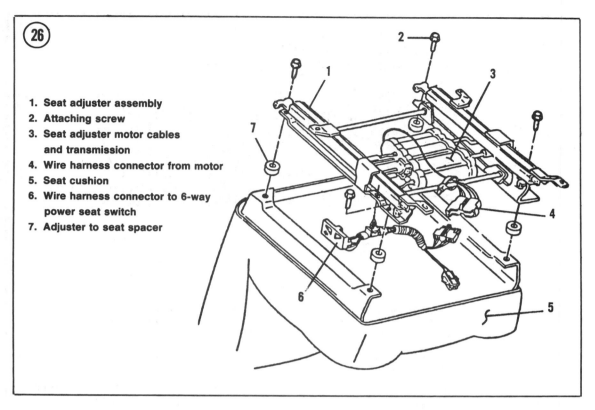

(26)

1. Seat adjuster assembly
2. Attaching screw
3. Seat adjuster motor cables and transmission
4. Wire harness connector from motor
5. Seat cushion
6. Wire harness connector to 6-way power seat switch
7. Adjuster to seat spacer

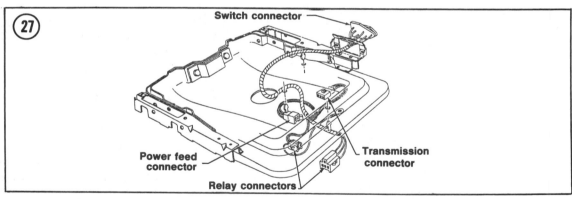

(27)

Switch connector

Power feed connector

Relay connectors

Transmission connector

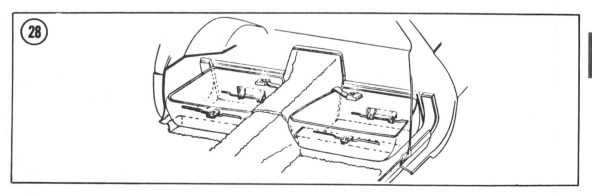

(28)

13

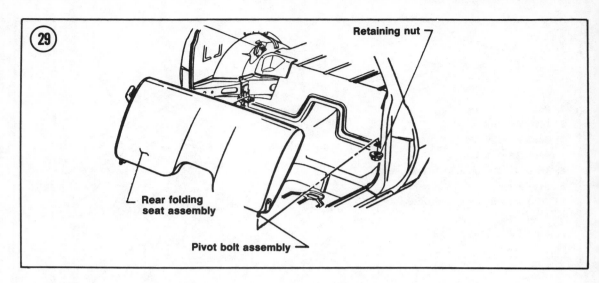

Retaining nut

Rear folding
seat assembly

Pivot bolt assembly

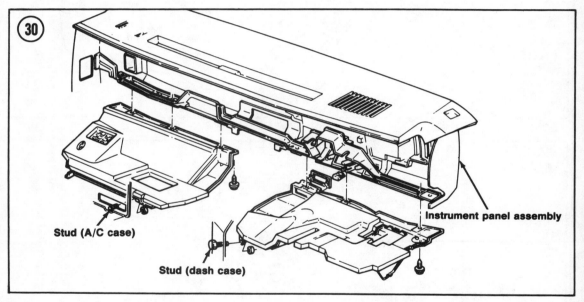

Stud (A/C case)

Stud (dash case)

Instrument panel assembly

INSTRUMENT PANEL

Removal/Installation

This procedure covers removal of the entire instrument panel assembly. To remove just the gauge cluster, see *Instruments*, Chapter Seven.

1. Disconnect the negative battery cable.

2. Remove the right- and left-hand hush panels. See **Figure 30** for Camaro and **Figure 31** for Firebird.

3. Disconnect the vent cables from the bottom of the panel.

4. Disconnect the heater control cables at the heater. Remove the lower air conditioning duct, if so equipped.

5. Remove the steering column trim cover (**Figure 32**). Remove the steering column support bolts. Lower the steering column.

6. Remove all instrument panel trim plates.

7. Pull the heater or air conditioning control unit out far enough to disconnect the wiring and vacuum harnesses. Remove the control unit.

8. Disconnect the bulkhead connector harness. Remove the nut from the bulkhead

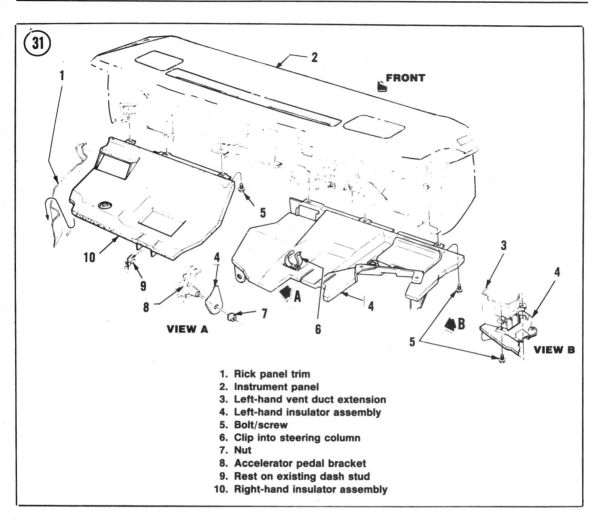

1. Rick panel trim
2. Instrument panel
3. Left-hand vent duct extension
4. Left-hand insulator assembly
5. Bolt/screw
6. Clip into steering column
7. Nut
8. Accelerator pedal bracket
9. Rest on existing dash stud
10. Right-hand insulator assembly

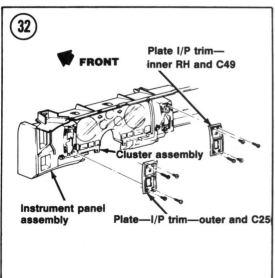

connector in the engine compartment. Remove the bulkhead connector.

9. Remove the upper instrument panel attaching screws from the panel carrier.

10. Remove 2 lower instrument panel screws at the corners.

11. Remove the center reinforcement brace.

12. Pull the instrument panel assembly out and disconnect the ignition, headlight dimmer and turn signal switches. Disconnect all remaining electrical leads, vacuum lines and the radio antenna lead.

13. Remove the instrument panel with the wiring harness.

14. Installation is the reverse of removal. If installing a new instrument panel, remove all components from the old panel and install them on the new one.

13

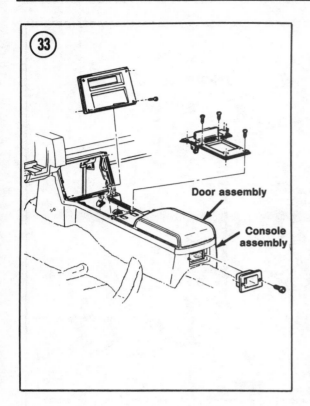

CONSOLE REPLACEMENT

Camaro

1. Refer to **Figure 33** and remove the trim panels shown.

2. Refer to **Figure 34** and remove the screws shown. Remove the console door and upper console assembly.

3. Refer to **Figure 35** and remove the screws shown. Remove the console assembly.

4. Installation is the reverse of removal.

Firebird

Refer to **Figure 36** for this procedure.

1. Remove the trim plate (3, **Figure 36**).

2. Remove the plate assembly (11 or 12, **Figure 36**).

3. Remove the console upper assembly attaching screws. Remove the upper assembly (1, **Figure 36**).

4. Remove the console lower assembly attaching screws. Remove the lower assembly (5, **Figure 36**).

5. Installation is the reverse of removal.

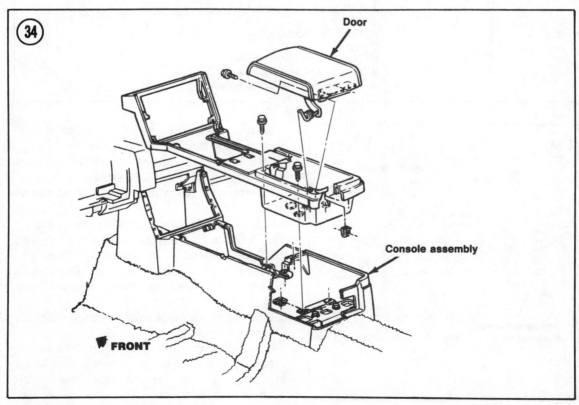

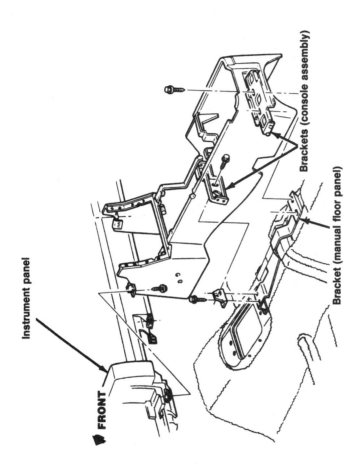

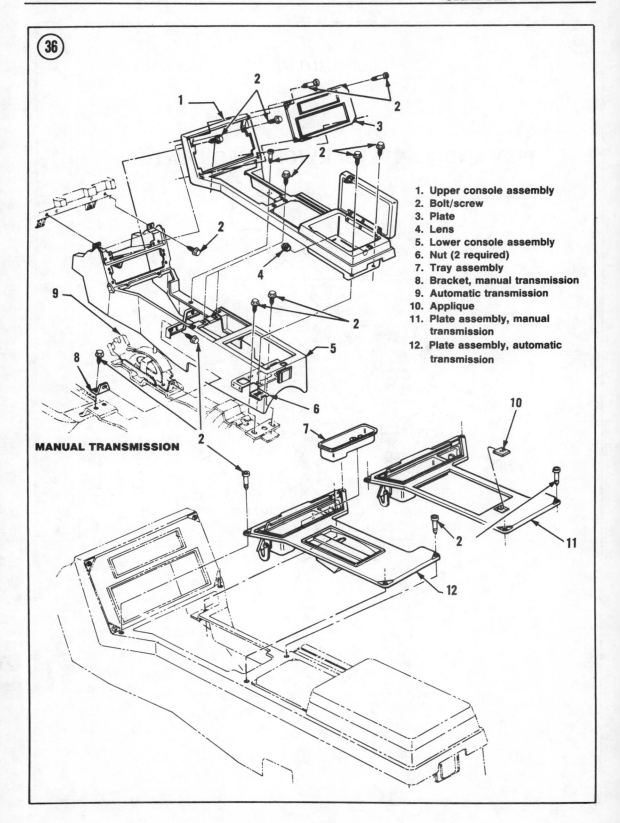

36

1. Upper console assembly
2. Bolt/screw
3. Plate
4. Lens
5. Lower console assembly
6. Nut (2 required)
7. Tray assembly
8. Bracket, manual transmission
9. Automatic transmission
10. Applique
11. Plate assembly, manual transmission
12. Plate assembly, automatic transmission

MANUAL TRANSMISSION

SUPPLEMENT

1983 AND LATER SERVICE INFORMATION

This supplement contains service and maintenance information for the 1983 and later Chevrolet Camaro and Pontiac Firebird models. The information supplements the procedures in the main body (Chapters One through Thirteen) of the book, referred to in this supplement as the "basic book."

The chapter headings and titles in this supplement correspond to those in the basic book. If a chapter is not included in the supplement, there are no changes affecting 1983 and later models.

If your vehicle is covered by this supplement, carefully read the supplement and then read the appropriate chapters in the basic book before beginning any work.

CHAPTER THREE

LUBRICATION, MAINTENANCE AND TUNE-UP

FUEL STOP CHECKS

The following fuel stop check reflects an addition to those specified in Chapter Three of the basic book for 1984 and later models:
1. Hydraulic clutch master cylinder—Check fluid level in the clutch master cylinder (bracket-mounted to the brake master cylinder attaching nuts). Clean the area around the master cylinder reservoir cover. Remove the cover and reservoir diaphragm. The fluid level should be even with the step inside the reservoir. Top up if necessary with DOT 3 brake fluid.

PERIODIC MAINTENANCE

Drive Belts

Drive belt tension specifications for 1983 and later models are provided in **Table 1**.

Oxygen Sensor

The oxygen sensor no longer requires periodic replacement. Change the sensor only if defective.

TUNE-UP

General Motors does not provide tune-up specifications for 1983-on models. Use the specifications on the Vehicle Emission Control Information (VECI) decal in engine compartment.

Spark Plugs

Spark plug wire routing on 1983 and later V8 engines has been changed to reduce the possibility of crossfire between cylinders 5 and 7 (left side) and cylinders 4 and 8 (right side). See **Figure 1** and **Figure 2** for carburetted engine. See **Figure 3** and **Figure 4** for fuel-injected engine.

Idle Speed Adjustment

Do not attempt to adjust the idle speed on fuel injected (PFI) V6 engines. An idle air control (IAC) assembly mounted on the throttle body maintains the correct idle speed according to electrical impulses from the electronic control module (ECM). Attempting to adjust the system will only make matters worse. If idle speed requires adjustment, see your GM dealer.

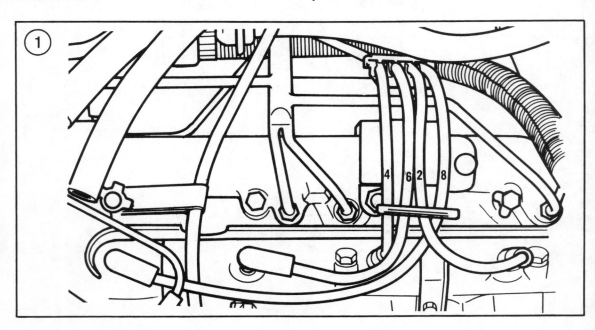

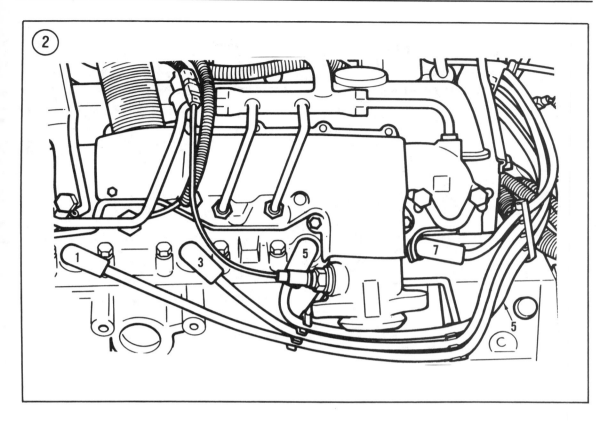

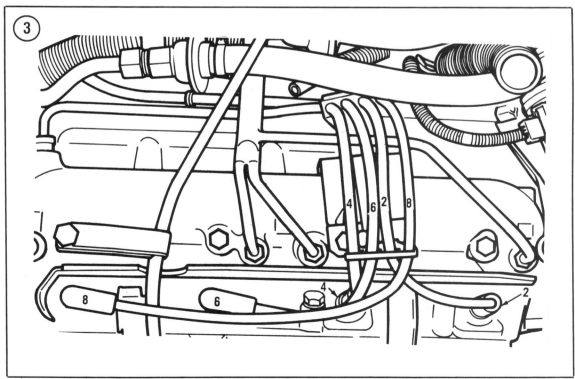

14

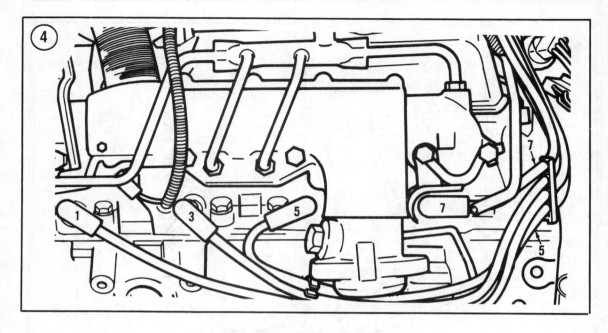

Table 1 DRIVE BELT TENSION

	Tension in lb.	
	New	**Used***
4-cylinder		
Air conditioning	135-165	65
All others	120-150	55
V6		
Air pump	100	45
Power steering pump	135	65-80
All others	145	65-80
V8		
Air conditioning	145	65-95
All others	130	65-80

* A belt is considered used after the engine has made more than one revolution and the belt has stretched or seated into the pulley groove.

CHAPTER FOUR

4-CYLINDER ENGINE

ROCKER ASSEMBLY AND PUSHRODS

The 1985-on 4-cylinder engine uses hydraulic roller lifters (**Figure 5**) to reduce valve train friction. The lifters are held in place and prevented from rotating by lifter guides and guide retainers. See **Figure 6**. Pushrods used with this engine have been shortened from 9.754 in. to 8.3996 in. and the camshaft profile slightly modified to accomodate the lifter change. The camshaft, pushrods, lifters and intake valves are not suitable for use as a replacement in earlier engines.

Service procedures remain unchanged with the additional step of removing the retainenrs and guides when lifters are removed. All lifters should be replaced whenever a new camshaft is installed.

Specification changes are provided in **Table 2**.

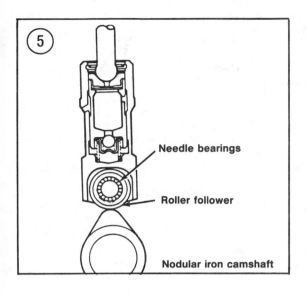

Needle bearings

Roller follower

Nodular iron camshaft

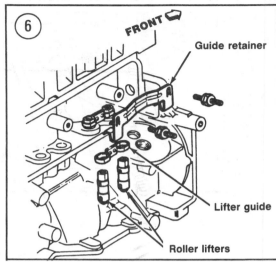

FRONT

Guide retainer

Lifter guide

Roller lifters

Table 2 4-CYLINDER ENGINE SPECIFICATIONS

Piston pin	
Diameter	0.938-0.942 in.
Fit in piston	0.0002-0.0004 in.
Fit in rod	Press
Piston rings	
Side clearance	
Top	0.002-0.003 in.
Second	0.001-0.003 in.
Oil ring	0.015-0.055 in.
Ring gap	
Compression	0.010-0.020 in.
Oil ring	0.020-0.060 in.
Valve system	
Head diameter	
Intake	1.75 in.
Stem diameter	
Intake and exhaust	0.342-0.343 in.
Valve spring load	
Open	170-180 lb. @ 1.26 in.

CHAPTER FIVE

V6 AND V8 ENGINES

ROCKER ARM COVERS

The rocker arm covers used on 1986 V6 and V8 engines have been modified to use a high-swell rubber-cork cover gasket instead of RTV sealant. The covers are designed to prevent splash oil from draining onto the cover gasket. Load spreaders or reinforcements are used under the cover bolts to distribute clamping pressure evenly. **Figure 7** shows the V6 cover design; the V8 is similar.

REAR MAIN OIL SEAL

A rubber split seal is used as a service replacement for the rope seal on 1982-1984 V6 engines. The rubber seal is factory-installed on 1985 and later V6 engines.

A one-piece rubber seal replaces the split seal on 1986 V8 engines. The new seal is housed in an aluminum retainer bolted to the rear of the block. A groove in the bottom of the retainer accepts the new one-piece oil pan

14

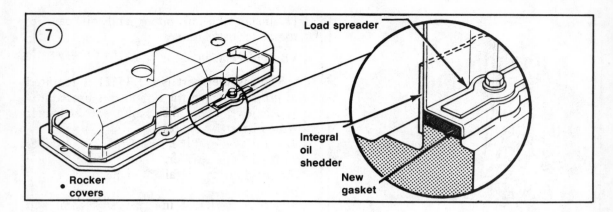

Rocker covers · **Load spreader** · **Integral oil shedder** · **New gasket**

gasket required by this design change. See **Figure 8**.

V6 Replacement

1. Remove the oil pan and oil pump.
2. Remove the rear main bearing cap.
3. Loosen the No. 2 and No. 3 main bearing caps.
4. Remove and discard the old rope seal. Clean the seal grooves in the main bearing cap and block to remove any pieces of the rope seal and oil.
5. Coat the outer diameter of the block half of a new rubber seal (not the seal lips) with a thin coating of GM gasket sealing compound (part No. 1050026) or equivalent. See **Figure 9**.
6. Using a piece of shim stock or equivalent like a shoe horn between the outer diameter of the seal and the edge of the seal channel in the block, roll the new seal into place in the block, rotating the crankshaft as required to help position the seal. When properly positioned, the seal dust lip will face the flywheel as shown in **Figure 9**.
7. Coat the outer diameter of the other half of the seal with GM gasket sealing compound or equivalent. Install seal half in main bearing cap.
8. Run a 1/32 in. (1 mm) bead of GM anaerobic sealant (part No. 1052357) or equivalent along the cap between the rear main seal and oil pan rear seal groove. Do not allow sealant to touch seal or bearing or to run into the drain slot.

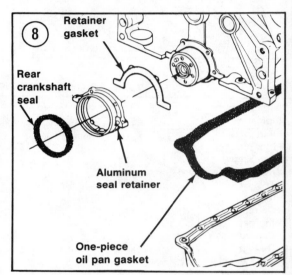

Retainer gasket · **Rear crankshaft seal** · **Aluminum seal retainer** · **One-piece oil pan gasket**

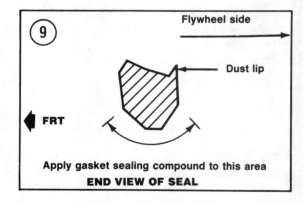

Flywheel side · **Dust lip** · **FRT** · **Apply gasket sealing compound to this area** · **END VIEW OF SEAL**

9. Lightly coat that part of the crankshaft surface that will come in contact with the seal with clean engine oil.
10. Install the rear main bearing cap. Tighten all loosened fasteners to 63-74 ft.-lb. (85-100 N•m).

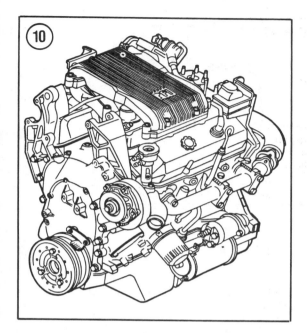

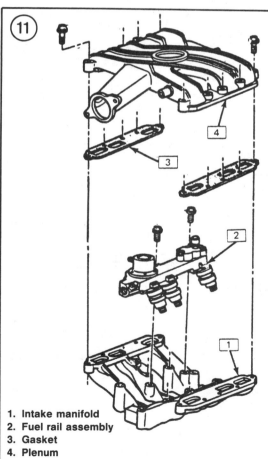

1. Intake manifold
2. Fuel rail assembly
3. Gasket
4. Plenum

11. Install the oil pump and oil pan to complete installation.

V8 Replacement

Seal installer part No. J-35621 is required to properly install the seal in this procedure.

1. Remove the transmission. See Chapter Nine of the basic book.

2. Carefully pry the seal from the retainer with a screwdriver. Three notches are provided in the retainer to be used as pry points.

3. Dip a new seal in clean engine oil and install it on tool part No. J-35621.

4. Position the tool and seal against the retainer and hand-start the tool attaching screws in the threaded crankshaft holes. Tighten all 3 screws evenly and snugly to assure seal installation without cocking.

5. Tighten the tool wing nut (handle) until it bottoms, indicating that the seal has been properly seated.

6. Loosen the tool attaching screws and remove the tool from the crankshaft.

7. Install the transmission. See Chapter Nine of the basic book.

OIL PAN AND PUMP

A one-piece pan gasket replaces the 2-piece gasket and front/rear seals on 1986 V8 engines. See **Figure 8**. The gasket is installed with a very slight amount of RTV sealant (part No. 1052751) at the front and rear corners of the pan. Excessive sealant will prevent the gasket from making a proper seal and can result in an oil leak.

PORT FUEL INJECTION (PFI)

The V6 engine used in 1982-1984 models is replaced in 1985 models by the PFI V6 (**Figure 10**). The 1985 V6 engine is the same design and displacement but it is equipped with port fuel injection (PFI) instead of a carburetor.

The new procedures required to service the PFI V6 are provided in this supplement. Specifications remain unchanged.

Plenum Removal/Installation

Refer to **Figure 11** for this procedure.

14

1. Disconnect the negative battery cable.
2. Disconnect all vacuum lines at the plenum.
3. Remove the 2 bolts holding the EGR tube to the plenum.
4. Remove the 2 throttle body bolts.
5. Remove the throttle cable bracket.

6. Remove the 10 bolts holding the plenum to the intake manifold. Remove the plenum and gaskets. Discard the gaskets.

7. Installation is the reverse of removal. Use new plenum gaskets. Tighten the plenum bolts to 18 ft.-lb. (25 N•m).

CHAPTER SIX

FUEL, EXHAUST AND EMISSION CONTROL SYSTEMS

Crossfire Fuel Injection is replaced on 1984 and later V8 engines by the Rochester E4ME/E4MC 4-bbl. carburetor. The E4ME (electric choke) and E4MC (hot air heated choke) are essentially the same except for calibration and can be serviced using the procedures in Chapter Six of the basic book.

ELECTRIC FUEL PUMP

The electric fuel pump used with 1984 and later fuel injected 4-cylinder engines has a back-up system programmed into the EMC in case of pump relay failure. A 2-circuit oil pressure sending unit controls the oil pressure light/gauge with one circuit and the fuel pump relay with the other circuit. If the relay fails, the oil pressure sending unit will turn the

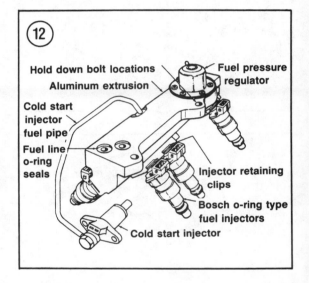

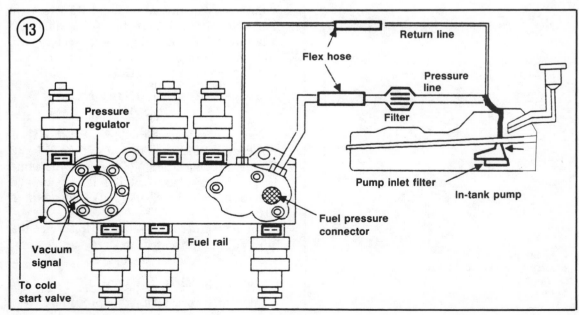

pump on as soon as oil pressure reaches approximately 4 psi.

This feature is useful in troubleshooting a defective fuel pump relay. If an engine that has been starting with no difficulty begins to require a cranking time of several seconds or more, have the fuel pump relay checked for a malfunction.

PORT FUEL INJECTION

The PFI V6 uses a fuel rail containing 6 fuel injectors located under the plenum (**Figure 12**). Each injector is installed in a cylinder intake port, All 6 injectors pulse once during each engine revolution. This provides 2 injections of fuel mixed withincoming air to provide the air-fuel charge for each combustion cycle. **Figure 13** shows the major components fo the PFI system.

System Operation

The PFI system operation is essentially the same as the TBI system used on the 4-cylinder engine. Since the system is electronically controlled, no attempt should be made to adjust the idle speed or fuel mixture. Owner service should be limited to replacement only. If the system is not working properly, take the car to a General Motors dealer for diagnosis and adjustment.

System Pressure Relief

The PFI fuel rail contains a pressure bleed orifice that bleeds off system pressure whenever the ignition is turned OFF. However, it is a good idea to bleed off any residual system pressure before opening any fuel connection to reduce the risk of fire and personal injury. Use the same procedure specified for the 4-cylinder engine in the basic book.

Fuel Rail Removal/Installation

Refer to **Figure 11** for this procedure.
1. Remove the plenum as described in the Chapter Five section of this supplement.
2. Disconnect the cold start valve at the fuel rail. See **Figure 13**.
3. Remove the fuel line retaining bolt at the cylinder head and disconnect the fuel lines at the fuel rail. Use one wrench to hold the fuel rail fitting and a second wrench to loosen the fuel line nut. Plug the lines to prevent leakage.
4. Disconnect the vacuum line at the fuel rail pressure regulator.
5. Remove the 2 fuel rail retaining bolts.
6. Carefully disconnect the electrical connectors at the injectors.
7. Remove the fuel rail and injectors.
8. Remove and discard all O-ring seals.
9. Installation is the reverse of removal. Install and lubricate new O-ring seals with clean engine oil. Tighten fuel rail bolts to 15 ft.-lb. (21 N•m).

Fuel Filter

The PFI V6 engine uses a disposable filter canister installed in the fuel line. See Chapter Three of the basic book for replacement procedure.

Fuel Pump

The PFI system uses an electric fuel pump attached to the fuel sending unit located in the fuel tank. To replace the pump, remove the fuel tank as described in Chapter Six of the basic book. Rotate the cam lock ring on the sending unit counterclockwise and lift assembly from the tank, then separate the lock ring from the sending unit. Installation is the reverse of removal.

Fuel Pump Relay

The PFI fuel pump relay is bracket-mounted to the shock tower relay assembly along with the fuel pump/ECM fuse. See **Figure 14**.

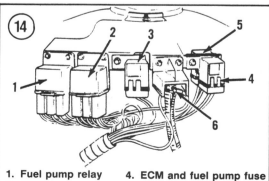

1. Fuel pump relay
2. MAF sensor
3. Cooling fan fuse
4. ECM and fuel pump fuse
5. MAF fuse
6. 12 volt junction

14

EGR Valve

EGR valve operation on the 1986 fuel-injected (RPO LB9) and high output (RPO L69) V8 engines is monitored by the ECM through a bi-metallic temperature switch installed in the base of the valve. See **Figure 15**. If the valve malfunctions, the ECM will turn on the "Check Engine" light and eliminates the supplemental spark advance provided during normal EGR operation until the valve malfunction is corrected.

Early Fuel Evaporation (EFE) System

The EFE system on 1984-on engines is no longer controlled by the ECM. A normally closed thermal electric switch (TES) controls the EFE grid operation. The TES should open at approximately 160° F (70° C) and shut the EFE grid off.

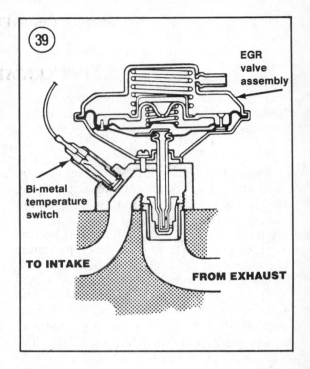

CHAPTER SEVEN

COOLING, HEATING AND AIR CONDITIONING

WATER PUMP

Table 3 provides water pump attaching bolt torques for 1984 and later engines.

RADIATOR

A lightweight aluminum radiator with plastic tanks is used on some models. The plastic tanks are fitted to the brazed aluminum crossflow core with cinched header tabs and sealed with a high-temperature rubber gasket.

Service and maintenance of this radiator is essentially the same as with the copper core design, but care must be exercised in hose removal/installation and hose clamp tightening to avoid damage to the tank fittings. Excessive pressure applied to a tank fitting can crack or break it.

Table 3 WATER PUMP TIGHTENING TORQUES

	ft.-lb.	N•m
4-cylinder	15	20
V6		
M8×1.25 bolt	15	20
M6×1 bolt	7	10
V8		
3/8-16 bolt	30	40
M8×1.25 nut	15	20
Fan-to-water pump bolts (all engines)	20	27

CHAPTER EIGHT

ELECTRICAL SYSTEMS

CHARGING SYSTEM

Three Delcotron SI alternators are used on 1984 and later models: the 10-SI, 12-SI and 15-SI. The 15-SI has delta stator windings and cannot be tested for opens. The 3 SI alternators differ primarily in slip ring bearing stack-up and output rating. The output rating is stamped on the alternator frame.

Three Delcotron CS alternators are used with 1986 models: the CS-121, CS-130 and CS-144. CS stands for "charging system;" the number after it indicates the outer diameter of the stator laminations in millimeters. The CS alternator is similar in design to the SI models, but has a new digital integral regulator, is smaller and lighter in weight and does not use a diode trio.

The regulator limits system voltage by cycling the rotor field current on/off about 400 times per second. This "duty cycle" changes according to engine operation and temperature. At lower speeds, the field may be on 90 percent of the time and off 10 percent of the time. As engine speed increases, less field current is required to generate the necessary system voltage. Thus, the field may be on 10 percent of the time and off 90 percent of the time at higher engine speeds.

Service to CS alternators is limited to replacement only at this time. Basic test procedures follow for diagnosing CS alternator problems.

CS Charging System Test

1. Check the alternator belt tension. See Chapter Three of the basic book.
2. Check the battery terminals and cables for corrosion and/or loose connections. Clean and tighten as necessary.
3. Check all wiring connections between the alternator and engine.

NOTE
If vehicle does not have a charge indicator lamp, proceed with Step 6.

4. With the engine off and the ignition switch ON, the indicator lamp should be on. If not, disconnect the wiring harness at the rear of the alternator and ground the L terminal.
   a. If the lamp lights, the alternator is defective.
   b. If the lamp still does not light, look for an open in the circuit between the ground lead and ignition switch.
5. Start the engine and run at idle. The indicator lamp should be off. If not, disconnect the wiring harness at the rear of the alternator.
   a. If the lamp goes off, the alternator is defective.
   b. If the lamp remains on, look for a grounded L terminal wire in the wiring harness.
6. If the battery is undercharged or overcharged:
   a. Disconnect the wiring harness connector at the rear of the alternator.
   b. Turn the ignition switch ON (engine OFF) and connect a voltmeter between the L terminal and ground. If the meter reads zero, there is an open in the circuit between the battery and L terminal.
   c. Reconnect the wiring harness to the alternator. Start the engine, run at idle and connect the voltmeter between the battery terminals. If the meter reads more than 16 volts, the alternator is defective.
   d. Shut the engine off. Disconnect the voltmeter and negative battery cable. Connect an ammeter between the BAT terminal and the wiring connector.
   e. Reconnect the negative battery cable. Turn on all accessories. Connect a carbon pile across the battery posts.

14

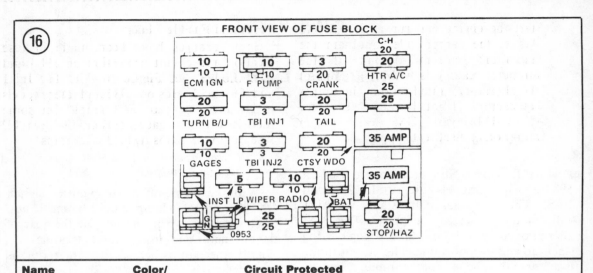

FRONT VIEW OF FUSE BLOCK

Name	Color/Size (amps)	Circuit Protected
ECM Ign	Red (10)	Computer command control, Electronic fuel injection
Fuel Pump	Red (10)	Electronic fuel injection
Crank	Purple (3)	Electronic fuel injection
C-H	Yellow (20)	Choke heater, charging system, computer command control, Trans Am hood louver
Turn/BU	Yellow (20)	Back-up lights, turn lights
TBI Inj 1	Purple (3)	Crossfire fuel injection (1983 V8 only)
Tail	Yellow (20)	Lights: Front park/marker, rear tail/marker/license, instrument panel, console, radio, digital clock
Htr/AC	White (25)	Air conditioning, computer command control (carburetted engine), electronic fuel injection, heater
Gages	Red (10)	Audio alarm system, brake warning system, computer command control, charging system, choke heater, cruise control, electronic fuel injection, instrument panel
TBI Inj 2	Purple (3)	Crossfire fuel injection (1983 V8 only)
Ctsy	Yellow (20)	Cargo compartment light, hatch release, horn, interior lights, cigar lighter, clock, power antenna, power door locks, power remote mirrors, radio and digital clock
WDO Circuit Breaker	(35)	Power windows, rear wiper/washer
Inst	Tan (5)	Audio alarm system, instrument panel, console
Radio	Red (10)	Radio, power antenna
Pwr acc Circuit Breaker	(35)	Defogger, power door locks, power seat
Wiper	White (25)	Wiper/washer, pulse wiper/washer
Stop Haz.	Yellow (20)	Audio alarm system, turn/hazard/stop lights

f. Start the engine and run at 2,000 rpm. Adjust the carbon pile to obtain the maximum current output. If the ammeter reading is within 15 amps of the alternator's rated output, the unit is satisfactory. If not, have the alternator checked by your GM dealer or an automotive electrical shop.

Fuses and Fusible Links

Some changes have been made in fuse location and circuit protection on 1983 and later models. See **Figure 16**. The TBI Inj 1 and TBI Inj 2 fuses on 1985 and later models is 20 amps instead of 3 amps. On some models with the gauge cluster, the Inst LP fuse may be 3 amps instead of 5 amps.

CHAPTER NINE

CLUTCH AND TRANSMISSION

The 5-speed Borg-Warner T-5 manual transmission is standard on 1983 and later Berlinetta/SE and Z28/Trans Am models and optional on Camaro/Firebird sport coupes. The 4-speed Turbo Hydramatic 700 R4 is optional on all models.

A hydraulic clutch is used on all 1984 and later models with manual transmission.

CLUTCH HYDRAULIC SYSTEM

The hydraulic clutch system on 1984 and later models is serviced as a complete

assembly—master cylinder, slave cylinder, reservoir and interconnecting lines. See **Figure 17**. If the system does not operate properly, the entire system should be removed and replaced as a complete assembly. Bleeding the system is not recommended by GM and should not be attempted. New assemblies are furnished pre-filled with fluid and bled at the factory. Clutch linkage and pedal position adjustments are not required.

Removal

> *CAUTION*
> *Before performing any service which requires removal of the slave cylinder pushrod from the release lever, the master cylinder pushrod must be removed from the clutch pedal. Depressing the clutch pedal with the slave cylinder removed will cause permanent damage to the slave cylinder.*

1. Disconnect the negative battery cable.
2. Remove the steering column trim cover and hush panel.
3. Remove the lockpin holding the clutch master cylinder pushrod to the clutch pedal. Disconnect the pushrod from the pedal. See **Figure 18**.
4. Working inside the passenger compartment, remove the 2 nuts holding the clutch master cylinder U-bolt to the cowl and braces (**Figure 19**).

17

1. Fluid reservoir
2. Clutch master cylinder
3. Boot
4. Push rod
5. Shipping strap
6. Boot
7. Clutch slave cylinder

14

5. Remove the fasteners holding the fluid reservoir to the reservoir mounting bracket (**Figure 20**). Remove the brake booster-to-cowl nuts.

6. Pull the brake master cylinder forward to provide access to the clutch master cylinder. Remove clutch master cylinder from cowl.

7. Raise the front of the vehicle with a jack and place it on jackstands.

8. Remove the 2 cylinder attaching screws from the mounting bracket (**Figure 21**). Disengage the pushrod at the release lever.

9. Remove the slave cylinder and heat shield.

10. Remove the jackstands and lower the vehicle to the ground.

> *NOTE*
> *Catch any plastic bearing inserts installed between the pushrod end and the release lever. Save for reuse if the old slave cylinder is to be reinstalled; discard when installing a new hydraulic system.*

11. Pull the master cylinder assembly through the cowl into the engine compartment and remove the entire hydraulic system from the vehicle.

Installation

1. Position the hydraulic system in the engine compartment and insert the master cylinder pushrod through the cowl opening.

2. Position clutch master cylinder to the cowl with the U-bolt. Install brake booster to cowl.

3. Insert master cylinder U-bolt through braces. Install U-bolt fasteners and tighten to 10 ft.-lb.

4. Install and tighten brake master cylinder attaching nuts to specifications.

5. Connect clutch cylinder pushrod to clutch pedal and install retainer clip.

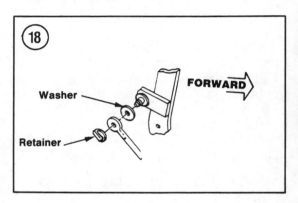

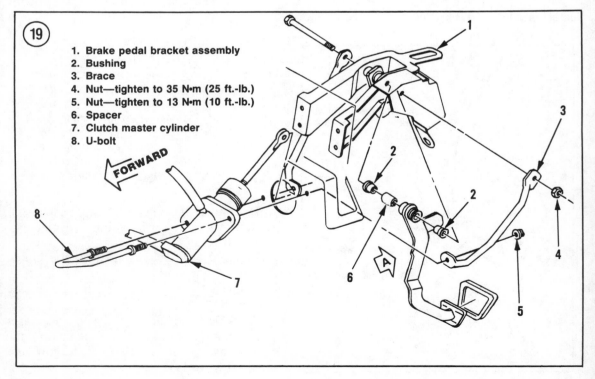

1. Brake pedal bracket assembly
2. Bushing
3. Brace
4. Nut—tighten to 35 N•m (25 ft.-lb.)
5. Nut—tighten to 13 N•m (10 ft.-lb.)
6. Spacer
7. Clutch master cylinder
8. U-bolt

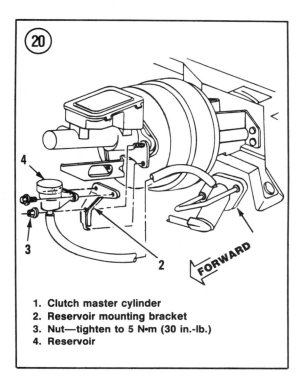

1. Clutch master cylinder
2. Reservoir mounting bracket
3. Nut—tighten to 5 N•m (30 in.-lb.)
4. Reservoir

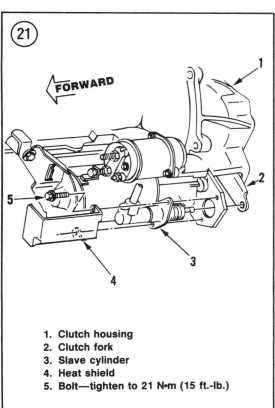

1. Clutch housing
2. Clutch fork
3. Slave cylinder
4. Heat shield
5. Bolt—tighten to 21 N•m (15 ft.-lb.)

6. Install hush panel and steering column trim cover.

7. Connect clutch reservoir to mounting bracket. Tighten fasteners to 30 in.-lb.

8. Raise the front of the vehicle with a jack and place it on jackstands.

9A. If the old slave cylinder is reinstalled, be sure to install the plastic bearing insert between the pushrod and release lever, if one was removed.

9B. New slave cylinders have a shipping strap attached to pre-position the pushrod for installation. This strap may also contain a plastic bearing insert. Install a new cylinder with the strap attached. Operating the clutch pedal when the system is installed will break the strap and provide normal system operation.

10. Insert the slave cylinder pushrod through the mounting bracket and into the clutch release lever. Position heat shield.

11. Install cylinder attaching screws and tighten to 15 ft.-lb.

12. Remove the jackstands and lower the vehicle to the ground. Reconnect the negative battery cable.

MANUAL TRANSMISSION

The Borg-Warner T-5 5-speed manual transmission is fully synchronized with blocker ring synchronizers and a sliding mesh type reverse gear. The gearshift lever assembly is mounted on top of the transmission extension housing and requires no adjustment.

Shift Lever
Removal/Installation

1. Working inside the passenger compartment, remove the screws holding the shift lever boot retainer. Slide boot up the lever.

2. Remove the shift lever-to-transmission bolts. Remove the lever.

3. Installation is the reverse of removal.

Transmission Removal/Installation

1. Remove the shift lever as described in this supplement.

14

2. Raise the car with a jack and place it on jackstands.

3. Drain the transmission lubricant.

4. Remove the torque arm. See Chapter Eleven in the basic book.

5. Remove the drive shaft. See Chapter Eleven in the basic book.

6. Disconnect the speedometer cable and all electrical connectors at the transmission.

7. Disconnect the clutch cable (1983) or slave cylinder (1984) at the transmission.

8. Support the transmission with a jack. Remove the transmission mount bolts.

9. Remove the catalytic converter hanger.

10. Remove the crossmember bolts and crossmember.

11. Remove the dust cover bolts.

12. Remove the transmission-to-engine bolts. Slide the transmission away from the engine and remove from under the car.

13. Installation is the reverse of removal. Tighten all fasteners to specifications (**Table 4**). Refill transmission with 3 1/2 pints of SAE 80W or SAE 80W-90 GL-5 gear lubricant.

T-5 Transmission Disassembly

Refer to **Figure 22** for this procedure.

1. Remove transmission case drain bolt. Drain lubricant, if not drained during removal.

2. Remove roll pin holding offset lever to shift rail with a hammer and punch (**Figure 23**).

> *NOTE*
> *Offset lever cannot be removed in Step 3 with extension housing bolted to transmission case.*

3. Remove extension housing-to-transmission case bolts. Remove housing and offset lever as an assembly. See **Figure 24**.

4. Remove detent ball and spring from offset lever (**Figure 25**), then remove roll pin.

5. Pry the plastic funnel from the rear end of the countershaft, then remove the thrust bearing and race. See **Figure 26**.

6. Remove transmission shift cover bolts. Note that 2 of the bolts are alignment-type dowel bolts—these must be reinstalled in the

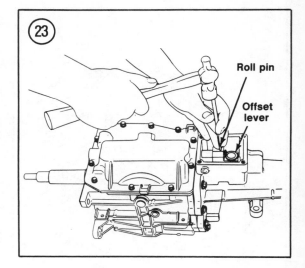

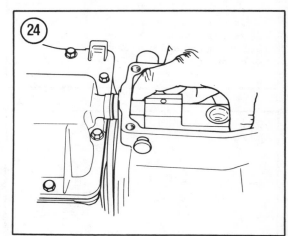

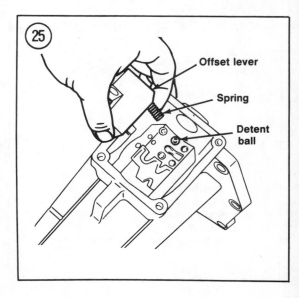

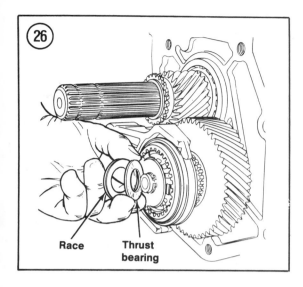

Race | Thrust bearing

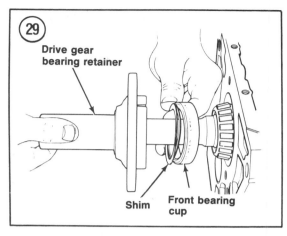

Drive gear bearing retainer

Shim | Front bearing cup

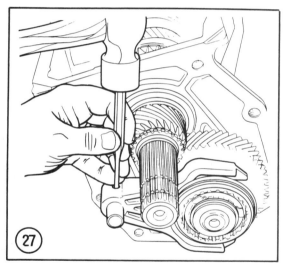

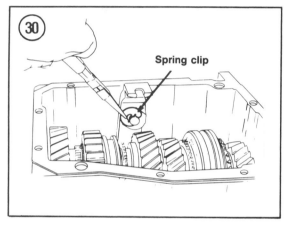

Spring clip

same location during assembly. Remove cover and shift assembly.

7. Support end of shaft with a block of wood and drive roll pin from 5th gear shift fork (**Figure 27**).

8. Remove 5th gear synchronizer snap ring, then remove shift fork, synchronizer sleeve, blocking reing and 5th gear from rear of countershaft.

9. Remove snap ring from 5th speed drive gear.

10. Mark bearing cap and case with a punch for reassembly. See **Figure 28**.

11. Remove front bearing cap bolts and cap. Remove front bearing race and end play shims from the cap. See **Figure 29**.

12. Rotate drive gear to align flat with countershaft, then remove drive gear.

13. Remove reverse lever C-clip and pivot bolt (**Figure 30**).

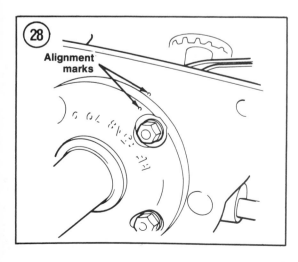

Alignment marks

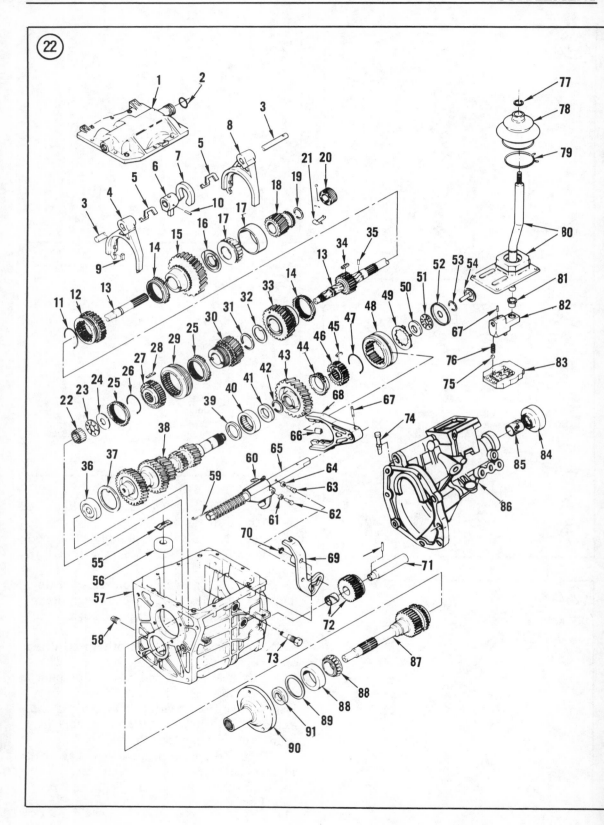

5-SPEED TRANSMISSION (77 MM)

1. Cover
2. O-ring
3. Shift shaft
4. 3rd and 4th shift fork
5. Shift fork plate
6. Control selector arm
7. Interlock plate
8. 1st and 2nd shift fork
9. Shift fork insert
10. Roll pin
11. Synchronizer spring
12. Reverse sliding gear
13. Output shaft/1st and 2nd synchronizer
14. Blocking ring
15. 1st gear
16. Thrust washer
17. Rear bearing
18. 5th driven gear
19. Snap ring
20. Speedometer drive gear
21. Clip
22. Main shaft bearing
23. Needle bearing
24. Bearing race
25. 3rd and 4th synchronizer ring
26. 3rd and 4th synchronizer spring
27. 3rd and 4th synchronizer hub
28. 3rd and 4th synchronizer key
29. 3rd and 4th synchronizer sleeve
30. 3rd gear
31. Snap ring
32. Thrust washer
33. 2nd gear
34. 1st and 2nd synchronizer key
35. Retaining pin
36. Bearing
37. Thrust washer
38. Counter gear
39. Spacer
40. Bearing
41. Spacer
42. Snap ring
43. 5th drive gear
44. 5th synchronizer ring
45. 5th synchronizer key
46. 5th synchronizer hub
47. 5th synchronizer spring
48. 5th synchronizer sleeve
49. Retainer
50. Bearing race
51. Thrust bearing
52. Bearing race
53. Snap ring
54. Funnel
55. Nut
56. Magnet
57. Case
58. Fill and drain plug
59. Reverse lock spring
60. Reverse shift fork
61. Fork roller
62. Reverse fork pin
63. Shift rail pin
64. Rail pin roller
65. 5th and reverse shift rail
66. Shift fork insert
67. Roll pin
68. 5th shift fork
69. 5th and reverse relay lever
70. Retaining ring
71. Reverse idler gear shaft
72. Reverse idler gear
73. Pin
74. Ventilator
75. Ball
76. Detent spring
77. Boot retainer
78. Boot
79. Boot retainer
80. Lever control
81. Damper spring
82. Offset shift lever
83. Detent and guide plate
84. Oil seal
85. Extension housing bushing
86. Extension housing
87. Main drive gear
88. Front bearing
89. Shim
90. Drive gear bearing retainer
91. Oil seal

14

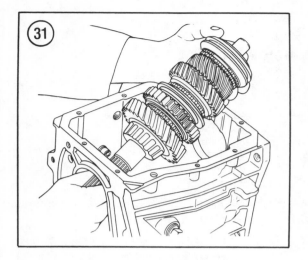

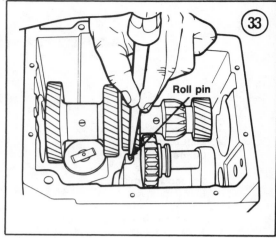

Roll pin

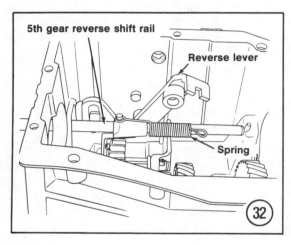

5th gear reverse shift rail

Reverse lever

Spring

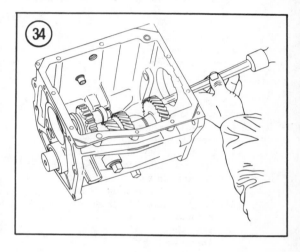

14. Remove main shaft rear bearing race. Tilt main shaft assembly up and remove from transmission case as shown in **Figure 31**.

15. Disconnect overcenter link spring at front of transmission case (**Figure 32**).

16. Rotate and disconnect 5th gear-reverse shift rail from reverse lever assembly. See **Figure 32**. Remove shift rail, reverse lever and fork assembly.

17. Drive roll pin from forward end of reverse idler shaft with a punch. See **Figure 33**. Remove shaft, O-ring and gear from transmission case.

18. Remove snap ring and spacer from rear of countershaft.

19. Carefully drive countershaft to the rear with a brass drift and remove rear countershaft bearing. See **Figure 34**.

20. Move countershaft to the rear, tilt upward and remove from case.

21. Remove countershaft front thrust washer and rear bearing spacer from case.

22. Remove countershaft front bearing from case with an arbor press.

Assembly

1. Wipe countershaft front bearing bore with Loctite 601 or equivalent. Press bearing in case until flush with case face.

2. Smear countershaft tabbed washer with grease and install with tab engaging case recess.

3. Place transmission case on its end. Install countershaft in the front bearing bore.

4. Install countershaft rear bearing spacer. Wipe rear bearing with grease and install with

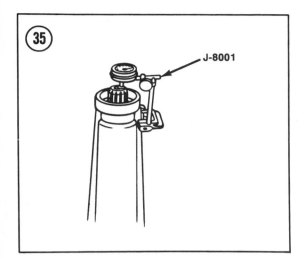

35 J-8001

protector sleeve (part No. J-33032) and installer tool (part No. J-29895) until bearing extends 0.125 in. (3 mm) from case surface.

5. Place reverse idler gear in case. Shift lever groove should face to the rear.

6. Install reverse idler shaft from rear of case and secure with roll pin.

7. Install main shaft assembly in case.

8. Install rear main shaft bearing race in case.

9. Install drive gear in case, engaging 3-4 synchronizer sleeve and blocker ring.

10. Install front bearing race in cap without shims and temporarily install cap.

11. Install 5th-reverse lever, pivot bolt and retaining clip. Coat bolt threads with nonhardening sealer. Make sure reverse lever fork engages reverse idler gear.

12. Install countershaft rear bearing spacer and snap ring.

13. Install 5th gear on countershaft.

14. Install 5th-reverse rail in rear of case with a rotating motion to ease engagement with the reverse-5th lever. Connect spring to front of case. See **Figure 32**.

15. Install 5th gear fork on 5th gear synchronizer, then position synchronizer on countershaft and shift fork on shift rail.

16. Align shift fork/rail roll pin holes. Support rail and fork with a wooden block and install the roll pin.

17. Coat thrust bearing and race with petroleum jelly and install on countershaft (**Figure 26**). Install plastic funnel in countershaft.

18. Temporarily install extension housing and turn case on end. Mount a dial indicator on extension housing as shown in **Figure 35**.

19. Rotate main shaft and zero dial indicator. Pull upward on main shaft and record end play reading.

NOTE
Main shaft bearings require a 0.001-0.005 in. (0.03-0.13 mm) preload.

20. Remove front bearing cap and install a shim pack that is 0.001-0.005 in. (0.03-0.13 mm) thicker than the reading obtained in Step 19.

21. Apply a 1/8 in. (3 mm) bead of RTV sealant No. 732 or equivalent to bearing cap mating surface.

22. Align bearing/case marks made during disassembly and install cap to case. Tighten bolts to specifications (**Table 4**).

23. Remove extension housing.

24. Position shift forks in cover and synchronizer sleeves in case in neutral.

NOTE
The offset lever-to-shift rail roll pin hole must be in a vertical position after completion of Step 25.

25. Apply a 1/8 in. (3 mm) bead of RTV sealant No. 732 or equivalent to transmission cover mating surface. Lower cover on case and install the 2 alignment dowel bolts. Install remaining bolts and tighten to specifications (**Table 4**).

26. Apply a 1/8 in. (3 mm) bead of RTV sealant No. 732 or equivalent on extension housing mating surface.

27. Slide extension housing over main shaft and shift rail until shift rail barely enters shift cover opening.

28. Install detent spring in offset lever and place steel ball in neutral guide plate detent. See **Figure 25**.

29. Place offset lever on steel ball. Apply pressure on lever while seating extension housing against transmission case. Install attaching bolts and tighten to specifications (**Table 4**).

30. Align offset lever and shift rail, then install roll pin.

14

Main Shaft Disassembly/Assembly

1. Remove thrust bearing washer on front of main shaft.

2. Scribe a mark on the 3-4 synchronizer hub and sleeve for reassembly reference.

3. Install a universal puller plate as shown in **Figure 36** and remove 3-4 synchronizer assembly and 3rd gear.

4. Remove 2nd gear snap ring, then remove tabbed thrust washer and 2nd gear (**Figure 37**).

5. Remove 5th gear with tool part No. J-22912-01 and an arbor press.

6. Remove 1st gear thrust washer, roll pin, 1st gear and synchronizer ring (**Figure 38**).

7. Scribe a mark on the 1-2 synchronizer hub and sleeve for reassembly reference.

> *NOTE*
> *The 1st-2nd-reverse hub and main shaft are machined as an assembly. If there are any defects in hub or shaft, replace the entire assembly.*

8. Remove synchronizer spring and keys from 1st-reverse sliding gear. Remove 1st-reverse gear from shaft.

9. Assembly is the reverse of disassembly.

Cleaning and Inspection

1. Wash the transmission case and components in clean solvent.

2. Inspect the aluminum case for cracks or signs of porosity. Check front and rear faces for burrs and dress off with a fine mill file, if necessary.

3. Remove and clean magnet at bottom of case.

4. Check all gear teeth for signs of wear or damage.

5. Inspect all roller bearings for excessive wear.

6. Inspect countershaft and reverse idler shaft for wear. Replace as necessary.

7. Check all washers for wear or distortion. Replace as necessary.

Oil Seal/Bearing Replacement

Procedures in Chapter Nine of basic book can be used to replace the drive gear bearing or retainer oil seal and the extension housing oil seal/bushing.

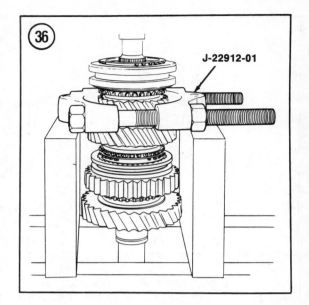

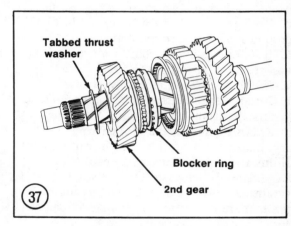

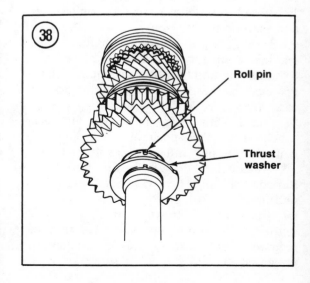

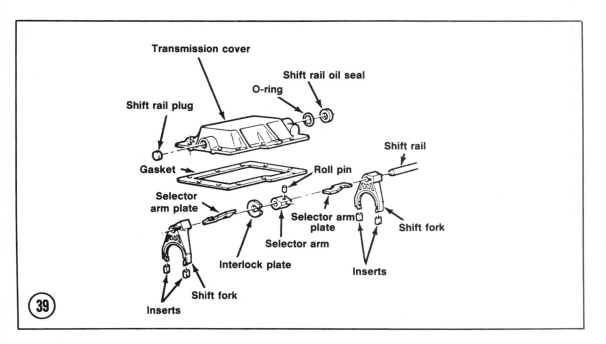

Transmission Cover

Refer to **Figure 39** for this procedure.

1. Center selector arm plates and shift rail (neutral position).
2. Rotate shift rail to disengage from selector arm plates.
3. Remove selector arm roll pin with a punch and hammer.
4. Remove shift rail, shift forks, selector arm plates, selector arm, interlock plate and roll pin.
5. Note position of nylon inserts and selector arm plates on shift forks, then remove.
6. To reassemble, install nylon inserts and selector arm plates on shift forks.
7. Coat shift rail and rail bore with lightweight grease, then insert rail in cover until flush with cover edge.

NOTE
The 1-2 shift fork is the larger of the 2.

8. Install 1-2 shift fork in cover. Fork offset should face rear of cover. Push shift rail through fork.
9. Install selector arm with C-shaped interlock plate in cover with widest part of plate facing away from cover. Install shift rail

through selector arm. Make sure selector arm roll pin hole faces downward and to the rear of the cover.
10. Install 3-4 shift fork in cover. Fork offset should face rear of cover, with selector arm plate underneath the 1-2 selector arm plate. Push shift rail through fork and into cover bore.
11. Rotate shift rail to position selector arm plate (at front of rail) away from but parallel with cover.

NOTE
If roll pin is not flush in Step 12, it may interfere with selector arm plates during shifting.

12. Align selector arm and shift rail roll pin holes, then install roll pin flush with selector arm surface.
13. Install a new shift cover-to-extension housing O-ring and coat with transmission fluid.

AUTOMATIC TRANSMISSION

Turbo Hydramatic 700 R4

All service procedures for the Turbo Hydramatic 200C given in Chapter Nine of the basic book apply to the 4-speed THM 700 R4 transmission.

14

Table 4 TIGHTENING TORQUES

Fastener	in.-lb.	ft.-lb.	N·m
HYDRAULIC CLUTCH			
Clutch reservoir-to-mounting bracket	30	1	5
Clutch master cylinder-to-cowl U-bolt nuts		10	13
Slave cylinder-to-bell housing		15	21
T-5 5-SPEED MANUAL TRANSMISSION			
Crossmember-to-frame bolts		35	50
Extension housing-to-case bolts		25	30
Fill plug		20	27
Front bearing retainer bolts		15	20
Reverse pivot bolt-to-case		20	27
Shift cover bolts		10	13
Transmission-to-engine bolts		55	75
Transmission mount bolts		35	50
THM 700 R4 AUTOMATIC TRANSMISSION			
Converter-to-flex plate		35	47
Cooler lines			
At transmission		10	14
At radiator		20	27
Oil pan screws		12	16
Parking brake bracket-to-case bolts		18	22
Transmission-to-engine bolts		55	75

INDEX

15

NOTES

NOTES

NOTES